Innovation, Technology, and Knowledge Management

Series Editor

Elias G. Carayannis
George Washington University, Washington, DC, USA

For further volumes:
http://www.springer.com/series/8124

Tugrul U. Daim • Melinda Pizarro
Rajasree Talla
Editors

Planning and Roadmapping Technological Innovations

Cases and Tools

Editors
Tugrul U. Daim
Engineering and Technology Management
Portland State University
Portland, OR, USA

Melinda Pizarro
Daimler Trucks North America
Happy Valley, OR, USA

Rajasree Talla
GE Healthcare
Hillsboro, OR, USA

ISSN 2197-5698 ISSN 2197-5701 (electronic)
ISBN 978-3-319-02972-6 ISBN 978-3-319-02973-3 (eBook)
DOI 10.1007/978-3-319-02973-3
Springer Cham Heidelberg New York Dordrecht London

Library of Congress Control Number: 2013953709

Printed on acid-free paper

Springer is part of Springer Science+Business Media (www.springer.com)

Series Foreword

The Springer book series *Innovation, Technology, and Knowledge Management* was launched in March 2008 as a forum and intellectual, scholarly"podium" for global/local, transdisciplinary, transsectoral, public–private, and leading/"bleeding"edge ideas, theories, and perspectives on these topics.

The book series is accompanied by the Springer *Journal of the Knowledge Economy*, which was launched in 2009 with the same editorial leadership.

The series showcases provocative views that diverge from the current "conventional wisdom" that are properly grounded in theory and practice, and that consider the concepts of ***robust competitiveness***,[1] ***sustainable entrepreneurship***,[2] and ***democratic capitalism***,[3] central to its philosophy and objectives. More specifically, the aim of this series is to highlight emerging research and practice at the dynamic intersection of these fields, where individuals, organizations, industries, regions, and nations are harnessing creativity and invention to achieve and sustain growth.

---

[1]We define *sustainable entrepreneurship* as the creation of viable, profitable, and scalable firms. Such firms engender the formation of self-replicating and mutually enhancing innovation networks and knowledge clusters (innovation ecosystems), leading toward robust competitiveness (E. G. Carayannis, *International Journal of Innovation and Regional Development* 1(3), 235– 254, 2009).

[2]We understand *robust competitiveness* to be a state of economic being and becoming that avails systematic and defensible "unfair advantages" to the entities that are part of the economy. Such competitiveness is built on mutually complementary and reinforcing low-, medium-, and high-technology and public and private sector entities (government agencies, private firms, universities, and nongovernmental organizations) (E. G. Carayannis, *International Journal of Innovation and Regional Development* 1(3), 235–254, 2009).

[3]The concepts of *robust competitiveness and sustainable entrepreneurship* are pillars of a regime that we call "*democratic capitalism*" (as opposed to "popular or casino capitalism"), in which real opportunities for education and economic prosperity are available to all, especially—but not only—younger people. These are the direct derivatives of a collection of topdown policies as well as bottom-up initiatives (including strong research and development policies and funding, but going beyond these to include the development of innovation networks and knowledge clusters across regions and sectors) (E. G. Carayannis and A. Kaloudis, *Japan Economic Currents*, p. 6–10 January 2009).

Books that are part of the series explore the impact of innovation at the "macro" (economies, markets), "meso" (industries, firms), and "micro" levels (teams, individuals), drawing from such related disciplines as finance, organizational psychology, research and development, science policy, information systems, and strategy, with the underlying theme that for innovation to be useful it must involve the sharing and application of knowledge.

Some of the key anchoring concepts of the series are outlined in the figure below and the definitions that follow (all definitions are from E. G. Carayannis and D. F. J. Campbell, *International Journal of Technology Management*, 46, 3–4, 2009).

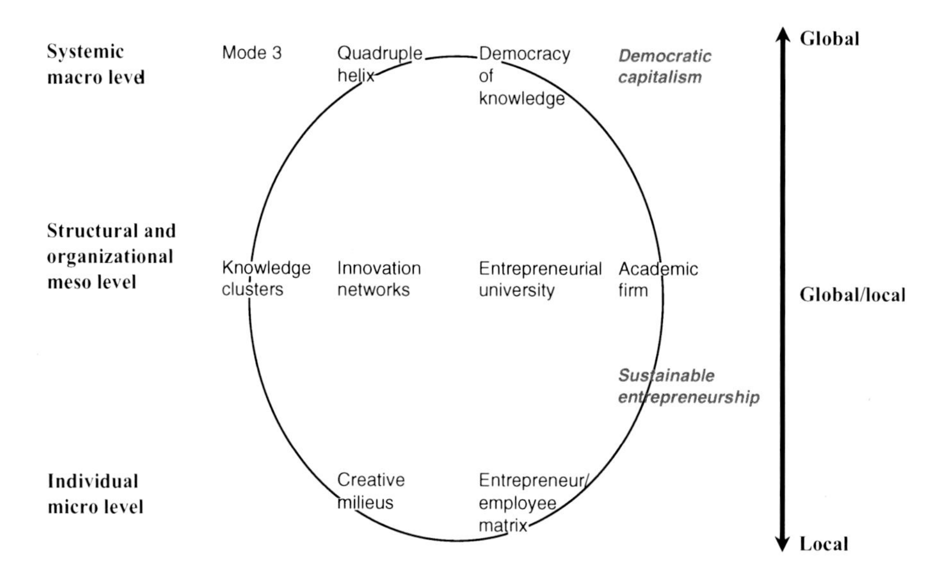

Conceptual profile of the series *Innovation, Technology,* and *Knowledge Management*

- The "Mode 3" Systems Approach for Knowledge Creation, Diffusion, and Use: "Mode 3" is a multilateral, multinodal, multimodal, and multilevel systems approach to the conceptualization, design, and management of real and virtual, "knowledge-stock" and "knowledge-flow," modalities that catalyze, accelerate, and support the creation, diffusion, sharing, absorption, and use of cospecialized knowledge assets. "Mode 3" is based on a system-theoretic perspective of socio-economic, political, technological, and cultural trends and conditions that shape the coevolution of knowledge with the "knowledge-based and knowledge-driven, global/local economy and society."
- Quadruple Helix: Quadruple helix, in this context, means to add to the triple helix of government, university, and industry a "fourth helix" that we identify as the "media-based and culture-based public." This fourth helix associates with "media," "creative industries," "culture," "values," "life styles," "art," and perhaps also the notion of the "creative class."

- Innovation Networks: Innovation networks are real and virtual infrastructures and infratechnologies that serve to nurture creativity, trigger invention, and catalyze innovation in a public and/or private domain context (for instance, government–university–industry public–private research and technology development coopetitive partnerships).
- Knowledge Clusters: Knowledge clusters are agglomerations of cospecialized, mutually complementary, and reinforcing knowledge assets in the form of "knowledge stocks" and "knowledge flows" that exhibit self-organizing, learning-driven, dynamically adaptive competences, and trends in the context of an open systems perspective.
- Twenty-First Century Innovation Ecosystem: A twenty-first century innovation ecosystem is a multilevel, multimodal, multinodal, and multiagent system of systems. The constituent systems consist of innovation metanetworks (networks of innovation networks and knowledge clusters) and knowledge metaclusters (clusters of innovation networks and knowledge clusters) as building blocks and organized in a self-referential or chaotic fractal knowledge and innovation architecture,[4] which in turn constitute agglomerations of human, social, intellectual, and financial capital stocks and flows as well as cultural and technological artifacts and modalities, continually coevolving, cospecializing, and cooperating. These innovation networks and knowledge clusters also form, reform, and dissolve within diverse institutional, political, technological, and socioeconomic domains, including government, university, industry, and nongovernmental organizations and involving information and communication technologies, biotechnologies, advanced materials, nanotechnologies, and next-Generation energy technologies.

Who is this book series published for? The book series addresses a diversity of audiences in different settings:

1. *Academic communities*: Academic communities worldwide represent a core group of readers. This follows from the theoretical/conceptual interest of the book series to influence academic discourses in the fields of knowledge, also carried by the claim of a certain saturation of academia with the current concepts and the postulate of a window of opportunity for new or at least additional concepts. Thus, it represents a key challenge for the series to exercise a certain impact on discourses in academia. In principle, all academic communities that are interested in knowledge (knowledge and innovation) could be tackled by the book series. The interdisciplinary (transdisciplinary) nature of the book series underscores that the scope of the book series is not limited a priori to a specific basket of disciplines. From a radical viewpoint, one could create the hypothesis that there is no discipline where knowledge is of no importance.
2. *Decision makers—private/academic entrepreneurs and public* (*governmental, subgovernmental*) actors: Two different groups of decision makers are being

[4]E. G. Carayannis, *Strategic Management of Technological Learning*, CRC Press, 2000.

addressed simultaneously: (1) private entrepreneurs (firms, commercial firms, academic firms) and academic entrepreneurs (universities), interested in optimizing knowledge management and in developing heterogeneously composed knowledge-based research networks; and (2) public (governmental, subgovernmental) actors that are interested in optimizing and further developing their policies and policy strategies that target knowledge and innovation. One purpose of public *knowledge and innovation policy* is to enhance the performance and competitiveness of advanced economies.

3. *Decision makers in general*: Decision makers are systematically being supplied with crucial information, for how to optimize knowledge-referring and knowledge-enhancing decision-making. The nature of this "crucial information" is conceptual as well as empirical (case-study-based). Empirical information highlights practical examples and points toward practical solutions (perhaps remedies), conceptual information offers the advantage of further driving and further-carrying tools of understanding. Different groups of addressed decision makers could be decision makers in private firms and multinational corporations, responsible for the knowledge portfolio of companies; knowledge and knowledge management consultants; globalization experts, focusing on the internationalization of research and development, science and technology, and innovation; experts in university/business research networks; and political scientists, economists, and business professionals.
4. *Interested global readership*: Finally, the Springer book series addresses a whole global readership, composed of members who are generally interested in knowledge and innovation. The global readership could partially coincide with the communities as described above ("academic communities," "decision makers"), but could also refer to other constituencies and groups.

Elias G. Carayannis
Series Editor

Preface

Technological innovations keep altering the way we do business at a rate increasing exponentially. This requires almost all organizations to plan carefully and efficiently. This book provides a review of practices in organizations in the Silicon Forest, Oregon, and demonstrates the use of one of the most efficient planning tools: Technology Roadmaps.

The first part of the book focuses on Research and Development (R&D). R&D management is crucial for technological companies, in order to develop new processes, services, or products, which are beneficial to society. Organizations are continually finding ways to radically and incrementally innovate technologies to remain at the forefront of the industry. Included chapters show that the concentration on the various segments of R&D, such as communication, project management, project selection, and information flow, can optimize a company's R&D organization.

While the first four chapters provide a general review of R&D management, the rest of the book focuses on and demonstrates the application of technology roadmapping, which is one of the most efficient planning tools, in different settings.

With continually fluctuating industry standards and customer requirements, it is becoming difficult to understand the market. Developing a product or service is more challenging in changing markets. The expectations on technology are always rising. To forecast any developments in a product requires a good understanding of the technology and market needs. Finding the correct resources at the appropriate time and using them in an efficient way is essential to develop a successful product or service. For any technology breakthrough to happen, planning is an important phase. To aid this process, roadmaps serve as an important tool. Developing a technology roadmap demands usage of different techniques besides the basic roadmap model.

Portland, OR, USA Tugrul U. Daim

Contents

Chapter 1
Communication

Fahad Aldhaban, James Eastham, Judith Estep, Dong-Joon Lim, David Tucker, and Tugrul U. Daim

Abstract This chapter compares R&D strategies from four companies and different sectors, specifically communication. The companies use communication to manage their R&D activities. Interviews were conducted with R&D managers, focusing on the communication element of R&D management while using a consistent framework obtained from literature. The case study will show that effective R&D management and strategy play a critical role in giving a company a competitive advantage.

Communication issues can exist between Research and Development (R&D) and other organizations which can create inefficiencies in R&D. Companies may not be aware of this communication breakdown or may not be conscious of tools and best practices which exist in literature and benchmarking which can address this gap. Effective R&D management and strategy formation can play a critical role in giving a company a competitive advantage and therefore make it successful in intense competitive environments. Good communication between R&D and other parts of the organization (e.g., marketing) is significant in developing and executing these strategies [1].

In this chapter, a case study methodology was utilized to compare how R&D strategies from different companies and different sectors compare and how these companies communicate and manage their R&D activities. The team conducted interviews with R&D managers, focusing on the communication element of R&D management.

F. Aldhaban (✉) • D.-J. Lim • T.U. Daim
Engineering and Technology Management, Portland State University, Portland, OR, USA
e-mail: aldhaban@yahoo.com

J. Eastham
Triquint Corporation, Hillsboro, OR, USA

J. Estep
Bonneville Power Administration, Portland, OR, USA

D. Tucker
Consolidated Metco, Portland, OR, USA

T.U. Daim et al. (eds.), *Planning and Roadmapping Technological Innovations: Cases and Tools*, Innovation, Technology, and Knowledge Management,
DOI 10.1007/978-3-319-02973-3_1,

Table 1.1 Business descriptions

Company	Revenue	Organization type	Business description	Customer	Number of employees
Bonneville Power Administration (BPA)	$3.3 billion	Government	Electric distribution and markets wholesale power	Consumer	3,000
Semiconductor manufacturer	$1.4 billion	Public	Semiconductor manufacturing	Businesses	4,200
Asian automotive manufacturer	$97 billion	Private	Automotive manufacturing	Consumers	80,000
Daimler Trucks North America (DTNA)	$3 billion	Private	Commercial truck manufacturing	Business/ consumer	24,000

These interviews were conducted using a consistent framework obtained from literature. Results were compiled from each company and recommendations were prepared based on lessons from benchmarking, literature, case studies [2], and lecture material.

To evaluate different methods of R&D communication and related tools and methods, we selected four companies from different sectors. The following table identifies the companies and their corresponding classifications (Table 1.1).

1.1 Literature Review

R&D management includes the process of transforming new knowledge to a more valuable level or to be a viable commercial product or service [3]. Although R&D includes multiple functions, we find that the effective communication of R&D activities and process to the organization is vital to improve the utilization of R&D and its overall efficiency and effectiveness. Communication is defined as "Exchange of information through various media, including face-to-face contact, telephone, letter, and electronic mail" [4]. Stimulating communication between researchers in R&D was indicated to be one of the R&D critical productivity problems [4]. Many scholars have studied R&D and its tools as they tried to explain and better communicate with the organization and improve performance. Vandaele and Decouttere studied the sustainability of R&D portfolios, and they indicated the power of communication to dissemination of the R&D assessment process [5]. Griffin and Hauser recognized the importance of communication tools in R&D, and they studied the patterns of communication among marketing, engineering, and manufacturing in R&D projects [6].

The importance of efficient team communications in R&D has become more critical and a key factor that influences the success of R&D. To better understand team communication in R&D, Hirst and Mann developed a model of team communications in R&D, and four team communication processes were identified: team boundary spanning, communication safety, team reflection, and task communication. The study concluded that communication is a critical key tool that affects project performances [3].

Communication is a very important tool that can help provide R&D with the right information needed for better outcomes. To improve the R&D processes, the quality of the input information has to be increased to gain a high-quality outcome [7]. Roadmapping was determined to be a valuable tool that can effectively improve R&D performance. Daim and Oliver proposed a framework, which consists of six steps in the development of a technology roadmap [8]. These six steps are identified below:

1. Identifying the needs and drivers
2. Identifying products or services to meet the needs and drivers
3. Identifying technologies to support the products or services
4. Establishing the linkages among steps one to three
5. Developing plans to acquire or develop the technologies
6. Assigning resources to accomplish the plans for acquisition and development

The framework proposed by Daim and Oliver [8] was used in this chapter as the basis for understanding how R&D strategies are developed and how R&D is managed at the different companies. The team used each element in this framework to guide the interviews. The application of each element is described for various industries; strengths, weaknesses, and opportunities are identified in the analysis section.

1.2 Case #1: Bonneville Power Administration

1.2.1 Company Background

Bonneville Power Administration (BPA) is under the Department of Energy and operates as a nonprofit organization in the Pacific Northwest. The agency provides transmission and markets wholesale electrical power to the region identified in Fig. 1.1.

The source of electrical power comes from 31 federal hydro projects in the Columbia River Basin, one nonfederal nuclear plant, and several other small nonfederal power plants. In total, one-third of the electric power used in the Northwest is provided by BPA. Related to transmission, BPA operates and maintains approximately three-fourths of the high-voltage transmission lines in the region, approximately 15,276 circuit miles. BPA's service territory includes Idaho, Oregon, Washington, California, Nevada, Utah, Wyoming, and parts of Montana. Overall, the area serviced by BPA covers approximately 300,000 mile^2 [9].

As part of their responsibility, BPA promotes energy efficiency, renewable resources, and new technologies. New technologies and energy-efficient solutions

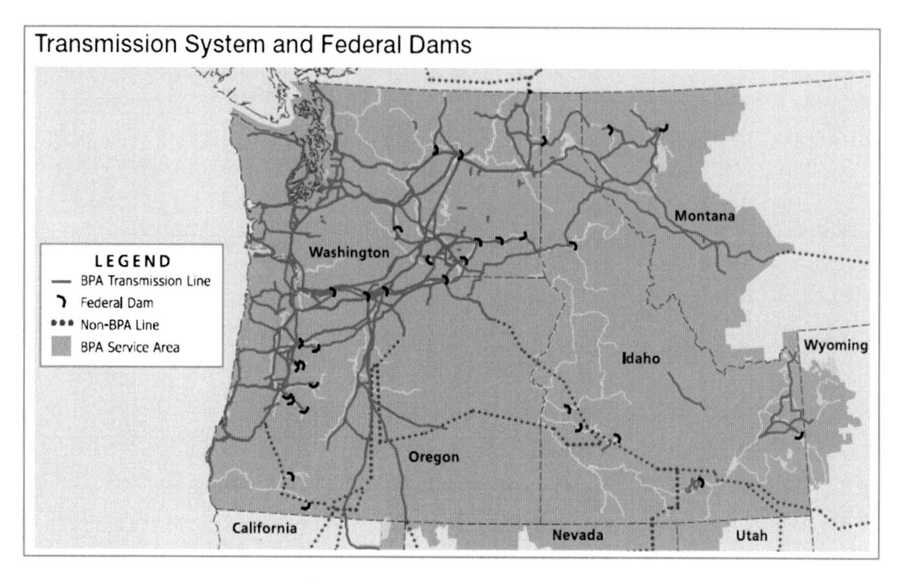

Fig. 1.1 Pacific Northwest transmission system and federal dams

are identified through the utilization of a roadmapping process. Roadmapping is widely used across the agency to ensure that product requirements are consistent with BPA's vision and are initiated through the Office of Technology Innovation at BPA, which is the Research and Development organization. The vision that BPA operates to is identified below:

> BPA will be an engine of the Northwest's economic prosperity, and environmental sustainability. BPA's actions advance a Northwest power system that is a national leader in providing: High reliability, Low rates consistent with sound business principles, Responsible environmental stewardship, and Accountability to the region. [9]

1.2.2 R&D Organization and Process

The Office of Technology Innovation is responsible for selecting and managing BPA's R&D portfolio of projects. Referencing Fig. 1.2, the process involves a rigorous portfolio selection, which is completed March through July of every year. Subsequently, a review cycle is conducted from January through March, implementing project management best practices, and once the research projects are complete, transferring the projects to application follows. Therefore, the primary function of this department is portfolio and project management and technology transfer.

Specific to roadmap (RM) development, Fig. 1.2 suggests that the roadmaps are reviewed as part of an annual research cycle. The input from the roadmaps is used to drive focus area decisions, which are used as the basis for the annual R&D

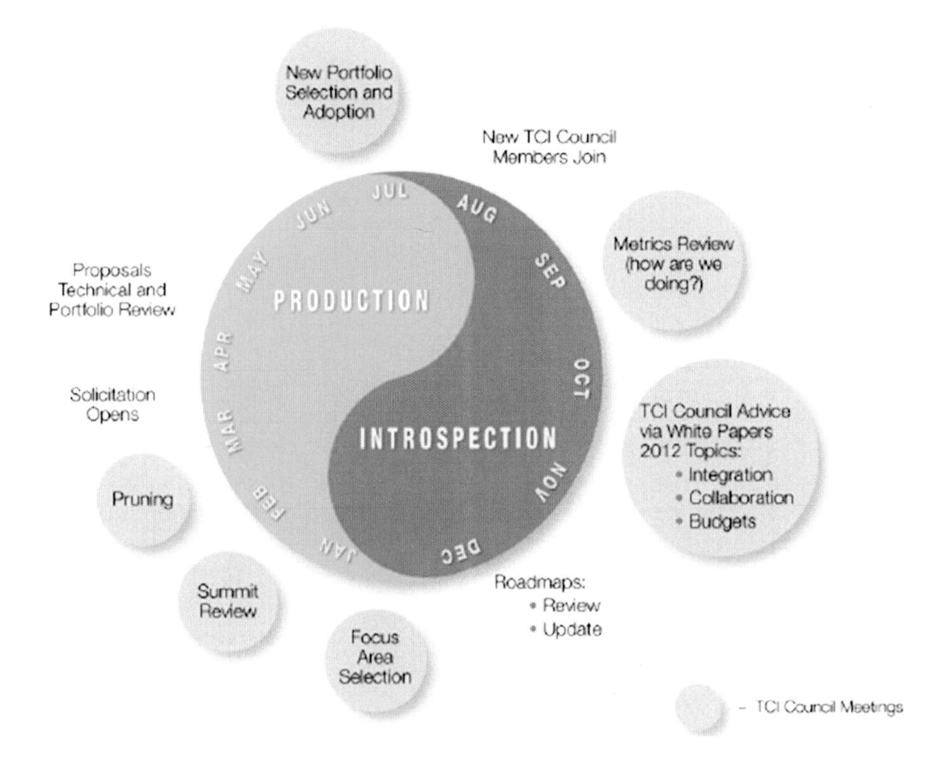

Fig. 1.2 TI office process diagram

solicitation. The roadmaps are representations of cross-functional efforts, involving many stakeholders, subject-matter experts (SMEs) within the agency, as well as soliciting input from external organizations.

1.2.3 Interview Results

The results for how BPA applies the framework elements are detailed in the article by Daim and Oliver for both transmission and energy efficiency technology roadmaps [8]. The results will be summarized in this chapter and analyses. Emphasis is placed on prevailing weaknesses and opportunities for improvement as they relate to communication.

For the first three roadmapping construction elements, the agency employs a similar strategy for collecting the requirements. Regarding the first element of identifying needs and drivers, the Technology Innovation Office takes the lead to develop and maintain the technology roadmaps. Needs and drivers are determined based on interviews and workshops with SMEs and reviewing these against recent R&D

portfolio of projects. The benefit of these brainstorming efforts is to encourage communication and participation from all levels within the organization as well as take advantage of pooled judgments [8]. Similarly, identification of products and services and supporting technologies follows a similar outreach and communication pattern. The agency solicits input from internal and external SMEs, leverages university partnerships, as well as engages in collaborative relationships with national labs and research consortiums to understand current R&D activities, which target the specific needs and drivers that were previously identified. In general, the agency does not conduct R&D independently. Rather the benefits of communication and collaboration with experts are highly valued and put into practice to develop nationally recognized processes and roadmaps.

While establishing linkages among the first three elements is addressed by extracting information from the experts, this stage of the roadmapping process aggressively engages the senior executives to set priorities. This is internally referred to as "bringing the right rock" to the executive committee and project sponsors. In other words, if decision-makers do not agree with the established direction or priorities, the outcome could be a lack of support in terms of resources or influence to move the project forward. The overall outcome of the R&D effort is to solve technical challenges by application of results. Without consensus among the stakeholders, this objective is at risk. A tremendous effort is made to establish agreement among priorities and alignment with the agency's strategic direction as they relate to the agency's technology needs.

Overall, roadmap elements one to four are very well developed and currently implemented at BPA. Opportunities for improvement are more readily identified when considering element 5 (developing plans to acquire or develop the technologies) and element 6 (assigning resources to accomplish the plans for acquisition and development). Related to these elements, the Technology Innovation Office has very well-defined and rigorous processes to select and manage a portfolio of projects that address identified gaps in the technology roadmaps. Most notable are the communication mechanisms that include project reviews by a cross-functional executive council, frequent informal and formal communication with project managers regarding project progress, integration of stage gates, and the start of a technology transfer process to facilitate the application of R&D projects. While there is no disputing the defined technology management processes in practice, the interviews and in-depth understanding of the BPA R&D methodology have identified a few opportunities for improvement.

- Assignment of resources – Because of the critical infrastructure service the agency provides, often R&D activities are not given a priority over solving operational problems. Communication about the benefits of investing in R&D *now* that could solve some of these same operational issues in the *future* is understood, but still, capacity is not freed up to pursue research in some cases.
- Stage gate implementation – Almost all BPA R&D projects have stage gates included as part of the project proposals; however, the practical application of the stage gates needs to be better understood and assessed. In some cases, the inclination

is to assess deliverables or project progress as acceptable or "GREEN," when in fact the project should be assessed as cautionary ("YELLOW") or, RED, and stop the project. Some project managers are inclined to overestimate progress, perhaps out of a concern that it is not acceptable for a project to fail. Rather it is quite the opposite, especially for an R&D project. In fact, the mantra at BPA is "fail early, fail cheap" – identify if a project is not making progress as soon as possible and stopping it while spending the least amount of money. Creating a culture where project managers understand and support failure is necessary.

- Developing and implementing a robust technology transfer process – Ultimately, the goal of developing roadmaps and subsequently creating an R&D portfolio is to apply the results of the project and solve operational and business problems. This is recognized by the agency, but to date, no formal technology transfer process is in place; the current focus is on understanding the potential for intellectual property (IP). In parallel, the technology transfer manager is reviewing literature and conducting benchmarking studies as the preliminary efforts to creating a technology transfer plan. Follow-up is recommended to update this perceived opportunity related to the roadmapping framework.

Overall, BPA has successfully implemented roadmapping and consequent portfolio and project management processes. The roadmapping process demonstrates many elements of communication among SMEs, research consortiums, and universities to ensure that needs, drivers, and technologies are comprehensively identified. In addition, the roadmap itself is used as a tool to communicate technology requirements which tie directly to the agency's whole strategy and mission for the Pacific Northwest.

1.3 Case #2: DTNA

1.3.1 Company Background

Daimler Trucks North America (DTNA) is the manufacturer of heavy-duty trucks in North America, and it is headquartered in Portland, Oregon, USA. DTNA is part of the Daimler family of products and services and represents one element of a global organization. Worldwide, the heavy-duty truck segment has 77,000 employees, 21,000 of which are based in the USA. Manufacturing facilities are located in the USA, Mexico, Brazil, Germany, and Japan (partners with Mitsubishi FUSO).

There is a strong US presence from the parent company as evidenced by the current CEO, other executive members in engineering and marketing, and many temporary detail positions. Equally, there are opportunities for US employees to travel abroad to work at Daimler Trucks in Germany, Brazil, Mexico, and Japan. These opportunities encourage knowledge sharing, cross-functional communications, and some standardization of processes. Ultimately, decision-making authority

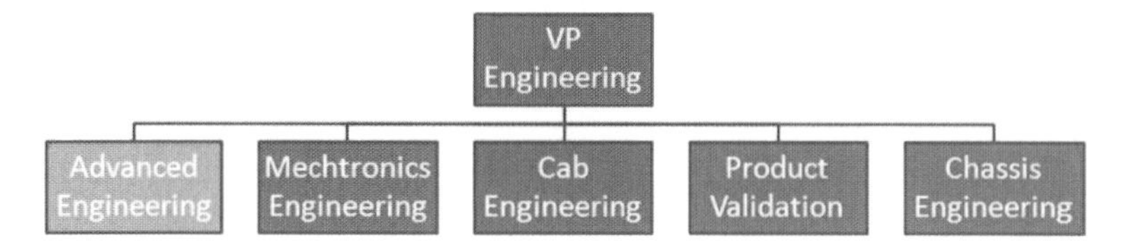

Fig. 1.3 DTNA engineering organization

resides at the corporate headquarters level in Germany, so the organization is not completely decentralized.

The engineering organization follows a matrix-based structure as identified in Fig. 1.3 (DTNA engineering organization). Research and development activity is managed by the Advanced Engineering group, which reports directly to the vice president of engineering.

1.3.2 R&D Organization and Process

Recently, the DTNA organization implemented the use of roadmaps to identify future technology requirements and set a strategic direction. The roadmap process is a joint effort between Advanced Engineering and Product Strategy, which is part of the Sales and Marketing organization. The two groups meet on a quarterly basis to discuss technology and customer trends. The information serves as the basis for keeping the roadmaps current. In preparation for these quarterly meetings, Advanced Engineering does preliminary research and fact-finding. The organization solicits information from their collaborative partners which includes suppliers, universities, customers, trade shows, and national labs. In conjunction with these activities, DTNA also closely monitors the activity of their competitors as well by conducting benchmarking activities. This information is then utilized to determine which technologies could be available 5–7 years into the future. In this capacity, Advanced Engineering sees their role as visionaries or technology leaders for the organization, being responsible for translating technology into a product, and commonly synthesizes several individual technologies together to create a product. One example is the predictive cruise control (PCC) system, jointly developed by Germany and the Advanced Engineering group in the USA. As defined "…PCC system looks for its route a mile in advance and adjusts engine output to the uphill and downhill gradients ahead. Based on this information, the on-board computer calculates the best acceleration response. This response is determined utilizing the same algorithms the driver will have learned during a driver training course, and therefore determines the optimum speed in terms of fuel economy" [10]. This technology integrates the capabilities of GPS location, digital mapping, and higher computational electronics for better fuel efficiency. A product was created that fulfilled a need on the roadmap.

When customer requirements and technology drivers are blended to create the roadmap and subsequent priorities, the results are presented to a global executive committee on a yearly basis. During the presentation, the executive committee reserves the right to overrule the priorities set by Advanced Engineering. The funding for R&D projects is determined through the product action request (PAR) process. Typically, Product Strategy will present a project proposal to a cross-functional team consisting of mid-level managers. Individual cost and resource estimates are collected from the cross-functional team to supplement the business case. Ultimately, the business case is presented to an executive committee who decides to move forward with a project, or not, based on how well it ties in with the organization's overall strategy.

In general, DTNA makes use of cross-functional teams and collaborative relationships to identify technology gaps. These gaps are communicated through technology roadmaps and are used to guide the organization's engineering and Product Strategy activities.

1.3.3 Interview Results

Roadmapping framework elements one to five are very well developed and currently implemented at DTNA. DTNA engages with SMEs that are internal to their organization as well as with external collaborative partners to identify needs and drivers and technologies which address these requirements. They have effectively implemented a process to review their RM on a yearly cycle in order to keep it current and up to date. As well, there is a process in place to approve and manage the R&D development opportunities. Opportunities for improvement are more readily identified when considering element six: assigning resources to accomplish the plans for acquisition and development. Related to this element, the interview with DTNA Advanced Engineering identified several opportunities for improvement.

- Assignment of resources: While there is a dedicated group to identify R&D opportunities at DTNA, execution of the projects requires resources from other engineering and manufacturing groups. In contrast, there are no dedicated R&D teams in these groups. Therefore, there are issues with prioritization of resources such as identifying if they work on operational problems or focus on R&D.
- Communication across all levels of the organization: There is good communication across executive levels, but information and priorities are not clearly communicated to mid-level managers and below.
- Building consensus: The lack of effective communication across all levels of the organization results in difficulties with aligning interest and building consensus. Mid-level managers develop their own perspectives on setting priorities. At this level, there is sufficient autonomy such that managers can decide not to dedicate resources to R&D resulting in conflict.

1.4 Case #3: Medium-Sized Semiconductor Company

1.4.1 Company Background

The selected semiconductor company designs, develops, and manufactures advanced high-performance solutions using various wafer process technologies for customers worldwide. The company participates in the mobile (e.g., cell phones, tablets) and network infrastructure market. The company is structured in two primary business units: mobile and network infrastructure. Each business unit manages its own profit and loss. The charter of the mobile business unit is to drive high volumes in the company factories, proving high utilization with lower profit due to the highly competitive market space. The mission of the network infrastructure business unit is to drive high margins with lower volumes. In addition to the two business units, a large corporate organization supports both business units. Some of these support functions include wafer fabrication, manufacturing, back-end assembly and test, logistics, and material planning. Roughly 80 % of the company revenue and profit comes from the high-volume mobile business unit.

Typical new product development (NPD) life cycles for each of the business units are different. For example, in the mobile unit, product development cycles are 9–24 months to high-volume production. Products become obsolete after approximately 3 years. For the infrastructure unit, product development cycles are similar in length, but product lifetimes are much longer, often greater than 5 years with some products staying in the market for 8–10 years.

1.4.2 R&D Organization and Process

The core of the R&D organization resides in "corporate." As mentioned above, these resources are shared among the three business units. The Advanced Technology team contains a separate subteam for Advanced Packaging as shown in Fig. 1.4. The Advanced Technology team focuses on wafer process technology development. Advanced Packaging focuses on technology development related to packaging of the integrated circuits along with other components. Advanced Design works to develop new circuit design approaches and component architecture in an effort to improve performance or reduce cost.

The technology development process is shown in Fig. 1.5. The process, a traditional stage/gate process, starts with a concept definition and a proposal being drafted. Once the proposal is drafted and reviewed internally with the group making the proposal, a feasibility analysis is conducted. The feasibility analysis includes the following items: return on investment (ROI) calculations, timeline, alternatives, risks, and required resources. If a project passes the feasibility gate, the project will move to the qualification stage.

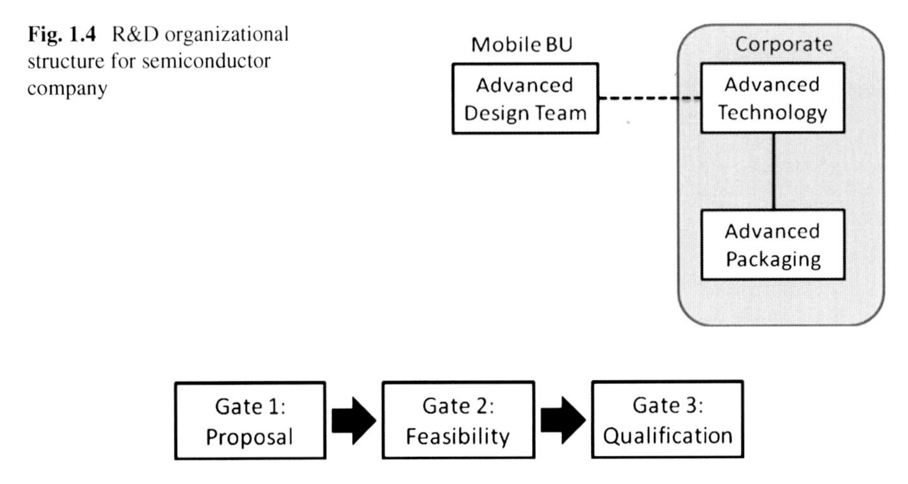

Fig. 1.4 R&D organizational structure for semiconductor company

Fig. 1.5 Technology development process

1.4.3 Interview Results

A series of interviews were conducted with the head of the Advanced Technology group. The team used the six-element framework methodology described above as a guide for the interviews. For the first element, identifying the needs and drivers, the R&D department obtains high-level needs directly from the chief executive officer (CEO). High-level drivers are provided by the CEO vision that technology initiatives need to address one of five areas: lower current consumption, higher linearity, low cost, higher efficiency, and device size. Technology needs tend to lag market needs due to the absence of a long-term product roadmap by marketing. There are no standing meetings between R&D and marketing. Specific business unit needs and drivers are primarily based on informal short-term needs as described in product roadmaps, because the bulk of the company's revenue comes from the mobile unit; most of the activity in R&D is geared toward the mobile unit needs. A long-term roadmap is not currently established and well communicated. As a result, R&D is mainly focused on short-term technology needs. Wafer process technologies typically take a minimum of 2 years to develop. Therefore, the lack of a longer-term roadmap creates challenges for the R&D department.

The second element, identifying products/services to meet needs and drivers, was discussed. Internal technologists together with design engineers work to identify the required products and services necessary to meet the needs and drivers. One problem mentioned during the interview was that sometimes needs and drivers can be addressed via multiple approaches, not just with wafer process technologies. According to the interviewee, the company sometimes lacks the collaborative synergies of the different R&D departments working together to address the needs and drivers. An example was provided where a new process technology was being developed to address a parametric market need while in reality a circuit design improvement could accomplish the same task and in some cases provide a superior result.

In terms of identifying technologies to support the products and services, technologists identify, sometimes in their own department, technologies based on their expertise and on benchmarking and competitive analysis. In this area as well, there is a lack of collaborative synergy between the different R&D teams. As mentioned above, this lack of teamwork can result in inefficient or inferior approach. Establishing the linkage between the first three items is attempted through technology review meetings with technologists. These meetings are held monthly, with each department hosting their own meetings with different attendees. There is no workshop or overall update meeting that combines the different R&D subteams.

In terms of developing plans to acquire or develop the technologies, the interviewee was confident the internal technologists understood the capabilities and boundaries of the internal capabilities and acquisition plans that were established when there are gaps in these capabilities. During the interview, past and active acquisitions were discussed as examples where internal capability was not available and outside capability was being acquired.

Assigning resources to accomplish the plans for acquisition and development is conducted in the subteams and not at a high level, where all resources and projects are considered. According to the interviewee, individual groups own the development and priorities are difficult to manage because these groups are also responsible for daily production issues. Often conflicting priorities exist, with R&D managers attempting to resolve them within their own realm of responsibility.

R&D and marketing do not have regular communications; therefore, a gap exists with identifying needs and drivers. Different business units have different drivers, but the bulk of R&D resources are focused on the high revenue mobile unit. Prioritizing projects, simply based on current revenue, can result in a longer-term technology lapse for the entire business. The team concluded the company had a weakness in the first element, identifying of the needs and drivers. When it came to product and service identification to meet the needs and drivers, the team concluded that the absence of a long-term roadmap could result in missed opportunities beyond 2–3 years. Process technologies take 2–3 years to develop, which requires a long-term product intersect plan to make sure the technologies are available for commercialization at the opportune time. Without such a plan, a panicked catch-up game may become the norm in terms of R&D development project definition. The company seemed to miss potential synergies between the different R&D subgroups when considering how to address needs and drivers because of the long-term roadmap gap coupled with the opportunities in the first three elements; a weakness exists in the fourth linkage element. The company has strength in the area of technology acquisition and development. The technologists have the competency to understand if internal technology development can meet the required needs or if external acquisitions are required. Resource management is also a weakness as the company does not have central program management for technology development projects or high-level resource management. Often, technologists manage R&D projects as well as supporting day-to-day factory production issues. Another issue is that often new technology developments impact several areas of the business. Managing these large development projects can be a full-time job unto itself. Currently, the entire management rests on the technologist's shoulders. In most cases, the technologists do not have the project management skills required or the desire to manage all the nontechnical aspects of the development project.

1.5 Case #4: Asian Automotive Manufacturing Company

1.5.1 Company Background

The interviewed company is the fourth largest automobile manufacturer in the world based on annual vehicle sales in 2010 [11]. The company is also known to operate the world's largest integrated automobile-manufacturing facility that can produce 1.6 million units annually. They have six R&D centers in Germany, Japan, Korea, and India. Additionally there is an American design center in California for specific US market utilization. In 2012, the company announced that it would invest $12.2 billion in its plants and research, up from $10.5 billion in 2011 [12]. R&D investment will increase about 11 % this year to $4.4 trillion, and 90 % of that total will be targeted toward boosting its vehicles' fuel economy and cutting their greenhouse gas emissions.

To continually improve proprietary technology, they have extended extraordinary efforts in the area of R&D. This ongoing investment has enabled them to use cutting-edge technology to produce world-class products. Their research and development centers focus on next-generation environmental, safety, and telecommunications technologies while offering an innovative and competitive model range to secure maximum productivity [13].

The company has built a global network of research facilities including R&D center in locations such as Ann Arbor, Michigan; Irvine, California; Tokyo, Japan; Frankfurt, Germany; and Mabuk, South Korea. The California Design & Technical Center, established in 1990, creates and develops both production vehicles and cutting-edge design concepts. The America Technical Centre in Ann Arbor, Michigan, opened in June 2005 as part of the company's ongoing commitment to the North American market. This facility has the capability of designing and developing vehicles and is responsible for all of their North American engineering activities. This center also operates in conjunction with the Irvine-based Design & Technical Centre and the California Proving Ground. This collaborative effort ensures that they will only market vehicles in the most modern design, which have been thoroughly engineered, developed, and tested. The company's extensive R&D efforts have led to favorable reviews and numerous awards from many independent automotive testing firms in North America.

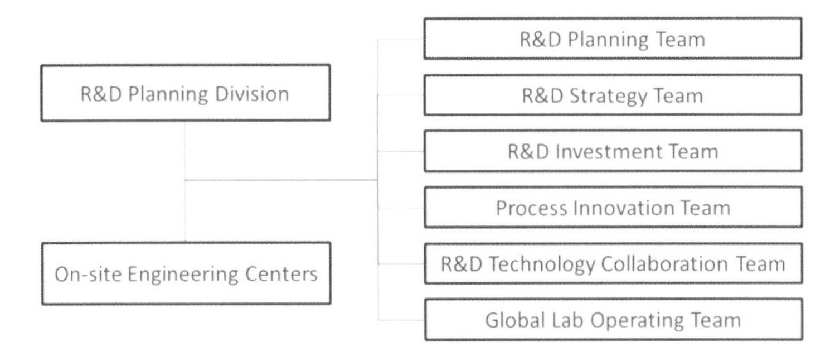

Fig. 1.6 R&D planning division structure

1.5.2 R&D Organization and Process

The interviewed company is well known for their systematic management [14]. R&D management is no exception to this rule, and "R&D planning division" is in charge of the entire R&D management process. Six teams are under the "R&D planning division" so that ten on-site centers can perform actual R&D activities efficiently and effectively. Figure 1.6 (R&D planning division and structure) identifies this structure.

1.5.3 Interview Results

The primary role of the R&D Planning Team is to aid the CTO (chief technology officer) so that they can make final decisions. They pull together pending issues from five other teams as well as on-site centers and report them to the CTO weekly. Once the decision is made by the CTO, they convey modified/determined plans to the subordinate groups. The CTO then organizes task force teams for urgent issues or priority projects. R&D Planning Team takes this responsibility by collaborating with on-site researchers or engineers. Additionally, they formulate a foreign policy plan to manage the publicity strategy with the marketing division.

R&D Strategy Team plays a major role in identifying needs and drivers by actively working with internal and external information sources. Several engineering- or science-focused universities including MIT, Stanford, and Caltech are affiliated with this team and are utilized to identify technology needs for next-generation automobile. The company also contracts with consulting firms when specific studies are required for benchmarking. In addition, they receive project proposals from research labs in the USA, Germany, Japan, and China. External information sources are utilized from journals or magazines and are also constantly monitored. Concurrently, they strategically utilize these media channels to publicize new design concepts. Combining all kinds of information from the aforementioned sources, the R&D Strategy Team conducts scenario planning integrating environment analysis, competitor analysis, and capability analysis.

Once R&D strategies are determined, R&D Investment Teams evaluate alternative decisions and set up investment plans. They first establish long-term investment strategies aligned with the company's R&D roadmap and then assign resources to medium and annual investment plans. Another major activity of R&D Investment Team is operational management. They monitor budget spending of on-site centers to capture bottlenecks or any unexpected occurrences. They also monitor their estimated spending and actual spending, on a weekly basis, as a means of operational management.

The major role of the Process Innovation Team is to standardize new product development process for efficiency improvement. Almost every time, new parts designs developed in on-site centers require advanced production process which is hardly connected to mass production. Therefore, the Process Innovation Team tries either to adapt current standards to the proposed design or to figure out how to achieve the same design performance with the current standard. Successful adjustment of this process can contribute to both cost reduction and flexible scheduling.

The R&D Technology Collaboration Team undertakes works related to collaboration with partners. They periodically evaluate their partners and classify them as 1st tier, 2nd tier, etc. The collaboration is purely based on this labeling system. For example, technology collaboration has taken place only with 1st tier and 2nd tier groups. In addition, only 1st tier parts suppliers are invited to the technology exhibition held by R&D Technology Collaboration Team. This exhibition is a popular technology transfer forum between partners and corporate labs where feasibility of new designs is actively assessed and adopted. The R&D Technology Collaboration Team also works in internal collaboration with other divisions such as sales division and business administration division to facilitate joint research projects.

The Global Lab Operating Team was separated from the R&D Planning Team in 2008 as managerial importance of fostering worldwide labs increased in China, India, and Germany. This team plays a key role of connecting the R&D planning division and global labs around the world. Specifically, as the R&D planning division supervises on-site centers, the Global Lab Operating Team manages every aspect of managerial functions including strategy establishment, investment planning, scheduling, and monitoring for worldwide labs.

1.5.4 Analysis and Findings

Currently, the company is experiencing an organizational transition from project-oriented structure to function-oriented structure, which is causing unexpected conflict among inter-functional centers. Previously, there was an executive director for each center that architecture design centers and test centers' functional areas used to cooperate well. However, since the organization has shifted to function-oriented structure, the architecture designers' wants to minimize design changes based on the results of tests and analytics have changed. Additionally, the organization operates sequentially rather than in parallel which penalizes innovativeness, which comes from the interactions. There is also existing conflict between architecture design centers (body and chassis) and design center (exterior/interior). The designers from design center tend to be as creative as possible, but architecture designers suppress them for the sake of impingement performance or road ability.

The utilization of a charismatic executive director was one of the unique cultures of the company, which allowed separate centers to be cooperative, controllable, and flexible enough to adapt to internal changes. Now this role of arbitrating conflicts among centers is taken over to project management center and functional managers. However, their authority is not only weaker than the executive director, but their role is limited by function-oriented structure. The company is trying to empower them. Nevertheless, function-oriented centers still do their best to have more power and look good at least than others.

1.6 Summary and Discussion

The analysis of the interviews and overall responses from the four companies identifies several key points for discussion. The following list identifies the key points:

1. The identification of strengths and weaknesses is based on perspectives.
2. No company performs perfect across all elements of the roadmap process.
3. Companies can learn and benchmark from other companies or perform publication research, which can provide additional insight into the best in class procedure and methodologies for roadmap.
4. Opportunities lie in transferring of power/authority to other groups within the organization and cohesive team involvement from all participating groups.

The identification of strengths and weaknesses is based on perspectives of analyzing a group as related to the roadmap techniques of the company as identified in the article by Oliver and Daim. Under this type of analysis, the corresponding recommendations do not take into account other perspectives such as financial or organizational knowledge and ability.

All four companies had areas for improvement under each of the six categories of measurement. The categorization of the method with a positive or negative perspective identifies that organizations must utilize continual improvement and self-evaluation, in order to develop a best in class methodology.

Companies can benchmark the processes and procedures of other companies in different business sectors and complete professional research in academic journals in order to develop the best in class system for technology roadmapping effectiveness. It is recommended that a business either collaborates with a consortium of companies or a minimum reviews case studies of other companies related to roadmap utilization.

Implementing this methodology would help the organization of interest at identifying the methods or techniques that will most help the organization.

Opportunities within companies exist when changing or restructuring the organization. This issue may pose problems when individuals resist reorganizing or do not see the value in the restructuring effort. Knowing this, it is important to utilize the correct internal strategies for developing consensus when communicating issues within the organization.

The results of the four interviews were analyzed and compared to best practices and benchmarking among the other companies in the sample as well. The team then assigned strengths or weaknesses to each element in the methodology; the results are summarized in the following tables.

1.6.1 BPA Recommendations

While BPA has demonstrated proficiency at developing technology roadmaps, there is always room for improvement. The interview and practical understanding of their roadmapping process identified some opportunities for incremental progress. A common theme among the organizations interviewed was the lack of sufficient resources to manage multiple projects. This theme is carried in literature. S. Elonen et al.'s research method involved interviews at R&D organizations to identify the issues with managing multiple projects simultaneously. Specific to shared resources their research team found that 24 % of the participants identified "…resource shortages and allocating resources properly…" as one of the biggest hurdles to managing a project [15]. Also, "…project work has often second priority…project work is frequently on the shoulders of the same experts…" [15]. One possible solution is presented by Fricke et al. Their research suggests a "divide and conquer" approach to managing resources and subsequent successful project outcome. In fact, the second most important factor to a successful project outcome is dividing resources [16]. The implication is that management in a multiproject environment will be more successful by creating a dedicated group of R&D project managers. This idea is further supported by McDonough and Spital. Their research suggests leaving some slack resources that could be allocated to development projects. Allocation of these resources would be done by a single senior manager [17]. In practice, McDonough and Spital's recommendation for slack resources might be difficult to implement in cash- and resource-strapped organizations.

As recently as 2012, the Office of Technology Innovation has taken the first steps to developing dedicated R&D teams in different business lines. It is an iterative process – project managers need to be cultivated to either assume the responsibilities of more senior engineers, thereby freeing them up to do R&D project management, or fulfill the role of an R&D PM themselves. Follow-up is recommended to understand if the expected benefits, specifically project success, were realized.

The second opportunity is to apply more rigors to stage gates. By definition, the stage gate approach is "…a phased project management approach that produces fact-based funding decisions based on a set of defined evaluation criteria…the Stage-Gate approach is used to:

- Provide consistent program and project management guidelines
- Characterize projects in terms of scope, quality, performance, and program integration
- Evaluate and monitor project progress against milestones
- Assess viability of technology commercialization
- Guide decisions on project funding (e.g. Go Forward, Stop, Hold, Return)" [18]

As mentioned, almost all of the R&D projects have stage gates identified. The BPA project management officer works with the individual project teams to emphasize the importance of stage gate assessments. Otherwise, for those projects with defined stage gates, the consistency of applying "go, no-go, or hold" criteria could be improved. As an example, one project was given additional time to satisfy the first stage gate after clearly missing the requirements. In this case, the concern was maintaining the delicate balance between exercising the stage gate criteria to kill the project while still encouraging a spirit of collaboration. Ultimately the project was stopped, but could it have been stopped sooner? The research conducted by R.G. Cooper et al. identified that over 50 % of the projects had deficiencies in defining stage gate criteria: "…no criteria have been established for making Go/Kill and prioritization decisions" [19]. To ensure more consistent processes, Cooper et al. suggested that senior management be more involved in the stage gate decision process (Table 1.2).

1.6.2 DTNA Recommendations

For DTNA, the identified weaknesses and opportunities in the roadmapping framework are not uncommon from the other organizations interviewed as part of the report. They manage multiple projects with no dedicated R&D project managers, requiring shared resources between day-to-day operations and research projects. The experiences at DTNA are echoed in literature. S. Elonen et al.'s research method involved interviews at R&D organizations to identify the issues with managing multiple projects simultaneously. Specific to shared resources their research team found that 24 % of the participants identified "…resource shortages and allocating resources properly…" as one of the biggest hurdles to managing a project [15]. Also, "…project work has often second priority…project work is frequently on the shoulders of the same experts…" [15]. One possible solution is presented by Fricke et al. Their research suggests a "divide and conquer" approach to managing resources and subsequent successful project outcome. In fact, the second most important factor to a successful project outcome is dividing resources [16]. The implication is that management in a multiproject environment will be more successful by creating a dedicated

Table 1.2 Interview response summary and analysis for BPA

Elements of technology roadmap process	Strength/weakness categorization	Description	Opportunities
Identifying of needs and drivers	Strength	Regular meetings between SME across organization ensures comprehensive identification	No opportunities identified
Identifying of products or services to meet the needs and the drivers	Strength	Company engages SMEs from industry, national labs, and universities; goal is to establish collaborative relationships to identify products and services	No opportunities identified
Identifying of technologies to support the products or services	Strength	Company engages SMEs from industry, national labs, and universities; goal is to establish collaborative relationships to identify products and services	No opportunities identified
Establishing the linkages among the first three steps above	Strength	Iterative process that relies heavily on internal/external SMEs to put the pieces together; final effort is to engage senior executives to ensure that the most pressing issues are reflected; training is provided on the benefits and process or roadmapping	No opportunities identified
Developing plans to acquire or develop the technologies	Strength/weakness	Yearly solicitation process; RMs are used as the basis for solicitation; very rigorous portfolio and project management practices are applied once a portfolio is determined; well-defined gate system	Improve resource (personnel/ facilities) allocation
		Insufficient resources available to review RMs on a predetermined frequency results in out-of-date RMs; gate criteria not always evaluated correctly	More rigor applied to gate go/ no-go criteria [19]
Assigning resources to accomplish the plans for acquisition and development	Strength/weakness	Financial resources are decided approx. 5 years out; in theory, projects are assigned to the organization most likely to apply the technology	Improve resource (personnel/ facilities) allocation
		Operational issues/priorities take precedence over R&D – do not have dedicated R&D teams in all organizations; immature technology transfer process	Consider formation of projectized projects [29] Develop and implement a robust technology transfer plan [30]

group of R&D project managers; this concept is more fully described in the BPA Analysis and Findings section. This idea is further supported by McDonough and Spital. Their research suggests leaving some slack resources that could be allocated to development projects. Allocation of these resources would be done by a single senior manager [17]. In theory, their recommendations make sense, but in an economy of reduced budgets and a declining workforce, it may be more of a luxury than a feasible solution.

Related to their difficulties building consensus, again, their issues are reinforced in literature. S. Elonen identified "...conflicts of interest between functional management and portfolio management..." [15] as a barrier to successful assignment of resources which are necessary to accomplish the acquisition and development plans. Fricke and Shenbar suggest that functional managers should be brought into the prioritization process and discussions [16]. Applying this to DTNA, lines of communication should be extended to the mid-level managers in an effort to build consensus regarding project priorities (Table 1.3).

1.6.3 Semiconductor Manufacturer Recommendations

For the semiconductor company, the recommendations are primarily focused around communication between internal groups (e.g., marketing and R&D, various R&D subgroups) and program management of R&D projects. By establishing regular meetings between the different business unit marketing teams and R&D, clear product and technology roadmaps [8] could be established. These roadmaps could be used to better understand technology/product intersects and improve the overall communication to the entire organization. Based on feedback from the interviews, the company lacks such a visual roadmap which could easily communicate the product and technology strategy. Such a visual roadmap tool could dramatically improve visibility into R&D projects.

As discussed in class, by "developing a strong interface between R&D and marketing" and "bringing marketing input into the R&D planning process," better alignment can be made between R&D projects and market needs [1]. The company lacked longer-term (>3 year) marketing product roadmaps which is a problem for the R&D teams. Many wafer process development projects take 24 months to qualify once approval is obtained. Without a longer product roadmap, the company could find themselves in perpetual "catch-up" mode.

The R&D teams are managed inside the "corporate" organization and in the mobile business unit. This dispersed, market-driven organization may not be optimum based on research [20] as compared to a more centralized or discipline-based organization. The R&D subteams should all be part of the planning and roadmapping process, as there are various approaches to common challenges. For example, one R&D team may be working to on a wafer process redesign to help address a market need, while in reality a much easier solution might exist in circuit design R&D. By improving communication between the subteams, making certain all

Table 1.3 Interview response summary for DTNA

Elements of technology roadmap process	Strength/weakness categorization	Description	Opportunities
Identifying of needs and drivers	Strength	Good communication between Advanced Engineering (AE) and Product Strategy	No opportunities identified
Identifying of products or services to meet the needs and the drivers	Strength	AE defines 5–7-year product roadmap AE conducts screening process which creates Product Strategy. AE conducts benchmarking/competitive analysis. Customer solicited for feedback. Company works with universities and national labs, trade shows, and national consortiums to identify products/services	No opportunities identified
Identifying of technologies to support the products or services	Strength	AE defines 5–7-year product roadmap AE conducts screening process which creates Product Strategy. AE conducts benchmarking/competitive analysis. Customer solicited for feedback. Company works with universities and national labs, trade shows, and national consortiums to identify products/services	No opportunities identified
Establishing the linkages among the first three steps above	Strength	RM is continually updated on a yearly process; executive committee in Germany has veto power on prioritization	No opportunities identified
Developing plans to acquire or develop the technologies	Strength/weakness	Have a very well-established product action request (PAR) system in place to manage project requests Gate criteria not always evaluated correctly	DTNA has identified a process to keep their RMs current – others could benefit from documenting this process in more detail
Assigning resources to accomplish the plans for acquisition and development	Weakness	Challenges occur at mid-manager level; these are the people who assign resources; at this level they have their own perspectives on what technologies/projects are important; there is autonomy at this level to push back	Assign resources using Design Structure or Responsibility Assignment Matrix [29] Communication across all levels of the organization [1] Reaching consensus [29]

teams are represented in the R&D planning process, and possibly combining the R&D subteams into one reporting structure, the company should be able to better leverage off of the expertise of the different teams.

The company struggles with prioritizing R&D projects as was mentioned several times in the interview. Implementing a process such as the one described in M.S. Brenner's paper [21] is suggested. In this process, five steps are defined which help teams "identify the key issues for success, build consensus among decision-makers, and require the project champions to state their project proposals in the framework most useful to decision makers."

Currently, R&D projects are managed by the project champion or head technologist responsible for the actual R&D work. This can create many issues; a few are identified below:

- Missed opportunities as technologists are spending time managing projects/people
- No centralized PM for R&D projects, limited synergies between subteams and projects
- Minimal rigor in terms of project planning, risk planning, resource management, facilitation of meetings, etc.
- No "one voice" in terms of program status supporting product and R&D roadmap

The Siemens case study reviewed in class provided some key lessons and suggestions related to a centralized program management approach for dispersed R&D teams [22]. Creating a dedicated project management (PM) function to manage R&D teams is suggested in order to avoid the key bullets above. The R&D teams are located at multiple global sites, which can create a unique set of challenges. V. Casey's paper [23] entitled "Virtual software team project management" focuses on the challenges of managing virtual disturbed teams. This paper provides recommendations in six specific areas, as they relate to global teams: risk management, conflict management, team structure and organization, implementation of virtual team process, and organization virtual team strategy. The lessons in this research are suggested to help with the management of the global R&D subteams *if* the company takes the suggestion of creating a dedicated R&D PM role (Table 1.4).

1.6.4 Asian Automotive Manufacturer Recommendations

According to literatures and industry analysts [24–26], the company's R&D management is heavily reinforced by the reflective observations and symbolic leadership of its CTO. He is both highly regarded and highly respected as a "decision-maker" of the company. In this regard, the company routinely makes use of a top-down approach to decision-making in which directives come down to employees in clear and explicit ways, and employees are expected to follow them to the letter. Employee participation levels tend to be lower. As a result, decisions are made more rapidly. However, the company is clearly an automobile-manufacturing firm, but it is also a technology company. Indeed, it might be suggested that the company is a

Table 1.4 Interview response summary for semiconductor manufacturer

Elements of technology roadmap process	Strength/weakness categorization	Description	Opportunities
Identifying of needs and drivers	Weakness	R&D and marketing not closely coupled. Different business units have different drivers; high-volume mobile business drives R&D. Can cause failure to develop key technologies	Set up regular meetings with R&D and marketing [1]. Create clear product roadmaps [8] short and long term with technology intersects
Identifying of products or services to meet the needs and the drivers	Weakness	Missing longer-term (3–5 year) product roadmaps. Wafer technologies take a minimum of 2 years to develop	Create short-/long-term roadmaps [8] as a guide. Use visual map as a tool for communication
Identifying of technologies to support the products or services	Weakness	Good at identifying wafer process technologies, but miss synergies with other R&D subgroups (packaging and design)	Improve communication between R&D subteams. Consider revising R&D organizational structure according to discipline instead of markets [20]
Establishing the linkages among the first three steps above	Weakness	Missing combined short- and long-term vision/roadmap for entire company leads to missing links	Use roadmap process [8] as a guide. Use visual map as a tool for communication. Create one master roadmap with product and technologies intersect
Developing plans to acquire or develop the technologies	Strength	Once technologies are agreed upon by BUs and CEO, development and/or acquisition is rapid	No opportunities identified
Assigning resources to accomplish the plans for acquisition and development	Weakness	R&D is fragmented between different business units, no overall priority and resource map. Shared resources support R&D and production. No central program management	Prioritize projects using process defined in [21]. Create resource map using Design Structure Matrix [31]. Create program management team to provide overall PM of R&D projects [22]. Use [32] to help manage global R&D teams

technology company on wheels. Modern cars today are more electronic than mechanical and are based on a number of core electronic and battery technologies that do not work always seamlessly in a planned strategic environment. A more flexible, impromptu competitive strategy may be preferable. In this endeavor, the executive role must focus more on entrepreneurial leadership than on steady-state behavior. The leader's role is here to create an environment or culture in which employees from top management down are capable of recognizing and then responding to continual change [27]. Hence, communication channel which allows linkage among R&D management activities throughout the organization could increase satisfaction level of both emerging market and CTO.

Interview results on "R&D Technology Collaboration Team" revealed their conservative approach on collaboration with its suppliers. The company collaborates only with 1st and 2nd tier partners for the sake of strategic information security. This "labeling" evaluation is conducted every 5 years. Even though collaboration should be based on mutual trust, this policy could restrict finding the best partners for the company. Excessive collaborations, of course, have been regarded as crucial issues by antitrust authorities [28]. However, today's fast-changing market even allows competitors often to collaborate by sharing a part of value-creating activities such as technology development, product design, and distribution, which are important elements for creating product distinctiveness. Although collaboration between competitors reduces their product distinctiveness, it may increase the distinctiveness between their products and a non-collaborator's product. Also, intensified competition between collaborators lowers their prices and imposes downward pressure on non-collaborator's pricing strategy that could compensate for the benefits by holding information alone. Therefore, it may be worthwhile for the company to consider more flexibility on their collaboration policy than 5 years of stigmatizing process that restricts interactions with their suppliers (Table 1.5).

1.7 Follow-on Research

This research provided several recommendations for organizations to improve their communication protocols based on the roadmapping framework presented by Daim and Oliver [8]. However, there are other opportunities to develop this research more completely – follow-on research is listed for consideration.

- There was no common theme among the organizations selected for interviews. Rather they were selected based on convenience – three of the team members had direct access to key individuals in the R&D departments. It could be interesting to interview similar organizations (e.g., all manufacturing and all government agencies) to determine if there are any industry-dependent communication issues. Or, it would be interesting to compare like industries but headquartered in different countries to understand how culture affects communication. Other divisions to investigate might be communication issues in large versus small organizations or the maturity of project management processes within an organization.

Table 1.5 Interview response summary for Asian automotive manufacturer

Elements of technology roadmap process	Strength/weakness categorization	Description	Opportunities
Identifying of needs and drivers	Strength	"R&D Strategy Team" collects scientific information from several engineering-focused universities all over the world and contract with consulting firms, journals, and magazine to monitor new drivers for next-generation design concept	No opportunities identified
Identifying of products or services to meet the needs and the drivers	Strength	"Global Lab Operating Team" and "R&D Planning Team" identify drivers from separate international labs to establish strategic product development plan	No opportunities identified
Identifying of technologies to support the products or services	Strength/weakness	"Process Innovation Team" tries to both standardize and customize development process. It depends on platform types (small/medium/large sedan/SUV). Weakness exists with new platform development due to desire to use existing standard internal process	Being more flexible to platform design could make the company launch more innovative auto designs [33]
Establishing the linkages among the first three steps above	Strength/weakness	"R&D Planning Team" supports CTO by reporting all kinds of R&D-related activities so that CTO can make decision to go or kill. This is purely top-down way rather than integrated decision process among subteams	Communication channel which allows linkage among driver, product, and technology identification activities could be improved [1]
Developing plans to acquire or develop the technologies	Strength	"R&D Technology Collaboration Team" manages collaboration with supply partners to ensure feasibility of proposed technologies. They also host a technology exhibition to encourage technology transfer between corporate labs and parts suppliers	No opportunities identified
Assigning resources to accomplish the plans for acquisition and development	Strength	"R&D Investment Team" plans development aligned with R&D strategies. They also participate in operational management to ensure that assigned resources are properly spent	No opportunities identified

- Follow-up with the participating organizations is suggested to understand how well (or not) the tools and processes are impacting their communication.
- While this research identified tools or processes to improve communication, additional research could develop metrics for measuring the success of these tools in an organization.

Chapter 1utilized case studies to compare R&D strategies from four companies, which are from different sectors of industry: BPA, DTNA, a semiconductor company, and automotive company. It was seen that these companies use communication to manage their R&D activities. Interviews were conducted with R&D managers, focusing on the communication element of R&D management. Effective R&D management and strategy formation play a vital part in giving a company a competitive advantage. Good communication between R&D and other parts of the organization is crucial for success.

References

1. Daim TU (2012) ETM536. Class lecture, topic: "Strategic R&D Planning" FAB 20. Faculty of Engineering, Portland State University, Portland, 10 July 2012
2. Badir YF, Buchel B, Tucci CL (2005) The role of the Network Lead Company in integrating the NPD process across strategic partners. Int J Entrep Innov Manage 5(1):117–137
3. Hirst G, Mann L (2004) A model of R&D leadership and team communication: the relationship with project performance. R&D Manage 34(2):147–160
4. Nobel R, Birkinshaw J (1998) Innovation in multinational corporations: control and communication patterns in international R & D operations. Strateg Manage J 19(5):479–496
5. Vandaele N, Decouttere C (2011) Sustainable R&D portfolio assessment. Available at SSRN. http://ssrn.com.proxy.lib.pdx.edu/abstract=1974873 or http://dx.doi.org.proxy.lib.pdx.edu/10.2139/ssrn.1974873
6. Griffin A, Hauser JR (1992) Patterns of communication among marketing, engineering and manufacturing-a comparison between two new product teams. Manage Sci 38:360–373
7. Palmer M (2002) How an effective project culture can help to achieve business success: establishing a project culture in Kimberly-Clark Europe. Ind Commer Train 34(3):101–105
8. Daim TU, Oliver T (2008) Implementing technology roadmap process in the energy services sector: a case study of a government agency. Technol Forecast Soc Change 75(5):687–720
9. Public Affairs Office, BPA (2011) BPA facts [Online]. http://www.bpa.gov/corporate/about_BPA/Facts/FactDocs/BPA_Facts_2011.pdf
10. Daimler Trucks North America celebrates the world premiere of Predictive Cruise Control. (26 March 2009) [Online]. http://media.daimler.com/dcmedia/0-921-899449-1-1193922-1-0-0-0-0-0-11701-614240-0-1-0-0-0-0-0.html
11. Top 10 car manufacturers. Craze for Cars (June 2010)
12. Adam B (2012) Home country hub. Site selection. (March 2012)
13. Scarlatoiu G (2012) Low carbon, green growth Korea. In: Korean science and Technology in an International Perspective. Physica-Verlag, Heidelberg, pp 239–258
14. Hong P, Kim S–C (2012) Business network excellence for competitive advantage: case of Korean firms. Int J Bus Excell 5(5):448–462
15. Elonen S, Artto KA (2003) Problems in managing internal development projects in multi-project environments. Int J Proj Manage 21(6):395–402
16. Fricke SE, Shenbar AJ (2000) Managing multiple engineering projects in a manufacturing support environment. Eng Manage IEEE Trans 47(2):258–268

17. McDonough EF, Spital FC (2003) Managing project portfolios. Res Technol Manage 46(3):40–46
18. U.S. Department of Energy, Energy Efficiency and Renewable Energy (2007) Stage-Gate innovation management guidelines, managing risk through structured project decision-making (v 1.7) [Online]. https://www1.eere.energy.gov/manufacturing/financial/pdfs/itp_stage_gate_overview.pdf
19. Cooper RG, Edgett SJ, Kleinschmidt EJ (2002) Optimizing the stage-gate process: what best-practice companies doII. Res Technol Manage 45(6):43–49
20. Burgelman RA, Christensen CM, Wheelwright SC (2008) Strategic management of technology and innovation. McGraw-Hill/Irwin, New York, pp 426–427
21. Brenner MS (1994) Practical R&D project prioritization. Res Technol Manage 37(5):38–43
22. Thomke S (2002) Siemens AG: Global Development Strategy (A). Harvard Business School Case Study, Cambridge, MA
23. Casey V (2010) Virtual software team project management. J Braz Comput Soc 16(2):83–96
24. Bensinger K, Vertabedian R (2011) Toyota to recall 2.17 million more vehicles. Los Angeles Times, pp C–1
25. Saporito B (2010) Toyota's blown engine. Time, pp 12–17
26. Mintzberg H, Waters JA (1985) Of strategies, deliberate and emergent. Strateg Manage J 6(3):257–272
27. Shim WS, Steers RM (2012) Symmetric and asymmetric leadership cultures: a comparative study of leadership and organizational culture at Hyundai and Toyota. J World Bus 47(4):581–591
28. Ghosh A, Morita H (2012) Competitor collaboration and product distinctiveness. Int J Ind Organ 30(2):137–152
29. Project Management Institute (2008) A guide to the project management body of knowledge, 4th edn. PMI, Newtown Square
30. Jain RK, Triandis HC (1997) Management of research and development organizations: managing the unmanageable, vol 27. Wiley, New York, pp 213–215
31. Daim TU (2012) ETM536. Class lecture, topic: "Design Matrix Structure" FAB 20. Faculty of Engineering, Portland State University, Portland, 6 Aug 2012
32. Daim TU et al (2012) Exploring communication breakdown problems in global virtual teams. Int J Proj Manage 30(2):199–212
33. Daim TU (2012) ETM536. Class lecture, topic: "Platforms vs. Derivatives" FAB 20. Faculty of Engineering, Portland State University, Portland, 6 Aug 2012

Chapter 2
Project Selection

Ritu Bidasaria, Aifang Guo, Namitha Shetty, and Rajasree Talla

Abstract Chapter 2 discusses the selection of projects with limited resources. Project selection is critical for an organization to be successful in the achievement of their corporate strategies and competitive advantages. Due to dynamic changes in the business environment, advancement in technology, and condensed product life cycles, companies need to focus their efforts on identifying, selecting, and maximizing their R&D projects to meet customer demands and develop a successful product. Failure to select the best R&D project can cause valuable resources to be spent on poor projects, which yield little result. The aim of this chapter is to identify the criteria that company uses to evaluate and rank R&D projects based on priorities and to select the most appropriate R&D project among several competing projects.

Research and development is critically important to the prolonged success of any manufacturing, product design, and information technology-driven company [1]. R&D project selection involves identification of all possible opportunities and the estimation of project options, along with qualitative as well as quantitative evaluation by different stakeholders [2]. Qualitative attributes are often associated with certain dubiety and unclearness, because of the different perceptions of organizational goals among various stakeholders within and outside the organization (government, financial organization, etc.). Differences in opinion often become an obstacle in the coordination and management of successful R&D projects. Therefore,

R. Bidasaria (✉)
Portland State University, Portland, OR, USA
e-mail: bidasar@pdx.edu

A. Guo
Zhejiang Sci-Tech University, Hangzhou, China

N. Shetty
TransUnion, Chicago, IL, USA

R. Talla
GE Healthcare, Portland, OR, USA

T.U. Daim et al. (eds.), *Planning and Roadmapping Technological Innovations: Cases and Tools*, Innovation, Technology, and Knowledge Management,
DOI 10.1007/978-3-319-02973-3_2, © Springer International Publishing Switzerland 2014

failures are frequent in R&D investment planning [2]. Successful R&D is the difference between leading a new wave of next-generation products and a slow decline into obscurity and bankruptcy [3]. It is not unusual for organizations to be wrestling with hundreds of new possible projects for new product development. This decision-making process is complicated because the probability that a project will be successful in its technical objectives is usually difficult to know. Furthermore, even if it could be predicted with 100 % certainty that a proposed R&D project will achieve its technical objectives and produce results, the ultimate impact of those results within the scientific and technological community is never totally apparent in advance. These factors make the successful selection of R&D projects a twofold challenge: first, to select projects that will be technically successful, have significant impact, and bring the organization great rewards and, second, not to overlook projects when they can be one of the project choices [4].

2.1 Literature Review

R&D management is most commonly practiced in the manufacturing, scientific, and product development sectors [1]. Companies allocate resources to research and development as part of their long-term management strategy [5]. An R&D program must accommodate both technical and commercial attributes of the company equally. Exploring the best idea and determining the top and appropriate technologies to invest in is a complex decision that requires expertise from across the company. In this process, a company faces numerous challenges. Listed below are few of them [5]:

- Creating an equilibrium between market opportunity versus technical viability within the realms of R&D budget
- Ensuring focus with the company's overall strategy/objective
- Gathering employees' input throughout the organization and from the R&D team
- Acquiring the best ideas and giving each idea a fair trial/thought
- Eliminating politics, biasing, prejudice, and personalities from the decision-making process.

In the rapidly changing business environment, R&D is an investment, which companies make for their future. Therefore, R&D project selection becomes even more important. Choosing the right project at the right time with the right tool can help determine the optimum allocation of resources. These days, project selection methods are no longer of minor importance. Both academic scholars and industrial R&D managers are keen to learn more about these methodologies. It has become literally a matter of survival for an industry [6]. The selection of projects is not an easy task [7]. Before choosing any project, one has to identify different criteria that project must meet: market needs, fulfilling organization goals, budget, employee skill set, etc. The criterion differs with specific organization strategies but usually includes a financial measurement, such as ROI, as well as nonfinancial criteria [6]. Research projects are high leverage types of projects, because nobody can forecast the future success of any project and their outputs can have a dramatic impact on the organization's future.

2.1.1 Method for Project Selection

Methods and techniques for selecting projects have appeared in the literature for at least 40 years, and there have been hundreds of published studies. Approaches tend to be either quantitative or qualitative, ranging from rigorous operations research methods to social-science-based interactive techniques [4]. Examples of some of the techniques and tools to help managers are screening models, evaluation models, and portfolio models. The choice of one type of method over another will depend on the nature of the projects being assessed and the decision problem at hand [6, 8].

2.1.2 Profile Model

The project proposals are compared on the basis of a subjective evaluation of their attributes. The ratings are qualitative in nature [6].

2.1.3 Checklists

Each project is subjectively evaluated by the decision maker and assigned a criteria score on each requirement. The criterion score is ascertained from a predestinated scoring scale that translates subjective evaluations into numerical score.

In general, for a checklist model,

$$Tj = \sum_i s_{ij},$$

where Tj is the total score for the *ith* project and s_{ij} is the score for project j on the *ith* requirement or criterion [6, 8].

2.1.4 Scoring Models

In a scoring model, each of $j = 1 \ldots n$ candidate projects are scored on each of $i = 1 \ldots m$ performance requirements or criteria. The criterion scores S_{ij} for each project are then combined with their respective criterion importance weights W_i to achieve a total score Tj for each project. Projects may then be ranked according to their Tj values [6, 8]. For example, a simple additive scoring model would be

$$T_j = \sum_i w_i s_{ij}$$

where s_{ij} is the score for project j on the *ith* criterion and W_i is the criterion weight.

2.1.5 Economic Models

An economic index model is simply a ratio between two variables, and the index is their quotient. Changing the values of the variables changes the value of their quotient or the index. An example of a commonly used index model is the return on investment (*ROI*) index model:

$$ROI\,Index =$$

where R_i is the net return expected from the project in the *ith* year, *Ii* is the investment expected to be made in the *ith* year, and *r* is an interest rate [6]. Economic models are the most popular project selection tool. Cooper (2001) [9] found that 77.3 % of businesses use financial approaches in portfolio management and project selection.

2.1.6 Net Present Value (NPV)

NPV is often used on capital budgeting. The basic idea is that value of money today is worth more than the value of money in some time in future and can earn money in the interim. Computation on NPV serves two purposes [10]. First it makes comparisons possible between early and late values in the same cash flow stream. For instance, how much is a profit worth 15 years from now, in comparison with the R&D expenditure now on the project. Second, it makes comparisons possible between cash flow streams that have different profiles of income and expenditure [6]. Thus, in comparing different income and expenditure streams, future financial values must be discounted back to the present, by the appropriate interest rate. With the help of NPV, we can compare projects with different streams of expenses and revenues and can take into account the time value of money.

2.1.7 Decision Theory Models

Decision theory models are based on the economics and strategic approaches to statistical decision making. These models are based on the idea that a rational decision maker will only adopt those policies, which maximize the expected value of the outcomes.

2.1.8 Analytic Hierarchy Process (AHP)

The AHP model developed by Saaty (1980) [11] is used to support decision makers to rationally select the best alternative based on the qualitative and quantitative approach (subjective and pairwise comparisons). The goal: evaluation criteria and sub-criteria are set in the hierarchical structure for order ranking. It then uses pair-wise comparison to find out the relative importance of one criterion over the other and select the best alternative.

2.2 Methodology

The general model for investigating approach in R&D project selection is shown in Fig. 2.1 below. The model graphically depicts a simplified approach in companies for project selection. There are five basic steps of selection, namely, define the opportunity, identify and analyze the alternatives, choose the best alternative, implement the alternative, and finally evaluate, document, and follow up the results [12].

2.2.1 Four Stages of Investigation Procedure

Figure 2.2 shows the steps followed during data collection.

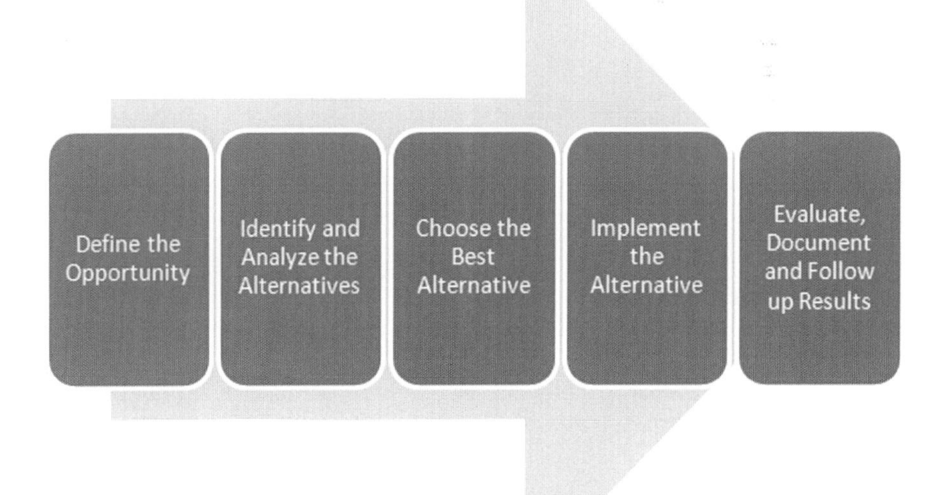

Fig. 2.1 Simplified project selection model

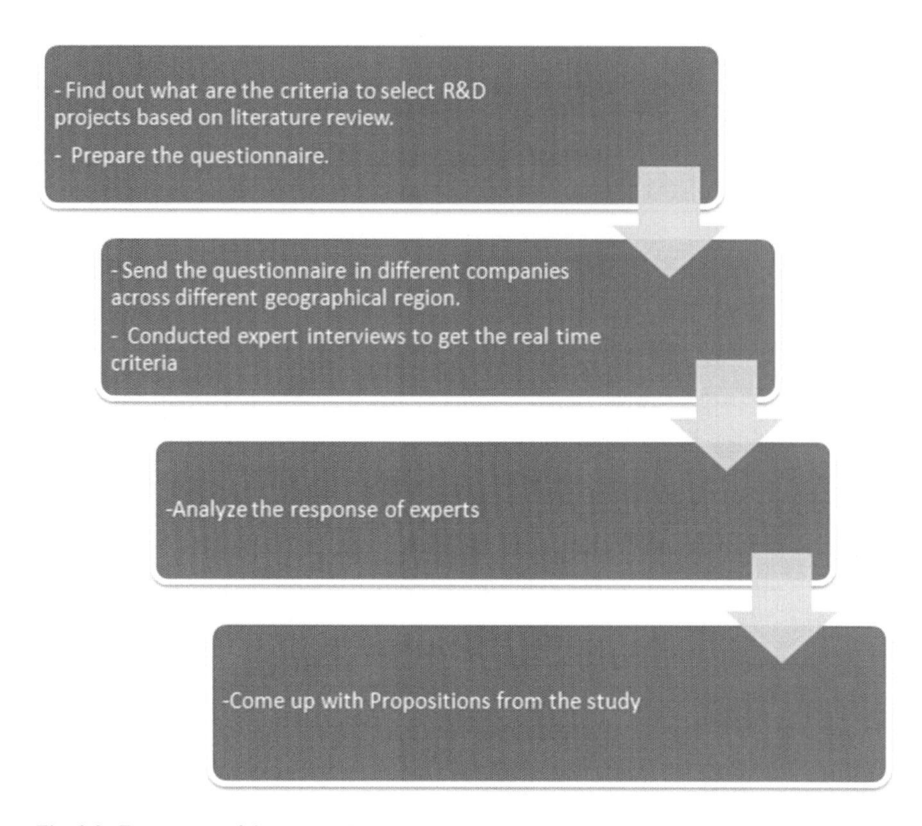

Fig. 2.2 Four stages of data collection

2.2.2 *Criteria and Sub-criteria*

There are various criteria considered by decision makers for choosing R&D project among several competing projects. Numerous researchers have pointed out the importance of criteria selection as follows [13]:

- The criteria reveal the firms target's ad visions.
- The criteria affect the qualities of proposed and selected projects and determine the output of R&D efforts.
- Decision makers decide what kind of projects is more favorable to the company.

Based on the literature study, below are questions that should be considered in determining the criteria for R&D projects [13]:

- What are the factors that make R&D project successful?
- What makes any R&D project successful?
- What should be avoided in an R&D project?

- What characteristics need consideration when evaluating technology and scientific R&D projects?
- What are the firm's strategies and goals?
- Where does our firm tend to be successful?

Identification of criteria, literature review, expert interviews, and discussions within the team reveal seven important aspects that one should consider in the selection of R&D project:

1. *Economic and financial* [3, 14]
   Total budget is considered to be one of the major criteria involved in the decision of evaluating and selecting a research project. Investing in R&D activities is a very crucial and sensitive issue, where the right allocated budget will enhance financial planning within the R&D institution and leads to maintenance of financial resources [14].
2. *Organizational and institutional* [15]
   Expected benefits of R&D project for the organization and compatibility with the firm's plan.
3. *Environmental* [16]
   It includes various ambient factors like safety considerations and environmental policy.
4. *Technical* [13]
   Factors related to the project itself, the technology required, and availability of technical resources.
5. *Risk factors* [13, 15]
   Potential risk for R&D projects such as technical risk or business risk. Organizations need to take some degree of risk in making a decision in project selection, in case the project fails or does not reach its predicted goals.
6. *Market* [14]
   Factors related to the success of the technology and its associated products as related to commercial and marketing.
7. *Managerial considerations* [14]
   Considerations include internal and external culture plus political factors that might influence decisions. Based on team discussions, additional criteria should be considered when selecting a project:

   (a) Frequency and timing of measurement of R&D performance
   (b) Whether company changes the criteria of project selection in time
   (c) Degree of uncertainty and complexity in chosen project
   (d) Type of R&D—basic, exploratory, applied R&D, product development
   (e) Technique used for R&D project measurement–subjective assessment by superior, assessment by independent third party, questionnaire/verbal feedback by internal or external customers, and objective score on quantitative criteria

Further based on the literature review and arguments made in the chapter, we have conceived the model shown in Fig. 2.3.

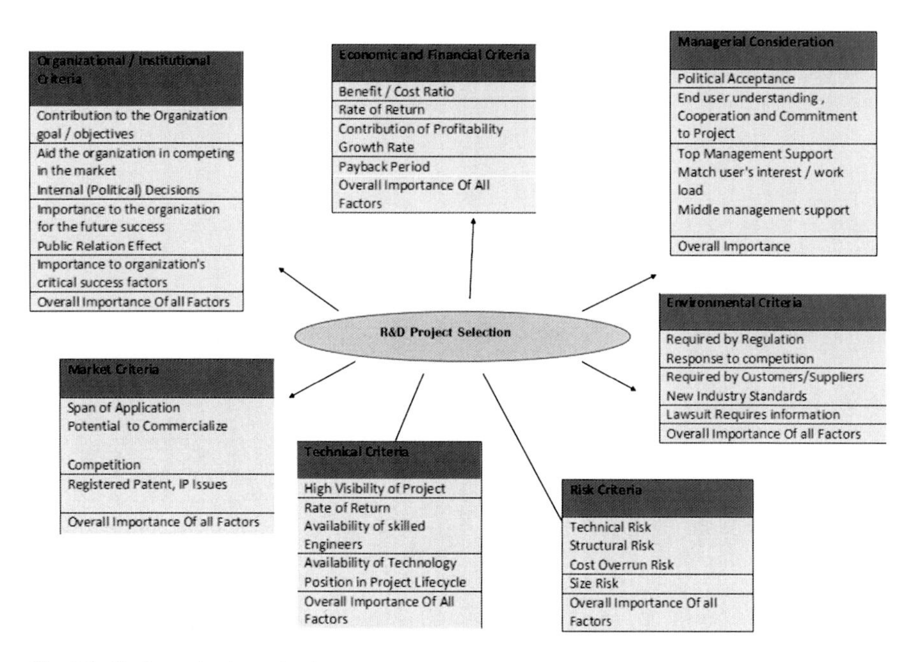

Fig. 2.3 Project selection criteria

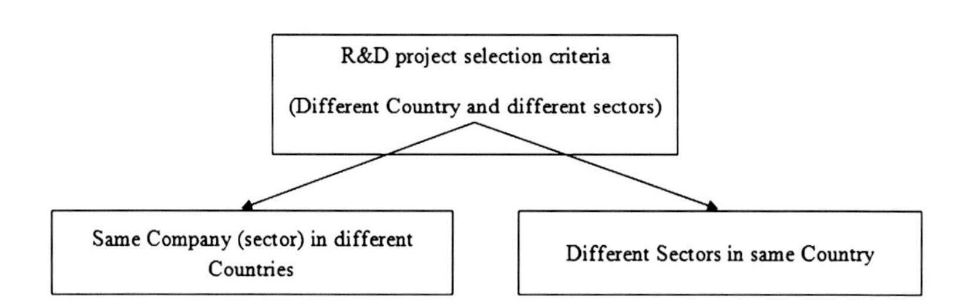

Fig. 2.4 Country project selection criteria

2.3 Results

In this section, we first compare the results across different countries and then we do comparison in different sectors but same location and finally we analyze the results of same sector but different locations (Fig. 2.4).

2.3.1 Selection Criteria Across Different Countries

In this section, we compared the results between US-based Synopsys having R&D arm and Electronic Design Automation (EDA) Software Pvt. Limited in India, called Synopsys (India) Pvt. Limited, focusing on local needs as an Indian company for the purpose of our study [17]. Chinese company known as "SUPCON" and US company called "General Electric" and Novellus for the purpose of the study.

Synopsys is a world leader in EDA, supplying the global electronics market with the software, IP, and services used in semiconductor design and manufacturing. Synopsys' comprehensive, integrated portfolio of implementation, verification, IP, manufacturing, and FPGA solutions helps address the key challenges designers and manufacturers face today, such as power and yield management, system-to-silicon verification, and time-to-results. These technology-leading solutions help give Synopsys customers a competitive edge in bringing the best products to market quickly while reducing costs and schedule risk. Synopsys is headquartered in Mountain View, California, and has more than 60 offices located throughout North America, Europe, Japan, Asia, and India [17].

SUPCON Group Co., Ltd. (SUPCON in short), established in 1993, is one of the leading high-tech enterprises in China with focus on research and development, manufacturing, marketing, engineering services, and system integration for industrial total solutions with innovative industrial control and information technologies. The core business of SUPCON is the development of innovative control and information technologies with hardware, software, system integration, and total industrial solutions to provide our customers with great values under today's competitive global market [18].

General Electric (GE) which is an established company in Healthcare sector, with the theme of "healthy imagination," always has R&D as its top priority. GE is widely spread in different markets. GE healthcare has six primary units [19].

- Healthcare systems
- Life sciences
- Medical diagnostics
- Healthcare IT
- Surgery
- Performance solutions (Fig. 2.5).

From the above graph, we can see that India has chosen risk as the most important criterion because they cannot afford to take high risk due to economic condition of the country, while the USA and China have chosen financial and market as the most important criteria for R&D project selection, because they think the project is successful only if they are able to meet market demands and earn more revenue.

2.3.2 *One Company in Different Geographic Locations*

In this section, we have analyzed the R&D results of the same company (GE) except in a different location (the USA and Singapore). To understand the difference in implementation and development of same product in different flavors, we approached experts with more than 15 years of experience in this area. The expert panel we

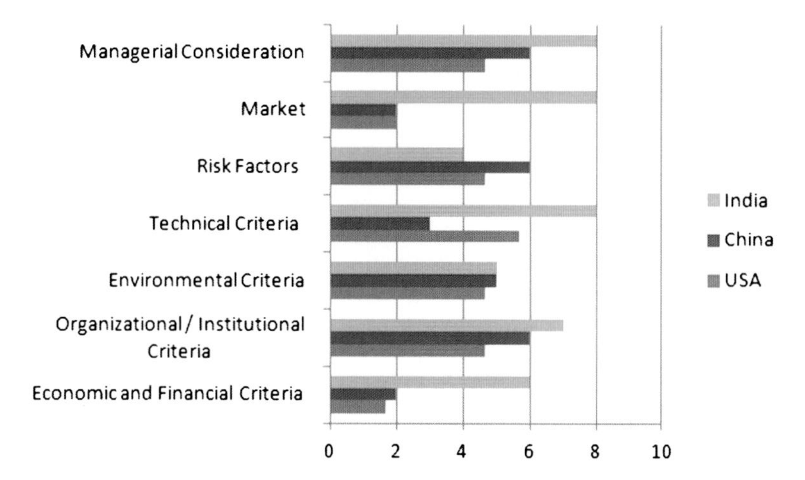

Fig. 2.5 Project selection criteria graph (Order of 1 to 7, 1 being highest and 7 being lowest)

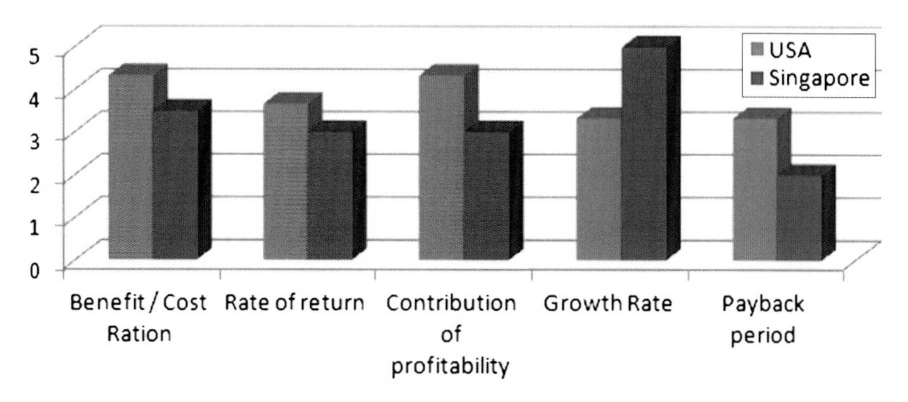

Fig. 2.6 Economic and financial criteria graph (With 5 being most important and 1 being least important)

selected has a managerial, architectural, and customer view on the application. We compared the survey results in both the USA and Singapore. There are few interesting findings from both Singapore and US study. Below is the analysis on the results after normalizing the results from all the experts (Fig. 2.6).

As medical records are new to Singapore compared to the USA, the criteria differed a lot in the financial sector. The return on investment or payback is not the major criterion in Singapore. Until the product is well established, commercialization is not the main criterion. We also observed that commercialization is not completely neglected. The only higher criterion with major difference to the USA is the growth rate. It is expected that potential growth rate is higher in Singapore as the product is not completely matured (Fig. 2.7).

In the organizational and institutional criteria, contribution towards organizational goals is similar in both countries. The competing market is less in Singapore

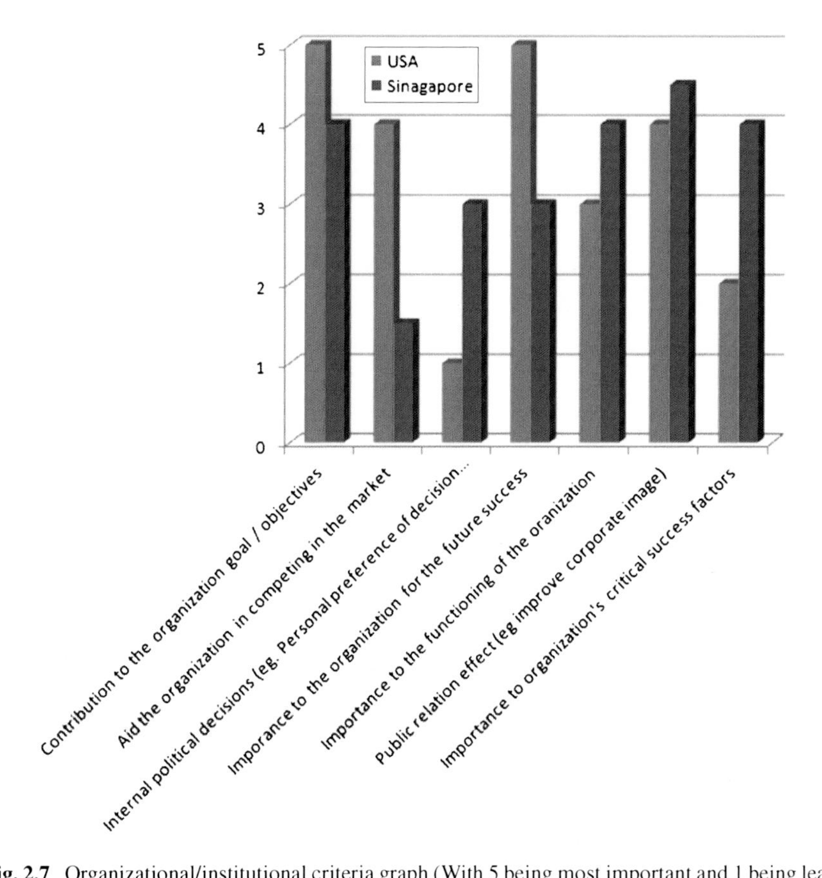

Fig. 2.7 Organizational/institutional criteria graph (With 5 being most important and 1 being least important)

as they are standardizing one product and introducing through the government. With internal political decisions, Singapore took the highest priority as it has more collaboration efforts than the USA. Future or long-term growth is still focused more in the USA. It is comparatively less in Singapore as it has more collaborations and success rate is divided among all of them. For the functioning of organization, both of them are similar. But Singapore gets the maximum as it takes points on globalization efforts. Image to the public is similar and is the highest important factor for the company in any environment. Regarding critical success, Singapore takes major points as it is a new move to the organization (Fig. 2.8).

All the environmental criteria are similar in both countries. Even though environment is really different in both scenarios, it is still important to work according to the specific federal regulations and industry standards. Competition is less in Singapore compared to the USA. Competition is less for this product in the market, but the competition exists while the project gets selected by the Singapore government (Fig. 2.9).

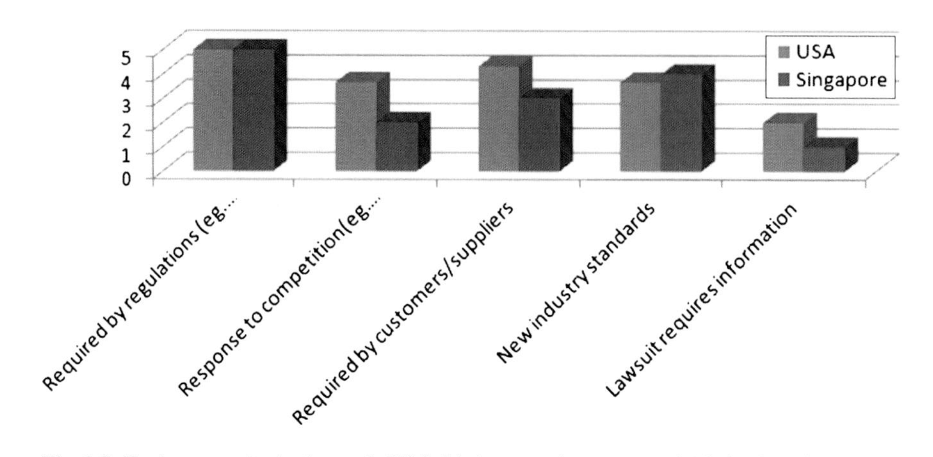

Fig. 2.8 Environmental criteria graph (With 5 being most important and 1 being least important)

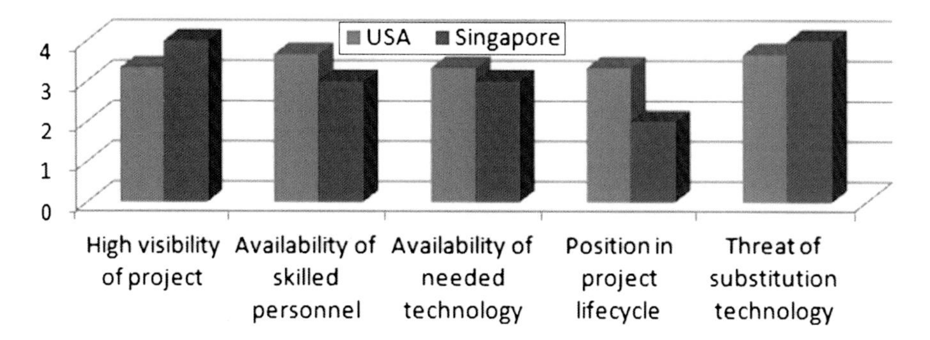

Fig. 2.9 Technical criteria graph (With 5 being most important and 1 being least important)

All the criteria in the technical criteria are important because any project needs the technical criteria met to make the software work. The important observation here is that the position of project's lifecycle is more important for the USA than Singapore. This is because of the dependencies the Singapore project has and also the project is still in the starting phase for Singapore's market (Fig. 2.10).

The risk factors are almost equally important for Singapore and the USA. Due to the integration of products that are new and government standards, the technical risk in Singapore is estimated to be higher compared to the USA. Structure risk is less in both areas as medical records are not a new technology for GE healthcare (Fig. 2.11).

All of the ratings are similar in both the USA and Singapore for these overall criteria. Except for the competition criteria, this is comparably less in the USA. This application is standardized and only GE's Centricity is allowed and encouraged by the government of Singapore. But in the USA there is no standardization like that. There are many companies that are in tough competition in the market for GE (Fig. 2.12).

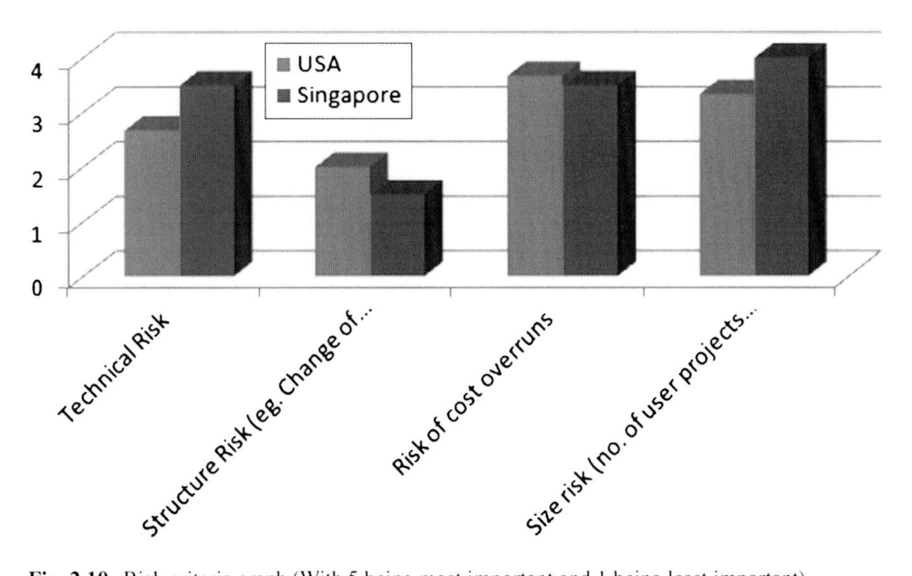

Fig. 2.10 Risk criteria graph (With 5 being most important and 1 being least important)

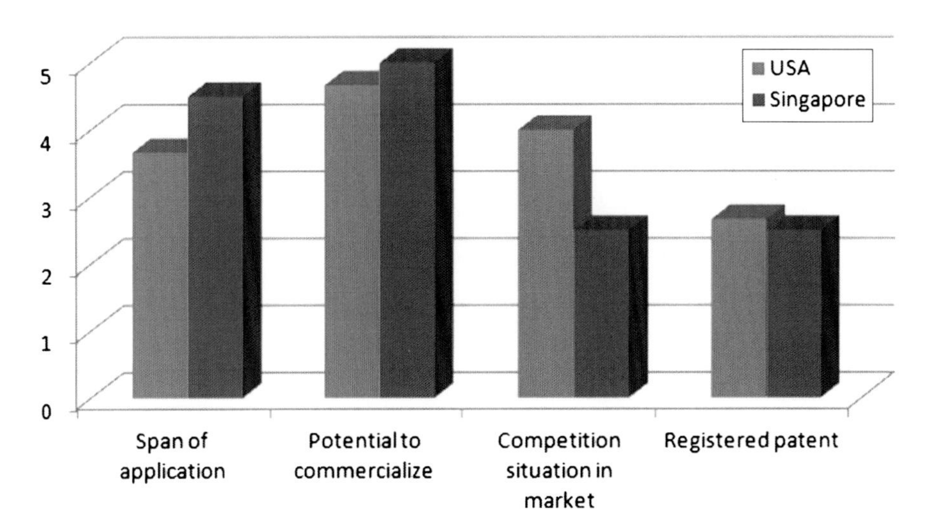

Fig. 2.11 Market criteria graph (With 5 being most important and 1 being least important)

Support from management is one of the top criteria for any project to be accepted. Almost all of the criteria are similar. But political acceptance and power is more reflected in the Singapore project selection because of the implementation. End user understanding is given a bit higher in the USA because the product is mature and users expect more. In Singapore, it is one way assumed to be pushed by the government and it will be a requirement to use this product (Fig. 2.13).

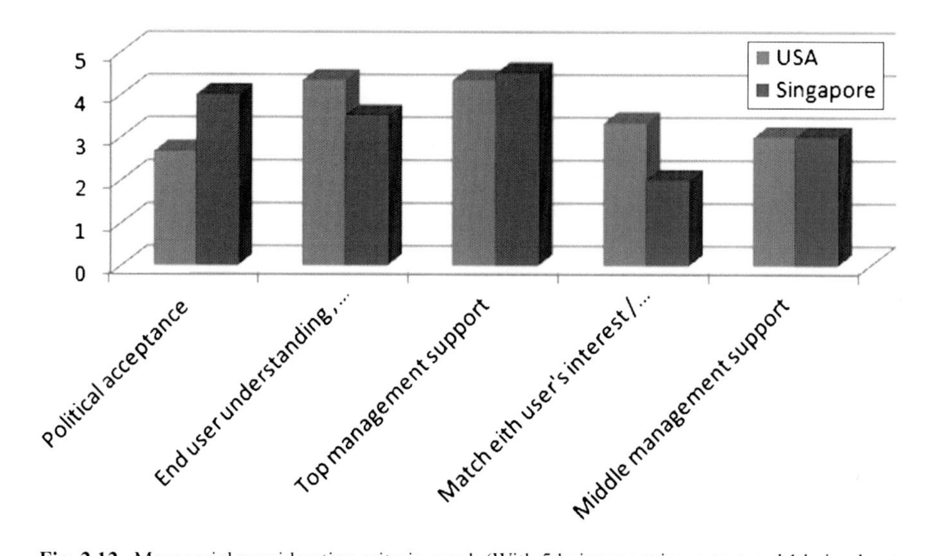

Fig. 2.12 Managerial consideration criteria graph (With 5 being most important and 1 being least important)

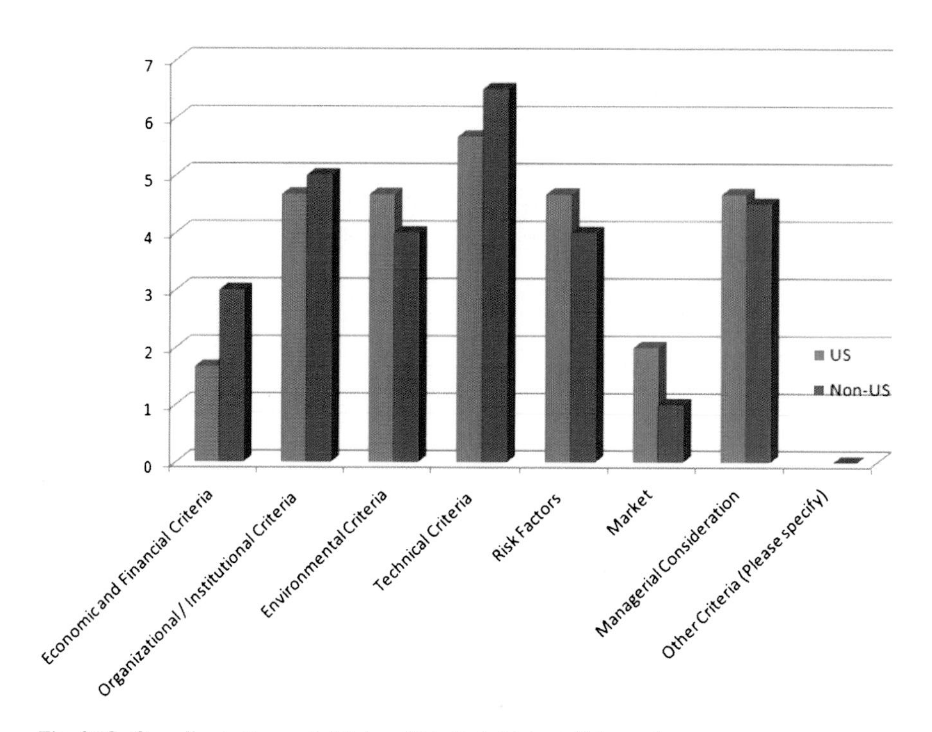

Fig. 2.13 Overall priority graph (Order of 1 to 7: 1, highest; 7, lowest)

As we observe from the graph, the rating of the criteria is almost similar in both the scenarios. The consideration of the criteria is in the same order. Market still takes the top criteria overall, because a project is not considered successful if it does not meet market requirements. Financial criteria have second place, because a company will not invest if revenue or profits are not realized. Organizational, environmental, risk, and managerial considerations take similar priority, because all of them are required to be considered to manage a project. A technical criterion is last, even though it is required. It is subject to change and is least important in a company's prospective, because users only feel the usability but nobody really cares about underlying technology until everything is working fine. Besides these criteria, other important factors that are considered for R&D in specific GE are as follows:

GE operates at multiple levels: R&D-centralized teams (Global Research Center) scouting next-generation/breakthrough technologies for technologies coming 1–3 years out; divisions have smaller principle engineer groups working on 1-year horizon technologies; product teams do targeted R&D for next major programs in 1–6 month cycle. Uncertainty and complexity have been higher in previous years (failure rate higher), but GE is working towards lowering both. GE has all levels of R&D—basic, exploratory, applied R&D, and product development, but the most focus is placed on product development.

2.3.3 *Different Sectors*

In this section, we compare the results received from Novellus and GE.

Novellus Systems, Inc., developed, manufactured, sold, and serviced semiconductor equipment used in the fabrication of integrated circuits. It was the leading supplier of chemical vapor deposition (CVD), plasma-enhanced chemical vapor deposition (PECVD), physical vapor deposition (PVD), electrochemical deposition (ECD), ultraviolet thermal processing (UVTP), and surface preparation equipment used in the manufacturing of semiconductors.

Novellus Systems was founded in 1984 and is headquartered in San Jose, California. The company maintains engineering and manufacturing facilities in Tualatin, Oregon, and San Jose, California. Also, Novellus has a component design and software development facility in Bangalore, India [20] (Fig. 2.14).

When we compared different sectors on the basis of some of the criteria, we found that healthcare companies pay more attention towards potential to commercialize and competition situation in the market because they want their product to stay in the market. For example, if they are launching a new drug for any disease, they do not want their product to fail and need to be pulled out from the clinic in say 6 months [21].

On the other hand, "technology" sector puts more stress on the availability of needed technology and technical risk because of fast obsolete technology and large manufacturing cost [22].

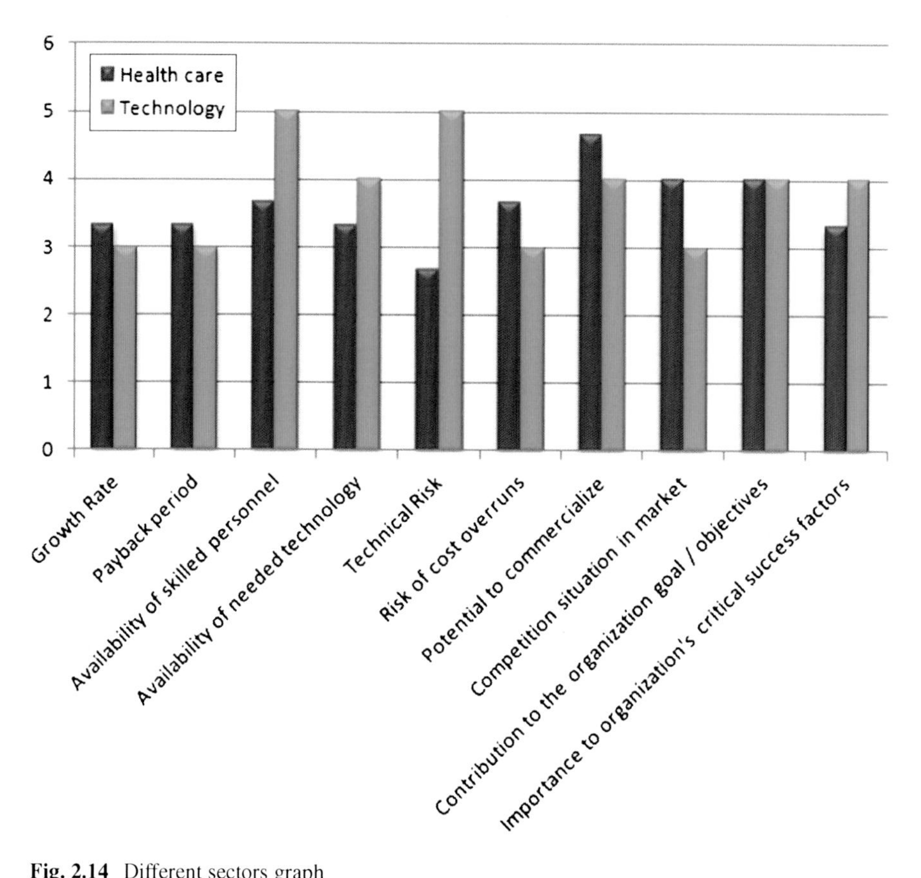

Fig. 2.14 Different sectors graph

2.4 Conclusion

This chapter made an attempt to identify factors that are important in selecting an R&D project. Based on the literature research and survey results that were collected from four companies from the USA and Asia, the following propositions are made:

P1: Market and economic criteria play an important role for project selection for most R&D companies in any country.
P2: Project selection is always aligned towards the organizational goals.
P3: Due to the high cost and commitment involved in any R&D project, understanding the end user acceptability and gaining the support from top management become a critical input into the process.
P4: Project selection is also dependent on the process of implementation of the project.
P5: Human capital is the single most important consideration in any R&D project.
P6: Companies choose projects which have medium to high degree of uncertainty and complexity.

P7: Project selection is also dependent on the process of implementation of the project.
P8: Healthcare projects are dependent on federal regulations and standards in any country in their respective manner.
P9: Technology criteria are important for project selection. Since they are also the continuous changing factors for any project, these are expected to be adaptable compared to any other criteria.

2.5 Recommendations

Although the chapter covers broader geography in understanding the process of selecting R&D projects, there are few limitations that can be overcome with these recommended future studies:

- Increase the sample size to include more companies to have greater confidence in the survey results.
- The study can be further enhanced by including industry-specific questions within the survey (e.g., healthcare, semiconductors). This will need literature search and domain experts from several fields.

Explore other approaches in evaluating the survey results (e.g., the use of pairwise analysis and other decision-making modeling techniques to quantify impact of each factor and subfactor on the R&D project selection).

Chapter 2 compared R&D strategies from four companies and different sectors to examine project selection. The analysis showed that companies use project selection criterion to choose R&D projects to be successful in the achievement of their corporate strategies and competitive advantages while constrained by limited resources.

Appendix 1: Survey

Page 1: Introduction

We are a group of students of "Research and Development Management" class at Portland State University. We are currently working on a project which identifies the criteria, best practices for selection of R&D project. The purpose of this survey is to establish the importance of different criteria that a person

R&D projects requires good amount of resources and therefore one need to consider a lot of factors before choosing it. Because R&D program must balance technical considerations with commercial potential, finding the best

We appreciate your help and support towards our project's success.

Page 2: Expert Details

Details about the Expert:

Name of the expert(optional)	
Designation/position held	
Place of work	
Years of experience in the field	
Additional comments if any	

Page 3: Selection Criteria

In this section, from *your* perspective, you will evaluate the importance of seven categories of R&D project selection criteria. Please use the following rating scale: *1* = Not important *2* = Slightly important *3* = Somewhat important *4* = Important *5* = Very important. (For Non US country, please mention the country name)

Economic and financial criteria

Benefit/cost ration	
Rate of return	
Contribution of profitability	
Growth rate	
Payback period	
The overall importance of the above financial criteria	

Organizational/institutional criteria

Contribution to the organization goal/objectives	
Aid the organization in competing in the market	
Internal political decisions (e.g. Personal preference of decision makers)	
Importance to the organization for the future success	
Importance to the functioning of the organization	
Public relation effect (e.g. improve corporate image)	
Importance to organization's critical success factors	
The overall importance of the above criteria	

Environmental criteria

Required by regulations (e.g. Federal, State)	
Response to competition (e.g. Response time better or equal competitors)	
Required by customers/suppliers	
New industry standards	
Lawsuit requires information	
The overall importance of the above criteria	

Technical criteria

High visibility of project	
Availability of skilled personnel	
Availability of needed technology	
Position in project lifecycle	
Threat of substitution technology	
The overall importance of the above criteria	

Risk factors

Technical risk	
Structure risk (e.g. Change of organization structure/procedures)	
Risk of cost overruns	
Size risk (no. of user projects involved, estimated project time)	
The overall importance of the above criteria	

Market

Span of application	
Potential to commercialize	
Competition situation in market	
Registered patent	
The overall importance of the above criteria	

Managerial consideration

Political acceptance	
End user understanding, cooperation and commitment to project	
Top management support	
Match either user's interest/work load	
Middle management support	
The overall importance of the above criteria	

Use of R&D project measurement techniques, please choose and write the serial number in the bracket (   )

1. Subjective assessment by superior(s)
2. Assessment by independent third party
3. Questionnaire/verbal feedback by internal and/or external customers
4. Objective score on quantitative criteria

Please use 1–8 sequentially to sort the following Criteria according their importance (1–means the most important)

Economic and financial criteria	
Organizational/institutional criteria	
Environmental criteria	
Technical criteria	
Risk factors	
Market	
Managerial consideration	
Other criteria (Please specify)	

Other criteria (Please specify)

Other questions	*Comments*
Frequency and timing of measurement of R&D performance	
Does your company change the criteria in time	
Degree of uncertainty and complexity in the chosen project	
Type of R&D (e.g. Basic, Exploratory, Applied R&D, Product Development)	

Appendix 2: Detailed Information About General Electric Healthcare Projects

General Electric (GE) is an established company in the healthcare sector with the theme of "healthy imagination." GE always has R&D as its top priority.

GE has invested a lot into the healthcare sector, and as part of this healthy imagination, one of the initiatives is Clinical Business solutions. Improvising electronic medical records is part of this initiative [23]. Electronic health records help physicians to deliver better quality of care. Delivering efficient and effective care is the focus for eHealth advantage. Globally all the countries are participating in eHealth. Few of them are Europe, North America, and Asia/Pacific [23].

EHR in North America

In North America, GE healthcare provides its services through a product called "Centricity." This patient information exchange system helps to work towards an effective care. Centricity Practice solution is an integrated medical records product that involves both practice management and patient's chart [24]. This is a well-established product in North America.

EHR in Singapore

As part of eHealth initiatives, the same Centricity product has been selected to be introduced in Singapore. The Singapore government is focusing on getting a common EHR system for all the hospitals. Centricity is the product that GE is introducing in collaboration with the Singapore government. As an integrated product, Singapore government is not considering this as information technology project [25].

The implementation of electronic health records is completely different in both North America and Singapore, even though the product is similar in foundation. We went through a couple of interviews with experts who worked both in North America and Singapore to come up with the criteria.

Expert Study

To understand the difference in the implementation and development of the same product in different flavors, we approached experts with more than 15 years of experience in this area. The expert panel we selected has a managerial, architectural, and customer view on the application. To come up with criteria that are considered for R&D project selection, our expert panel included the following:

- Chief architects
- Business analysts
- Engineering manager
- Product manager
- User physicians.

These interviews were focused on the first step of our research process, which is the criteria selection.

From the interviews, the vital areas that influenced the criteria in this specific project were as follows.

Hospital System

In Singapore, the hospital management system is different from the USA.

USA—Types of hospitals in the USA include community hospitals, federal government hospitals, nonfederal psychiatric hospitals, and long-term care and hospital units of institutions [26]. The workflow in any hospital is almost the same when the patient enters or leaves the hospital [27]. Pharmacies are separate business from hospitals.

Singapore—In Singapore, hospitals are government, private owned and clinics. Primary care physicians, also known as the general physicians, play an important role in hospital system [25]. Workflows might not involve all the members as US workflows; the clinics do not have all the staff. Pharmacies are sometimes not separate to the medical facilities.

Government Incentives

The USA and Singapore have different approaches to incentives.

USA—It was not a requirement to use medical records, or there was no government policy for that, but recently government realized the way the healthcare market is growing and this made them to work on the incentives. The government recently introduced Medicare ($44,000) and Medicaid ($63,750) incentives when they have the appropriate attestation [28]. This is expected to bring in $5 billion to US EHR market [29]. This gives a great push for the adoption of electronic medical records.

Singapore—The government of Singapore has taken EMR adoption as separate platform integrating with others like networking and referral processing systems [24, 25]. This will provide the standardization efforts way earlier in the game compared to North America. Experts mentioned that components like networking, EMR, BizTalk, and CMS (clinical medical systems) vendors are collaborating to complete the project in Singapore.

Insurance Programs

USA—In the USA, insurance programs are predefined and are in practice many years ago. This is also a requirement in North America to receive quality care and affordable care. Few of them include Medicare, Medicaid, and all other private and nonprofit insurance providers [30]. This is an established market in North America.

Singapore—Insurance in Singapore is a common term, but not everybody has to have insurance. Patients can pick their own primary care providers. Only few companies are getting insurance policies established for their employees. Both public and private companies offer insurance in Singapore [31]. The government is trying to provide financial incentives for encouraging the adoption of insurance plans.

Users

USA—In the USA, besides physicians, there are many other persons who access EMR on a regular basis like receptionists, nurses, and assistants.

Singapore—Singapore also has similar users as the USA. The only difference occurs in the workflows. It is not always required to go through a receptionist or any other medical staff. Physicians in small clinics which are common in Singapore do not really have any staff.

These were few common comparisons that occurred in our expert study in understanding the implementation of EMR. The input from this study is transferred into some of the common criteria mentioned in the questionnaire.

References

1. What is R&D management?. http://www.wisegeek.com/what-is-rd-management.html
2. R&D project selection. www.progrid.info/rd-project-selection
3. Otaibi AA, Sultan YA, Khadra WA (2006) Integrated model for project evaluation in R&D institution: a case study of Kuwait. Kuwait Institute for Scientific Research, Safat, Kuwait

4. Begičević N., Divjak B., Hunjak T. Desicion making on project selection in high education sector using the Analytic Hierarchy Process. In: Proceedings of the ITI 2009 31st international conference on information technology interfaces, pp. 547–552
5. Henriksen AD, Traynor AJ (1995) A practical R&D project selection scoring tool. IEEE 46: 158–170
6. Cooper RG, Edgett SJ, Kleinschmidt EJ (2001) Portfolio management for new product development: results of an industry practices study. R&D Management 31(4):361–380
7. Martino JP (1995) R&D project selection. Wiley, New York
8. Saaty TL (1990) How to make a decision: the analytic hierarchy process. Eur J Oper Res 48(1): 9–26
9. Powers M (2008) The five basic steps involved in systematic decision making, 07 Nov 2008. http://voices.yahoo.com/the-five-basic-steps-involved-systematic-decision-2123858.html
10. Adnan N (2006) An integrated tool for ranking and selecting research and development projects. Kuwait Institute for Scientific Research, Kuwait
11. Jiang JJ, Klien G (1999) Project selection criteria by strategic orientation. Inform Manage 36(2):63–75, Elsevier
12. Pitts J (2010) R&D project selection: best practices for suppliers. In: Massachusetts Institute of Technology. Department of Mechanical Engineering; Sloan School of Management; Leaders for Global Operations Program, 2010
13. Coldrick S, Longhurst P, Ivey P (2003) An R&D options selection model for investment decisions. *Elsevier, Technovation*, pp 185–193
14. Pourkazemi A, Ghoreyshi SM (2010) A possiblistic programming model for R&D project portfolio selection in fuzzy environments. APIEMS: pp. 7–10
15. Synopsys. http://www.synopsys.com/Company/officelocations/india/Pages/default.aspx
16. Supcon. http://en.supcon.com/aboutus.htm
17. Waukesha, Wisconsin, USA Medical (2010) GE healthcare systems – case study. *Brüel & Kjær*
18. Lam Research/Novellus Systems. http://www.novellus.com/
19. Pisano G, Fleming L, Strick E (2006) Vertex pharmaceuticals: R&D portfolio management (A). Harvard Business School, Boston
20. Shih W, Pisano G, King A (2008) Radical collaboration: IBM microelectronics joint development alliances. Harvard Business School, Boston
21. GE Healthcare healthy imagination Investor Update, *GE healthcare*. http://www.ge.com/investors/events/event_id11092010.html
22. GE, *GE healthcare*. http://www.gehealthcare.com/centricity-advance
23. Singapore's National Electronic Health Record Architecture, 04 Jun 2009. http://www.omg.org/news/meetings/workshops/SOA-HC/presentations-09/04-03_Tan-Seng.pdf
24. American Hospital Association (2012) *Fast facts on US hospitals*, 03 Jan 2012. http://www.aha.org/research/rc/stat-studies/fast-facts.shtml
25. UML Diagrams for Hospital Management, *Programs & notes for MCA*. http://www.programsformca.com/2012/03/uml-diagrams-for-hospital-management.html
26. Kim A (2009) eHealth best practices – optimizing efficiency and quality of care: global case studies in Asia/Pacific, Europe and Americas
27. Pizzi R (2007) U.S. EHR market to approach $5 billion by 2015, 05 Feb 2007. http://www.healthcareitnews.com/news/us-ehr-market-approach-5-billion-2015
28. EHR Incentive Programs (2012) 02 Aug 2012. https://www.cms.gov/Regulations-and-Guidance/Legislation/EHRIncentivePrograms/index.html?redirect=/EHRIncentivePrograms/
29. Guide me Singapore http://www.guidemesingapore.com/relocation/introduction/healthcare-in-singapore
30. Habib M, Khan R, Piracha JL (2009) Analytic network process applied to R&D project selection. In: International conference on information and communication technologies, Karachi 2009. ICICT '09. pp 274–280
31. Souder WE (1980) Project screening, evaluation and selection: Chapter 9. In: Souder WE (ed) Management decision methods for managers of engineering and research. Van Nostrand Reinhold, New York, pp 137–190

Chapter 3
Design Structure Matrix

Bing Wang, Farshad Madani, Xiaowen Wang, Liying Wang, and Corey White

Abstract Trial and error are inevitable in the process of software development; unfocused communication wastes valuable resources during redesign. To speed up this development process, an optimization of the information flow and a redesign of the development organization were initiated, specifically by creating "chunks" or groupings of tasks and people. First, we investigated the information flow between tasks and utilized the Design Structure Matrix (DSM) to couple tasks into phases, thereby reducing information exchange among chunks of tasks and eliminating the redundant iterations of tasks. Meanwhile, we also grouped the engineers into groups in order to eliminate wasteful communications between the groups of engineers. We depicted the social network defined by the information flow within the software development sector and compared the new arrangement to the old arrangement in a visible way. This new arrangement will facilitate the communications between engineers and speed up the process of software development.

3.1 Introduction

As we all know, software development fails and developers fail to meet their goals if they spend all their time fighting against an inappropriate organizational structure, task assignments, or information exchanges. Therefore, understanding the importance and advantages of the proper organizational structure is vital to the ultimate

B. Wang • F. Madani (✉) • X. Wang
Portland State University, Portland, OR, USA
e-mail: wbing2000@gmail.com; farshad.madani@gmail.com

L. Wang
Jiliang University, Hangzhou, China

C. White
Morpho Detection, Camas, WA, USA

T.U. Daim et al. (eds.), *Planning and Roadmapping Technological Innovations: Cases and Tools*, Innovation, Technology, and Knowledge Management,
DOI 10.1007/978-3-319-02973-3_3, © Springer International Publishing Switzerland 2014

success of a software development organization. Many chief information officers recognize that the organizational structure of their software development group has an impact on the success of their application development efforts. An organization is defined by much more than job titles and a reporting structure. Each individual in an organization has the skills; these skills are usually formal or informal performance, future performance incentives, and rewards (compensation) measurements. The information flow in the organization is related largely to the assignment of tasks to different persons and the cooperation among them.

We chose to research how to develop and maintain a good way to do task assignment and effective information exchange in project teams [1]. While many articles have addressed the importance of such issues, few have conducted systematic investigations about their operation in software development.

There are three reasons for a greater emphasis on the organizational and social contexts of software processes. First, the human element is a critical and dominant factor in most tool-intensive parts of software development such as the system-building process. There are the efficiency and appropriateness tools that are obviously important; for example, the crucial job of tracking down the sources of inconsistency and negotiating their resolution is performed by people. Second, many process studies have indicated a large amount of unexplained variance in performance suggesting that significant aspects of the process are independent of the technological context [2, 3, 4]. Finally, it is noted that a significant proportion of project effort is devoted to non-programming activities, with some estimates indicating as much as 50 % of a work week typically absorbed by machine downtime, meetings, paperwork, company business, and sick and personal days [1, 2].

The design and development of complex engineering products requires hundreds of participants from different backgrounds, leading to the efforts and cooperation of the complex relationship between people and tasks. Many traditional project management tools such as PERT, Gantt, and CPM methods do not address problems stemming from this complexity. These tools allow the modeling of sequential and parallel processes, but they fail to address interdependency (feedback and iteration), which is common in complex product development (PD) projects. To address this issue, a matrix-based tool called the Design Structure Matrix (DSM) has evolved. This method differs from traditional project management tools because it focuses on representing information flows rather than work flows. The DSM method is an information exchange model that allows the representation of complex task (or team) relationships in order to determine a sensible sequence for the tasks (or grouping for the teams) being modeled. This chapter will cover how the basic method works and how organizations can employ the DSM to improve the planning, execution, and management of complex PD projects using different algorithms (i.e., partitioning, tearing, banding, clustering, simulation, and eigenvalue analysis) [5].

Software development is predominantly a social activity. It is important to view software development groups, departments, and corporations as social bodies. We learned to use a new data collection method, combined with several techniques commonly used in social network analysis of software organizations. We cataloged the social network diagrams by using a variety of visualization techniques. Based on the architectural pattern of emerging design technologies, we provided a communication and organizational model [6].

3.2 Methodology

In this chapter, we examined an innovative approach to this problem by seeking to combine the strengths of two existing ways, the DSM and spectral clustering, into improved task assignments which yields a more efficient information flow in the software development process.

The DSM is a powerful tool that aids in business analysis through visualizing, analyzing, innovating, and improving systems including product architectures, organizational structures, and process flows.

The DSM makes the processes of management easier to visualize, allowing for identifying and representing the elements in a project, keeping track of cyclic task dependencies as well as task flows, and aiding in analyzing how and where to make improvements in the dependencies between systems. The Design Structure Matrix management tool can generate a good flow of information between departments so that each department is aware of others' and plans accordingly. The DSM has also been used to solve the problems of a software development and system architecture. The DSM has been utilized by many of the top blue-chip companies since its development in the 1970s, and it has been shown to help solve problems and improve organizations [7]. It is a suitable process model and very pivotal for product developing. The DSM emphasizes the interdependencies of information, task sequences, and product design to provide an effective modeling method. In this chapter, the establishment of the principle was introduced. As an example, DSM customized corrected stent-based process models. Additional models are proposed such as task decomposition and the establishment and optimization of the DSM. The method of establishment and optimization of process model of product design based on DSM can shorten design cycle of product effectively, which will improve competitiveness of developers.

In recent years, analyzing social networks based on data clustering has become a popular topic owing to its significance to a variety of industries. It can be used to prevent terrorist attacks and detect the spread of diseases by identifying communities. Moreover, an understanding of the structure of social networks makes it easier to boost social development and social cooperation; because social networks are dynamic, data clustering can predict changes of social ties [6]. Effective knowledge among team members is a critical factor that can facilitate team knowledge and innovation and increase organizational knowledge as a whole. Thus, effectively understanding and taking advantage of social networks analysis is beneficial to any organization. From the data mining aspect, social networks are incomplete, huge, complex and dynamic networks, and traditional data clustering methods do not work well in social areas due to these features. Conversely, spectral clustering, as one of most popular modern data clustering algorithms, offers a systematic, flexible, and practical solution to problems about social networks [8]. This chapter attempts to depict the spectral clustering and its advantages to the information flow within the software development sector and compare the new arrangement to the old arrangement in a visible way.

3.3 Data Collection

We interviewed the software development department in a Chinese company named "Datashine" located in Shanghai, China. This software company is focused on the development of enterprise information management systems, consulting, and implementation services. Datashine is the leading enterprise-class information management system and service provider. We collected all the related development data including the relationships between each developer and each task.

Firstly, we interviewed the manager of the software department of the Datashine company. They identified 17 tasks for the development of Customer Relationship Management (CRM) platform as in Table 3.1. CRM platform development is a regular business of Datashine, which has engaged in it for about 5 years.

We then defined the 17 tasks as shown in Table 3.1.

We presented a DSM to them in a form of a questionnaire according to the work tasks. There are totally 20 persons in the CRM software department who undertake different tasks. Every one of them filled out the questionnaire according to their information flow facts in working for the allocated tasks. This questionnaire is suitable for DSM as well as SNA because it not only addresses the information flow among tasks but also depicts the information flow between persons. We gathered the data for the analysis of DSM and SNA.

3.4 Data Analysis and Result

As discussed, we first depict the DSM matrix as shown in Table 3.2.

When we received the initial DSM, we found that Task 1, Task 2, and Task 3 formed the first chunk. This chunk prepares for the development and forms the development design including the framework and database design. This chunk periodically gives information to the programming tasks. Task 17 forms a specific chunk, which is testing. This task has inflow and outflow to the programming tasks. The other tasks are programming tasks, which the "W" and "M" are distributed randomly across. So we tried to align all the "W" and "M" closer to the diagonal of the matrix. This helps us to identify the chunks in the programming tasks as shown in Table 3.3.

In this way we divided the CRM software department into five chunks as shown in Table 3.4. We then looked at the persons responsible for the tasks and find out that

Table 3.1 Project schedule

Phase (results)	Task	Work content	Plan	Person(s)
Preparatory phase (the project plan document)	Task 1	Development preparation	(1) To determine the demand for programs and the development of the development process (2) To prepare the database and test server address (3) To determine the development environment (4) To complete the project flowchart (5) To determine the user rights Personnel to freeze the activities automatically obtain and page functions	Tom
Design phase (database and project design document)	Task 2	Software framework design	Build solutions to determine the application development framework	Joe
	Task 3	Database design	(1) The design of the database table fields (2) Completion of the database documents	Robert
Development stage (program code, the solved problems, BUG report)	Task 4	Schedule	Module programming, test and BUG report	Jesse Jack
	Task 5	Attendance management	Module programming, test and BUG report	Jesse Jack
	Task 6	Reimbursement of expenses	Module programming, test and BUG report	Jesse Jack
	Task 7	Internal messaging	Module programming, test and BUG report	John Ben
	Task 8	External mail	Module programming, test and BUG report	John Ben
	Task 9	SMS	Module programming, test and BUG report	George Apple
	Task 10	Reminding system	Module programming, test and BUG report	George Apple
	Task 11	Process management	Module programming, test and BUG report	Martin Alan Dean
	Task 12	Attachment upload	Module programming, test and BUG report	Jim
	Task 13	Online contract modification	Module programming, test and BUG report	Daniel Kevin
	Task 14	Order management	Module programming, test and BUG report	Daniel Kevin
	Task 15	Receivables management	Module programming, test and BUG report	Peter Vincent
	Task 16	Invoice management	Module programming, test and BUG report	Peter Vincent
Test phase (test documentation)	Task 17	Program test and optimization	(1) To complete the internal testing procedures in the test server (2) To hand it over to the testing group (3) To improve the database document (4) To complete the development documentation (5) To sum up the development experiences	Simon Alice Rose

Table 3.2 The information flow among the 17 tasks

	1	2	3	4	5	6	7	8	9	10	11	12	13	14	15	16	17
Task 1	#																
Task 2	D	#	D														
Task 3	D	D	#														
Task 4		D	W	#			M										M
Task 5		D	W		#												M
Task 6		D	W			#					M	M					M
Task 7		D	D	M			#						M	M	M	M	M
Task 8		D	W					#						M	M	M	M
Task 9		D	W						#				M				M
Task 10		D	W							#				M	M		M
Task 11		W	D			M					#		M	M	M	M	M
Task 12		W	D			M						#				M	M
Task 13		W	D				M		M		M	M	#			W	M
Task 14		W	D				M			M	M			#	W		M
Task 15		W	D					M		M	M			W	#		M
Task 16		W	D					M			M	M	W			#	M
Task 17	M			W	W	W	W	W	W	W	W	W	W	W	W	W	#

Blue characters are feedback, and red characters are feed forward
D daily information flow from the task in the column to the task in the row
W weekly information flow from the task in the column to the task in the row
M monthly information flow from the task in the column to the task in the row

many of the staff belonged to different chunks, which makes the communication more frequent than it should be. In order to eliminate the unnecessary communication between chunks, we rearrange the tasks conducted by the staff, as shown in Table 3.5. The rearranged tasks are identified in Table 3.6.

In order to show the relationship of persons in the CRM software department, we depicted the social network chart derived from the questionnaire before and after the rearrangement of tasks, as shown in Tables 3.7 and 3.8, Figs. 3.1 and 3.2.

We cannot see big changes to the social network diagram since the change is not very prominent. However, from the matrix, we can see that we added 4 connections which are red "1"s; the 6 grids with blue background are the eliminated connections, while the social network cannot embody the improvement totally since it does not show the frequencies of communications. It can, however, see that Task 14 and Task 15 need communication to occur weekly. We rearranged these tasks to the same people, Peter and Vincent, which eliminated the weekly communication. In a similar fashion to the previous reassignment, we rearranged Daniel and Kevin (Task 13 and Task 16) in order to eliminate the weekly communication between these two tasks.

Table 3.3 The DSM with chunks optimized

	1	2	3	7	4	1	1	1	8	1	1	1	6	1	9	5	1
1	#																
2	D	#	D														
3	D	D	#														
7		D	D	#	M	M	M				M	M					M
4		D	W	M	#												M
15		W	D			#	W	M	M	M							M
14		W	D	M		W	#	M		M							M
10		D	W			M	M	#									M
8		D	W			M	M		#		M						M
11		W	D			M	M			#	M	M	M				M
16		W	D						M	M	#	W		M			M
13		W	D	M						M	W	#		M	M		M
6		D	W							M			#	M			M
12		W	D								M		M	#			M
9		D	W									M			#		M
5		D	W													#	M
17	M			W	W	W	W	W	W	W	W	W	W	W	W	W	#

Yellow areas are the weekly communications that we try to eliminate by rearrangement of persons in order to speed up development. We rearrange the same persons for Task 14 and Task 15 and the same persons for Task 13 and Task 16. In this way the frequent weekly communications are all avoided

Table 3.4 The chunks of tasks

Task1	Development preparation	Chunk1	Tom
Task2	Software framework design	Chunk1	Joe
Task3	Database design	Chunk1	Robert
Task7	Internal messaging	Chunk2	John Ben
Task4	Schedule	Chunk2	Jesse Jack
Task15	Receivables management	Chunk2 / Chunk3	Peter Vincent
Task14	Order management	Chunk2 / Chunk3	Daniel Kevin
Task10	Reminding system	Chunk3	George Apple
Task8	External mail	Chunk3 / Chunk4	John Ben
Task11	Process management	Chunk3 / Chunk4	Martin Alan Dean
Task16	Invoice management	Chunk4	Peter Vincent
Task13	Online contract modification	Chunk4	Daniel Kevin
Task6	Reimbursement of expenses	Chunk4	Jesse Jack
Task12	Attachment upload	Chunk4	Jim
Task9	SMS	Chunk4	George Apple
Task5	Attendance management	Chunk4	Jesse Jack
Task17	Program test & optimization	Chunk 5	Simon Alice Rose

Table 3.5 The rearrangement of persons to tasks

Task	Work content	Chunk	Persons
Task1	Development preparation		Tom
Task2	Software framework design	Chunk1	Joe
Task3	Database design		Robert
Task7	Internal messaging		Martin Alan Dean
Task4	Schedule	Chunk2	Jesse Jack
Task15	Receivables management		Peter Vincent
Task14	Order management		Peter Vincent
Task10	Reminding system	Chunk3	Jim
Task8	External mail		John Ben
Task11	Process management		John Ben
Task16	Invoice management		Daniel Kevin
Task13	Online contract modification	Chunk4	Daniel Kevin
Task6	Reimbursement of expenses		Jesse Jack
Task12	Attachment upload		George Apple
Task9	SMS		George Apple
Task5	Attendance management		Jesse Jack
Task17	Program test & optimization	Chunk 5	Simon Alice Rose

Table 3.6 The person change to tasks

Task	Work content	Prior rearrangement	Post rearrangement
Task7	Internal messaging	John Ben	Martin Alan Dean
Task10	Reminding system	George Apple	Jim
Task11	Process management	Martin Alan Dean	John Ben
Task12	Attachment upload	Jim	George Apple
Task14	Order management	Daniel Kevin	Peter Vincent
Task16	Invoice management	Peter Vincent	Daniel Kevin

3.5 Discussion

As demonstrated in Table 3.1, in software development, most of the information is communicated weekly and monthly. Around half of the said communication is feedback, i.e., blue characters, since they are above that of the diagonal. We learn from the position of the weekly and monthly communications that the associated people and tasks have not been well organized. This culminates to a software development project that is very vulnerable to wasting time and money due to rework and wasted communications. As stated by [9], gaining awareness of existing information

Table 3.7 The communication matrix of persons before rearrangement

	Tom	Joe	Robert	Jesse	Jack	John	Ben	Georg	Apple	Martin	Alan	Dean	Jim	Daniel	Kevin	Peter	Vincent	Simon	Alice	Rose
Tom	#	1	1															1	1	1
Joe		#	1	1	1	1	1	1	1	1	1	1	1	1	1	1	1			
Robert		1	#	1	1	1	1	1	1	1	1	1	1	1	1	1	1	1	1	1
Jesse				#		1	1			1	1	1	1					1	1	1
Jack					#	1	1			1	1	1	1					1	1	1
John				1	1	#								1	1	1	1	1	1	1
Ben				1	1		#							1	1	1	1	1	1	1
George								#						1	1	1	1	1	1	1
Apple									#					1	1	1	1	1	1	1
Martin										#										
Alan				1	1						#			1	1	1	1	1	1	1
Dean				1	1							#		1	1	1	1	1	1	1
Jim				1	1								#	1	1	1	1	1	1	1
Daniel						1	1	1	1	1	1	1		#		1	1	1	1	1
Kevin						1	1	1	1	1	1	1			#	1	1	1	1	1
Peter						1	1	1	1	1	1	1	1	1	1	#		1	1	1
Vincent						1	1	1	1	1	1	1	1	1	1		#	1	1	1
Simon				1	1	1	1	1	1	1	1	1	1	1	1	1	1	#		
Alice	1			1	1	1	1	1	1	1	1	1	1	1	1	1	1		#	
Rose				1	1	1	1	1	1	1	1	1	1	1	1	1	1			#

Table 3.8 The communication matrix of persons after rearrangement

	Tom	Joe	Robert	Jesse	Jack	John	Ben	George	Apple	Martin	Alan	Dean	Jim	Daniel	Kevin	Peter	Vincent	Simon	Alice	Rose
Tom	#	1	1															1	1	1
Joe		#	1	1	1	1	1	1	1	1	1	1	1	1	1	1	1			
Robert		1	#	1	1	1	1	1	1	1	1	1	1	1	1	1	1	1	1	1
Jesse				#		1	1	1	1	1	1	1						1	1	1
Jack					#	1	1	1	1				1					1	1	1
John				1	1	#								1	1	1	1	1	1	1
Ben				1	1		#							1	1	1	1	1	1	1
George								#						1	1	1	1	1	1	1
Apple									#					1	1	1	1	1	1	1
Martin										#										
Alan				1	1						#			1	1	1	1	1	1	1
Dean				1	1							#		1	1	1	1	1	1	1
Jim				1	1								#	1	1			1	1	1
Daniel						1	1	1	1	1	1	1	1	#		1	1	1	1	1
Kevin						1	1	1	1	1	1	1	1		#	1	1	1	1	1
Peter						1	1	1	1	1	1	1	1	1	1	#		1	1	1
Vincent						1	1	1	1	1	1	1	1	1	1		#	1	1	1
Simon				1	1	1	1	1	1	1	1	1	1	1	1	1	1	#		
Alice	1			1	1	1	1	1	1	1	1	1	1	1	1	1	1		#	
Rose				1	1	1	1	1	1	1	1	1	1	1	1	1	1			#

Blue characters indicate the information flow from the task in the row to the task in the column

Red characters indicate the information flow from the task in the column to the task in the row

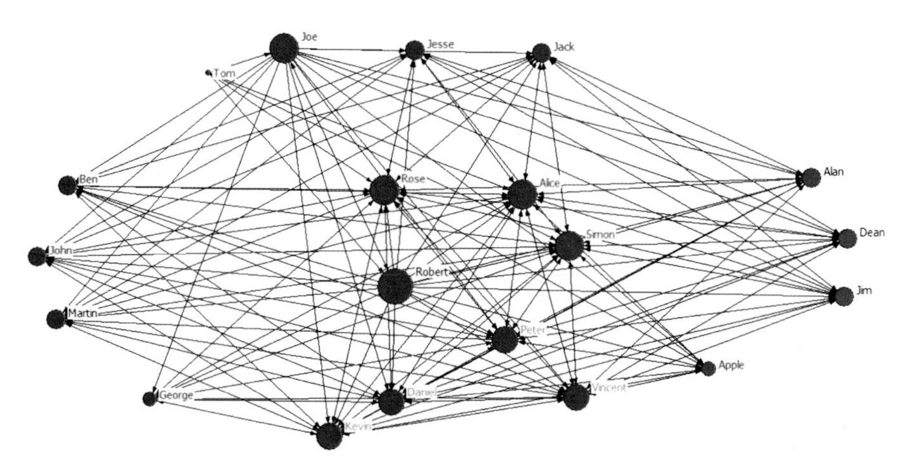

Fig. 3.1 The social network diagram before rearrangement

exchange routes, information providers can act on information opportunities and make changes to information routes to improve the delivery of information services. Upon analysis, we discovered that they were opportunities to optimize the software development in the development state. Opportunities to optimize software

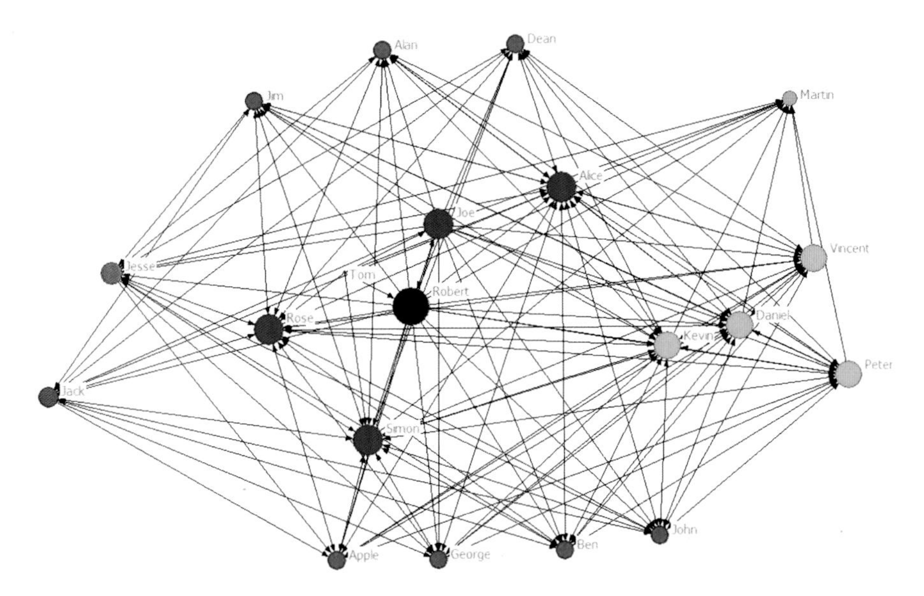

Fig. 3.2 The social network diagram after rearrangement

development are mostly available in development stage including all programming tasks, Task 4 through Task 16 in this case, as other tasks in other stages comprise preparatory, design, and test and are inherently independent and cannot be assigned to other teams. Majority of the information fed forward to other tasks resides in the top of the DSM without any change (to include Task 17, test phase). Therefore, Task 1, Task2, and Task 3 are considered a chunk.

In this case, the main reason that the programming tasks have the potential to get optimized is that Datashine is a small company; they have to assign more than one subsystem to each programmer. Since managers may have not assigned the subsystems well based on their technical and organizational aspects, DSM can help to improve this assignment. Optimized DSM showed that reassigning some subsystems can lead to better information flow and less feedback in the CRM department.

3.6 Recommendation

Datashine company as a software company must be cautious about its new product development projects to avoid delays. Optimization information in the projects by rearrangement of the people is a vital solution but not enough. Datashine can make information flow more efficient in software development projects by:

- Preparing more efficient feedbacks
- Classifying feedback from *ordinary* to *critical*
- Using prior lesson to recognize critical feedbacks to focus on them, accelerating critical feedbacks (monthly to weekly, or even weekly to daily)

- Preparing feedbacks among projects to transfer experiences and lessons to the others
- Capturing feedbacks and organizing them to use for future projects by applying knowledge management techniques.

Additionally, Datashine could utilize a skill-based allocation in conjunction with the DSM presented above. As described previously, human resource allocation or staffing, i.e., given a group of available developers and a set of project activities, which developers' activity allocation yields more value to the organization, is a major problem in software development [10]. Reassignment of tasks based on the skill of the developer is a wise financial decision as it will lead to less project rework due to error and as a result save the company resource [10]. This skill-based reallocation in conjunction with the DSM suggested previously could be a viable solution to Datashine.

3.7 Conclusion

Software development is potentially vulnerable for wasting time and money due to reworks made in development stage. Most of feedbacks come from development stage and some from test stage. DSM matrix as a powerful tool can help to improve new product development process such as software development process. DSM focuses on information flow, but relation among people is another critical aspect which can be improved by rearrangement of people to tasks. Social network analysis (SNA) can be applied to visualize the improvement made by DSM and task reassignment.

References

1. Brooks FP Jr (1975) The mythical man-month. Addison-Wesley, Menlo Park
2. Boehm BW, Papaccio PN (1988) Understanding and controlling software costs. IEEE Trans Softw Eng 14(10):1462–1477
3. Brooks RE (1980) Studying programmer behavior experimentally: the problems of proper methodology. Commun ACM 23(4):207–213
4. Vosburgh J, Curtis B, Wolverton R, Albert B, Malec H, Hoben S, Liu Y (1984) Productivity factors and programming environments. In: Proceedings of the 7th international conference on software engineering. IEEE Computer Society, Washington, DC, pp 143–152
5. Yassine AA (2005) An introduction to modeling and analyzing complex product development processes using the Design Structure Matrix (DSM) method. Product Development Research Laboratory, University of Illinois, Urbana-Champaign Urbana
6. LIU Hongli, FU Yao, CHEN Zhigao (2009) Effects of social network on knowledge transfer within R&D team. In: 2009 International conference on information management, innovation management and industrial engineering, 978-0-7695-3876-1/09 © 2009 IEEE, Xian. doi: 10.1109/ICIII.2009.348
7. Browning TR (2001) Applying the design structure matrix to system decomposition and integration problems: a review and new directions. IEEE Trans Eng Manage 48(3):292–306

8. Cain BG, Coplien JO, Harrison NB (1996) Social patterns in productive software development organizations. Ann Softw Eng 2(1):259–286. doi:10.1007/BF02063813
9. Haythornthwaite C (1996) Social network analysis: an approach and technique for the study of information exchange. Soc Inform Sci Res 18(4):323–342, ISSN 0740–8188, 10.1016/S0740-8188(96)90003-1. http://www.sciencedirect.com/science/article/pii/S0740818896900031
10. Gonsalves T, Itoh K (2011) Multi-objectives optimization for software development projects. In: Proceedings of the international multi conference of engineers and computer scientists 2010, vol 1, IMECS 2010, Hong Kong, 17–19 Mar 2011

Chapter 4
Critical Elements of R&D Management: Case Study of Three Firms from Different Sectors of Industry

Baraa Abudawod, Nertila Bregaj, Zack Khalifa, and Melinda Pizarro

Abstract Chapter 4 is conducted to holistically evaluate the critical elements of R&D management—R&D planning, R&D organization, R&D portfolio management, R&D project management, and R&D knowledge transfer—by assessing R&D management from different sectors. The research methodology is based on an intensive literature review by delving into the literature to have a full understanding of the critical elements of R&D management. In addition, R&D managers from the three firms were interviewed in order to gain insight on how R&D management functions within the critical elements of R&D management.

Research and development (R&D) is a term broadly heard in the industry in this era of technology and innovation. It is used to describe the processes that take place in firms where scientists and engineers are working together. R&D is imperative for organizations to radically and incrementally innovate technologies that are underlying organizations' endeavors to develop new products, processes, or services that benefit the society [1]. Firms that fail to enhance its products and supplant those that become outdated will struggle declining profitability as a result of the "heat" of the market place and the advancement of the technology—i.e., "if you snooze you lose."

B. Abudawod (✉)
GSK, Jeddah, Saudi Arabia
e-mail: babudawod@gmail.com

N. Bregaj
Intel Corporation, Hillsboro, OR, USA

Z. Khalifa
Schlumberger, Denver, CO, USA

M. Pizarro
Daimler Trucks North America, Portland, OR, USA

T.U. Daim et al. (eds.), *Planning and Roadmapping Technological Innovations: Cases and Tools*, Innovation, Technology, and Knowledge Management,
DOI 10.1007/978-3-319-02973-3_4,

Some companies point out that 30 % of their income at any one time are generated from product developed in the preceding 3 years [1]. Conventionally the pipeline of R&D has been described by the process that is initiated by pure research, applied research, development, testing, engineering, and so forth until releasing the products to the market place. Moreover, R&D process is categorized based on its strategic implication as follows: [1]

- *Incremental R&D* is a process that generates definable and enhanced products or processes or services.
- *Radical R&D* is a process that creates breakthrough products, processes, or services.
- *Fundamental R&D* is described as a process that does not intended to generate specific business advantages; however, it is aimed to create scientific and technical information.

There are some concerns on how R&D generates and runs, how R&D managers should evaluate the proposed research projects, and how they should manage the workforce of their R&D. Due to plenty of uncertainties resulted from "managing the unmanageable"—stemmed from risky experimentation for discovery, managing "out of the box thinkers," and managing "fuzzy front end"—enterprises need to implement efficient and effective R&D management. Thus, it is imperative for firms to develop reliable mechanisms for R&D management by integrating methods or approaches to resist the global competition in this era of technology. Putting mechanisms in place requires interlinking the firm's R&D management, knowledge innovation, workforce, end users, organization development, tangible and intangible assets, and organization strategies [2]. Intuitively, there are lots of critical elements, which need to be taken into account to run R&D management effectively and efficiently. Thus, in this framework, we conduct a holistic study at the macroscale to evaluate three different firms from different sectors—Intel, Daimler Trucks North America, and Bonneville Power Administration. The case study is established by delving into the literature to understand the critical elements of R&D management as depicted in Fig. 4.1. Accordingly, a questionnaire template was developed for R&D managers' interviews from the three different companies.

4.1 Methodology

In this framework, two methodologies have been conducted in order to have a comprehensive insight of the R&D management processes and practices of the three aforementioned firms. Therefore, the research methods adopted in this study are described as follows:

(A) Literature Review: An intensive research was carried out in an in-depth induction and analysis intended to have a clear vision of the five critical elements of R&D management. According to the research findings, we constructed a survey for R&D managers from the three different companies.

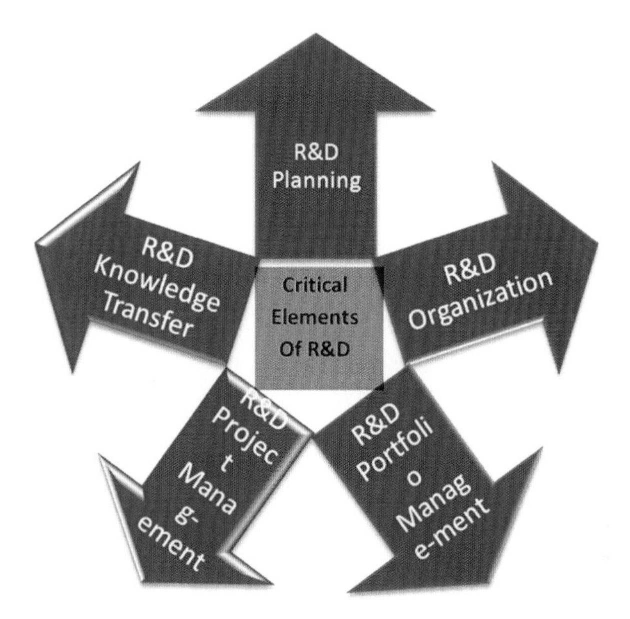

Fig. 4.1 Five critical elements of R&D framework

(B) Questionnaire: In order to implement the knowledge delivered from the ETM class and extracted from the literature, we developed a questionnaire asking R&D managers from the three different firm's general questions with respect to the critical elements of R&D management. The questions were developed in a generic manner in order to avoid confidentially concerns from the R&D managers' point of view. The data needed to be investigated was collected through targeted personal interviews with the R&D managers from the three different companies.

4.2 Literature Review

Nowadays, the marketplace is increasing with respect to competition and globalizations, which makes it imperative for companies to enhance their innovation capabilities in order to increase profitability and growth. Therefore, the success of the companies is highly dependent on their innovation capabilities, i.e., innovative product development [3]. However, the innovative product development process is very complex, and it requires a well-studied strategic plan. Uncertainties in the technology and market present crucial issues to the innovative product development process. The uncertainties introduce high R&D risks, which lead to significant number of failures in the R&D projects. Thus, effective management of R&D risks to improve the success rate of product launches has become a "hot" topic for managers [3]. All the aforementioned challenges/issues in the R&D projects have established the need for effective R&D planning strategies.

4.3 R&D Planning

When planning R&D projects, it is very important to determine the investments necessary for the company to meet its short-term goals of improving current products while simultaneously developing next-generation innovative products [4]. This would eventually enable the company to grow and increase its overall profit. Thus, a well-planned process is essential to improve the quality of the decisions that are made. This process must also be flexible in order to be updated and adjusted as R&D projects advance and move forward [3]. A study by Gray D. McCord presents a guide for strategic R&D planning process [4]. The study investigates a typical scenario of a strategic new product development plan. In his study, McCord mentions the fact that the overall process is iterative and requires multiple passes to achieve the desired results.

Below is a description of each task involved in the strategic R&D planning process [4]:

1. *Defining the Business Assumptions*—It is a very important task for making the right decisions in terms of investment and resource allocation. This task involves the evaluation of three important planning phases—launch, transition, and production [4].
2. *Identifying and Categorizing Current Product Issues*—Under this task, the list of issues for the current product is listed and documented, which includes issues preventing building new systems, reliability and maintenance, user interface, human factors, operational cost, and functionality issues [4].
3. *Prioritizing Existing Product Issues*—After the issues are listed and documented, the next task is to prioritize them on the basis of criticality, importance, and desirability [4].
4. *Defining the Basic Requirements for the Next-Generation Product*—This task requires the development of a "living" document that is updated over time. This task has some advantages as well as some disadvantages [4].
5. *Identifying Dependencies and Leverages*—Planning for dependencies and leverages is a very important task when managing multiple development projects in parallel [4].
6. *Creating the Product Roadmap*—After the completion of the aforementioned tasks, the next task is to translate this information into a graphical representation—product roadmap [4].
7. *Updating the Plans*—This task requires keeping the process "alive" and updating it on a regular basis [4].

As mentioned above, technology/product roadmap (TRM) is used extensively in R&D planning. It is a robust management tool that is used to support strategic and long-term R&D planning. It provides a framework for linking business to technology [5]. Thus, it is very useful when it comes to R&D management strategies that focus on markets and customers. A study by Lee et al. introduces a TRM framework called "TechStrategy," which used technology roadmapping for R&D projects [6]. It provides a framework for planning and coordinating R&D efforts with operational requirements. TechStrategy puts more emphasis on R&D planning activities by investigating technology needs, evaluating the company's technology in comparison to other competitors in the market, and creating a development plan/strategy to satisfy the company's needs [6].

Moreover, the TechStrategy consists of six consecutive phases. A description of every one of these phases is listed below [6]:

1. *TRM Initiation*—This phase consists of preliminary TRM development activities. In general, a TRM team is assigned, TRM reports are developed, and roadmapping schedule is completed [6].
2. *Subject Selection*—This phase is considered as the actual starting point of roadmapping. In this phase, the customer needs and inputs are gathered, and the items that need to be improved are proposed and selected [6].
3. *Technology Needs Assessment*—The main objective of this phase is to identify specific technology needs for the selected items. Under this phase, each selected item is divided into its sub-components in order to select the sub-components that should be developed with the available resources. The item can be a product or technology [6].
4. *Technology Development Plan*—In this phase, development goals and strategies are created for sub-components that have been selected in the previous phases of the process [6].
5. *TRM Implementation*—The TRM report is finalized and released for implementation in this phase of the process. The TRM report contains details about the future outlook of the selected item (macro-TRM) as well as the development plan for the item's sub-components (micro-TRM). The information in the TRM report is used as the basis for R&D budgets and project plan [6].
6. *Follow-Up Activity*—This phase is the final phase in the TRM process. In this phase, the TRM report and process are updated on a regular basis [6].

4.4 R&D Organization

Research and development is of significant importance in business as production methods and processes are ever changing. It is necessary for firms to continually update their designs and rethink their product portfolio, because of the rapidly changing technological advancements. Factors such as customers' preferences and the level of market competition call for new innovations, continuous product revisions, and new designs. R&D becomes essential for firms to compete and survive in industry. Therefore, R&D strategy is a key factor for attaining superior R&D performance. To aid in this endeavor, firms have established R&D organizations, both internal and external, to align their work with the changing needs of their businesses. In addition, the firm should be aware of the impact that R&D organizational culture plays towards the company's success.

4.4.1 Internal R&D Organization

Firms with R&D project management offices manage R&D process, project portfolios, and resources. The R&D process established by an organization typically has a management team who decides on R&D concepts to pursue. The creative ideas proposed to management are subject to an innovation process, which consists of stages or phases and gate reviews. The decision-making process is used to filter projects. "The ability to select the 'correct' R&D programs has proven to be one of the leading components of a successful R&D organization" [7]. The simplified innovation process has three phases: conception, implementation, and marketing. A brief description of activities during each phase follows:

- *Phase one*: Conception—requirement analysis, idea generation, idea evaluation, and project planning activities take place [8].
- *Phase two*: Implementation—development and construction, prototyping, pilot application, and testing activities take place [8].
- *Phase three*: Marketing—production, market launch and penetration activities occur [8].

It can be seen later in the case studies that the firms analyzed have similar R&D processes.

The internal organization utilizes the company's resources to conduct R&D work. "Internal R&D network is important because it enables the firm to gain and develop critical human resources, to actively participate in the corporate R&D program and to be internally connected information-wise" [9]. The employees gain a sense of ownership in the product they are developing. "Thus, an R&D program can be readily accelerated by tapping into their technology platform and internal network to select focused team members" [7]. Firms pull from their pool of talent for specific project needs and also keep knowledge and information internally. Also, R&D activities can begin immediately because project teams can form quickly.

Internal R&D organizations can be either centralized or decentralized. "Centralized R&D is more conducive to more pioneering research, research that explores new markets, and more fundamental advances" [10]. Therefore, centralized research produces innovations that extract from a wider range of technologies.

Centralized organizations are broader in the research it conducts with emphasis on science, but decisions are made at the primary R&D center. "The advantage of this type of structure is control and coordination of technology development, and provision for discovery research" [11]. Firms are able to span a fuller range of development work and have better control over the contents and direction of the research projects. Centralization provides a better connection between the primary R&D center and the dispersed research facilities, which is easier to manage due to open communication.

In contrast, decentralized R&D is more conducive to focused and incremental research. "A decentralized R&D organization is one in which there is no corporate or central laboratory" [11]. The secondary research centers make their own project decisions, which may make judgments faster but may cause coordination issues with the primary center.

4.4.2 External R&D Organization

Oftentimes, R&D organizations go outside their firm to leverage technology advancement by tapping into innovations of others. "Open innovation is the use of purposive inflows and outflows of knowledge to accelerate internal innovation, and expand the markets for external use of innovation, respectively" [12]. Firms form strategic alliance and collaborative networks with government agencies, academic institutions, and other companies in order to acquire inventions or intellectual property. Collaboration between firms fosters rise to success and prosperity. As partners learn from one another and leverage the strengths of their associates, they gain an advantage to develop new technologies and reach new markets. There are situations where companies are limited in their vision. Therefore, a different point of view can bring creativity and a new outlook. Collaborative ventures paves the way for these companies to access a broader means of expanding R&D, because "collaboration, in and of itself, becomes a means to innovation" [13]. Firms are able to gain insight into new concepts and develop new technologies faster due to the partnerships. The advantage is that research has already been conducted and the knowledge that the partners possess can be combined. Therefore, a company is not starting from a blue ocean. The shared research saves the partnership R&D resources, which contributes to profit margins because of cuts in overhead costs.

Open innovation has become a useful tool to acquire collective research information. Yet, firms should be cautious with the strategic partnerships that it establishes. These collaborations should contain defined boundaries. Proprietary information should be kept within the partnership, in order to protect themselves from passing on too much information that can be detrimental to their core business. The alliances are beneficial to the firms creating a win-win situation. The key is to have good communication and trust.

4.4.3 R&D Organization Culture

R&D organizational culture is the dynamics of how the firm operates: traditions, values, structure, behavior, and expectations within the company. "The culture of an organization is an amalgamation of the values and beliefs of the people in that organization. A commonly used definition of organizational culture is 'the way we see and do things around here'" [14]. Values, therefore, define what employees of the organization care about, because they know what is expected of them. Culture plays a significant role in the way a company functions.

R&D organizational structure has changed throughout the years [15]:

- The first generation shows a simple model, one person in charge directing the employees, the creative leader.
- The second generation has evolved into an administrative leader and a management team due to the creation of R&D organizations within big firms.
- The third has transformed from an administrative leader to an entrepreneurial leader with an administrative team because of the surge in marketing. Business-minded management skills were necessary.
- The fourth generation emerges entrepreneurial leader and entrepreneurs. The entire organization should be engaged in making the projects successful, a collaborative effort to work together.

R&D organizations can be internal and external, as well as centralized or decentralized, adjusting to align their position with the changing needs of their businesses. Furthermore, R&D organizational culture can significantly affect company's success, because of its dynamics.

4.5 R&D Portfolio Management

R&D portfolio management is one of the most critical elements in R&D management. The challenges that are associated with it render this element as one of the most important functions for R&D managers. This process consists of making decisions regarding investment mix and policy, linking business strategies to objectives, allocating available assets for individuals and institutions, and balancing between risk and performance [16]. The main goal of portfolio management is really to capture the highest financial returns from the constrained resources within an acceptable level of risk. This process is classified as a dynamic decision process as the business list of active R&D is consistently updated and revised [17]. In this element of R&D management, new projects are assessed, selected, and prioritized in a way that meets the business missions. Moreover, ongoing projects might be accelerated, by putting more efforts and injecting more resources into them; terminated, not worth continuing; or de-prioritized as other projects might be more important than the ongoing ones [17]. Generally, this element of R&D management is described by hesitant and changing information, dynamic prospects, multiple objectives and strategic goals, interdependency between projects, and multiple decision makers and locations [17].

Organizations have different approaches to handle their respected R&D portfolio management. However, generally, portfolio management links a number of approaches/methods to select projects and prioritize them accordingly based on organizations' view and vision of R&D. Speculatively, the approaches or the methods undertaken by organizations' aim for aligning the firms' missions to their dynamic strategies optimize the utilization of resources within the window of the available resources and maximize the organization returns.

Some organizations look at portfolio management as if it is a "top-down" statement of desires, allocating resources to a wide range of tasks. Other organizations view it as a "bottom-up" pile of available projects [18]. The spot where "top-down" and "bottom-up" meet is where the criticality of portfolio decisions becomes significantly important [18].

The criticality of the importance of portfolio management is stemmed from many factors. Robert G. Cooper et al. highlighted eight factors [17]—according to the case study they conducted—that tend to make this element of R&D management to be very vital. These factors are described as follows:

1. Financial: tend to be critical as it shoots for maximizing organizations' returns, maximize the R&D outputs to reach the horizon of the firms' intentions.
2. To maintain the viable spot of the organizations in the market space, thereby increasing sales and market share.
3. To tactically and strategically allocate resources.
4. To form a bridge between project selections and firms' missions—i.e., the portfolio is the "expression" of business strategies. Thus, it is essential to support the business missions.
5. To tailor the focus towards the projects that seem to generate high returns to the firms and allocate resources to the "fruitful" projects.
6. To manage the balance between long-/short-term projects and high-/low-risk projects—with respect to the business objectives.
7. To healthily communicate priorities within organizations vertically and horizontally.
8. To provide a reliable "objectivity" selection by filtering out the good projects that seem to be worth undertaken.

The main target of fruitful portfolio strategy is generating the most value of an organization—i.e., the same as the goal of the technology strategy [18]. Portfolio strategy should undertake and merge the mission of an organization with technology strategy by establishing a set of projects and opening new gates for new innovations [18]. Furthermore, portfolio strategy signifies a firms' selection with respect which set of projects need to be undertaken to meet the potential outputs of R&D overt time. Aside from that, portfolio strategy highlights where the "spotlights" need to be pointed at on various segments of the portfolio—business lines, technologies, market, etc. [18].

Portfolio strategy enables the organization to ensure that all projects receive the needed resources to drive/accelerate them towards the aimed objectives. Such strategy needs to be forged in a way if sufficient resources are not obtainable for a project, project must be suspended or eliminated in order to allow the constrained resources to be utilized for other projects [18]. One of the critical issues encountered in portfolio strategy is developing the correct balance between innovations—but risky projects—and incremental projects with positive returners. This is where the traits of managers play a role—managers who are classified as risk takers as oppose to the ones who "follow the book."

Matheson pointed out some concerns that are needed to be taken into consideration upon developing strategic decisions in the portfolio management [18]. These concerns are presented in question format for R&D portfolio managers as follows:

1. How should managers combine their opportunities into obtainable strategic projects?
2. Who is in charge of the overall process and who will facilitate the analytical process?
3. How can managers assure a sufficient level of credibility that top management and projects leadership will be convinced with the results and support the proposed recommendations?
4. How can managers react to the results of a portfolio evaluation? Meaning, how do managers prioritize the projects based on their outcomes? If the portfolio outcomes have remarkable strategic implications, how will managers establish discussion of new paths and subsequent implementation?
5. How will business and marketing units interact with the process? Meaning, is there a need for "cross-functional" decision team for the entire portfolio, to distribute responsibilities by business or technical areas within the firm, or to employ multilevel review structure?
6. How can the portfolio management be kept immortal?

The decision process in R&D portfolio management can be modeled and tackled by mathematical models, integer liner programming, data envelopment analysis, or economical models, using benefit/cost ration, payback period, net present values, annual equivalent worth, sensitivity analysis, etc. However, hierarchical decision models (HDMs) seem to be very convenient for decision making in R&D portfolio management. HDMs enable decision makers to have a "360-degree" view of R&D portfolio management where managers can incorporate all the possible criteria needed for deciding on alternatives within the portfolio.

4.6 R&D Project Management

Project management has a significant impact in R&D. It is the creativity and skills of the project manager that drive a project from birth to death. Though project management is a fairly new concept that has been around for a few decades, we see many industries where project managers are needed. In a case study of Siemens AG-Global

Development Strategy, its 17 regional development centers' (RDCs) approach to projects was by having project managers [19]. Siemens' project managers would act as midwives for subprojects and deliver milestones. Sometimes issues would get resolved a few management levels above. However, for other RDCs projects not in Munich, meetings would be held every 6 weeks. Unfortunately this would call for delay in decisions because of time constraints between upper management.

The classical responsibilities of the PM are usually described in terms of four activities: (1) planning, (2) organizing, (3) directing, and (4) monitoring [20]. The *planning* activity is dominant in the early stages of a project, especially with respect to the preparation of the project plan. At this step, the PM also thinks about problems and contingencies that may arise and how to handle them. The planning phase begins with the development of a project plan. Such a plan contains six essential elements:

1. Needs, goals, objectives, and requirements
2. Task statements, work breakdown structure (WBS)
3. The technical approach to the project
4. A project schedule
5. The project budget
6. Risk analysis

In the PM world, the project plan (PP) is at the core of the planning function for the project team and is a blueprint for the work to be performed. All project plans should contain the above elements, although it is recommended that a project plan should be as short and concise as possible. These six project plan elements provide the input to the organizing function.

The *organizing* responsibility involves deciding how to organize the project itself. This step also involves assigning resources to the various tasks of the project by preparation of initial tasking, work breakdown structures (WBS), responsibility matrices for the project, and the like. The organizing function is divided into two essential activities, namely, work activities and activities having to do with project organization. The work activities have four parts, all flowing from the project plan. These are:

1. The tasks, WBS
2. The technical approach
3. The schedule
4. The task responsibility matrix

Next is the *directing* activity which is the formal and informal tasks on a daily basis running of the project that can include meetings as well as description of assignments when changes are required to solve problems. In the *directing* stage, problem solving and leadership skills are necessary and utilized well as it is a critical stage to continue the project.

The *monitoring* duty involves keeping updates with the status of all aspects of the project in relation to the requirements and the project plan. At this step, when problems are discovered, immediate action is taken. "Monitoring is collecting, recording, and reporting information, concerning any and all aspects of project performance that the project manager or others in the organization wish to know" [21]. In the PM world, scope, cost, and time are what's monitored. In project management, we stress the need to plan, check on progress, compare progress to the plan, and take corrective action if progress does not match the plan. Then *control* is the last element in the implementation cycle of planning-monitoring-controlling. It is useful to perceive the control process as a closed-loop system, with revised plans and schedules following corrective actions. Under controls there is go/no-go controls with a popular form known as phase-gated processes [22]. Rather than waiting until the project is completed, and then finding out that it doesn't achieve the objectives of the organization, the phase-gate process controls the project at various points throughout its life cycle to make sure it stays on track. Phase gates get placed at project milestones where milestones are natural "end-of-phase" points with a project, whereas gates are meant to catch problems early on.

One of the crucial aspects in PM as part of the organizing stage is the schedule. "A schedule is an expression of the tasks and activities to be performed along a time line." Two main methods of describing a schedule are in use today, namely, (1) a Gantt chart and (2) a program evaluation and review technique (PERT) Chart [22]. Besides Gantt chart, PERT chart in PM has each circle represent an event—a specific point in time at which a measurable activity is either started or completed. The lines between the events are activities during which resources are directed to achieve the designated end event. This useful method places in evidence the longest path through the network, which is known as the critical path.

4.7 R&D Knowledge Transfer

For R&D organizations, technology transfer may be defined as the process by which science and technology are transferred from one individual or group to another that incorporates this new knowledge into its way of doing things. A new technology has to have considerable relative advantage and has to provide significant value to the customer before it is embraced by the wider user community [22]. The new technology can be more expensive than the older technology, but the value in terms of quality, flexibility, and responsiveness it provides motivates the user to take the necessary steps in adopting this technology.

4.7.1 Stages of Technology Transfer

Transferring technology from an R&D lab to manufacturing, marketing, and the ultimate user is an important function. Different organizational elements can play useful roles in successfully reaching this goal. There are five main steps leading to the adoption of technology [22]:

1. Knowledge
2. Persuasion

3. Decision
4. Implementation
5. Confirmation

Knowledge occurs when a potential user learns about the new technology and gains some understanding of its capabilities and usefulness. At this stage, the user wants to know what the innovation is, what its capabilities are, and how it works. *Persuasion* occurs when the user forms a favorable or an unfavorable attitude towards the innovation. Here the user is looking at comparative advantages and disadvantages of the innovation. *Decision* occurs when the user engages in activities that lead to adoption or rejection of the innovation. *Implementation* occurs when the user incorporates the innovation into the way of doing things. *Confirmation* occurs when the user seeks to confirm the implementation decision and continues to use the innovation. This step is not always well understood, which is why many innovations first implemented are later discontinued. Certain activities to reinforce user acceptance of the innovation need to continue after implementation.

Adoption of innovation involves considerable uncertainty and thus some risk since it is not always clear what benefits will follow. Operational problems can often occur during the implementation stage, thus increasing costs and reducing benefits. Some of the uncertainty can be reduced by demonstration projects and by implementing the innovation on a partial basis. Organizations that do not reward prudent risk-taking are less likely to adopt innovations. Innovation adoption typically follows an S-curve. In general, early adopters are prudent risk takers, are better informed and educated, and act as opinion leaders for the organization. The role of the early adopters is to decrease the uncertainty about an innovation by adopting it and by adjusting it to fit the organization's needs. Early adopters then communicate this information to other potential users within the organization and to peers outside the organization. Adoption of innovation requires resources (people, funds, and time), some training in using the innovation, and, at times, some changes in the way organizations operate.

4.7.2 Technology Transfer Strategy

The challenges of technology transfer are based on the uncertainty of individuals doing specific tasks, getting support from top management, and because of the difficulties in finding the necessary people and resources on a timely basis. More often than not, technology moves from research and development to the user in small increments. The size of the transfer effort varies. For some large projects, resources required for effective tech transfer may indeed be extensive. For most projects, the tech transfer effort may have to be accomplished within existing resources. Real literature research and reviews have been conducted on an approach that might allow one to develop a strategy. To understand this approach clearly and to operationalize the concept, real research project execution and actual organizational experiences are needed. In addition, a general approach of allocating resources, based on the size and complexity of the project and the availability of resources, consists of user manuals, design criteria, patents, licensing, sponsor at high levels, operation and maintenance document, and so forth. Based upon the knowledge of the R&D staff and the user community, it is best to prepare a preliminary list of tech transfer activities and documents that foster technology transfer.

4.8 Case Studies

4.8.1 Case #1: Bonneville Power Administration (BPA)

Bonneville Power Administration is a federal agency that supplies electrical power in the Pacific Northwest, and it is a part of the US Department of Energy. The agency was founded in 1937 and is headquartered in Portland, Oregon. It generates the electrical power from 31 federal hydroelectric projects, 1 non-federal nuclear plant, and other small non-federal resources. The US Army Corps of Engineers and the Bureau of Reclamation are responsible for operating the dams. About one-third of the electric power used in the Northwest comes from BPA. It supplies the electrical power to Oregon, Washington, Idaho, western and eastern Montana, Wyoming, Nevada, Utah, and California [23, 24].

Moreover, the agency operates and maintains a high-voltage transmission grid consisting of approximately 15,276 miles of lines and 300 substations. The agency employs approximately 3,117 employees, and it provides about 35 % of the electricity used in the Pacific Northwest [24]. It spends 1 % of its revenue on R&D activities [25].

4.8.1.1 R&D Planning

BPA has a research and development department called "Technology Innovation Office" with a headcount of 12 people (3 contract, 1 detail position, and 8 permanent employees). It focuses the agency's technology initiatives on a coherent and disciplined R&D approach and aligns them with BPA's strategic objectives. The Technology Innovation Office obtains project ideas from the competition, market changes, and continuous improvement in R&D areas such as smart grid, effective renewables and storage integration, aging infrastructure, energy efficiency, and CO_2 sequestration. Thus, BPA engages in incremental and radical R&D projects. BPA's Technology Innovation Office uses a cross agency council of executives and technologists to guide its research and development efforts [25].

According to the interview with one of the experts at BPA, BPA takes into consideration the internal and external forces when planning the agency's R&D efforts. Those forces guide the direction of the R&D efforts. In terms of internal forces, BPA considers forces such as updating aging infrastructure as well as creating innovative technology for renewable energy. External forces, on the other hand, include forces like quality of customer as well as low costs.

In terms of business strategy, BPA has a very well-defined business strategy, which aligns the research and development activities with the business strategies. BPA wants to make an agency connection with the business and technology challenges facing the utility industry. The agency also uses other techniques to improve its business strategy as it looks to what others are doing in the industry in both national and international markets in order to benchmark the agency's progress against other industry leaders. The agency also uses some tools such as technology roadmaps to capture the logic and business framework for research and development. Subject matter experts within BPA develop the roadmaps. However, the inputs are solicited from industry, national lab, and universities. In fact, the roadmaps identify the factors that are driving the technology needs as well as the areas of great potentials for BPA [26].

4.8.1.2 R&D Organization

As mentioned above, BPA has Technology Confirmation/Innovation Council, which is run by a number of executives and technologists. This council is on top of the hierarchy for BPA's R&D department, and its goal is to provide direction and principles, select portfolio, and ensure that decisions and results are applied. Under BPA's hierarchical R&D structure comes the Technology Innovation Office that is run by a chief technology innovation officer. The office is responsible for developing and managing portfolio, developing project management model, managing projects, and developing policy analysis [25]. Figure 4.2 [25] below depicts the relationship between the Technology Confirmation/Innovation Council, Technology Innovation Office, and the technology roadmaps. The technology roadmaps define the technologies that are important to BPA, identify the gaps between the current and future technologies, and also help in prioritizing research choices [25].

In terms of external R&D organization, customer/end user needs are considered as areas to look for market incentives. BPA understands the customer/end user need of cheaper power. Thus, offering low-cost power is one of BPA's strategic goals. Figure 4.3 [25] below shows the hierarchical flow of BPA's business strategy. BPA is constantly looking at continuous improvements to infrastructure and ways to integrate renewable energy options in order to offer customer power with low cost. As previously discussed, roadmaps enable BPA to understand the R&D needs and plan accordingly. From BPA's point of view, the internal customers are the transmission, power services, energy efficiency, and physical security.

External customers, on the other hand, are ultimately the ratepayers in the Pacific Northwest. Direct external customers include research partners (universities, national labs, and industry) and other local utilities. To ensure the quality of research and development efforts, BPA makes sure that the best people available are hired. This is done through a very rigorous screening and hiring process. Key success criteria (both technical and qualitative) are determined. Interviews are conducted using a competency-based method and ranked against the key success criteria.

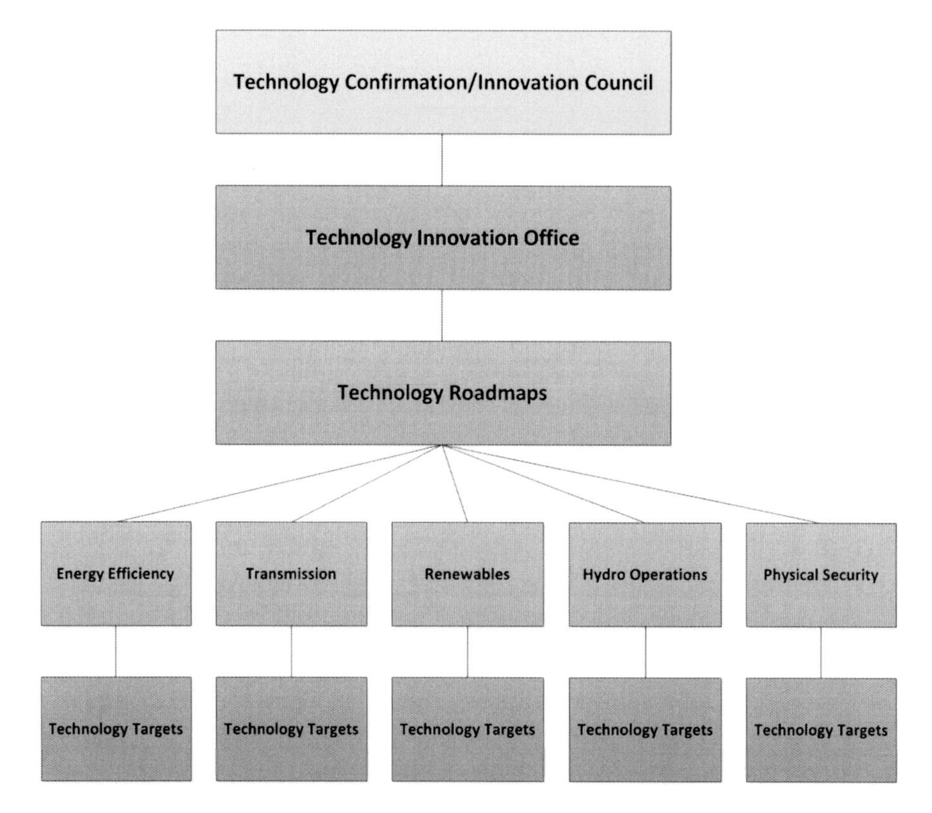

Fig. 4.2 BPA's technology innovation council

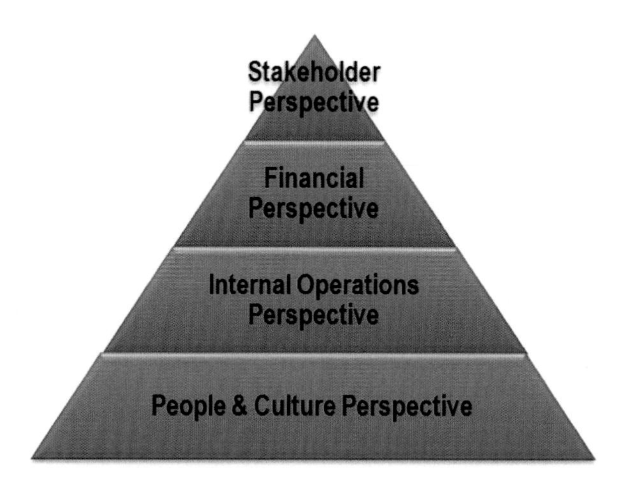

Fig. 4.3 Hierarchy of BPA business strategy

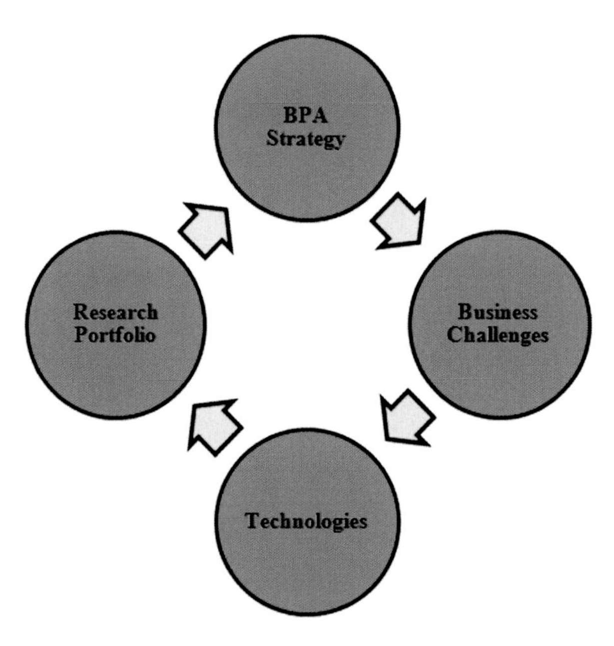

Fig. 4.4 Relationship between BPA strategy and research portfolio

4.8.1.3 R&D Portfolio

A big agency like BPA has many projects under its portfolio. Therefore, a portfolio management strategy is necessary to coordinate the funding and resource allocation among the different projects. BPA follows a "bottom-up" approach when managing their portfolio. BPA engages in a lot of projects and filters them based on their importance and priority to the agency. Roadmaps are used to determine the importance and priority of the projects to the agency. One of the main criteria for BPA when making a portfolio decision is the contribution to the agency's mission [25].

Moreover, BPA has direct linkages between the agency's strategy, business challenges, technologies, and research portfolio. Figure 4.4 [25] above shows the relationship between BPA's strategy and its research portfolio. This relationship consists of making decisions with regards to investment mix and policy, linking the business strategy to research portfolio. Under this relationship, allocation of resources is determined as well as the balance between risk and performance [3]. At BPA, all R&D projects are assessed using the same criteria and to ensure that they still align with the agency's strategic objectives. Roadmaps are refreshed to increase the likelihood of targeting the right technologies to fill technical gaps. The agency tries to balance technical and market uncertainties when managing the agency's portfolio. BPA is considered to be a risk taker as the Technology Innovation Office operates under the assumption that 80 % of the projects in the portfolio will fail. Therefore, BPA understands that the success of the projects in the portfolio has direct correlation to the level of risk involved in these projects—high risk results in big success and vice versa [25].

Along the same lines of R&D portfolio management, the technology innovation initiative at BPA follows an annual cycle of portfolio funding system, which is mainly based on the strategic needs identified in BPA's technology roadmaps. In February, all the projects in the portfolio have to be reviewed by the Technology Innovation Council, and then in March the door opens for new R&D project ideas, which opens from March to May. In June, the proposals for the new R&D projects are reviewed, and then in July the council selects the projects that will be included in the following fiscal year's portfolio. In general, BPA's portfolio is considered to be a medium long-term portfolio, and it is expected to generate direct financial benefits to the agency and eventually add value to the Pacific Northwest electric system [25, 26].

4.8.1.4 R&D Project Management

R&D project management is very important for a highly innovative organization like BPA. The agency uses the Project Management Body of Knowledge (PMPOK) as a guide/methodology for managing its R&D projects. Hence, BPA uses the five process groups when managing its projects—initiating, planning, executing, monitoring and controlling, and closing. The initiating phase of the R&D projects usually starts by collecting the requirements needed for the projects. The planning phase is where the projects are being selected and prioritized based on the technology roadmaps. The main criterion used for selecting and prioritizing R&D projects at BPA is the alignment with the roadmaps and focus areas. Project proposals are peer reviewed within the agency as well as from outside participants. Ultimately, they are evaluated on their likelihood of success and the value of the project to the agency. In general, the projects that best fit BPA's mission are the ones that get selected [27].

Moreover, the execution phase is the point where work on the R&D project actually gets started, which then requires the monitoring and controlling activities. At BPA, the monitoring of the R&D projects is done through informal monthly meetings with project managers, formal written quarterly status reports, and a yearly review of the R&D portfolio by the executive council, and stage gates are used to terminate projects.

At BPA, the chief technology innovation officer acts as the program manager who is in charge of coordinating R&D projects. The agency uses some tools for effective management of its R&D projects. These tools include training, best practices, maturity model, templates, formal and informal meetings, formal/informal communication, sponsor, project review, and stage gates. In terms of the triple constraints (scope, time, and cost), scope is the number one goal that BPA focuses on when managing the agency's innovative projects. Time and cost are important but not as significant to the R&D projects as scope [25].

4.8.1.5 R&D Knowledge Transfer

Knowledge transfer is a common practice across big technology innovation organizations. However, BPA is still in the process of further developing its knowledge and technology transfer processes, and the agency is not considered to be mature enough in this area. Currently, BPA is practicing benchmarking in order to improve the capability for lining the agency's technology with other related technologies worldwide.

Moreover, knowledge transfer is good practice that innovative organizations adopt to learn from each other's experiences. However, this practice surfaces and introduces some issues. One of the most important issues is the intellectual property (IP) issue. Since BPA is not very mature when it comes to the knowledge transfer area, the IP issue doesn't seem to cause a significant threat to the agency as it does for other companies that are involved heavily in the knowledge transfer practice.

4.8.2 Case #2: Intel Corporation

Intel Corporation is the largest semiconductor manufacturer in the world, headquartered in Santa Clara, California. The company employs approximately 100,100 people in its eleven fabrication facilities and six assembly and test facilities around the world, which have combined advanced chip design capability with a leading-edge manufacturing capability. It is the inventor of the ×86 series of microprocessors, the processors found in most personal computers. Intel Corporation was founded in July 18, 1968, by semiconductor pioneers Robert Noyce and Gordon Moore and widely associated with the executive leadership and vision of Andrew Grove. Intel also makes motherboard chipsets, network interface controllers and integrated circuits, flash memory, graphic chips, embedded processors, and other devices related to communications and computing.

One of Intel's major investments is in R&D. What makes Intel the biggest chip manufacturing company is keeping up with rapid changes in the microprocessor industry and constantly investing in R&D. Intel is number four in the list of top ten R&D spending companies at $8.4 billion in the last 12 months [28]. For the scope of this paper, we interviewed knowledgeable people from two main sectors of Intel's R&D: Intel Labs and Intel Manufacturing, which is part of the Logic Technology Development Group (LTD) and consists of 17,000 employees. The interview consisted of focusing in the five major areas of R&D as described in this paper.

4.8.2.1 R&D Planning

Both Intel Labs and Intel Manufacturing R&D integrate technology into business strategy, through a structured process which involves several meetings. These meetings cover challenges they are facing. They consider case studies such as—how technology can be used in hospitals or office-future usages. They work with OEM's and government agencies that have big challenges or even with healthcare organizations. Intel's global technology plan gets formed by having technology roadmaps, reaching out to expand into new things, and looking at new trends by utilizing global factories in Ireland and Israel to get into emerging markets.

4.8.2.2 R&D Organization

Intel's R&D organization works with major customers. Only a small research goes into just one customer. Intel looks into the industry trends, and if a technology is big, then they look into market research. Intel gives direction to its customers. For example Intel came up with the Ultrabook concept and worked with the OEMs on how to develop the product. Intel works with many universities. Intel hires the best people available through the partnerships with the universities and top school tiering. Intel's collaborative research is important because it does not have a product more than 5 years old so it has to move quickly and without product research that could mean "no product."

4.8.2.3 R&D Portfolio Management

Intel keeps a technology portfolio that tracks all research programs. It manages it through gate meetings to provide funding and investment. Intel invests into companies that emerge with them. Within the portfolio, it evaluates market uncertainties by use of option analysis and risk analysis to understand if project risk makes it less attractive.

4.8.2.4 R&D Project Management

Intel monitors projects by use of stage gates from phase to phase with regular review and support with funding. If funding provided exceeds the expenses, then the project is shut down. According to the Intel expert interviewed, in the project's life cycle, there are three main stages [34]: (1) concept—fairly light; (2) proof of concept—path finding; and (3) technology transfer—stage to lend into product group.

Under the triple constraint of time–cost-scope, Intel is most concerned with time. Time for the semiconductor industry and Intel is crucial as it needs to move rapidly. If they are not aggressive enough and drop things that they cannot keep up with, it gets beat with the competition. Other items that are important to the projects are program and operations managers. The program manager is external to the program and works on bigger projects at later stages. Operations managers are involved in the whole process and operations of the research.

4.8.2.5 R&D Knowledge Transfer

In manufacturing development, Intel does what's called "seeding"—after development when Intel is ready to ramp up, product "seeds" from all ramp sites come in to learn the new process. Seeds involve people from different positions from area managers to operations managers, to engineers and technicians. Usually it takes 3–6 months or even a year. Then they take that information back to their sites. Also Intel follows "copy-exactly" method as it transfers every new process development technology into all its manufacturing sites around the world. IP is a major concern especially during this process as there are IP gates set in each area or department so that "seeds" get trained and gain information only in the area applicable to them.

Intel Labs

Intel's R&D network consists of 22 labs across 10 countries in areas such as open innovation and research, enterprise systems and services, sustainability, and embedded and automotive. Intel has five major Intel Labs; the biggest ones are in the USA, Europe, and China. Within them, there are many academic programs and research areas—to mention a few, Academic Programs and Research, Circuits and Systems Research, Integrated Platforms Research, Interaction and Experience Research, and Microprocessor and Programming Research. External organization in R&D and, collaborative partnerships with research areas and universities play a crucial role for Intel as well. For example, the Academic Research Office funds research with grants of various sizes as well as large strategic programs championed by Intel employees. The academic programs office manages academic relationships with focus schools and proliferates Intel technologies on campuses. The lablets, staffed by Intel employees, conduct research with close partnership with the university researchers and students, primarily in the areas of Connected Systems for Communities (with University of California at Berkeley), Cloud Computing Systems and Embedded Real-Time Intelligent Systems (with Carnegie Melon University in Pittsburgh), and Sensor-Driven Computing Systems (with University of Washington, Seattle).

Intel Labs Europe

Intel R&D/Innovation in Europe is driven by a network of research labs, product development labs, and innovation labs spanning the region as well as a variety of Intel business units. Intel Labs Europe (ILE) was formally established in early 2009 as the central means of coordinating activities across this diverse and extensive network and to strengthen and improve Intel's alignment with European R&D. Today ILE consists of more than 40 R&D locations employing more than 3,700 R&D professionals [29]. The mission of ILE is to advance Intel research, development, and innovation and to partner with European stakeholders to help improve European competitiveness. To achieve this ILE aims to strengthen Intel's relationships and collaborations with European researchers and to align the company's technology vision with European policy makers across a broad technology agenda. ILE has grown existing initiatives and continually seeks new opportunities to advance the value of ICT solutions for society and business. Recent exciting areas of focus include next-generation Intel architecture, visual computing, software service development, enterprise solutions, sustainability, embedded computing, and high-performance computing.

Intel Labs China

Intel Labs China strives to become a world-class embedded systems research institute delivering breakthrough technologies to enable, foster, and improve Intel business opportunities in China and around the world with teams in system integration, architecture, software, and hardware co-design. Intel Labs China is one of five Intel Labs and is the largest non-US Intel research group. Through world-class research, with a commitment to understanding and adapting to local development requirements, Intel Labs China strives to forge a strong partnership with China in technological innovation and economic development endeavors.

Intel into the Future

Intel has invested a big portion of its revenue in R&D. In the last 2 years, Intel produced 32 nm chips called "Sandy Bridge" and just this year released its first 22 nm tri-gate technology called "IVY Bridge." Intel is the first one to have come up with the 22 nm technology after 10 years of research. Up until now, transistor layouts were "planar" or flat, in relation to the die. As Skaugen, Intel's head of PC client, says, "the difference here is that 3D tri-gate transistors enable us to pack significantly higher transistor density on the die, helping increase the chips' performance and energy efficiency" [30]. Each processor contains over 1.4 billion transistors. The process has become so difficult that to go even smaller to 14 nm next year and reducing the power to half will be a great challenge.

Intel has its own collaborative partnerships with research centers, universities, and other companies. In fact, Intel is working on its next 450 mm wafer manufacturing Intel Labs in NY and partnerships with Google, Samsung, and IBM. Intel's mission is to form a US-based research consortium that is looking into ways to move to bigger, next-generation wafers[31]. Going from 300 to 450 mm wafer means increasing tremendously equipment size and cost, but it will allow building more chips per wafer at a lower cost. "Intel hopes the agreement will shorten the timeline to create bigger and more cost-efficient 450-millimeter (mm) wafers and a new generation of advanced extreme ultraviolet lithography"[32]. For this reason, Intel is already building its manufacturing factories now, including D1X in Hillsboro where 450 mm wafer technology will start, as well as two other new fabs, one in

Arizona and one in Israel. The way Intel is able to do this and continue to keep up with new innovation in such a rapid market is by having its factory ability and continuous upgrade. Intel is also preparing to upgrade fabrication plants in the United States and Ireland to make chips using the 14 nm fab method. Intel's R&D is quite deep and looks decades in advance. If it all goes to plan, Intel would start shipping 10 nm processors in 2015, with work on 7 nm technology starting shortly after. In order to stay a few steps ahead of the competition, process technology is not the only key to the customer puzzle. Intel will also have to break into the mobile space with powerful but energy-efficient chips [33].

Research Breakthrough: Hybrid Silicon Laser

Intel and the University of California, Santa Barbara (UCSB), announced the demonstration of the world's first electrically driven hybrid silicon laser. This device successfully integrates the light-emitting capabilities of indium phosphide with the light-routing and low-cost advantages of silicon [34]. As Intel's chief technology officer, Justin Rattner, puts it, *"Silicon Photonics is a critical part of tera-Scale computing as we need the ability to move massive amounts of data on and off these very high performance chips"* [34]. The researchers believe that with this development, silicon photonic chips containing dozens or even hundreds of hybrid silicon lasers could someday be built using standard high-volume, low-cost silicon manufacturing techniques. This development addresses one of the last hurdles to producing low-cost, highly integrated silicon photonic chips for use inside and around PCs, servers, and data centers. The hybrid silicon laser is a key enabler for silicon photonics and will be integrated into silicon photonic chips that could enable the creation of optical "data pipes" carrying terabits of information. These terabit optical connections will be needed to meet the bandwidth and distance requirements of future servers and data centers powered by hundreds of processors. When voltage is applied to the contacts, current flows, and the electrons (−) and holes (+) recombine in the center and generate light. With highly integrated silicon photonic transceiver, it is possible to imagine a future world in which most computing devices are endowed with high-bandwidth optical connectivity.

4.8.3 Case #3: Daimler Trucks North America (DTNA)

Daimler Trucks North America Corporate Headquarters is located on Swan Island in Portland, Oregon, with its parent company DAIMLER in Stuttgart, Germany. DTNA is the largest commercial truck manufacturing company in North America as well as the leading producer of specialized and medium duty vehicles. The company employs approximately 16,000 people, dispersed among its affiliates: DTNA, Detroit Diesel, Thomas Built Bus, Freightliner Custom Chassis, Western Star, SelecTrucks, and Alliance Parts.

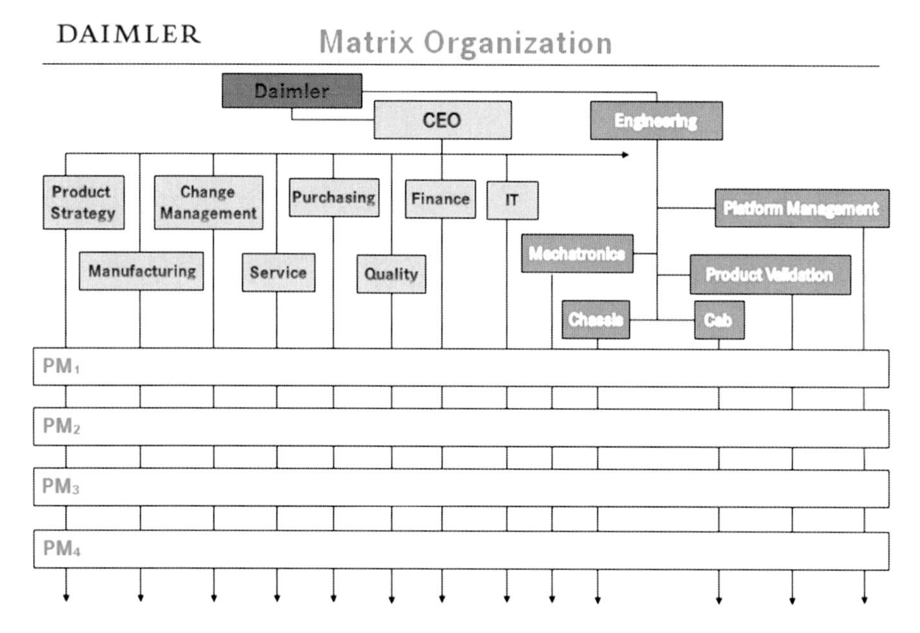

Fig. 4.5 DTNA project management organization structure

DTNA engineering has broken down project work into vehicle platforms, which include heavy duty and medium duty. Commercial truck classification is determined based on the vehicle's gross vehicle weight rating (GVWR), ranging from one to eight. It is also done more broadly under the US DOT Federal Highway Administration (FHWA), which groups Class 1, 2, and 3 as "Light Duty"; 4, 5, and 6 as "Medium Duty"; and 7 and 8 as "Heavy Duty" [35]. In addition to the vehicle classes, the platforms include Western Star, Aggregates, Vocational, Exports, and Specialty Vehicles.

DTNA is a matrix organization, a mix or hybrid structure, which incorporates both the functional and project approaches, with the hope of optimizing the strengths and minimizing the weaknesses of each. Figure 4.5 [38] illustrates DTNA's organizational structure. "The objective of the matrix is, control and technical excellence" [20]. Cross-functional teams are formed to accomplish projects. Representatives from the various departments come together as a project team, led by a project manager. When the project is complete, they disband and return to their respective areas.

4.8.3.1 R&D Planning

DTNA has a research and development department called "Advanced Engineering," comprised of 16 people, which is project based. The R&D organization utilizes technology forecasting by scanning the transportation industry, looking for market changes and trends. Also, suppliers and competitors are monitored for innovative technology changes. The company does not develop for specific customers but is driven by customer criteria and needs:

- Fuel efficiency
- CO_2 Reduction
- Reliability/quality
- Safety
- Styling
- Noise/vibration
- Serviceability
- Ride and handling
- Powertrain/drivetrain performance

The Advanced Engineering Organization receives project concepts and ideas from different sources, such as government regulatory standards, customer feedback, continuous cost-saving initiatives, and engineering, quality, and manufacturing departments. The R&D organization is driven by the desire to develop better products than the competitors and provide new technological improvements to current products. DTNA is part of DAIMLER AG, which is a global organization, thus when planning, varying factors should be taken into consideration. Different markets have different needs and specifics are unique according to applications used. Therefore, a balance between local and global R&D should be maintained. Framework schedule, specification for project definition, and project goals are established during the planning phase. Gantt charts and Microsoft Project are used to layout schedules with milestones and deadlines.

4.8.3.2 R&D Organization

DTNA is an internal and centralized organization, which utilizes open innovation. DTNA is a centralized organization because of the proximity of the corporate office and R&D center. DTNA has formed strategic partnerships with academic institutes, government agencies, and other businesses in order to explore and develop new product ideas. Advanced Engineering has partnered with the following schools: Oregon State University and Portland State University. Collaboration is specific to these institutes because their labs are geared towards automotive technology. Furthermore, DTNA has strategic alliances with Detroit Corporation and Cummins Engine manufacturers. These partnerships have been able to produce new technology to meet the stringent standards that the Environmental Protection Agency (EPA) has imposed on original equipment manufacturers (OEM) of commercial vehicles. DTNA has also partnered with the US government, having contracts to provide military vehicles. DTNA also has partnerships with DAIMLER Trucks Financial and Travel Centers of America. Again, DTNA is part of a larger global company, which has other R&D departments: DAIMLER in Stuttgart, Germany; Detroit Corporation in Detroit, Michigan; and Mercedes Benz in Palo Alto, California. Therefore, a collaborative network has been established between each R&D center, in order to avoid duplicate work. Also, individual centers can focus on conducting their own research projects, and knowledge can be shared internally.

4.8.3.3 R&D Project Portfolio

The Advanced Engineering group at DTNA uses "roadmapping" to manage their project portfolio. Presently, the project focus is on fuel efficiency, CO_2 emissions, and aerodynamics due to an energy regulation "EO 13514" [36] that the EPA has required of the transportation industry by the year 2020. Project selection is driven by various factors, but the primary factor is customer buy criteria. Also, project selection is dependent on active projects in the pipeline as well as work load and resources available. As projects close, new ones are activated according to the project roadmap. Important criteria of portfolio management are decision making and risk management. The decisions made can have serious impacts not only on the project but the company as well. This can be seen with DTNA's competitor Navistar. The CEO of Navistar, Daniel Ustian, made the decision to pursue "Exhaust Gas Recirculation, or 'EGR' technology that Navistar has, in effect, bet the ranch on. The rest of the industry uses more conventional Selective Catalytic Reduction, or SCR, technology" [37]. This bold decision has had severe consequences on their company, which is now on the verge of bankruptcy. Due to the nature of R&D, there are numerous uncertainties; thus, in the decision-making process, lots of questions should be asked, and the alternatives should be considered. "A project manager should decide whether or not to continue the project, because not every idea works," states Derek Rotz, Advanced Engineering Project Manager. Termination of a project is done in a review process, usually initiated due to failure to meet gate deliverables. Some projects that are in the termination category have not reached a maturity level that is acceptable. Therefore, it is evaluated by the review committee which can decide to postpone and reposition the project on the R&D roadmap or stop the project altogether.

4.8.3.4 R&D Project Management

The R&D organization uses an "innovation creation process" to manage departmental projects. This process has three phases and four quality gates to aid the project manager in the R&D project life cycle. Figure 4.6 [38] depicts an example of the innovation quality gates. The key feature of this process is the ability to measure and direct activities towards project targets using the four gate system: (QG3) innovation draft, (QG2) project maturity, (QG1) functional proof, and (QG0) integration suitability. At each gate, there are deliverables that must be accomplished in order for the project to pass the gate. A brief description of each gate is given below.

(a) *Quality gate 3—innovation draft*

- A preliminary study has been developed from a concept idea. The innovation draft is a description of the creative idea.

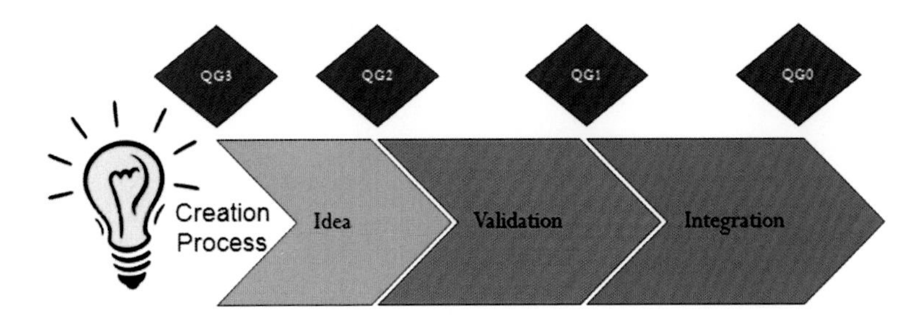

Fig. 4.6 DTNA innovation quality gate process

(b) *Quality gate 2—project maturity*

- A project can be started with the information gathered from the preliminary study. Project proposal is created, which includes project expectations or targets. Initialization of market and benefits analysis started. At this gate, patents needs are evaluated.

(c) *Quality gate 1—functional proof*

- Definition can be given to the project or product. A feasibility study is conducted, as well as the market and benefits analysis is completed. At this time, patent applications are filed.

(d) *Quality gate 0—integration suitability*

- Technical risks have been evaluated, feasibility of the project/product has been proven, and definition of objectives has been met. Economic feasibility and market acceptance has also been confirmed, and the patent process has been completed. A business case has been developed.

Projects are managed using the triple constraint: budget, schedule, and scope. In R&D project management, budget is usually the most important constraint, schedule being the least.

4.8.3.5 R&D Knowledge Transfer

Once a project has passed through quality gate 0, this is the birth of an engineering project. The product project then transfers to the Engineering Project Life Cycle, a project management process called Commercial Vehicle Development System (CVDS). This process is used as a means to manage internal engineering projects through planning, steering, and reporting. The key feature of this process is the ability to measure and direct activities towards project targets using a 12 quality gate system. The project is handed over from Advanced Engineering to our product strategy and marketing groups, which will identify the business need. Joint work between the departments will bring the new technology into the market place.

Fig. 4.7 DTNA innovation truck

Transferring knowledge can be difficult when it comes to intellectual property. Patents are used to try to capture IP rights and knowledge protection. Also, DTNA has our suppliers sign a nondisclosure agreement. At the working level, DTNA Human Resources has corporate employees sign a nondisclosure contract when they are hired into the company.

R&D Products

The Advance Engineering department has an innovation truck which features advanced technologies developed from DTNA's research and development labs. Figure 4.7 [39] is a picture of the truck that has a cutting edge aerodynamic package for fuel economy. Prototype parts for new technologies are installed, tested, and verified using this vehicle along with the product validation engineering test fleet.

Earlier this year, DTNA also debuted a second generation of the innovation concept vehicle at the Mid-America Truck Show 2012. The vehicle is called the "Revolution Innovation Truck." Again, it features new technological advancements in electronics, fuel economy, and new cab interior. Figure 4.8 [39] is a picture of the prototype vehicle.

4.9 Lessons Learned

- Strategic R&D planning enables organizations to develop strategic plans for their respective R&D efforts as an important element of their business mission. R&D plans are very crucial and embodies the quality of R&D's outcomes. Therefore,

Fig. 4.8 DTNA revolution innovation truck

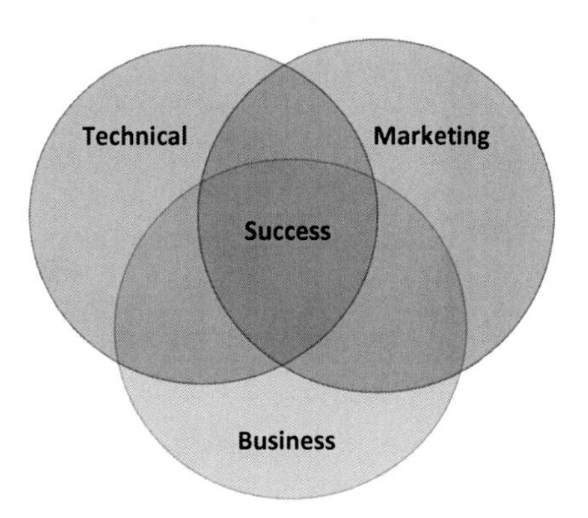

Fig. 4.9 Three factors versus success

the systemic approach of R&D planning enables organizations to incorporate the three critical inputs of R&D—marketing, technical, and business. The overlap between the inputs of the R&D planning shapes the "sweet spot" that organizations aim for—namely, success as illustrated on Fig. 4.9 [40] above (R&D constraints).

- Interestingly, the three case studies investigated in this framework utilize TRM as a main tool for R&D planning. Technology roadmapping is a very powerful tool that allows firms to support strategic and long-term R&D planning [6]. This can be done by establishing explicit R&D plans with regards to technology development, forecasting, and identifying the technological gaps between the firm's existing state of technology and the advanced levels that firms desire to reach [6].

- R&D organizations fuel the outcomes of their R&D departments by developing matrices to integrate the knowledge across the different segments within an organization. In order words, establishing culture of innovation within a firm is the key success of steering the wheel of R&D.
- Decisions in R&D management of an organization are handled by systematic and well-structured approaches across the organization. Having a solid approach established by R&D management enables organization to have 360 view of their portfolio.
- The criticality of portfolio management is stemmed from managing a reliable balance between objectives, timeframes, and risks that are associated with R&D projects.
- The success of R&D does not rely on how many patents are generated by the R&D division; instead, it depends immensely on how R&D management integrates the technology (radical and incremental technology) with the market needs.
- R&D management needs to carry a periodic review of their portfolio in order prioritize projects according to their progress. Meaning R&D management needs to have a consistent review of the stage gates on the pipeline of a project. This approach allows R&D management to allocate the constrained resources as needed for the highly important projects.
- As far as reviewing the progress of a project in R&D is a major concern, R&D management needs to designate a gatekeeper to monitor the development of a project.
- It is imperative for the senior management of an organization to provide the required support, empowerment, and authority to the project manager and members. This is critical as projects sometimes need to be terminated.
- In order for an organization to move swiftly with the dynamic of the market, the organization needs to pull all the capabilities and potentials they have got and integrate them securely with their business activity horizontally, across not just their organizations but their entire value chain from customers to suppliers.
- Organizations have different views in terms of how they evaluate the triple constraints. For instance, Intel's biggest concern in a project is the time factor. On the other hand, Daimler considers the budget of a project to be the most important constraint. Furthermore, BPA views the scope of the R&D project as the most curial factor. The heart of the argument of such considerably different views is resulted from the nature and the background of the different sectors.

4.10 Recommendations

Despite the differences between the three organizations—stemmed from the different sectors and organizations' size—the core of the R&D management of the three companies is interestingly the same in terms of the process. All of the investigated organizations in this framework operate within the five critical elements of R&D

management. However, by drilling more in a deeper level, to understand the process at the microscale for each of the three organizations would require us to delve into the following propositions:

Proposition 1: Financial matters are very critical in organizations; thus, it is imperative to understand how an organization handles their R&D operation from this perspective.

Financial matters embody business hampering factors for organizations. Consequently, a deeper understanding of the financial matters with an organization is imperative to have an insight of how budgets and cost are being evaluated within a company, meaning, how each of the three organizations handles the financial matters of their R&D nationally and internationally. Moreover, how are funds granted for R&D? Are they funded by a proponent within a company—business line or top management—after certain approvals that follow the organization standards and polices?

Investigating such proposition may reveal surprising outcomes due to the different business orientations of each of the three organizations.

Proposition 2: As far as performance measurements of R&D are a significant concern, comparative R&D intensities between the three organizations need to be analyzed.

Since the three companies are from different sectors of R&D, intensity needs to be evaluated in terms of the R&D and sales ratio. This can be done by having information about the inputs lunched in the pipeline of each of the R&D of the three companies and the sales generated out of them. Such analysis can be conducted by using the model proposed by Pietro Moncada et al. [41].

Proposition 3: Intellectual property is another critical factor that needs to be studied.

It would be more interesting to highlight the difference between how government organizations such as BPA deals with IP as oppose to an organization like Intel.

Proposition 4: The geographical culture differences seem to be one of the factors that influence the decisions of the decision makers within organizations. Hence, it will be more interesting to see how culture influences decisions in terms of risk taking. This proposition can be tackled by excavating into the management of Daimler and see how the German culture deals with risk taking versus Intel.

4.11 Conclusion

R&D represents the backbone of any industrial organizations. Managing R&D differs from one organization to another based on the sector that organizations operate in as well as business orientation. The criticality of R&D management is resulted from the rate of increasing both of radical and incremental innovation. The study, which was carried out, attempted to comprehensively evaluate three organizations from different sectors in the light of the five critical elements of

R&D management—R&D planning, R&D organization, R&D portfolio management, R&D project management, and R&D knowledge transfer. The study is built on a foundation constructed by the literature review followed by personal interviews with R&D managers from Daimler, Intel, and BPA. Despite the difference of the business orientations of each of the three organizations, the findings of this framework indicated that the principals of R&D management of the evaluated companies are the same in terms of the process at the macroscale. Each of the three companies enjoys systematic pipelines with multiple gates starting from the discovery, experimentation, design, development, and testing of the product/technology all the way through commercializing the final product/technology. For a deeper analysis to carry this investigation for future research, four propositions have been proposed to have a clear vision of R&D management of each of the three organizations at the microscale.

Chapter four evaluates the five critical elements of R&D management: R&D planning, R&D organization, R&D portfolio management, R&D project management, and R&D knowledge transfer. Assessment of R&D management from different sectors was conducted. The research indicates that the companies have similar framework when it comes to project management.

References

1. Reeves R (1997) The management of R&D. http://www.richardreeves.net/aboutrd/slim-1.htm. 12 July 2012
2. Liu P, Tsai C (2008) A study on R&D competence for R&D management personnel in Taiwan's high-tech industry. Int J Comput Internet Manage 16(1):1–17
3. Wang J, Yang CY (2011) Flexibility planning for managing R&D projects under risk. Int J Prod Econ 135:823–831
4. McCord G (2010) R&D planning process guide. http://www.m3design.com/strategic-rd-planning-process/. Accessed 11 Aug 2012
5. Phaal R, Farrukh CJP, Probert DR (2004) Technology roadmapping—a planning framework for evolution and revolution. Technol Forecast Soc Change 71(1):5–26
6. Lee S, Kang S, Park YS, Park Y (2007) Technology roadmapping for R&D planning: the case of the Korean parts and materials industry. Technovation 27(8):433–445
7. Via FA (2003) Industrial innovation with external R&D programs. http://www.ncbi.nlm.nih.gov/books/NBK36327/. Accessed 2 Aug 2012
8. TUHH (2012) The innovation process. http://www.global-innovation.net/innovation/index.html. Accessed 8 Aug 2012
9. Helble Y, Chong LC (2004) The importance of internal and external R&D network linkages for R&D organizations: evidence from Singapore. R&D Manage 34(5):608
10. Arora A, Belenzon S, Rios LA. The organization of R&D within firms: measures, characteristics and consequences, 17 Oct 2010
11. Larson CF (2000) R&D in industry. AAAS report XXIV: research & development FY 2000. http://www.aaas.org/spp/rd/xxiv/chap4.htm. Accessed 8 Aug 2012
12. Chesbrough HW. Program in open innovation. http://openinnovation.berkeley.edu/what_is_oi.html. Accessed 7 Aug 2012
13. HMS Inspiring Ideas. What is collaborative competition? http://us.hsmglobal.com/notas/57674-what-is-collaborative-competition. Accessed 13 July 2012

14. Saxena S, Shah H. Effect of organizational culture on creating learned helplessness attributions. http://www.vikalpa.com/pdf/articles/2008/V33203-025to045.pdf. Vikalpa Vol 33 No 2, p 34, April–June 2008
15. Zlotin B, Zusman A (2005) Revolutionary innovation tools for the ultimate R&D organization. Ideation International Inc. http://www.ideationtriz.com/new/materials/r&dbook.pdf
16. Investopidia (2012) Portfolio management. http://www.investopedia.com/terms/p/portfolio-management.asp#axzz22zgRox5Q. Accessed 15 July 2012
17. Cooper RG, Edgett SJ, Kleinschmidt EJ (2006) Portfolio management for new product development : results of an industry practices study. http://www.techrd.com/files/Portfolio/Cooper,%20Edgett,%20Kleinschmidt%202006.pdf. Accessed 18 July 2012
18. Matheson (1997) R&D portfolio strategy. http://www.roundtable.com/lib/file/Workshop/SmartOrg-Chapter10.pdf. Accessed 25 July 2012
19. Thomke S, Siemens AG (2002) Global development strategy. Harvard Business School, Cambridge, Boston MA
20. Eisner H (2008) Essentials of project and systems engineering management, 3rd edn. Boston MA, pp 22–24, 43–44
21. Meredith JR, Mantel SJ Jr (2008) Project management—a managerial approach, 8th edn. Wiley, New York, pp 22–24, 43–44, 182, 481
22. Jain RK, Triandis HC (1997) Management of research and development organizations. Wiley, New York, pp 200–221
23. InsideView (2012) Bonneville power administration. http://www.insideview.com/directory/bonneville-power-administration. Accessed 12 Aug 2012
24. 2011 BPA facts (2012) https://www.bpa.gov/corporate/about_BPA/Facts/FactDocs/BPA_Facts_2011.pdf. 11 Aug 2012
25. Kim J. Guest Lecture—ETM 536/636 R&D management: "Technology Innovation Office", Department of Engineering & Technology Management, Portland State University, Portland, 31 July 2012
26. Bonneville Power Administration. http://www.bpa.gov/corporate/business/innovation/. Accessed 12 Aug 2012
27. Haughey D. The Project Management Body of Knowledge (PMBOK). http://www.projectsmart.co.uk/pmbok.html. Accessed 12 Aug 2012
28. Knatz M, USA Today (2012) Microsoft, Google, Intel outspend Apple on R&D. http://www.usatoday.com/money/perfi/columnist/krantz/story/2012-03-20/apple-marketing--research-and-development-spending/53673126/1. Accessed 5 Aug 2012
29. Intel Labs (2012) Enabling a digital Europe. http://www.intel.eu/content/www/eu/en/research/intel-labs/enabling-digital-europe.html. Accessed 5 Aug 2012
30. Intel Corporation (2012) Intel unveils quad-core Ivy Bridge chips. p 1. www.circuit.com. 6 July 2012
31. Intel Corporation (2012) Will Intel continue manufacturing in the U.S?, p 1. www.circuit.com. 6 July 2012
32. Intel Corporation (2012) Keeping Moore's Law alive and kicking. p 1. www.circuit.com. 17 July 2012
33. Garreffa A (2012) Intel's R&D teases 10nm chips by 2015, already hard at work on 14nm. http://www.tweaktown.com/news/24093/intel_s_r_d_teases_10nm_chips_by_2015_already_hard_at_work_on_14nm/index.html. Accessed 11 Aug 2012
34. Intel Labs (2012) Hybrid silicon laser: project. http://www.intel.com/content/www/us/en/research/intel-labs-hybrid-silicon-laser.html. Accessed 5 Aug 2012
35. Wikipedia. Truck classification. http://en.wikipedia.org/wiki/Truck_classification. Accessed 5 Aug 2012
36. US Environmental Protection Agency (2012) Federal energy requirements. http://www.epa.gov/oaintrnt/energy/fedreq.htm. Accessed 11 Aug 2012
37. Market Insider (2012) Bankruptcy as an option for Navistar? http://www.cnbc.com/id/47871323/Bankruptcy_as_an_Option_at_Navistar.Accessed 11 Aug 2012

38. Truck Product Creation (2011) Ensuring technical & economical maturity. Daimler Chrysler: Innovation Quality Gates & Business Cases Trucks, p 5, 15 May 2011
39. Freightliner (2012) Advanced engineering. http://www.freightlinertrucks.com/TruckInnovation/Advanced-Engineering. Accessed 11 Aug 2012
40. Tips & Facts—Organizing R&D for success (2010) http://www.sensors-research.com/articles/tips.htm. Accessed 14 Aug 2012
41. Moncada-Paternò-Castello P, Ciupagea C, Smith K, Tübke A, Tubbs M (2010) Does Europe perform too little corporate R&D? A comparison of EU and non-EU corporate R&D performance. Res Policy 39(4):523–536

Chapter 5
Technology Roadmapping for Medical Imaging: Toward Improved Value

Larry Ball, Ritu Bidasaria, Ignacio Castillejos, Pinprapa Pakdeekasem, Chakaphan Pornsatit, and Tugrul U. Daim

Abstract This study creates technology roadmaps for medical imaging. Four roadmaps were created for future products to include advanced imaging, high-tech imaging, super-tech imaging, and ultra-tech imaging. A literature review of academic and medical sources was conducted to collect data and review TRM (technology roadmapping) methodologies.

An analysis was performed for each level of the roadmaps to include market drivers, product features, technology capabilities, and resources. The aforementioned levels were linked and timelines provided to construct the roadmaps. The probable future products were advanced computed tomography, magnetic resonance imaging, and positron emission and ultrasound devices. To generate the technology roadmap layers, this chapter explores different tools like SWOT, QFD, scenario analysis, and gap analysis.

5.1 Introduction

Medical imaging is an important component of modern healthcare. Medical imaging has been driven by the need of medical professionals to view the human body's internal condition without the need for invasive exploratory surgery. Advances in technology allow modern physicians to view a patient's internal functions easily and have been implemented in primary diagnostic tools. Several primary technologies are currently in use for medical imaging to include X-ray, computed tomography (3D X-ray), magnetic resonance imaging (MRI), ultrasound, and the emerging technology of positron emission tomography (PET).

L. Ball (✉) • R. Bidasaria • P. Pakdeekasem • C. Pornsatit • T.U. Daim
Engineering and Technology Management, Portland State University, Portland, OR, USA
e-mail: larryb545@gmail.com

I. Castillejos
Tektronix, Beaverton, OR, USA

T.U. Daim et al. (eds.), *Planning and Roadmapping Technological Innovations: Cases and Tools*, Innovation, Technology, and Knowledge Management,
DOI 10.1007/978-3-319-02973-3_5,

To understand what medical imaging devices will be developed in the future, technology roadmapping (TRM) may be used. TRM for medical imaging is market driven by the health practitioner's needs. In this study, we seek to roadmap the technology of medical imaging and predict possible future medical imaging products in the next 2 years, 5 years, 10 years, 15 years, and beyond.

Using the methodology espoused in the literature by Phaal, Daim, and others [1, 2], we will construct the roadmap by sequentially examining the market drivers, desired product features, desired technology capabilities, and supporting resources necessary for future technology needs. The results of this process are four TRMs for new products to be introduced in 2, 5, 10, and 15+ years, respectively.

A literature search of existing, emerging, and future market drivers, product features, technology capabilities, and supporting resources, in the form of required research and development (R&D), was conducted. These four primary components are analyzed and technology roadmaps developed for future enhanced and new products.

5.2 Methodology

5.2.1 Literature Review

The literature review included a search of academic journals, papers, and web sites from academic, governmental, and medical sources. Methodology for development of the TRM was drawn from the academic literature [1, 2]. Literature review findings for medical imaging are included in the following four subsections to include market drivers, product features, technological capabilities, and resources (R&D).

5.3 Market Drivers

The first step in building a TRM using a market pull approach is finding out what the market wants and needs are. The tools used to elicit the market drivers were largely based on previous studies in the TRM field [3]. Following this methodology, the tools used in the market drivers are described in the table below (Table 5.1).

The literature review was performed using resources from the academia, organizations of professionals in the field, and industry players. Multiple articles were

Table 5.1 Market drivers research methodology

	Tools used	Primary findings
Market drivers	Literature review	15 medical imaging industry market drivers
	SWOT	Internal analysis, opportunities, threats (SWOT)

Table 5.2 SWOT analysis for MRI products

Strengths	Weaknesses
Resolution	Price
Noninvasive procedures	Portability
Real-time procedures	Acoustics
Imaging of soft tissue	High-power consumption
Imaging of brain activity	Expensive supporting infrastructure (cooling systems, cabling)
Opportunities	**Threats**
Increased demand for medical imaging:	Improved CT technology
Developed world – aging population	Impact of government regulation in MRI R&D
Developing world – growing middle class	PET (position emission tomography)
Increased number of healthcare professionals	

analyzed and assessed by the team members in order to form an expert opinion on the matter; the market drivers were initially elicited based on this expert opinion. Furthermore, other inputs were provided by the team members based on the current trends in IT adoption by other industries, including other branches of healthcare and personal experiences as patients in local hospitals.

Additionally a SWOT analysis was performed to identify market drivers for one of the technologies in the medical imaging industry. The SWOT analysis was limited in scope and developed for MRI drivers only, and after this exercise was performed, the scope of the project was changed to include the whole range of driver possibilities within the medical imaging realm. However, going through this exercise helped our team to get a better understanding of the multiple market drivers in the industry regardless of the technology and products. This is consistent with Phaal et al.'s observations that "roadmaps and the roadmapping process can provide a means for enhancing an organization's 'radar', in terms of extending planning horizons, together with identifying and assessing possible threats and opportunities in the business environment" [4] (Table 5.2).

Based on the literature review and the SWOT analysis, 15 market drivers were identified and were assigned id codes (Table 5.3). These codes will be used in the team presentations and through the rest of this chapter as follows:

5.4 Product Features

The ability to image the human body, both to diagnose disease and guide biopsy and surgery, has become central to the practice of medicine during the 105 years since Röntgen's discovery of X-rays [9]. In the subsequent time, radiology has developed to include the use of many forms of electromagnetic radiation (ultrasound, gamma radiation, magnetic fields, radio frequency radiation, etc.) to make powerful diagnostic images of the body.

Table 5.3 Market driver definitions

Market drivers	Definition
D1 – low cost	Refers to a cost of acquisition and ownership below other products with the same features [5]
D2 – high resolution	Refers to the quality of the images captured with the medical image device [6]
D3 – no side effects	Refers to the effects to both the patient and the medical imaging technician [7]
D4 – portability	Refers to the ability to transport the medical imaging device with ease [5]
D5 – soft tissue imaging	Refers to the ability to capture images of soft tissue, as opposed to only hard tissue (bones and cartilages) [8]
D6 – full body imaging	Refers to the ability to scan all parts of the body, as opposed to body-part-specific scanner like mammogram scanners [8]
D7 – 3D imaging	Refers to the ability to capture images in 3D [8]
D8 – real-time info	Refers to the ability to monitor/image the human body in real time [5][8]
D9 – exposure duration	Refers to the time it takes for a medical imaging device to capture the information from the patient [5]
D10 – app in a mobile device	Refers to the ability to perform medical imaging in a mobile/handheld device
D11 – medical social networking	Refers to the ability to share the information captured with medical imaging professionals in a secure fashion [5]
D12 – easy to operate	Refers to the ease of use of the imaging device
D13 – IT infrastructure	Refers to the infrastructure that needs to be put in place so that the information captured with the medical imaging device can be shared over computer networks, including the Internet [5]
D14 – noninvasive	Refers to the ability to perform medical imaging tasks without needing to force an entry in the patient, e.g., cut or injection. In this context, this also refers to the ability to perform these tasks without being intrusive, which would be entering the patient via an existing opening [8]

Existence of different specialties (radiology, nuclear medicine, medical physics, nuclear pharmacy, information science, etc.) has led to hospital and university departments being variously called "diagnostic imaging" or "radiology" or "radiological science." The power of modern computers to allow the rapid display of sectional images of the body using technologies such as ultrasonography (US), computed tomography (CT), single-photon emission tomography (SPECT), positron emission tomography (PET), or magnetic resonance imaging (MRI) has been central to the growth of the new technologies. Previously, because of the limitations of "radiology," physicians had to diagnose the disease based on the patient's symptoms.

In the twenty-first century, "imaging" is being used not only to identify the lesion, and to do so more powerfully, but to guide the needle used in its biopsy; not only to locate an abscess but to guide its drainage; not only to identify a blocked blood vessel but to guide its dilatation, etc. It is evident that imaging services can replace some expensive surgical procedures (biopsies, drainages, exploratory operations) and have done much to facilitate dramatic falls in the patient's length of hospital stay. Therefore, diagnostic imaging is a strategic tool vital to the health and sickness care in the future.

The newer technologies (CT, MRI, PET, etc.) produce images that are intrinsically digital, and radiology as a whole is moving away from film-based image storage.

Table 5.4 Product feature definitions

Product features	Definition
P1 – battery powered	Product can operate on battery
P2 – Wi-Fi	Product can have Wi-Fi which enables it to retrieve information through the Internet
P3 – handheld	A medical imaging machine will be as small as a sugar testing machine or blood pressure measuring machine
P4 – no radiation	It will not use any radiation for imaging
P5 – imaging software for mobile apps	The patient can have an application of imaging software in his/her mobile
P6 – no high voltage required	Product will not require high voltage to operate
P7 – no liquid nitrogen cooling	No liquid nitrogen cooling is required to destroy the diseased tissue
P8 – no film required	Future medical imaging products will not require any films to scan the output
P9 – 3D imaging	Product should be capable of producing 3D images of internal body parts
P10 – faster imaging process	This refers to the time the patient needs to be exposed to the imaging device plus the time it takes for the device to present the image data
P11 – no noise	Machines will not make any noise while in operation
P12 – safe for pacemakers	People who have pacemakers inside them can also go for medical imaging treatments
P13 – electronic transmission of medical image	Medical image can be transmitted electronically to different devices
P14 – videoconferencing	Imaging products will have the feature of videoconferencing so that doctors can communicate and discuss in real time
P15 – reliable data storage	Product would be able to store huge imaging files
P16 – automated disease interpretation	Product would be having artificial intelligence (AI) in it so that it can detect the disease by comparing it with the information present in its database

The opportunities this fact creates are boundless. In the last 100 years, imaging technologies have greatly refined the study of structure. Imaging methods have also been directed to studies of tissue and organ function beginning with nuclear medicine methods including single-photon emission computed tomography (SPECT) and positron emission tomography (PET) and expanding into functional magnetic resonance imaging (fMRI) and magnetic resonance spectroscopy (MRS) [9].

Similar to the previous section, all of our product features have been put in the table below with a brief explanation (Tables 5.4 and 5.5).

From the last step, we had matched the product features to the market drivers. In this section, we have tried to come up with technological capabilities that supported those product features. According to our literature research, there were eight possible technological capabilities which consisted of digital signal processing (DSP), teleradiology, computer-aided diagnosis (CAD), positron emission tomography (PET), magnetic resonance imaging (MRI), ultrasound, computed tomography, and advanced battery technology, respectively.

Table 5.5 Linkage between market drivers and product features

Market priority	Market drivers	Linked product features	Product features
7	D1 – low cost	P6, P7, P8	P1 – battery powered
10	D2 – high resolution	P8, P9	P2 – Wi-fi
7.5	D3 – no side effects	P4, P10, P13, P14	P3 – handheld
4.5	D4 – portability	P1, P2, P3, P6, P7	P4 – no radiation
8	D5 – soft tissue imaging	P9	P5 – imaging software for mobile ops
10	D6 – full body imaging	P8	P6 – no high voltage required
9.5	D7 – 3D imaging	P13	P7 – no liquid nitrogen cooling
9.5	D8 – real time info	P13, P16	P8 – no film required
9	**D9 – exposure duration**	**P10**	P9 – 3D imaging
5.5	D10 – app in a mobile device	P2, P3, P5, P16	**P10 – faster imaging process**
7.5	D11 – medical social networking	P2, P5	P11 – no noise
9	D12 – easy to operate	P13, P15	P12 – safe for pacemakers
9	D13 – IT infrastructure	P2, P5	P13 – electronic transmission of medical images
8	D14 – non intrusive	P4, P10, P11, P12, P13, P14	P14 – videoconferencing
			P15 – reliable data storage
			P16 – automated disease interpretation

5.4.1 *T1. Digital Signal Processing (DSP)*

Digital signal processing (DSP) is the mathematical manipulation of an information signal to modify or improve it. It is characterized by the representation of discrete time, discrete frequency, or other discrete domain signals by a sequence of numbers or symbols and the processing of these signals. Subfields of DSP are signal processing for communications, control of systems, biomedical signal processing, seismic data processing, etc. The main goal of DSP is usually to measure, filter, or compress real-world analog signals. Although DSP is more complex than analog processing and has a discrete value range, it provides more advantages over analog processing in many applications such as error detection and correction in transmission as well as data compression [10]. Nowadays, by using digital signal processing (DSP), X-ray signals can be converted to digital images at the point of acquisition with high image resolution. Plus, digital files eliminate the time and cost of processing film as well as provide more reliable storage. Most significantly, being able to render digital images in real time enables the doctor to view a precise image at the exact time of surgery [11].

5.4.2 *T2. Teleradiology*

Teleradiology is the digital sharing of medical images among radiologists for the purpose of collaboration or interpretation. It has the potential to improve patient care by transmitting medical images to those with expertise, allowing patients to have the most appropriate people review their images, regardless of geographical boundaries. Currently, despite the low rate of hospitals with electronic medical records (EMRs), some doctors have already begun to take advantage of using electronic medical images [12].

5.4.3 T3. Computer-Aided Diagnosis (CAD)

Computer-aided diagnosis (CAD) works by using different learning software to compare new medical images to the past ones that have already had abnormal markers or lesions identified by radiologists. The software then reports its conclusion as to whether the new medical image contains an abnormal marker or lesion, and this conclusion is used as a second opinion by a radiologist. CAD is currently a fast-developing research field that provides a way to make medical image interpretation much more efficient. CAD has already been successfully implemented for a number of different cancers such as breast, lung, and melanoma, as well as vertebral fractures and intracranial aneurysms [13].

5.4.4 T4. Positron Emission Tomography (PET)

Positron emission tomography (PET) is a nuclear medicine imaging technique that produces three-dimensional physiologic images of functional processes in the body based on radiation emissions from the body. These emissions are generated by radioactive chemical elements taken by the patient, which are designed to target specific organs or tissues. The three-dimensional imaging is often accomplished with the aid of a CT X-ray scan performed on the patient during the same session, in the same machine [14]. It has emerged as a powerful imaging tool for detecting cancer and occult tumors. Sometimes when cancer is treated with radiation or chemotherapy, X-ray, CAT, or MRI scan, they cannot clearly justify whether something left behind is tumor, scar tissue, fibrous tissue, or just necrotic dead tumor cells. However, with a PET scan, it is possible to see changes in a tumor much sooner than with a CAT scan or MRI [15].

5.4.5 T5. Magnetic Resonance Imaging (MRI)

Magnetic resonance imaging (MRI) is a noninvasive diagnostic technology that uses a strong magnetic field, radio frequencies, and a computer to produce images of the soft-tissue structures of the body. The MRI system uses powerful magnets to create a magnetic field which forces hydrogen atoms in the body into a particular alignment or resonance. Radio frequency energy is then distributed over the patient, which is disrupted by body tissue. The disruptions correspond to varying return signals which, when processed, create the image. It is mainly used for diagnosing a broad range of conditions, including cancer, heart and vascular disease, and muscular and bone abnormalities [16]. MRI is known for its radiation-free and quality images. However, it is not appropriate for those who have implanted metallic materials inside the body, have allergic reaction to a special dye, and have claustrophobia [17].

5.4.6 T6. Ultrasound

Ultrasound imaging uses high-frequency sound waves to view soft tissue inside the body. It basically consists of two main parts which are the transducer and the monitor. The transducer's duty is to send and receive the high-frequency sound waves while the monitor reports the result as an image. The quality of image depends on the amplitude and frequency of the sound signal as well as on how long the sound signal takes to return from the patient. The advantage of this method is that it involves no radiation. Although ultrasound may heat up the viewed tissue or create gas in bodily fluids or tissues, it has so far not been reported to cause any long-term effects [18].

5.4.7 T7. Extensible Imaging Platform (XIP)

XIP is a platform being developed by a group of Siemens researches that provides a standardized system for analyzing images from any medical imaging source. XIP would enable a much faster analysis of the resulting information, thus supporting earlier detection of diseases [19].

5.4.8 T8. Computed Tomography (CT)

Computed tomography (CT) is a medical imaging technique that produces three-dimensional images of internal human body parts from a large series of two-dimensional X-ray images taken around a single axis of rotation. When compared with a conventional X-ray radiograph, which is an image of many planes superimposed on each other, a CT image exhibits significantly improved contrast. A CT scan is useful in the examination of bone structures, lung and chest imaging, and cancer detection. It also pinpoints the location of a tumor, infection, or blood clot. However, using CT involves risks of radiation exposure, harm to babies, and reactions to contrast material [20].

Table 5.6 Technological capability definitions

Technological capabilities	Definition
T1 – digital signal processing (DSP)	Refers to a mathematical manipulation of an information signal to filter or compress real-world analog signals [10]
T2 – teleradiology	Refers to the digital sharing of medical images among radiologists for the purpose of collaboration or interpretation [12]
T3 – computer-aided diagnosis (CAD)	Refers to the software that reports its conclusion as to whether the new medical image contains an abnormal marker or lesion compared to the past ones [13]
T4 – positron emission tomography (PET)	Refers to a nuclear imaging technology that produces three-dimensional physiologic images of functional processes in the body based on radiation emissions from the body [14]
T5 – magnetic resonance imaging (MRI)	Refers to a noninvasive diagnostic technology that uses a strong magnetic field, radio frequencies, and a computer to produce images of the soft-tissue structures of the body [16]
T6 – ultrasound	Refers to a medical imaging technique that uses high-frequency sound waves generating from a transducer for viewing soft tissue inside the body [18]
T7 – extensible imaging platform (XIP)	Refers to a platform that is capable of integrating microscopic and macroscopic imaging data [19]
T8 – computed tomography (CT)	Refers to a medical imaging technique that produces three-dimensional images of internal human body parts from a large series of two-dimensional X-ray images taken around a single axis of rotation [20]
T9 – advanced battery technology	Refers to battery backup power systems used in emergency situations

5.4.9 T9. Advanced Battery Technology

Even though the most talked about things about medical imaging are the quality of images and its applications, advanced battery technology also plays an important role in medical imaging. Nowadays, medical imaging technologies such as permanent and portable X-ray, CT scans, and MRI all use batteries for backup or extended use away from AC power supply. These batteries are typically the same ones found in backup power systems used in emergency situations that supply power to homes in the case of electricity failure. The two basic components of battery-based storage systems are an inverter/charger and a set of DC batteries. The inverter/charger converts AC power from the grid to DC to charge the batteries. When power from the grid is lost, the inverter converts the DC battery power to AC to power the unit. The length of time that a battery-based storage system can provide emergency power to these medical units depends on its overall capacity and the type of medical appliance used.

As done in the previous two sections, all of our technological capabilities have been put in the table below with a short description (Table 5.6).

Finally, the nine technological capabilities were matched with the product features as shown below (Table 5.7).

Table 5.7 Linkage between product features and technology capabilities

Product features	Linked tech capabilities	Technology capabilities
P1 – battery powered	T9	T1 – digital Signal Processing (DSP)
P2 – Wi-fi	T1, T2, T6	T2 – teleradiology
P3 – handheld	T6	T3 – computer – aided diagnosis
P4 – no radiation	T4, T5, T6	T4 – nuclear imaging using PET
P5 – imaging software for mobile ops	T3	T5 – magnetic imaging with MRI
P6 – no high voltage required	T3	T6 – single-chip ultrasound imaging
P7 – no liquid nitrogen cooling	T4	T7 – XIP
P8 – no film required	1	T8 – computed tomography (CT)
P9 – 3D imaging	T3, T4, T5, T6, T8	T9 – advanced battery tech
P10 – faster imaging process	T1, T7	
P11 – no noise	T4, T6, T8	
P12 – safe for pacemakers	T4, T6, T8	
P13 – electronic transmission of medical images	T2, T3, T7	
P14 – videoconferencing	T1	
P15 – reliable data storage	T1	
P16 – automated disease interpretation	T3	

5.5 Resources

In our case, there are eight resources: semiconductor industry, networking technologies, artificial intelligent technology, software, biomarker technology, nuclear medicine R&D, materials engineer (magnets), and materials engineer (battery).

5.5.1 R1. Semiconductor Industry

Since the medical devices have been developed to become smaller, more adaptable, and more portable, semiconductor industry would be one of the most critical sources for medical technology. For instance, latest technology imaging devices require technology capabilities which provide higher resolution, 3D imaging, lesser image capturing time, small handheld devices, faster processing, more sensing for transmitter, and higher analog capability. Therefore, with a diverse application of semiconductor technology will enable new type of medical images for specific treatments with shorter processing time [22]. In advanced ultrasound technology, semiconductors have improved the quality of image by using 3D and 4D imaging technological capabilities [23]. Also, new applications provide more energy-efficient devices and consume less power. The imaging technologies supported by semiconductor resources are digital signal processing (DSP), positron emission tomography (PET), magnetic imaging with MRI, ultrasound imaging, and computed tomography (CT) [24].

5.5.2 R2. Networking Technologies

The wide world of imaging technologies can be integrated with modern networking technologies. The networking technologies enhance medical imaging communication. Since the application of information technology, or IT, plays an important role in telecommunication, this would let teleradiology become feasible and more efficient. Examples of networking technology are the use of preoperative images during surgery, remote surgery, and a further-reaching integration of digital data in the hospital [25].

5.5.3 R3. Artificial Intelligence Technology

In today's hospitals, diagnosis relies remarkably on computer support. Artificial intelligence technology or medical AI is the program that performs diagnosis and makes therapy recommendations. Medical AI programs are based on symbolic models of disease entities. With a variety functions supported by the intelligent computers, the physicians should be able to provide more accurate diagnosis (CAD) [26].

5.5.4 R4. Software

Software has played an important role in developing the technology roadmapping process. Also, it helps to integrate advanced systems which bring the breakthrough technology to medical imaging industry. As a result, the advanced software programs have the ability to enable imaging devices to best serve patients. The imaging technologies that are supported by software are computer-aided diagnosis (CAD) and extensible imaging platform (XIP).

5.5.5 R5. Biomarker Technology

Biomarker technology is developed to understand the fundamental biological processes and relationships. The biomarker is a new tool in the development of therapeutics, and it is used to segment the population for specific treatments. The benefits of biomarker technology are to screen subjects to determine clinical possibility, detect early toxicology, and support the diverse goals of BioPharma research and healthcare. Also, a biomarker helps to eliminate drug failure rates. Studying the genes, proteins, and metabolites will enhance the utility of medical imaging technology. The imaging technologies supported by biomarker technology are positron emission tomography (PET), magnetic imaging with MRI, and computed tomography (CT) [27, 28].

5.5.6 R6. Nuclear Medicine R&D

Nuclear medicine is a medical application of radioactive material to diagnose a variety of diseases, including heart disease, gastrointestinal and neurological disorders, and other abnormalities. The nuclear medical R&D has the ability to pinpoint molecular activity within the body. Also, it can identify the disease at an early stage. The nuclear medicine function allows the information from two different exams to be correlated and interpreted on one image. Its performance is enabled by the three systems: gamma camera, single-photon emission computed tomography (SPECT), or positron emission tomography (PET). The imaging technology supported by nuclear medicine technology is positron emission tomography (PET) [29].

5.5.7 R7. Materials Engineer (Magnets)

Magnetic imaging material is a new imaging technology which uses the magnetic properties of iron-oxide nanoparticles injected into the bloodstream in order to generate unprecedented real-time images of arterial blood flow and volumetric heart motion. The goal of this imaging tool is to improve diagnosis and therapy planning for many diseases, such as heart disease, stroke, and cancer. Also, developing a process for building large superconducting magnets will enable the imaging technology to generate more power and carry lighter weight. The imaging technology supported by the material magnet resource is magnetic imaging with MRI [30].

5.5.8 R8. Materials Engineer (Battery)

The new material battery technology provides a better performance than current electrical energy storage systems. The new advanced energy storage system is lithium-ion battery (LIB) technology. The advantages of this specific element are providing short time frame for data collection, small sample size, and short range order probing, especially in situ and noninvasive tools. The material battery technology provides an alternative for many mobile and stationary applications, because of its high-energy and high-power performance characteristics (Tables 5.8 and 5.9). The imaging technology supported by the material battery resource is advanced battery technology [31].

Table 5.8 Resources definitions: medical imaging

Resources	Definition
R1 – semiconductor industry	Semiconductor industry provides higher resolution, 3D imaging, lesser image capturing time, small handheld devices, faster processing, more sensing for transmitter, and higher analog capability
R2 – networking technologies	The application of information technology or telecommunication
R3 – artificial intelligence technology	Medical AI is the program that performs diagnosis and makes therapy recommendations
R4 – software	The integration of advanced systems which bring the breakthrough technology to medical imaging industry
R5 – biomarker technology	A new tool in the development of therapeutics that is used to segment the population for specific treatments
R6 – nuclear medicine R&D	A medical application of radioactive material to diagnose a variety of diseases, including heart disease, gastrointestinal and neurological disorders, and other abnormalities
R7 – materials engineer (magnets)	The use of magnetic properties of iron-oxide nanoparticles injected into the bloodstream in order to generate unprecedented real-time images of arterial blood flow and volumetric heart motion
R8 – materials engineer (battery)	Advanced energy storage system is lithium-ion battery (LIB) technology. Providing high-energy and high-power performance characteristics

Table 5.9 Linkage between technology capabilities and resources

Technology capabilities	Linked resouces	Resources
T1 – digital signal processing (DSP)	R1	R1 – semi-conductor industry
T2 – teleradiology	R2	R2 – networking technologies
T3 – computer-aided diagnosis	R3, R4	R3 – art Intell technology
T4 – nuclear imaging using PET	R1, R5, R6	R4 – software
T5 – magnetic imaging with MRI	R1, R5, R7	R5 – biomarker tech
T6 – single-chip ultrasound imaging	R1	R6 – nuclear medicine R&D
T7 – XIP	**R4**	R7 – materials engr (magnets)
T8 – computed tomography (CT)	R1, R5	R8 – materials engr (battery)
T9 – advanced battery tech	R8	

5.6 Analysis

Using the TRM analysis techniques of Phaal and Daim [1, 2], the four levels of TRM are analyzed. For market drivers, expert surveys were conducted and priorities calculated by response weight. Product features were analyzed using market drivers and the product feature grid with weighted scoring using the expert survey data. Technological capacities were analyzed using the scenario technique. Resources were analyzed using gap analysis and were prioritized for R&D requirements.

Table 5.10 Market survey results

Market drivers	OHSU researcher	Technician 1	Technician 2	Technician 3	Total (scale of 20)	Prioritization (scale of 10)
D1	3	3	5	3	14	7
D2	5	5	5	5	20	10
D3	4	5	1	5	15	7.5
D4	2	2	3	2	9	4.5
D5	3	5	3	5	16	8
D6	5	5	5	5	20	10
D7	5	4	5	5	19	9.5
D8	4	5	5	5	19	9.5
D9	4	4	5	5	18	9
D10	4	2	3	2	11	5.5
D11	5	2	3	5	15	7.5
D12	5	3	5	5	18	9
D13	4	4	5	5	18	9
D14	4	4	5	3	16	8

5.6.1 Market Drivers Analysis

Once these market drivers were defined, additional field market research was performed with a survey among medical imaging professionals at local hospitals in Portland, Oregon. Our team surveyed three medical imaging technicians at the Emmanuel Medical Center and one researcher at Oregon Health and Sciences University (OHSU). The results of the survey are listed above:

Based on the results of the survey, the market drivers were prioritized and assigned weights on a normalized scale of 0–10 (Table 5.10).

5.6.2 Product Features Analysis

For identifying product features, we talked to experts, performed brainstorming, and referred to some articles [11, 30–32] and then came up with some features which could be available in the upcoming imaging products. In the market drivers and product features analysis grid below, we have evaluated the relationships between product features and market drivers and ranked the impact of each feature on each market driver [33] (Table 5.11).

After ranking, we found that 3D imaging contributes most toward the market drivers. Therefore, it would be most beneficial to launch a product with this feature. For this project, we have identified four products called "advanced imaging machine," "high-tech imaging machine," "super-tech imaging machine," and "ultra-tech imaging machine." The release date of each product along with the specific features of the product is decided on the basis of technology and market drivers available at different time periods (Tables 5.12, 5.13, 5.14, and 5.15).

Table 5.11 Market drivers and product features analysis grid

Market driver weighting	7	10	7	4	8	10	9	9	9	5	7	9	9	8		
	Market/business drivers															
Product feature concepts	D1 – lowcost	D2 – high resolution	D3 – no side effects	D4 – portability	D5 – soft tissue	D6 – ull body imaging	D7 – 3D imaging	D8 – real time info	D9 – exposure duration	D10 – app in a mobile device	D11 – medical social networking	D12 – easy to operate	D13 – IT infrastructure	D14 – non intrusive	Total	Normalized
P1 – battery powered				4							0	2			34	2.1
P2 – Wi-fi				2						4	5		4		99	6.1
P3 – handheld				5					1	4	2	2			81	5.0
P4 – no radiation			5						3					3	86	5.3
P5 – imaging software for mobile oss	1									5	5		4	3	127	7.8
P6 – no high voltage required	3			3											33	2.0
P7 – no liquid nitrogen cooling	3			2											29	1.8
P8 – no film required	2	3				4		4							120	7.4
P9 – 3D imaging		5			4		5		4						163	10.0
P10 – faster imaging process								4						5	76	4.7
P11 – no noise														4	32	2.0
P12 – safe for pace makers				0						0	0	0	0	3	24	1.5
P13 – electronic transmission of medical image			5				1					2		4	94	5.8
P14 – videoconferencing			4											4	60	3.7
P15 – reliable data storage												2			18	1.1
P16 – automated disease interpretation		2	0			3	2	4		3					119	7.3

Table 5.12 Market/product features mapping: advanced imaging product

Advanced imaging (2012)	
Features	Market drivers
P4 – no radiation	D1 – low cost,
P7 – no liquid nitrogen cooling	D2 – high resolution
P8 – no film required	D3 – no side effects
P9 – 3D imaging	D5 – soft tissue imaging
P14 – videoconferencing	D6 – full body imaging
P15 – reliable data storage	D10 – app in a mobile device
	D12 – easy to operate
	D14 – nonintrusive

Table 5.13 Market/product features mapping: high-tech imaging product

High-tech imaging (2014)	
Features	Market drivers
P10 – faster imaging process	D1 – low cost
P11 – no noise	D3 – no side effects
P16 – automated disease interpretation	D4 – portability
	D8 – real-time info
	D14 – nonintrusive

Table 5.14 Market/product features mapping: super-tech imaging product

Super-tech imaging (2017)	
Features	Market drivers
P2 – Wi-Fi	D4 – portability
P3 – handheld	D10 – app in a mobile device
P6 – no high voltage required	D11 – medical social networking
P12 – safe for pacemakers	D13 – IT infrastructure
	D14 – nonintrusive

Table 5.15 Market/product features mapping: ultra-tech imaging product

Ultra-tech imaging (2022)	
Features	Market drivers
P1 – battery powered	D3 – no side effects
P5 – imaging software for mobile apps	D4 – portability
P13 – electronic transmission of medical images	D10 – app in a mobile device
	D11 – medical social networking
	D12 – easy to operate

5.6.3 Technology Capabilities Analysis

In our case, based on what we had learned about T-plan from our class lecture, we decided to choose the scenario analysis as our tool to forecast and estimate what the impacts would be if certain technological progress were made. To perform the scenario analysis, we first determined what the future of some technological capabilities would look like based on our literature research. After that, we as a team discussed and tried to come up with pros and cons if the technological progress were executed.

5.6.4 The Future of Our Technological Capabilities

First of all, the future of CAD software most likely lies in software packages that will be incorporated directly into the viewing display of radiologists. In this case, related images can be linked to the viewing display, allowing radiologists to instantly examine past conclusions of similar images. Some researchers believe that the software packages will be web based, allowing radiologists to simply upload a medical image and then have the areas of concern highlighted [12].

PET is currently developing toward molecular imaging. With molecular imaging, a doctor will be better able to make an early diagnosis of cancer, see what is happening inside atherosclerotic plaques in coronary arteries, study arthritic joints, and know if the patient is in the earliest stage of Alzheimer's disease [15].

Meanwhile, scientists are developing newer MRI scanners that are smaller, portable devices. These new scanners apparently can be most useful in detecting infections and tumors of the soft tissues of the hands, feet, elbows, and knees. The application of these scanners to medical practice is now being tested [16].

Over the past several years, ultrasound equipment has become more compact, with cart-based systems increasingly complemented or replaced by portable and handheld ultrasound machines. Thus, the future goal is to create a single-chip ultrasound machine that allows the probing, receiving, transmitting, and processing chains to be integrated. That in turn allows all of the ultrasound machine electronics to reside in the probe head, which then can use a wireless link to transmit information to the display [11].

For CT, increases in resolution and quality of medical images are expected to continue. As a result, CT scans will continue to improve their slice counts, allowing for large volumes to be visualized in a single pass [21]. This allows for faster CT scans as well as higher image quality.

Consequently, over the next decade, there are quite a few expectations from medical imaging technologies. First of all, medical software is expected to be developed for better disease detection and diagnosis. Second, medical imaging devices are expected to become more portable, thus bringing care to patients in rural and remote areas instead of forcing them to travel. Third, increases in resolution and quality of medical images are likewise expected to continue. In this case, the fields of 3D medical imaging and molecular imaging are also expected to develop and grow. 3D medical imaging allows radiologists to view high-quality 3D images in real time and helps them make clinical decisions with accuracy. On the other hand, with molecular imaging, we will see what is happening at a molecular level in our cells. In other words, imaging the actual disease process is a radical change, and it will

Table 5.16 Scenario analysis: medical imaging

	Software (computer-aided diagnosis, XIP, teleradiology)	Portability (PET, ultrasound, CT, MRI, advanced battery)	Image quality (DSP, PET, ultrasound, CT, MRI)
Positive impacts if the technological progresses were made	Better diagnosis	Medical imaging will reach rural areas	More accurate diagnosis
	Reliable result	Reduce patients' traveling time	See tissues in 3D or molecular size which aids diagnosis
	Reduce time required for diagnosis	Good solution for those who have claustrophobia or are allergic to special dye used in most cart-based systems	Reduce time required for diagnosis
Negative impacts if the technological progresses were made	Costly for patients who do not need a very detailed computer-aided diagnosis	Small screen size Fair resolution Need reliable battery Radiologists have to travel more	In the case of molecular imaging, the best radiologist is required for diagnosis, which is very difficult to find
	Similar images linked to the viewing display cannot always be trusted		Costly for patients who do not need very high image quality

radically alter medicine. After we identified the key expectations from medical imaging technologies, we discussed each of them in the team meeting and compiled all of the advantages and disadvantages that would occur if the expected technological progresses were made, which is shown in the table above (Table 5.16).

5.6.5 Resources Analysis

After integrating the technology roadmapping process, the three main levels of the roadmap, which are market driver, product feature, and technological capability, also require extra factors in order to increase market opportunity and approach the development of new technologies. Technology resources are addressed as significant sources because they have the potential to fill the technology gaps and deliver good roadmaps. Moreover, having sufficient resources will allow the capability of technology to overcome the barriers of technology application and also improve the diagnosis and treatment of patients.

1. *Current Level of Technology Capabilities*
   Nowadays, imaging devices have been developed to be incorporated in a variety of different types of applications. Also, some of them can be adapted to enable diagnosis for a particular part of the body or organ. The imaging

techniques that have already been used in medical imaging industry provide high resolution; lesser image capturing time; smaller, portable devices; real-time diagnosis; and so on. The capabilities of imaging technology are different than each other, depending on the characteristic of the technology. The current stage for each technology is described in more detail in the text below.

T1. Digital Signal Processing (DSP)
A digital signal processor (DSP) is a microprocessor having a lot of software capabilities to support imaging functionality, for example, searching and retrieving images from the database and reducing the redundancy in the image data to optimize transmission. It can also manipulate signals after being converted from analog voltages and currents into digital form in order to build high-performance communications systems. The advantages of a DSP are eliminating the time and cost of processing film as well as providing more reliable storage, allowing doctors to view a precise image at the exact time of surgery. Also, a DSP can be simply reprogrammed for other applications or ported to different hardware. A DSP provides better control of accuracy requirements as digital signals can be easily stored without deterioration. Although a DSP works as a microprocessor and provides high effective resolution, it involves some technology gaps. A DSP has low ability to distinguish between higher and lower frequencies, as a result of limited frequency resolution. Sometimes the disturbance during system operation causes loss of information [34].

T2. Teleradiology
The capability of teleradiology at the current stage is in transmitting radiologic images from one location to another for the purpose of diagnosis or consultation. Thus, teleradiology can improve the interpretation and improve patient care as well. However sometimes image quality is reduced due to loss of data during the transmission [35].

T3. Computer-Aided Diagnosis (CAD)
The capability of computer-aided diagnosis at the current stage is in detecting abnormalities in mammograms. The advantages of CAD are detecting early breast cancer and reducing mortality rates. However, CAD requires a computer expert because, during transmission, there are chances of system error [13].

T4. Positron Emission Tomography (PET)
PET has been used with many technologies, such as radioactive materials called radiotracers and imaging devices that can detect the radiotracers. A PET scanner is a large machine with a round, doughnut-shaped hole in the middle, similar to a CT or MRI unit. The capability of PET at the current stage is in pinpointing molecular activity within the body and measuring body functions such as blood flow, oxygen use, and sugar level. PET has many advantages of its application, for example, it offers the potential to identify the disease in its earliest stage, is noninvasive, is painless, has no side effects mostly, allows the patient to wear his/her own clothing, gives

detailed information on both function and structure, is less expensive, and yields more precise information than exploratory surgery. There are also some disadvantages of PET regarding the efficiency. Mostly PET relies on other exams such as CT scan for accurate diagnosis. Food and drinks are not allowed several hours before the scan. The scan takes at least 20–30 min, and also it usually takes 60 min for the radiotracer to travel through the body. Additional tests involving other tracers may be used for specific examination such as heart disease, which could take up to 3 h. Patients may have discomfort in having to remain still during imaging. Plus, they would feel anxiety while being scanned if they are claustrophobic [36].

T5. Magnetic Resonance Imaging (MRI)

The technologies MRI are magnetism, radio waves, and advanced computer application. The MRI unit is a tube surrounded by a giant circular magnet and is used to detect tiny changes of structures within the body. Also, it produces cross-sectional images of organs and internal structures in the body. The advantages of MRI are its precise accuracy, it is painless, has no known side effects, and uses no radiation. Moreover, MRI provides detailed images of ligaments and cartilage like no other tests can. MRI also has some disadvantages which could lead to technology gaps for its future development. MRI can cause heart pacemakers and other implants to work improperly. Some exams require a special dye (contrast) which may cause an allergic reaction to the patient. MRI does not involve metallic materials. So, coils may be placed around the head, arms, legs, or other areas. The test lasts for 30–60 min, but sometimes it may take longer. Therefore, food and drinks are not allowed 4–6 h before the test. Also, patients need to be given a medicine if they have claustrophobia. The MRI machine produces loud humming noise [16–18].

T6. Ultrasound Imaging

Ultrasound imaging (sonography) at the current stage is used for viewing soft tissues such as muscles and internal organs in real time. It uses a transducer creating high-frequency sound waves and a monitor as a current technology. Ultrasound imaging uses a handheld ultrasound device with a monitor mounted on it. The benefit of ultrasound imaging is that it does not involve ionizing radiation. The drawbacks of ultrasound imaging are that it heats the tissues slightly produces small pockets of gas in body fluids or tissues [18].

T7. Extensible Imaging Platform (XIP)

Extensible imaging platform (XIP) involves imaging software technology. XIP is an open platform that offers a standardized basis for analyzing images from any source. The capabilities of XIP at the current stage are in supporting advanced multi-resolution imaging technology and integrating the image from the full spectrum of modalities. The advantages of XIP are that it provides a faster analysis of the resulting information and has the ability to detect the disease at an early stage. But XIP's software program cannot be used for different types of imaging files [19].

T8. Computed Tomography (CT)

Technologies in computed tomography (CT) are CT scanner creating X-ray and computer. CT is a large, boxlike machine with a tunnel in the center and with the X-ray tube and detectors located inside and a narrow examination table slid into and out of this tunnel. The advantages of CT are that it produces a three-dimensional image, takes only a few minutes for operation, and gives the result with detailed pictures. CT has some disadvantages which could lead to technology gaps for its future development. CT involves exposure to radiation, and the patient may also cause allergic reaction to contrast dye. Food and drinks are not allowed 4–6 h before the test. Mostly, CTs are for patients who weigh less than 300 pounds. Also, patients are required to remove all jewelry and wear a hospital gown only [17, 36].

T9. Advanced Battery Technology

Advanced battery still requires lighter weight for future because advanced battery was designed to have more weight to be able to generate more power. Therefore, advanced battery should have light weight and still be able to generate efficient energy.

2. *Required Level of Technology Capabilities*

   The required level of technology capabilities has been set as an R&D requirement for roadmap planning. The process aims to emphasize a great potential for supporting business strategy, reducing technology gaps which would impede the efficiency of technology capability, increasing competitive advantages, and building sustainability in business. All required levels of technology capabilities would help the industry to develop a better technology for medical imaging in the future with faster processing and higher resolution, coupled with more sensing and transmitter channels. Therefore, new technology capability will be utilized for more precise diagnosis. The required level or future solution for medical imaging roadmap planning is derived from our brainstorming and literature research. We also consider the future trend for imaging devices which have the capability to support both product feature level and market driver level. The analysis of the required level is given in more detail for each technology in the table below.
3. *The Critical Capability Gaps*

   We used gap analysis as our analysis tool. In order to customize the technology gaps, we will interpret from disadvantages or drawbacks of technology capability the technology need for our future imaging market. Thus, we expect in the future that imaging devices will be made proficient enough to have all feasible capabilities without their disadvantages. Most importantly, the consideration of imaging device development would allow our scenarios from technology analysis to become a reality and more accurate for future projections. The result of the analysis is presented in the table below (Table 5.17).
4. *Prioritizing Resources*

   Resources were prioritized using a scoring system. First, a single market driver was selected, and the linked path from the driver to product features to technology capabilities to resources was traced. Referring to layer linking tables X, Y, and Z, the path from driver D1 to the resources may be mapped as follows: D1, low cost, has a weight of 7.0 from the expert surveys. The result scores for D1 are 0 for R2 and R8, 14 for R1, and 7 for R3, R4, R5, and R6. Likewise, scoring for D2 to D15 can be made and values assigned to R1–R8 (Table 5.18).

Table 5.17 Resource gap analysis: medical imaging

Technology capabilities	Required level	Critical capability gaps
T1 – digital signal processing (DSP)	No information lost during transmission	Loss of information during processing
	Can distinguish between a wide range of frequencies	Cannot distinguish between higher and lower frequencies
	Better frequency resolution	Limited frequency resolution
	Increases utilization of functional image transported	
T2 – teleradiology	Highly efficient transmitter	Low transmission quality
T3 – computer-aided diagnosis (CAD)	Develops better CAD software	Related images cannot be linked to the viewing display
T4 – positron emission tomography (PET)	No need to rely on other technologies	Relies on other technologies such as CT for accurate diagnosis
T5 – magnetic resonance imaging (MRI)	No dye required	A special dye required
	Pacemakers or other implants allowed	Can cause heart pacemakers work improperly
	No noise	Produces loud noise
T6 – ultrasound imaging	No side effect at all on scanned tissues	Heats the tissues slightly
	Four-dimensional sonography	Produces small pockets of gas in tissues
T7-extensible imaging platform (XIP)	A platform to process different imaging data	No imaging platform to analyze imaging data
T8 – computed tomography (CT)	No dye required	A special dye required
	Uses no radiation	Exposure to radiation
T9 – advanced battery technology	Light weight	Needs more efficient resolution
	Requires more power and energy storage	

5.7 Results

5.7.1 Medical Imaging Technology Roadmap

To create the roadmaps, we first verified the links between the market drivers, product features, technology capabilities, and the resources from the literature search. We then established the timeline for the levels and produced future product timelines derived from the literature search (Tables 5.19 and 5.20).

Each of the following TRMs is subdivided by level to include market drivers, product features, technology capabilities, and resources (R&D). Criteria are provided for the product feature and technology capabilities levels. The lengths of the level parameters indicate the time span that the particular driver, feature, or capability is ready for product development use (Tables 5.21, 5.22, 5.23, and 5.24).

Table 5.18 Resource priorities: medical imaging

Resources	Priority	10	9.5	9	8	7.5	7	5.5	4.5	Score
R1 – semi-conductor industry	**1**	5	0	3	6	4	2	3	4	**203.5**
R2 – networking technologies	**5**	0	1	2	0	2	0	1	1	**52.5**
R3 – art intelligence technology	**4**	0	1	2	0	2	1	2	1	**65**
R4 – software	**3**	0	1	3	0	2	1	2	1	**74**
R5 – biomarker tech	**2**	3	0	0	5	1	1	0	1	**89**
R6 – nuclear medicine R&D	**6**	0	0	0	4	0	1	0	1	**43.5**
R7 – materials engr (magnets)	**7**	0	0	0	2	1	0	0	0	**23.5**
R8 – materials engr (battery)	**8**	0	0	0	0	0	0	0	1	**4.5**

Table 5.19 Advanced and high-tech imaging products timeline

Advanced imaging			High-tech imaging		
2012–2014			2014–2017		
Features	Market drivers	Tech capabilities	Features	Market drivers	Tech capabilities
P4 – no radiation	D3 – no side effects	T4 – PET	P10 – faster imaging process	D3 – no side effects	T1 – DSP
	D14 – non intrusive	T5 – MRI			
P7 – no liquid nitrogen cooling	D1 – low cost	T5 – MRI	P11 – no noise	D3 – no side effects	T4 – PET
				D4 – portability	
P8 – no film required	D2 – high resolution	T1 – DSP	P16 – automated disease interpretation	D8 – real time info	T3 – computor aided dDiagnosis
	D6 – full body image				
P9 – 3D imaging	D6 – full body imaging,	T4 – PET			
	D14 – non intrusive	T5 – MRI T8 – CT			
P14 – video conerencing	D10 – app in a mobile device	T1 – DSP			
P15 – reliable data storage	D12 – easy to operate	T1 – DSP			

5.8 Conclusions

Technology roadmaps provide a guide for technology and product development. To predict the most likely resultant products can be difficult. Use of economic and probabilistic models can reduce uncertainty but cannot eliminate it from predicting future products. TRMs are best suited as guides to determine which technologies and/or product features should be developed to improve a product or develop a new product.

Using the data and analysis tools of this study, several broad conclusions may be derived about future medical imaging products. In the short term, 0–2 years,

Table 5.20 Super- and ultra-tech imaging products timeline

Super-tech imaging			Ultra-tech imaging		
2017–2022			2022+		
Features	Market drivers	Tech capabilities	Features	Market drivers	Tech capabilities
P2 – Wi-fi	D4 – portability D10 – app in a mobile device D11 – med social networking	T1 – DSP T2 – tele-radiology	P1 – battery powered	D4 – portability	T9 – advanced battery tech
P3 – handheld	D4 – portability D10 – app in a mobile device	T6 – single chip ultrasound	P5 – imaging software for mobile ops	D3 – no side effects D10 – app in a mobile device D11 – med social networking	T3 – computer aided diagnosis
P6 – no high voltage required	D1 – low cost	T6 – single chip ultrasound	P13 – electronic transmission of medical images	D10 – app in a mobile device	T2 – tele-radiology T3 – computer aided diagnosis
P12 – safe for pacemakers	D14 – non-intrusive	T4 – PET T6 – single chip ultrasound			

Table 5.21 Advanced medical imaging TRM

Medical imaging TRM – Advanced Imaging		
Level	**Criteria**	**Now – 2014**
Market drivers	Market drivers	D1 low cost D3 no side effects D2 high resolution D6 full body imaging D10 mobile app D12 easy to operate D14 non-intrusive
Product	Power	
	Accessories	P7 No liguid nitrogen P14 video conferencing P15 reliable data storage
	Usability	P8 no film P9 3D imaging
	Safety	P4 no radiation
	Appearance	
	Portability	
Technology	Power	T4 PET T5 MRI
	Software	T1 DSP
	Electronics	T4 PET T5 MRI T8 CT
	Communications	
	Materials	T4 PET T5 MRI T8 CT
Resource	R&D	R1 semi conductor industry R5 biomarker tech R6 nuc med tech R7 matls engr (magnets)

advanced medical imaging products would most likely be upgraded CT, PET, and MRI imaging devices driven by cost and ease of use with improved accessories. High-tech medical imaging devices, 2–5 years, would most likely be an upgrade of PET imaging devices with improved performance to include the speed of imaging and resolution. The super-tech products, 5–10 years, would most likely be a PET upgrade or PET derivative device and a new ultrasound device. The improved

Table 5.22 High-tech medical imaging TRM

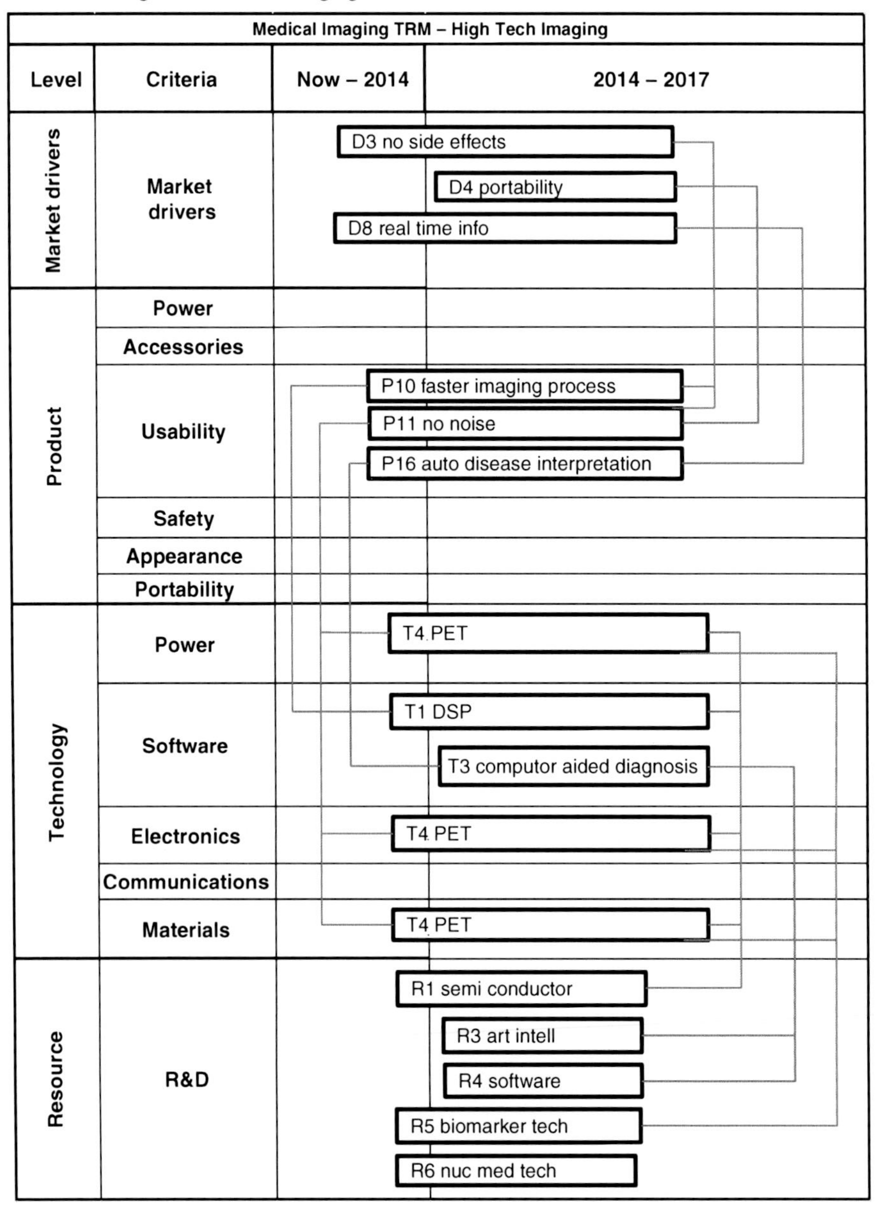

PET devices would utilize advances in materials science and communications. The ultrasound devices would be smaller and more portable than existing devices and be able to communicate from remote locations.

And finally after 10 years, the ultra-tech devices will have improved portability features, software, and communications technology. They will be mobile, highly

Table 5.23 Super-tech medical imaging TRM

Medical imaging TRM – super techimaging				
Level	Criteria	Now – 2014	2014 – 2017	2017 – 2022
Market drivers	Market drivers	D1 low cost		
		D3 no side effects		
			D4 portability	
		D10 mobile app		
				D11 med soc networking
		D14 non-intrusive		
Product	Power			P6 no high voltage
	Accessories			P2 Wi-Fi
	Usability			P12 pacemaker safe
	Safety			
	Appearance			
	Portability			P3 handheld
Technology	Power	T4 PET		
	Software	T1 DSP		
			T3 comp aided diagnosis	
	Electronics	T4 PET		
				T6 single chip ultrasound
	Communications			T2 teleradiology
	Materials	T4 PET		
Resource	R&D	R1 Semi Conductor		
				R2 networking tech
			R3 art intell	
			R4 software	
		R5 biomarker tech		
		R6 nuc med tech		

effective, able to remotely communicate with other devices, and cost effective. What scanning technology these devices would possess is difficult to predict at this point in time, based on our limited research and analysis.

Table 5.24 Ultra – tech medical imaging TRM

Medical Imaging TRM – Ultra Tech Imaging					
Level	Criteria	Now – 2014	2014 – 2017	2017 – 2022	2022+
Market drivers	Market drivers	D3 no side effects			
			D4 portability		
		D10 mobile app in a med device			
				D11 med soc networking	
Product	Power				P1 battery powered
	Accessories				
	Usability				P13 elec trans of images
	Safety				
	Appearance				
	Portability				P5 mobile apps software
Technology	Power				
	Software		T3 comp aided diagnosis		
	Electronics				
	Communications			T2 teleradiology	
	Materials				T9 adv battery tech
Resource	R&D			R2 networking tech	
			R3 art intell		
			R4 software		
		R9 adv battery tech			

5.9 Future Research

To obtain a more focused technology roadmap for medical imaging, further analysis is shown to be conducted to include cost benefit, patent search, bibliometric search, and other methods to quantify uncertainty. Reference to medical libraries and journals is recommended. Surveys of experts, including medical imaging manufacturer's marketing professionals and state-of-the-art researchers, are also recommended.

Appendix

Expert Surveys

Survey Forms and Responses

In this section, from *your* perspective, you will evaluate the importance of different market drivers for medical imaging technology. Please use the following rating scale: *1* = Not important *2* = Slightly important *3* = Somewhat important *4* = Important *5* = Very important

Market Drivers	Scale				
D1 – Low Cost	1	2	(3)	4	5
D2 - High Resolution	1	2	3	4	(5)
D3 - No side effects	1	2	3	(4)	5
D4 - Portability	1	(2)	3	4	5
D5 - Aging population	1	2	3	4	5
D6 - Soft Tissue	1	2	(3)	4	5
✓ D7 - Full body imaging	1	2	3	4	(5)
✓ D8 - 3D Imaging	1	2	3	4	(5)
D9 - Real time info	1	2	3	(4)	5
D10 - Exposure duration	1	2	3	(4)	5
✓ D11- App in a mobile device	1	2	3	(4)	5
✓ D12- Medical Social Networking	1	2	3	4	(5)
D13 - Easy to operate	1	2	3	4	(5)
D14 - IT Infrastructure	1	2	3	(4)	5
✓ D15 - Non intrusive	1	2	3	(4)	5

"✓" for: future need.

We are a group of students of "Technology Roadmapping" class at Portland State University. We are currently working on a project that identifies the current and future market drivers of Medical Imaging Technology. The purpose of this survey is to establish the importance of different market drivers that a person takes into account when deciding to develop a new product on medical imaging.

We appreciate your help and support towards our project's success.

Expert Detail

Name of the Expert (Optional)

Designation/Position held CT TECHNOLOGIST

Place of Work LEGACY EMANUEL

Years of Experience in the field 15

Additional comments

In this section, from *your* perspective, you will evaluate the importance of different market drivers for medical imaging technology. Please use the following rating scale: *1* = Not important *2* = Slightly important *3* = Somewhat important *4* = Important *5* = Very important

Market Drivers	Scale				
D1 – Low Cost	1	2	(3)	4	5
D2 - High Resolution	1	2	3	4	(5)
D3 - No side effects	1	2	3	4	(5)
D4 - Portability	1	(2)	3	4	5
D5 - Aging population	1	2	3	(4)	5
D6 - Soft Tissue	1	2	3	4	(5)
D7 - Full body imaging	1	2	3	4	(5)
D8 - 3D imaging	1	2	3	(4)	5
D9 - Real time info	1	2	3	4	(5)
D10 - Exposure duration	1	2	3	(4)	5
D11- App in a mobile device	1	(2)	3	4	5
D12- Medical Social Networking	1	(2)	3	4	5
D13 - Easy to operate	1	2	(3)	4	5
D14 - IT Infrastructure	1	2	3	(4)	5
D15 - Non intrusive	1	2	3	(4)	5

We are a group of students of "Technology Roadmapping" class at Portland State University. We are currently working on a project that identifies the current and future market drivers of Medical Imaging Technology. The purpose of this survey is to establish the importance of different market drivers that a person takes into account when deciding to develop a new product on medical imaging.

We appreciate your help and support towards our project's success.

Expert Detail

Name of the Expert (Optional)

Designation/Position held CT Technologist

Place of Work Emanuel

Years of Experience in the field 7 yrs

Additional comments

In this section, from *your* perspective, you will evaluate the importance of different market drivers for medical imaging technology. Please use the following rating scale: *1* = Not important *2* = Slightly important *3* = Somewhat important *4* = Important *5* = Very important

Market Drivers	Scale				
D1 – Low Cost	1	2	3	4	(5)
D2 - High Resolution	1	2	3	4	(5)
D3 - No side effects	(1)	2	3	4	5
D4 - Portability	1	2	(3)	4	5
D5 - Aging population	1	2	(3)	4	5
D6 - Soft Tissue	1	2	(3)	4	5
D7 - Full body imaging	1	2	3	4	(5)
D8 - 3D Imaging	1	2	3	4	(5)
D9 - Real time info	1	2	3	4	(5)
D10 - Exposure duration	1	2	3	4	(5)
D11- App in a mobile device	1	2	(3)	4	5
D12- Medical Social Networking	1	2	(3)	4	5
D13 - Easy to operate	1	2	3	4	(5)
D14 - IT Infrastructure	1	2	3	4	(5)
D15 - Non intrusive	1	2	3	4	(5)

We are a group of students of "Technology Roadmapping" class at Portland State University. We are currently working on a project that identifies the current and future market drivers of Medical Imaging Technology. The purpose of this survey is to establish the importance of different market drivers that a person takes into account when deciding to develop a new product on medical imaging.

We appreciate your help and support towards our project's success.

Expert Detail

Name of the Expert (Optional)

Designation/Position held CT tech

Place of Work Emanuel Medical Center

Years of Experience in the field 14 yrs.

Additional comments

In this section, from *your* perspective, you will evaluate the importance of different market drivers for medical imaging technology. Please use the following rating scale: *1* = Not important *2* = Slightly important *3* = Somewhat important *4* = Important *5* = Very important

Market Drivers	Scale				
D1 – Low Cost	1	2	3	4	5
D2 - High Resolution	1	2	3	4	5
D3 - No side effects	1	2	3	4	5
D4 - Portability	1	2	3	4	5
D5 - Aging population	1	2	3	4	5
D6 - Soft Tissue	1	2	3	4	5
D7 - Full body imaging	1	2	3	4	5
D8 - 3D Imaging	1	2	3	4	5
D9 - Real time info	1	2	3	4	5
D10 - Exposure duration	1	2	3	4	5
D11- App in a mobile device	1	2	3	4	5
D12- Medical Social Networking	1	2	3	4	5
D13 - Easy to operate	1	2	3	4	5
D14 - IT Infrastructure	1	2	3	4	5
D15 - Non intrusive	1	2	3	4	5

References

1. Phaal R, Muller G (2009) An architectural framework for roadmapping: towards visual strategy. Technol Forecast Soc Change 76(1):39–49
2. Daim T et al (2012) Technology roadmapping: wind energy for Pacific NW. J Clean Prod 20(1):27–37
3. Lamb AM et al (2012) Wood pellet technology roadmap. IEEE Trans Sustain Energy 3(2):218–230

4. Phaal R et al (2004) Technology roadmapping – a planning framework for evolution and revolution. Technol Forecast Soc Change 71:5–26
5. Everton KL, Mazal J (2012) White paper report of the 2011 RAD-AID conference on international radiology for developing countries: integrating multidisciplinary strategies for imaging services in the developing world. J Am Coll Radiol 9(7):488–494
6. Hillman B et al (2004) The future quality and safety of medical imaging: proceedings of the third annual ACR FORUM. J Am Coll Radiol 1(1):33–39
7. Galbrun J, Kijima K (2010) Innovation in medical imaging technology: toward a systemic service perspective. In: Service Systems and Service Management (ICSSSM), 2010 7th international conference on 28–30 June 2010, pp 1–7
8. Kunio D (2005) Current status and future potential of computer-aided diagnosis in medical imaging. Br J Radiol 78:S3–S19
9. Law D (2000) Future needs for medical imaging in health care. http://publications.gc.ca/collections/Collection/C21-30-1-2000E.pdf. Accessed 10 Aug 2013
10. Oppenheim A, Schafer R (1989) Discrete-time signal processing, 3rd edn. Prentice Hall, Upper Saddle River
11. Nadeski M, Frantz G (2008) The future of medical imaging [Online]. http://www.ti.com/lit/wp/slyy020/slyy020.pdf. Accessed 10 Aug 2013
12. Leiserson M (2010) Insights: the future of medical imaging [Online]. http://s3.amazonaws.com/tuftscope_articles/documents/97/TSS10_-_Leiserson.pdf. Accessed 10 Aug 2013
13. Kunio D (2007) Computer-aided diagnosis in medical imaging: historical review, current status and future potential. Comput Med Imaging Graph 31:198–211
14. Bailey D (2005) Positron emission tomography: basic sciences, 1st edn. Springer, Secaucus
15. Schimpff S (2010) Molecular imaging: the future of medicine [Online]. http://medicalmegatrends.com/imaging.html. Accessed 10 Aug 2013
16. Shiel W Jr (2012) Magnetic resonance imaging (MRI scan) [Online]. http://www.medicinenet.com/mri_scan/article.htm. Accessed 10 Aug 2013
17. Wilkinson I (2008) Diagnostic radiology: a textbook of medical imaging, ch. 5, 5th edn. Churchill Livingstone, New York
18. U.S. Food and Drug Administration (2012) Radiation-emitting products: ultrasound imaging [Online]. http://www.fda.gov/Radiation-EmittingProducts/RadiationEmittingProductsand Procedures/MedicalImaging/ucm115357.htm. Accessed 10 Aug 2013
19. Pease F (2008) The future of medical imaging [Online]. http://www.siemens.com/innovation/pool/en/publikationen/publications_pof/pof_fall_2008/early_detection/imaging/pof208_med_imaging_pdf_en.pdf. Accessed 10 Aug 2013
20. Lawrence M (2012) CT scan (CAT scan, computerized axial tomography) [Online]. http://www.emedicinehealth.com/ct_scan/article_em.htm. Accessed 10 Aug 2013
21. Murray C (2010) Electronic innovation spearheads medical imaging revolution [Online]. http://www.designnews.com/document.asp?doc_id=228821. Accessed 10 Aug 2013
22. Patelay W (2009) Industrial & medical semiconductors: new growth area in 2009 and beyond [Online].http://www.eetimes.com/electronics-news/4197930/Industrial-Medical-Semiconductors-new-growth-area-in-2009-and-beyond-. Accessed 10 Aug 2013
23. Santa C (2010) Siemens and national semiconductor align to advance ultrasound technology [Online]. http://www.siemens.com/press/en/pressrelease/?press=/en/pressrelease/2010/healthcare/hus2010090710.htm. Accessed 10 Aug 2013
24. Rosso D (2012) Semiconductors at the heart of life-saving medical imaging & devices [Online]. http://www.sia-online.org/events/2012/09/18/public-event/sia-texas-instruments-tech-boot-camp-briefing-on-capitol-hill/. Accessed 12 Aug 2012
25. Kuijpers FA (1995) The role of technology in future medical imaging [Online]. http://www.healthcare.philips.com/phpwc/main/about/assets/docs/medicamundi/mm_vol40_no3/kuijpers.pdf. Accessed 10 Aug 2013
26. Coiera E (2003) Artificial intelligence in medicine: an introduction [Online]. http://www.openclinical.org/aiinmedicine.html. Accessed 10 Aug 2013

27. McCormick T, Martin K, Hehenberger M. Advancing the utility of imaging biomarkers [Online]. http://www-935.ibm.com/services/us/gbs/bus/pdf/g510-6560-00-biomarker.pdf. Accessed 10 Aug 2013
28. Scaros O, Pharm D, Fisler R (2005) Biomarker technology roundup: from discovery to clinical applications, a broad set of tools is required to translate from the lab to the clinic [Online]. http://www.biotechniques.com/multimedia/archive/00004/BTN_A_05384SU01_O_4221a.pdf. Accessed 10 Aug 2013
29. Radiological Society of North America, Inc. (RSNA) (2012) General nuclear medicine [Online]. http://www.radiologyinfo.org/en/info.cfm?pg=gennuclear. Accessed 10 Aug 2013
30. Medical News Today (2009) Philips announces breakthrough in new medical imaging technology [Online]. http://www.medicalnewstoday.com/releases/140578.php. Accessed 10 Aug 2013
31. Liaw B, Kostecki R (2011) In situ characterization of lithium ion battery materials, electrodes, and cells [Online]. http://ne.ucsd.edu/smeng/images/files/ecs%20highlight.pdf. Accessed 10 Aug 2013
32. GE Healthymagination (2010) Annual report [Online]. http://www.healthymagination.com/progress. Accessed 10 Aug 2013
33. GE Healthymagination (2009) Annual report [Online]. http://www.healthymagination.com/progress. Accessed 10 Aug 2013
34. Pradhan D (2010) Multicore processors bring innovation to medical imaging [Online]. http://www.ti.com/general/docs/lit/getliterature.tsp?baseLiteratureNumber=slyy024&track=no. Accessed 10 Aug 2013
35. The American College of Radiology (2003) General diagnosis radiology: teleradiology [Online]. http://imaging.stryker.com/images/ACR_Standards-Teleradiology.pdf. Accessed 10 Aug 2013
36. Radiological Society of North America, Inc. (RSNA) (2012) Positron Emission Tomography – Computed Tomography (PET/CT) [Online]. http://www.radiologyinfo.org/en/info.cfm?pg=pet. Accessed 10 Aug 2013

Chapter 6
Technology Roadmap: The "Complete EHR" Toward Higher-Quality Patient Care

Saranya Durairajan, Amit Hulme, Sean McGraw, Sajeda Tamimi, Jubin Dilip Upadhyay, and Tugrul U. Daim

Abstract The objective of this study is to explore the current trends and the future adoption of products, technologies, and resources in the EHR industry (electronic health records) by means of a detailed technological roadmap. Demographics, governmental healthcare reforms, and mobile health are considered as the primary market drivers and the various T-plan analysis tools such as Porter's five forces model, SWOT analysis, quality function deployment (QFD), and S-curve analysis were employed for the purposes of this study. The result of this paper is a technology roadmap for the "complete EHR" system by the end of the next 4-year timeline. The paper is based on data collected from sources that have been subject matter experts in the relative fields for many years. This report intends to illustrate the roadmapping process by bringing the cognitive thinking onto a swim lane chart to direct the critical path for an organization.

6.1 Introduction

Technology roadmapping is unique in the sense that not only it can be looked upon as a system to map the future of an organization but also has been put in practice in real-world organizations [1]. Healthcare technologies are becoming more and more

S. Durairajan (✉)
Infosys Technologies Ltd, Hillsboro, OR, USA
e-mail: saranya.durairajan@pdx.edu

A. Hulme
Health Data Specialists LLC, Portland, OR, USA

S. McGraw
Intel Corporation, Hillsboro, OR, USA

S. Tamimi • T.U. Daim
Engineering and Technology Management, Portland State University, Portland, OR, USA

J.D. Upadhyay
Ampcus Inc, Washington, DC, USA

T.U. Daim et al. (eds.), *Planning and Roadmapping Technological Innovations: Cases and Tools*, Innovation, Technology, and Knowledge Management,
DOI 10.1007/978-3-319-02973-3_6, © Springer International Publishing Switzerland 2014

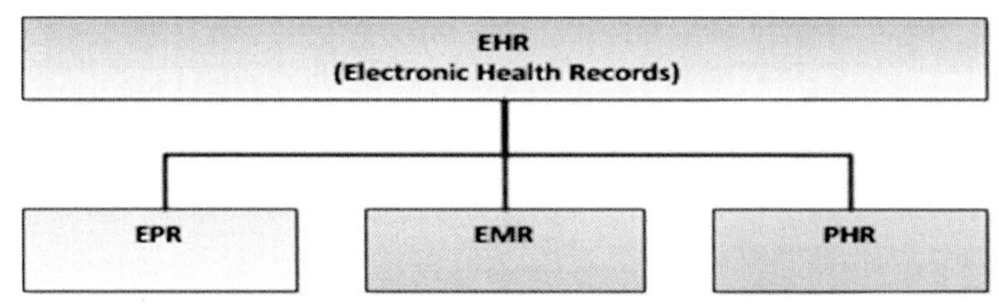

EHR – An electronic health record, may be of many types, and used for many varying purposes, but primarily for setting goals and planning customized care provision for patients, documentation of care and associated expenses, and to assess the impact and improvement of care and its quality. (ref)

(Essentially an umbrella that comprises of EPR*, EMR** & PHR***)
* Electronic Patient Records
** Electronic Medical Records
*** Personal Health Records

Fig. 6.1 Basic EHR overview

evident and apparent due to several factors, government policy, industry push, etc. The goal of this paper is to primarily map the path to a "complete EHR" solution for a healthcare organization over time (Fig. 6.1).

Roadmapping illustrates the cognitive thinking of a group of subject matter experts and intellectuals within an industry on a swim lane graphical map, showing the development and potential gaps over time [1]. It is a methodology that has the potential of taking into account the strengths of all the techniques that make technology management a unique field. The techniques of data mining, tools such as technology surveys and interviews, strategic vision development, technology assessment and evaluation, technology forecasting, research identification, and technology transfer challenges all form a part of the bigger design of a roadmap.

6.2 Methodology

The research was conducted using a series of interviews, three repeat iterations of interviews, and telephone surveys with a pre-identified group of subject matter experts. The research sample consisted of experts from GE Healthcare, Virginia Neurology Clinics, Pennsylvania State Healthcare, Methodist Hospital—Texas, Providence St. Vincent—Oregon, and many IT organizations that have been contracting for EHR applications such as Computer Sciences Corporation.

After the identification of SMEs was done, appointments and telephone interviews were scheduled for three iterations, consecutively for 3 weeks. Inputs from every expert were noted and grouped into clusters, based on short-term, medium-term, and long-term perspectives, and also grouped into product, services, enablers,

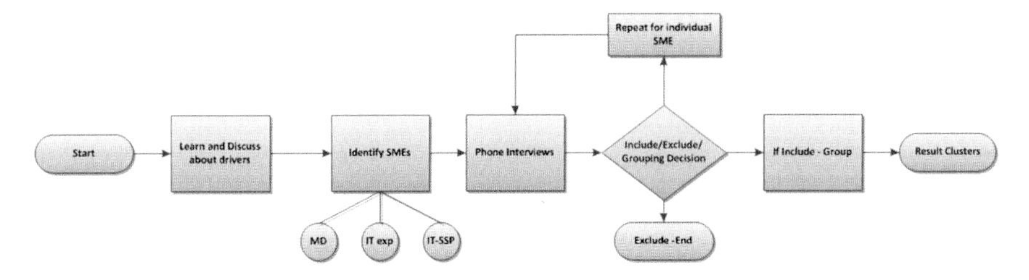

Fig. 6.2 Research methodology—flow diagram

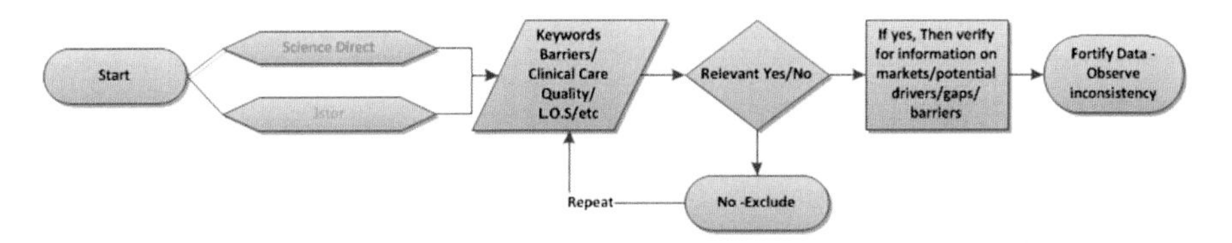

Fig. 6.3 Literature review

resources, or policy issues. If an inconsistency was noted, it was skipped and the interview for that expert was repeated again. This was similar to a Delphi approach but different in the way that building consensus was not the objective, but the objective was to extract accurate inputs and unbiased feedback (Fig. 6.2).

A parallel literature review was conducted so that standard terminology could be referred and verified. The following figure illustrates the literature review model. Literature was also referred to facilitate identification of inconsistencies in technology availability, technology maturity verification, and technology research gaps (Fig. 6.3).

6.2.1 Literature Review

A multi-perspective literature review was incorporated as an essential step in the development of this roadmap [2]. It was essential to understand the process of road-mapping and mark relevant examples that could be used as pointers to control and understand the process. ScienceDirect, PubMed, Google Patent Search, Google Scholar, and IEEE Xplore were used to mine articles and templates and to create a list of potential surprises that might be encountered when the roadmapping process was actively in use. It was observed that roadmapping not only created a map of various paths to achieve a vision, but the process also became a driver for instituting a corporate vision and facilitating a corporate change [3]. Roadmapping has been applied to select healthcare technologies and niches within medicinal science such as neurology [4]. Telemedicine, termed as Telecare, was studied for the purpose of roadmapping in perspective of geographic locations [5]. Roadmapping as a tool for early assessment of technologies has been proposed by Ijzerman and Steuten, 2011 [6].

6.2.2 Research Gap Identification

Many more articles and reports were examined, including the sudden spurt in patents related to EHR. There is a clear gap in roadmapping of EHR adoption in healthcare organizations. With the intent of filling this gap, further research was conducted using telephone surveys and personal interviews as tools to extract information from subject matter experts.

6.3 Market Drivers

6.3.1 Enterprise EHR Industry Overview

Enterprise EHR systems fall in the healthcare technology sector, and the industry is comprised of companies that provide integrated software platforms and consulting services to doctors, hospitals, and healthcare businesses. The adoption of EHRs is enhancing the market, and as a result, the healthcare IT software market increased in revenues from $6.8 billion in 2010 to $8.2 billion in 2011 [7]. The US healthcare IT software sector is forecast to grow at a compound annual growth rate (CAGR) of more than 30 % from 2012 to 2014 [7]. The growth is attributed to three primary market drivers.

6.3.2 Primary Market Drivers

6.3.2.1 Demographics

The USA has an aging population with escalating healthcare needs. The number of older adults in the USA is increasing dramatically as the baby boomers retire and life expectancy increases. Persons reaching age 65 have an average life expectancy of an additional 18.8 years [8]. The 65+ population in 2030 is projected to be twice as large as their counterparts in 2000, growing from 35 million to 72 million people and representing nearly 20 % of the total US population [9].

Enterprise EHR systems have the potential to play a transformational role in advancing patient care for the aging population. EHR systems are effective in managing hospital costs and improving quality of care, motivating health systems to invest more in EHR software. EHR adoption will accelerate as older physicians retire and are replaced by younger, more tech-savvy physicians.

6.3.2.2 Government Healthcare Reform

In February 2009 the Obama administration passed the American Recovery and Reinvestment Act, of which $25.9 billion was allocated to the Health Information Technology for Economic and Clinical Health (HITECH) Act. HITECH designated funding to modernize the healthcare system by promoting and expanding the adoption of health information technology and more specifically EHR adoption.

The act provides incentives in the form of Medicare bonus payments to eligible professionals and hospitals that "meaningfully use" certified EHRs by fiscal years 2011–2016. HITECH furthermore imposes penalties on those organizations who have not yet demonstrated "meaningful use" of such technology by 2015, in the form of up to 5 % lower Medicare and Medicaid reimbursement rates [10].

Healthcare costs, Medicare bonus payments, and the potential of lower Medicare and Medicaid reimbursement rates are driving the EHR adoption rate by hospitals and eligible professionals currently at 19–82 % by the end of 2013 [11]. This tremendous projected growth, induced by the government, is propelling the EHR industry to contract with health organizations to help demonstrate "meaningful use" per government standards in the stipulated time frame.

6.3.2.3 Mobile Health

The mobile health market has a year-over-year growth rate of around 17 % since 2010 and is estimated to be worth $2.1 billion at the end of 2011. In addition, the mobile health market is expected to grow with a CAGR of nearly 22 % from 2012 to 2014. The main driver of mobile health's growth is the increasing adoption of smartphones during the past few years. At the end of 2009, smartphone penetration was around 21 % and is expected to be 50 % by the end of 2011. Further, over 72 % of physicians are smartphone users, and mobile health applications embedded in smartphones are a main reason for this increased usage [7].

Mobile health is in an infancy stage and will play a key role in various areas of healthcare delivery. Through mobile health there is tremendous potential for improved quality of care in education and awareness, remote data collection, remote monitoring, disease tracking, and treatment support. EHR systems will remain the "hubs" of data, while numerous mobile applications extend the access to critical information from that data.

6.3.3 Enterprise EHR Industry: Five Forces of Competition

The adoption of EHRs is driving the healthcare IT software market, and in this paper Porter's five forces analysis was utilized to evaluate the attractiveness of the enterprise EHR industry (Fig. 6.4).

6.3.3.1 Threat of New Entrants [Low]

Barriers to new enterprise EHR software companies entering the market are high due to three main factors:

1. The move toward a fully interoperable health IT environment requires a complete enterprise solution, which is a huge barrier for new entrants not already

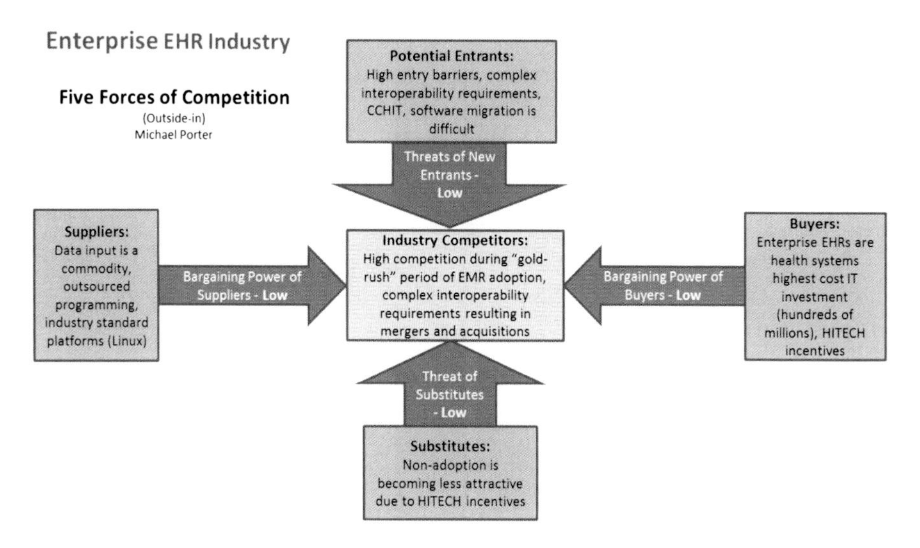

Fig. 6.4 Enterprise EHR—Porter's five forces of competition

established in the market. Interoperable standards are critical in e-prescribing, communication between systems, health information exchange, and integration with mobile devices.

2. Eligible healthcare professionals and eligible hospitals must use *certified* EHR technology in order to achieve "meaningful use" and qualify for incentive payments. The Certification Commission for Healthcare Information Technology (CCHIT) certifies EHR technologies that offer the necessary capabilities, functionalities, and security to help achieve "meaningful use."
3. Migration from a legacy EHR system to a new EHR system poses serious cost considerations to health systems as well as the complexity of the implementation project. The new EHR system must provide significant value in cost reduction and increased quality of care for a hospital to invest.

6.3.3.2 Bargaining Power of Suppliers [Low]

The clinical data from user input and system information exchange are commodities to EHR systems, used to provide "meaningful use" value to health organizations. Software programmers that develop new functionality and upgrades to EHR systems are being outsourced to cheaper labor regions or supplied by recent IT college graduates, reducing employee negotiating power. In addition, the hardware and operating system platforms on which EHR systems are developed are industry standard and can be purchased at market rates through software licensing contracts from big vendors such as Oracle or Microsoft.

6.3.3.3 Threat of Substitutes [Low]

Non-adoption is the most viable substitute, in which organizations continue to operate with a network of healthcare applications that are limited and will not meet "meaningful use" guidelines. Those health organizations with any Medicare or Medicaid business will be penalized by foregoing certified EHR adoption due to HITECH incentives that will go into effect by 2015. Non-adoption of a certified EHR system is not a sustainable option.

6.3.3.4 Bargaining Power of Buyers [Low]

Buyers in the enterprise EHR market have capital as well as multiple vendors to choose from, but in order to take advantage of government incentives, they must follow strict timelines to adopt a certified EHR and achieve "meaningful use" standards. The penalty associated with late adoption of a certified EHR system neutralizes the bargaining power of buyers.

6.3.3.5 Competitive Rivalry [High]

The enterprise EHR industry is highly competitive and expected to mature in the coming years. Due to HITECH incentives, health systems are buying certified EHR systems with the goal of achieving "meaningful use" standards as quickly as possible. As a result, enterprise EHR vendors are aggressively vying to gain market share by establishing long-standing business relationships with enterprise health systems. Vendors unable to acquire a significant industry presence will be acquired by a larger vendor or phased out of the market altogether. EHR vendors are also heavily investing into R&D to develop new features to meet "meaningful use" standards and the growing demands of mobile health. The enterprise EHR vendors that can provide innovative technologies with a focus on the patient, provider, and health mobility, while at the same time balancing the needs of health information exchange and efficient revenue cycle, will solidify their place in the market.

6.3.4 *SWOT Analysis*

6.3.4.1 Strengths

Boom of Information Technology (IT)

IT has introduced healthcare industry including doctors and medical professionals to the digital world, thereby allowing digitization, automation, and organized storage on a virtual platform.

Need for Storage of Digital Versions of Clinical Records

Conventionally, people would use bulky and cumbersome paper reports as clinical data records. With the IT boom it is more convenient to have electronic medical records (EMRs), which are digital records safely kept at a digital repository. This eliminates the possible loss of a paper-based report and therefore crucial information and the manual transportation of bulky records to medical consultations.

Need for an Integrated Information Management System for Clinical Data

With time, managing huge amounts of data and storing them safely as a record became an enormous problem for every hospital and clinic. Digital data makes it possible for hospitals to have such records organized, formatted, processed, and stored on a virtual platform, which could later be transferred to compact discs.

Need to Have Ready Access to Clinical Data

EMRs allow patients to have access to their clinical data no matter where they are, if they have access to the Internet. Through the World Wide Web (WWW), patients can access their records and also save a copy for ready reference. This speeds up medical treatment and relieves patients from having to physically carry their records when they travel.

Huge Data Storage and Faster Data Processing Capabilities of Mainframes

EMRs have central server-based models for data storage where patient data is finally stored. This centralized repository is also mainframe based as it is faster and can accommodate huge amounts of data.

6.3.4.2 Weaknesses

Keeping a mainframe as back end is less user-friendly and requires time-consuming upgradations. Mainframe is actually an old technology that is robust but not as user-friendly as the present-day systems. People prefer ease of access and better user interactions. Keeping a mainframe as back end also means that the work has to be performed in languages such as NATURAL and COBOL, which are not easy to work upon. A line of coding written by a software engineer in COBOL or NATURAL is costlier than a line of Java code. Hence, upgradations become expensive and troublesome [12].

Low Security

Hackers the world over can hack into a particular low-end clinical data repository (server-based) and have ready access to someone else's data. So there is now a problem of identity crisis and invasion of privacy. Hence, digital security needs to be hiked [12].

6.3.4.3 Opportunities

Development of Platform-Independent Coding Languages

If a Java virtual machine is installed in any system, then many other high-end coding languages can be used in parallel with Java. Additionally, upgradations are easily made in Java or any other present-day platform-independent coding languages [12].

Efficiently Networked Servers as an Alternative to Mainframes

There is a need for having a properly connected multiple server infrastructure, which will aid in storing data while rendering easy access to that data for patients or end users.

More Efficient and More User-Friendly Interfaces

Developing the front end and adding more and more features to the front end of any information system is critical for any industry, and healthcare is no exception.

Development of Better and More Effective Security Protocols

Security is both a need and a threat to any modern society or industry, which largely rely on digital or electronic modes of operation. Security concerns need to be addressed to prevent the invasion of privacy using an individual's clinical data.

Development of Efficient and Intuitive Data Processing Software and Bioinformatics Tools

Attractive front ends of information systems should be provided with efficient interactive multimedia tools for high-end data processing since it will play an extremely important part. These tools are software algorithms such as the algorithms used for heart rate variability analysis. Such advanced diagnosis can be a very effective tool for judging an athlete, for example [12].

6.3.4.4 Threats

Security Concerns

As already mentioned, malpractices using any other person's data is the biggest threat to the clinical information systems industry. Hence, the threat to digital security due to hacking needs to be tackled [12].

6.4 Product

6.4.1 Quality Function Development (QFD)

Originating at Mitsubishi's Kobe shipyard in 1972, the quality function deployment is a thought process that states products should be engineered to reflect customer's desires and tastes [13]. That is to say that the model is set up in a way that the customer's needs can be linked in a relationship to the technical features of a product (Fig. 6.5).

Customer needs were determined through interviews with SMEs from both the doctor using the EHR system and healthcare IT professionals working to develop technologies. One of the major customer needs is to have a standardized system that meets all the regulation requirements of the HITECH portions of ARRA. As part of the standards laid out in HITECH, healthcare providers need to meet meaningful use requirements which include the ability to move patient's health information from one point to another by 2014 [14]. During interviews for this report, it became evident that not only do providers want a product that is easy to use but was comprehensive as well. Many of the SMEs suggested that the use of voice recognition

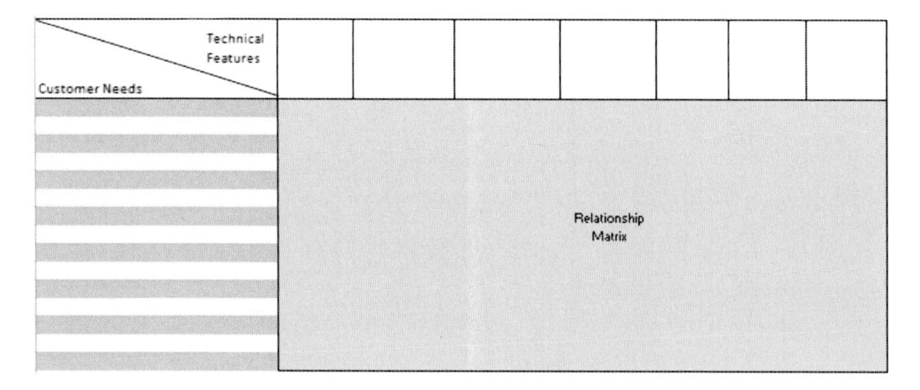

Fig. 6.5 Basic QFD matrix

and optical character recognition (OCR) technologies was useful but does not integrate fully into many EHR systems.

During analysis of technical features, it became evident that there are gaps within EHR systems that currently limit the software and need to be improved upon in creating the complete EHR system. These gaps were determined by matching those technical features to customer needs that are currently not being met, and a future relationship can be seen in the figure below (Fig. 6.6).

The QFD process identified many of the technological gaps that exist in EHR systems that while may exist in some form or fashion need to be developed for integration into a complete EHR to occur. Much of the feedback from SMEs matches the technological gaps that were determined and will be further discussed in this research.

6.4.2 *Statistical Patent-Based Research: For EHR Development and HIT Tools and Applications to Study and Explore a General Trend*

Intellectual property is a vast field directly related to the technology arena. Patents and patent searches have long been employed to mine and map developments and also to carry out competitive analysis [15]. CobaltIP and USPTO were used to extract patent information and assignee numbers.

The results show that a maximum number of patents have been filed and published for the cost reduction and price determination technologies in the healthcare sector, followed by EHR data processing as the second biggest group, followed by user-friendliness, and user interface development and improvement for healthcare applications and equipment. The following bubble chart shows the growth in respective US class clusters (Fig. 6.7).

Studying survival rates/renewal and maintenance rates for a specific sector may also indicate the interest and focus on that area [16]. This report studied the survivorship rates for the EHR patents and found that most had a survival rate of 97–100 % which is unheard of in the IP industry. This may be an indicator that organizations view EHR as a futuristic revenue and competitive edge offering growth point. Figure 6.8 illustrates the survival rates. Keywords were used to locate these patents, and clusters were formed based on their generic groups. Observations were then made by citing their renewal and extension histories that were mapped and documented using Excel to create this chart.

6.4.3 *Technology Diffusion*

The diffusion of innovations has been researched and modeled by Rogers [17] as a bell-shaped advancement through populations of innovators, early adopters, early

S - Strong
M - Medium
W - Weak
Future relationship needed

Customer Needs	Technical Features: Easy UI	Clinical Industry Standards	Customizable charting verification	Voice Recognition Charting	RFID Patient Tracking	Central EHR Database	Integrated Security	Redundant and Failover Architecture	Automated Access	RFID/NFC embedded software	Cost
Easy to use	S			S	M			M	S	S	
Standardized	W	S	W					S			
Meets Regulations		M									
Error Free Charting			M	W							
Voice Recognition				W							
RFID/NFC capable					W				S	M	
Efficient Database Access			M			W					
Biometric Access							W		W		
Secure						S	S	S	M		
Integrates all clinical systems		M	S								
Reliable				W				S			
Cost Effective		M	M								W
RTLS					W						
Mobile App Base										W	M
Cloud Computing											M
Reportability		S	S			S					

Fig. 6.6 QFD—EHR

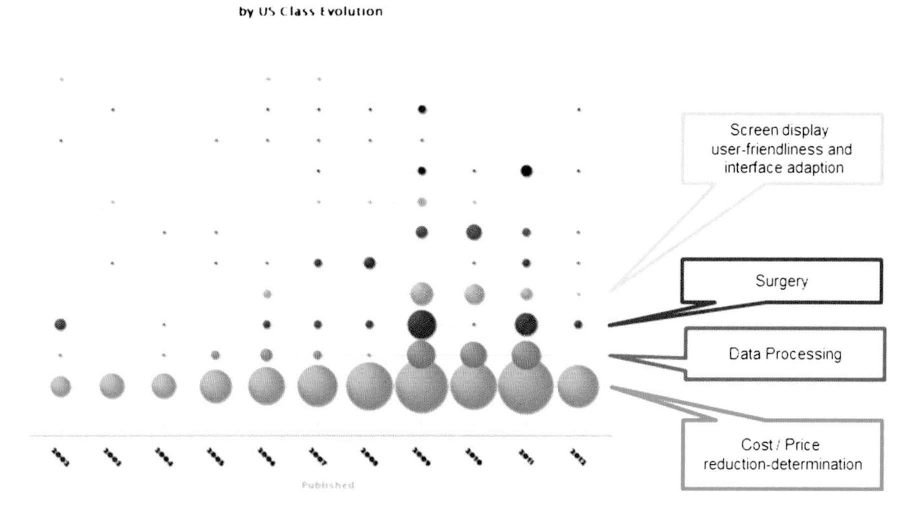

Fig. 6.7 Bubble chart showing the growth in respective US class cluster

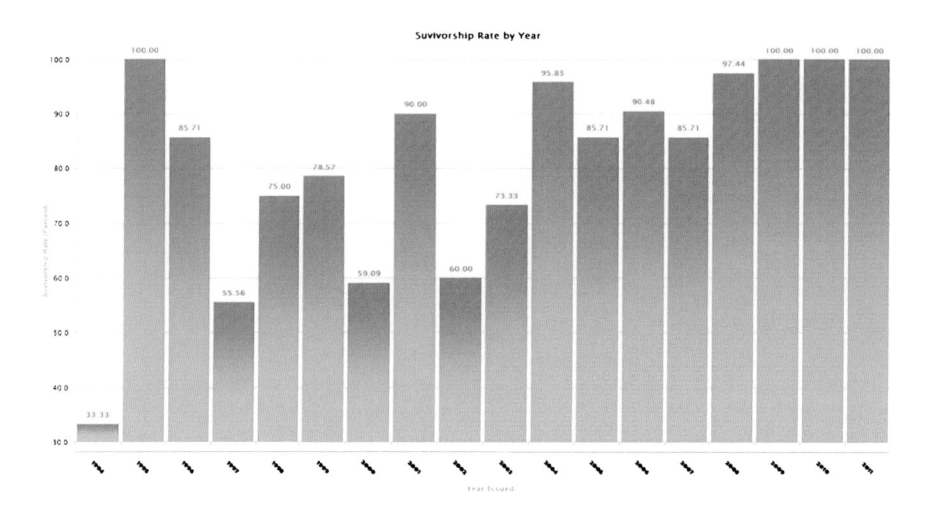

Fig. 6.8 Survivorship rates for the EHR patents

majority, late majority, and laggards. At some point during this spread of an innovative solution, a critical mass of adopters, or tipping point, is reached and the innovation is assured widespread diffusion [18]. Adoption is usually described by an S-shaped curve of adopters vs. time, and the rate of adoption is the slope of the S-shaped curve at any given time, i.e., with successive groups of consumers adopting the new technology, its market share will eventually reach the saturation level typically forming the S-curve.

In order to analyze whether the tipping point is visible for EHR adoption yet, there is a need to examine the various elements affecting the diffusion of new ideas. Rogers propose four main elements that influence the spread of a new idea: the innovation, communication channels, time, and a social system. That is, diffusion is the process by which an innovation is communicated through certain channels over time among the members of a social system [17].

6.4.4 Innovation

Rogers defines an innovation as "an idea, practice, or object that is perceived as new by an individual or other unit of adoption." Rogers defines several intrinsic characteristics also known as Rogers' five factors of innovations that influence an individual's decision to adopt or reject an innovation. They are relative advantage, compatibility, complexity or simplicity, trialability, and observability [17].

Relative Advantage—To what degree is the EHR perceived to be better than the practice it aims to supersede—paper charts? For some, EHRs are increasing efficiency and improving quality of care for patients. For others, EHRs are impediments to quality of care and an endless money pit for the practice. The biggest advertised advantage of EHRs, interoperability, is little more than a promissory note issued by EHR proponents to prospective adopters. The government is adding an advantage in the form of stimulus incentives and future financial penalties for non-adoption. This advantage seems to be significant for hospitals and large groups, but less so for small private practices.

Compatibility—Are EHRs compatible with existing values, past experiences, and needs of potential adopters? Here EHRs are being propelled onto the much larger stage of healthcare reform. They are no longer a humble replacement of pen and paper and fax machines. EHRs are instruments of change, a change from treating one patient at a time the best you can, to considering value-based strategies for the benefit of entire populations and considering those right at the point of care. This seems to be a major departure from a value system created and enriched across many generations of medical doctors.

Complexity—Simplicity is always a virtue. The complexity of hospital EHRs, with their unwieldy CPOE modules, has created a perception of EHRs being rigid and unduly complicated tools, which take years to master. The simple ambulatory EHRs available today have failed to change these perceptions. To be fair, EHRs are inherently more complex than a piece of paper, but that should not necessarily deter adoption.

Trialability—Experimenting with small parts of an innovation before taking the final leap reduces adopters' risk and anxiety. EHRs can be, and mostly are, implemented in stages, particularly in hospitals. In the ambulatory sector there was a trend to implement electronic prescribing as a trial before complete computerization. Perhaps the best exercise of trialability for EHRs is the free trials offered by too few vendors.

Observability—An innovation is more likely to be adopted if its results are easily visible to others. This of course assumes that the results are positive. Unfortunately, successful implementations of EHRs are uneventful and largely anonymous, while their failing counterparts, usually associated with astronomic losses in funds and sometimes lives, are very visible, heavily advertised, and frankly more interesting [19].

6.4.5 Communication Channels

A communication channel is "the means by which messages get from one individual to another" [17]. The news and evaluation of an innovation are spread throughout the community by various means, from mass media to informal peer-to-peer communications. As every EHR vendor knows, the latter is the most prevalent and effective method of disseminating messages among physicians and also it is a very slow method of creating awareness. The government's intervention, with all its glorious publicity and billions of dollars in support of the innovation, has both positive and negative impacts on EHR [19].

6.4.6 Time

"The innovation-decision period is the length of time required to pass through the innovation-decision process." "Rate of adoption is the relative speed with which an innovation is adopted by members of a social system [17]." Time is involved in diffusion of innovation in several ways.

- On an individual level the innovation–decision process goes through five stages known as knowledge, persuasion, decision, implementation, and confirmation. In EHR industry parlance, these translate to research, assessment, selection, implementation, and adoption. The shorter the innovation–decision individual cycle is and the more people actually complete it without dropping out in its midst and the more positive their adoption experience is, the faster an innovation is expected to diffuse. For EHRs this cycle can range anywhere between a few months for a small practice to several years for a large hospital. The government-imposed meaningful use schedules are shortening the innovation–decision cycle for those racing to qualify for maximum incentive. Perversely, the inadequate time allowed for implementation will also increase failure rates and adverse events, which does not bode well for long-term diffusion rates.
- Diffusion is also affected by the innovativeness of the population targeted by the innovation. Research here has encountered accusations of physicians being inher-

ently opposed to technological advancements and the counterarguments based on the number of iPhones and iPads already owned by physicians, not to mention all the advanced technologies in imaging, surgery, and other medical fields, which are readily embraced by the medical community. When it comes to EHRs though, most doctors don't mind being very late adopters or even laggards.

- The rate of adoption dictates how much time it will take for an innovation to diffuse throughout the system. Unfortunately for EHRs, the rate of adoption is heavily dependent on the five characteristics of an innovation and none of those are particularly stellar for EHRs. This is why the rate of EHR adoption prior to HITECH has been lingering at the bottom of a very wide S-curve. The government intervention, which as mentioned above is increasing the financial advantage, is making a marked difference in the rate of adoption effectively pushing EHRs up the S-curve [19].

6.4.7 Social System

"A social system is defined as a set of interrelated units that are engaged in joint problem solving to accomplish a common goal [17]." The structure, norms, and leadership of a system also affect the diffusion of innovations. Systems whose members are similar in education, social status, and beliefs are not well suited to rapid change and innovation. Physicians arguably do form such system. The historical low rates of EHR adoption could be attributed to lack of accepted opinion leaders in general and those who view EHRs as a positive innovation in particular. Innovations are not always an individual choice and sometimes the decision to innovate is authority driven. Authority-driven innovations are faster to be adopted and, depending on the level of coercion, may follow a completely different path. Up to HITECH, individual physicians in private practice considered EHRs optional. Those employed by hospitals or large groups were experiencing the effects of authority-driven innovation all along, thus the much larger adoption rates in those sectors. Although EHRs are not yet mandatory, the increasing pressure exerted by government incentives, regulations, and penalties is changing the diffusion patterns of the EHR innovation. The government exertions may continue only until a critical mass of EHR adopters is created and the mythical tipping point is reached. The tipping point is usually observed at about 15 % adoption under normal circumstances and is marked by the emergence of opinion leaders who adopted the innovation, and EHRs can also be expected to follow the same pattern [19].

Despite increases over the past decade, no category of physicians has achieved a high level of adoption of basic EHR systems. In accordance with the Health Information Technology for Economic and Clinical Health provisions, the Office of the National Coordinator and the Centers for Medicare and Medicaid Services are addressing this gap by developing standards for certified systems and providing financial incentives to healthcare providers whose systems meet the criteria for meaningful use. This broad initiative is intended to raise overall adoption levels. Federal programs initiated by the 2009 legislation are targeting primary care providers and physicians in small practices. According to the study, to achieve the stated aims of widespread use, the programs will need to continue to aim incentives and support at small practices. Programs may also need to focus on physicians outside of primary care to narrow the persistent and widening gap in the adoption of EHR systems [20].

One noteworthy future trend in healthcare IT is *mobile health*. The tools of mobile computing—smartphones, PDAs, tablet PCs, patient monitoring devices, and an avalanche of apps among them—are opening new vistas of opportunity for clinical collaboration. It's an evolutionary cycle. Telemedicine, voice recognition, and home monitoring have been around for years, but the trending mHealth devices have made dramatic leaps forward in terms of cost, bulk, weight, durability, and performance. And there are thousands of mobile healthcare apps already on the market, with more on the way. They include e-prescribing, medical calculators, decision support tools, personal health records, health and fitness, and patient medical and eligibility queries for starters. The potential universe of mHealth applications spans the payer, provider, and healthcare consumer markets. Another trend that extends beyond the structure of the app is the use of text messaging in public health campaigns [21]. RFID and OCR technologies have been around for few years now, and the next generations of those technologies are accounted in the technology layer of the roadmap. Near Field Communication (NFC) is a wireless connectivity technology evolving from a combination of contactless identification and networking technologies. It enables convenient short-range communication between electronic devices and smart objects [22]. While talking about mobile health technologies, mHealth security can be attributed as solutions to secure products, health information, and the organization as a whole. Improvements in telecommunications, information, and medical technologies are greatly expanding opportunities for the application of telemedicine and telehealth. With the availability of high-resolution imaging, noninvasive telemetric sensors, robotics, and high-speed broadband connections, providers have the capability of remotely monitoring, diagnosing, and treating patients in a manner that both makes optimum use of clinicians' time and delivers care when and where needed by the patients. Speech recognition tools are part of complementary technologies that are being employed via mobile devices for documentation, charge capture, scheduling, and notes. Currently real-time location systems (RTLS) are being merged with mobile devices to accelerate patient throughput, manage staff, monitor at-risk family members, and schedule utilization of high-value equipment [21]. A widespread use of these next generation technologies can be expected in the future. The ultimate focus is to use mobile technology in conjunction with cloud-based models for a secure, high-speed ecosystem that can influence health—instead of just healthcare.

The ultimate EHR software should be supported by state-of-the-art semiconductor chips, switches and encryption technologies, augmented reality, novel object and voice recognition technologies, broadband telecommunications services, and ultra-low power remote monitoring devices.

6.5 R&D and Resources

During a literature review this report found many areas discussing the EHR development, application, infrastructure, future insight, etc. For the purpose of creating the complete EHR, there are four main categories that will be discussed, which are RTLS, OCR, and RFID adoption in healthcare; e-healthcare system implementation; Internet of things (IoT) and medical data acquisition system, and Wireless Body Sensor Network (BSN).

6.5.1 RTLS, OCR, and RFID Adoption in Healthcare

Real-time location system (RTLS), optical character recognition (OCR), and radio frequency identifications (RFID) are some of the hot topics now in terms of HW and SW adoption in healthcare world. As mentioned before, some of these SW and HW are not in the shape this report envisioned to be used in healthcare. So, even though some of them are already in the market, R&D is still ongoing for more enhancements such as common applications, benefits, barriers, and critical success factors. Also, better-designed systems are needed to increase acceptance and proper use in healthcare world [23, 24].

However, in order to have a successful application of the R&D, some resources are required for the implementation process among healthcare facilities like global standards, privacy and interference solutions, technological media adoption, and reasonable affordable costs.

6.5.2 e-Healthcare System Implementation

Some of the healthcare facilities have moved beyond the implementation phase of EHRs in their practice. But, more research is still needed and is ongoing to analyze and review the outcomes of the implementation process of EMRs and exploring the experiences of primary healthcare providers and staff who had moved beyond that phase in their practice [25].

Required resources for this stage are federal regulations, funding, and incentives that facilitate the adoption process in every healthcare facility. Federal regulations would help take a stab at working toward consistent data entry and use. Developing strategies to address issues such as electronic connectivity are needed resources that will ease implementation. Moreover, some regulations are required in assessing and enhancing computer skills, for example, conducting training courses in data entry and computer skills for all staff who are going to use EHRs.

6.5.3 IoT and Medical Data Acquisition System

R&D is now introducing an approach based on Internet of things (IoT) in medical environments to achieve a global connectivity with the patient, sensors, and everything around it.

This feature makes the patient's life easier and the clinical process more effective since it provides awareness for both the patient and healthcare provider [26].

Medical data acquisition system is one of the available resources that helps in managing IoT for an easy and efficient data management system in medical world. This wireless system could allow medical staff to monitor and update a patient's database easily and will increase the productivity of medical staff [27].

Required resources for this stage are efficient wireless communication and Bluetooth technologies.

6.5.4 Wireless Body Sensor Network (BSN)

Another category of R&D determined through research is moving toward a wireless approach of body sensor network (BSN). Research fields are exploring the requirements, architecture, and implementation of smart body-worn medical sensors [28]. The main required resource for this stage is an integrated wireless communications network that is secure and safe and would help in eliminating the mixing-up of medical data from different patients. Other required resources are cloud-based architecture, Wi-Fi backhaul networks, and real-time indoor localization systems [29].

6.6 Technology Roadmap

Fig. 6.9 shows the finalized roadmap.

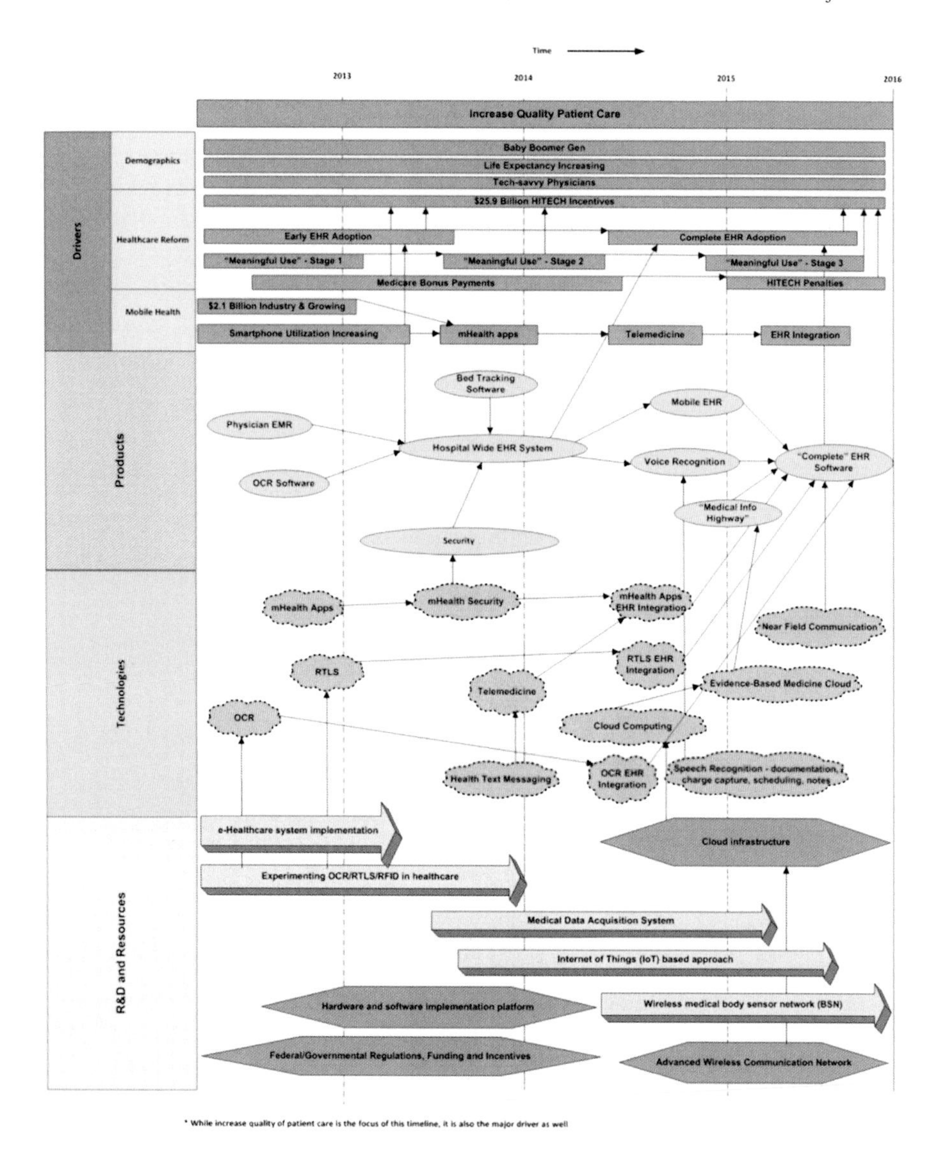

Fig. 6.9 Technology roadmap—complete EHR

6.7 Conclusion

Like other industries, the technology globalization has affected healthcare world in every aspect. IT has introduced doctors and medical professionals to the digital world, thereby allowing digitization, automation, and organized storage on a virtual platform. This raised the need to have complete EHRs that have an integrated information management system for clinical data with global standards.

It was noticed during this report that healthcare is moving toward EHRs at a fast pace without having an organized process that allows for a smooth transition. Some elements on the roadmap are already in the market, while others are under the stage of research and development. It is the conclusion of this report that continuing research in the integration of peripheral applications into the EHR bundle be done. Over the next few years, with research, it is expected that this integration will become plausible and the complete EHR can be put to market to improve quality patient care and meet federal regulations.

6.8 Future Research

Future research can focus on the continuation of defining more roadmaps as the technology and regulation are changing on regular bases. Moreover, a real path needs to be drawn to demonstrate the integration process between regulations, globalized infrastructure, and hardware and software adoption process in healthcare industry since every facility is now using its own EMRs. The area of "healthcare IT" is very transient and highly affected by policy push rather than a market pull, and hence the dynamics of the healthcare industry force researchers to be aware and educated about the ever-changing state and federal policies that determine the future of the healthcare services and revenue associated with it. It is needless to say that apart from a technical, organizational, and personal dimension to technology growth and development, there is another dimension that this report cannot afford to overlook or ignore, and this is the political dimension of health IT. The political scenario is looked upon as a driver of change and a driver of "people's needs."

In the future, it will be interesting to see the policy push by the federal and state governments to improve efficiency and reduce cost in the health services arena with the help of new technologies and improving EHR. Future research can hence focus on integrating a political dimension to the roadmap.

References

1. Phaal R, Farrukh CJP, Probert DR (2004) Technology roadmapping—a planning framework for evolution and revolution. Technol Forecast Soc Change 71(1–2):5–26
2. Linstone H (1999) Decision making for technology executives—using multiple perspectives to improved performance. Artech House, Boston
3. Phaal R, Muller G (2009) An architectural framework for roadmapping: towards visual strategy. Technol Forecast Soc Change 76(1):39–49
4. Ruijters D, Homan R, Mielekamp P, van de Haar P, Babic D (2011) Validation of 3D multimodality roadmapping in interventional neuroradiology. Phys Med Biol 56(16):5335–5354
5. Oudshoorn N (2012) How places matter: telecare technologies and the changing spatial dimensions of healthcare. Soc Stud Sci 42(1):121–142

6. Ijzerman M, Steuten L (2011) Early assessment of medical technologies to inform product development and market access. Health Policy 9:331–347
7. Lewis N (2011) Healthcare IT spending to reach $40 billion. InformationWeek.May 2011. http://www.informationweek.com/healthcare/electronic-medical-records/healthcare-it-spending-to-reach-40-billi/229500682. Accessed 8 Aug 2012
8. Department of Health & Human Services (2011) Profile of older Americans: 2011. Administration on Aging. http://www.aoa.gov/aoaroot/aging_statistics/Profile/index.aspx. Accessed 30 Jul 2012
9. National Institute on Aging (NIA) (2011) Older Americans 2010: key indicators of well-being, AgingStats.gov, 14 Jan 2011. http://www.agingstats.gov/agingstatsdotnet/main_site/default.aspx. Accessed 30 Jul 2012
10. Department of Health & Human Services (2010) Medicare and Medicaid incentives and administrative funding. HHS.gov/Recovery, June 2010. http://www.hhs.gov/recovery/reports/plans/pdf20100610/CMS_HIT%20Implementation%20Plan%20508%20compliant.pdf. Accessed 6 Aug 2012
11. Accenture (2010) Overview of international EMR/HER markets. Accenture, Aug 2010. http://www.accenture.com/SiteCollectionDocuments/PDF/Accenture_EMR_Markets_Whitepaper_vfinal.pdf. Accessed 7 Aug 2012
12. World Wide Web. http://www.growthconsulting.frost.com/web/images.nsf/0/7E4EDBCB0C54FA71862573B200386E4B/$File/TI%20Alert.htm. Accessed 5 Aug 2013
13. Hauser JR, Clausing D (1988) The house of quality. Harv Bus Rev 66(3): 63–73. Business Source Premier. Web. 9 Aug 2012
14. Pfister H, Frohlich J, Ingargiola S (2012) Driving interoperable health data exchange under HITECH. Rep. iHealthBeat, 30 Apr 2012. Web. 6 Aug 2012. http://www.ihealthbeat.org/features/2012/driving-interoperable-health-data-exchange-under-hitech.aspx
15. R&D METRICS PATENTS AS PREDICTORS: corporate patent analysis provides quantitative predictive indicator of a company's wall street performance. (1998) Chem Eng News (0009-2347) 76 (36), p 24
16. Chen Y-S (2011) Using patent analysis to explore corporate growth. Scientometrics 88(2): 433–448
17. Rogers EM (1995) Diffusion of innovations, 4th edn. Free Press, New York
18. Gladwell M (2000) The tipping point: how little things can make a big difference. Little Brown, New York
19. World Wide Web (2010) http://onhealthtech.blogspot.com/2010/09/diffusion-of-ehr-innovation.html. Accessed 5 Aug 2013
20. Decker SL, Jamoom EW, Sisk JE (2012) Physicians in nonprimary care and small practices and those age 55 and older lag in adopting electronic health record systems. Health Aff 31(5): 1108–1114 (published online 24 April 2012; 10.1377/hlthaff.2011.1121)
21. Mobile health. J Healthc Info Manag. HIMSS Publication. Vol 26 Number 3/Summer 2012
22. Morak J, Hayn D, Kastner P, Drobics M, Schreier G (2009) Near field communication technology as the key for data acquisition in clinical research. First international workshop on near field communication. IEEE, New York
23. Yao W, Chu CH, Li Z (2012) The adoption and implementation of RFID Technologies in Healthcare: a literature review. J Med Syst. 36(6):3507–3525
24. Kamel Boulos MN, Berry G (2012) Real-time locating systems (RTLS) in healthcare: a condensed primer. Int J Health Geogr 11:25
25. Terry AL (2012) Perspectives on electronic medical record implementation after two years of use in primary health care practice. J Am Board Fam Med 25:522–527
26. Jara AJ, Zamora MA, Skarmeta AFG (2010) An Architecture Based on Internet of Things to Support Mobility and Security in Medical Environments. In: 7th IEEE Consumer Communications and Networking Conference (CCNC), 9–12 Jan. 2010, Las Vegas, NV

27. Abdul Karim MF, Muhamad R (2006) Integration of near field communication (NFC) and Bluetooth technology for medical data acquisition system. In: ISCGAV'06 Proceedings of the 6th WSEAS International Conference on Signal Processing, Computational Geometry & Artificial Vision, 147–152
28. Jacobsen RH et al (2011) A modular platform for wireless body area network research and real-life experiments. Int J Adv Netw Serv 4(3,4):257–277
29. Ho Q, and Le-Ngoc T (2011) An integrated wireless communications platform for smart electronic healthcare applications. In: Proceedings of the 24th Canadian Conference on Electrical and Computer Engineering, CCECE 2011, Niagara Falls, page 1544–1547

Chapter 7
Technology Roadmap for Automotive Flexible Display

Byung Sung Yoon, Corey White, Greg Wease, Lokesh Honnappa, Sheng-Te Tsai, Xiaowen Wang, and Tugrul U. Daim

Abstract Flexible displays are thin, lightweight, unbreakable, and energy saving, which can be fabricated using the existing display manufacturing facilities, reducing the significant cost of building new facilities. In addition to displays, the flexible solution can be beneficial for a multitude of applications: automotive, medical, technical, and educational applications. The objective of this chapter is to develop a technology roadmap for flexible display technology. The research focuses on the application of flexible display in automotive industry. We will introduce market drivers, product, and technology analysis and also provide research on the necessary resources needed within R&D in the coming years. This chapter also presents tools like QFD – quality function deployment – matrix to perform the mapping between appropriate products and technologies. An extensive literature is conducted to gather information for the different layers of technology roadmap.

7.1 Introduction

In 2011, Toyota announced a new concept car, the Fun Vii, at the Tokyo Auto Show in Japan. This car has a specific appearance which is different from other typical concept cars in prominent motor shows. A distinguishing feature of this concept car

B.S. Yoon (✉) • S.-T. Tsai • X. Wang • T.U. Daim
Engineering and Technology Management, Portland State University, Portland, OR, USA
e-mail: yoon3@pdx.edu

C. White
Morpho Detection, Camas, WA, USA

G. Wease
Leadspoke, Portland, OR, USA

L. Honnappa
Lam Research, San Jose, CA, USA

T.U. Daim et al. (eds.), *Planning and Roadmapping Technological Innovations: Cases and Tools*, Innovation, Technology, and Knowledge Management,
DOI 10.1007/978-3-319-02973-3_7,

is that its exterior color can be changed by a driver's intention. In addition, the exterior which consists of curved surfaces can show even motion pictures. Also, its interior is covered by numerous curved display units, which enable a user to change interior illumination or communicate with others [1]. The core technology which facilitates this concept is the flexible display technology.

Flexible display technology may bring a new world in communication or information electronics design. In other words, with this technology, it is possible to make not only curved display panels but also foldable or collapsible display units. As a result, away from typical design limited to flat surfaces, it is feasible to design various shapes of display units or to reduce size and weight of a product more freely. Furthermore, mass production, which is necessary for cost reduction, is possible with innovative manufacturing technology such as roll-to-roll processes which enable production on large scale as well as lowering costs [2]. Therefore, numerous organizations such as display manufactures and laboratories have been researching this technology. A number of prototype display units from firms and laboratories have been unveiled in electronics exhibitions, such as Consumer Electronics Show (CES) and similar conferences. Moreover, display manufacturers like Samsung Display, LG Display, and Universal Display are preparing initial stage of mass production lines for flexible display units.

However, in the automobile industry, though interest in the flexible display technology is increasing, still, there are a lot of technological problems that have accumulated that have to be solved. Because environmental conditions in automotive applications are more severe/demanding than in general consumer electronics applications, a more robust performance has to be achieved in order for widespread acceptance to be achieved. Also, because competition in this industry has intensified, economic advantages are regarded as a superb value. Consequently, the level of requirements and standards on performances like vividness, durability, and economic feasibility is stringent [2].

Therefore, as a components supplier for the automotive industry, establishing appropriate strategies for research and development (R&D) is required. According to Phaal, Farrukh, and Probert, technology roadmapping is a proper tool to build up strategic and long-term planning by assessing potentially disruptive technologies and market changes [3]. Accordingly, the objective of this chapter is to develop a technology roadmap for flexible display technology. In particular, this research focuses on the application of flexible displays in the automotive industry as an automotive parts supplier.

7.2 Methodology

Initially, our research was focused on the use of OLED technology in a military, consumer electronics, or industrial application. Due to compliance and security reasons, we determined the military would not supply the necessary information to complete a full-blown roadmap in a timely manner. Further, with consumer electronics being highly fragmented, we decided to focus our efforts on an industrial application, more specifically, the use of OLED in the automotive sector.

Our Research Methodology is a combination of in-depth literature reviews backed up by interviews with subject matter experts. By tapping into a diverse set of articles, along with interviews/correspondents, we were able to follow the many suggestions of previous roadmapping research techniques by not relying too much on one particular set of research findings to draw significant conclusions. We were able to cross-reference and corroborate findings among these articles/interviews.

That said, and with one caveat, due to the current volume of data points collected, we cannot state the results are statistically valid. Additional research via surveys, interviews, and possibly focus groups will be required to state the findings are statistically valid.

We conducted the article reviews and interviews with the mind-set that we are a company that currently manufactures flexible OLED solutions – and that our target customer base is comprised of luxury automakers, primarily: Acura, Audi, BMW, Cadillac, Infiniti, Mercedes-Benz, Lexus, etc. Further, our product/services platform enables us to partner with automotive component companies such as Continental Automotive System, Delphi Automotive System, and Bosch and flexible display companies such as Samsung Display, LG Display, AUO, and Universal Display.

7.2.1 Literature Research

Semiconductor technology is the birthplace for the lineage of technology which gave advent to flexible display systems. First is light-emitting diode technology, which is a semiconductor light-generating source. Invention of such technologies as light-emitting diode displays in 1989 [4], dense LED matrix for high-resolution full color video in 1989 [5], and wide band gap semiconductor light-emitting devices in 1990 [6] set the path to automotive applications. LED technology gave way to OLED technology or "organic light-emitting diode" [7] and, since its invent, has seen a period of rapid development. The difference between the two is the light-generating layer is a film of organic compound that responds when a current passes through it [8]. Used in displays, organic materials are more vivid, consume less energy, and are easier to make when compared to options based on previous liquid crystal technology [9] which was the first of such technology to appear in an automotive application (think first-generation dashboard digital clocks).

The current technologies in automobiles that will be eventually phased out are analog gauges. The move from analog to a fully digital environment has been gradual as the trickle down of technology not originally intended for automotive application makes its way into the industry. The first adaptation of true led display technology in the automotive industry debuted in the audio market segment. Pioneers such as Alpine, Sony, and JVC were among the first to adapt the technology. Purely audio display systems gave way to audio/GPS units. Next, OEM manufacturers evolved to a consolidated HVAC/audio/GPS unit that utilized an integrated center panel. The near-term evolution of automotive displays will evolve to a singular control bezel with touch or gesture control [10]. Information management and effectively minimizing driver distractions while enhancing driver experience is the goal [10, 11]. The increased web connectivity, smartphone capability, entertainment, and HVAC management functions have led to the need for large intelligent informatics displayed in a well-designed platform that is all encompassing and enhances the drivers' experience while not intrusive to the driving function [11]. These drivers have forced OEM manufactures to incorporate the latest R&D efforts in flexible display systems.

Flexible display systems have allowed designers to push the envelope as displays no longer have to be flat. As a result flexible display systems have the ability to solve challenging and therefore expensive design solutions, changing the way the interior and exterior of the automobiles will look and function [12]. Full spectrum OLED on flexible glass or plastic substrate or projected is the emerging generation of technology that could be utilized in redesigned instrument clusters, new "rollup" displays, and interior and exterior smart lighting systems that according to [11] by 2017 the North American market size for such central displays, touch screens, and head-up displays will reach 6 million, 3 million, and 0.4 million, respectively.

7.3 Roadmap Development

In developing our roadmap, we analyzed market drivers as they are indicators of the basic criteria to meet a potential buyer's needs. Figure 7.1 will demonstrate the primary drivers behind this change from LCD to OLED technology and the primary market drivers behind flexible displays in an automotive application as we have

Market Drivers		Code
Smart	Unmanned Vehicle Technology	D1
	Car Intelligent System – provide interface	D2
Eco-friendly	High Energy Efficiency	D3
	No Toxic Material	D4
	Environmental Regulations	D5
	Greater likelihood to purchase green products	D6
Driver Experience	Car Entertainment System	D7
	More Flexible, Dynamic and Adaptable interior/Exterior	D8
	Wireless Communication Connectivity	D9
	Color Tunability and immobility	D10
Safe	More durable, safer & impact resistant	D11
	Free from distraction and overload.	D12
Economic	Increase market share	D13
	Reduce total product cost	D14

Fig. 7.1 Market drivers – automotive flexible display

discovered through the research conducted for this chapter. We also analyzed the gaps between the current states of technology against the automotive context. The aforementioned efforts allow us to develop the technology roadmap as presented below.

7.3.1 Market Drivers

Based on current research and development in the automotive industry, we identified five categories as the primary drivers behind this TRM.

7.3.1.1 Market Drivers: Smart

Unmanned Vehicle Technology

Unmanned vehicle technology enables a vehicle to operate while in contact with the ground without the assistance of on board human interference. This technology incorporates sensors, cameras, and display systems to observe the environment and will make driving decisions either remotely guided or completely autonomously. This technology was originally developed to replace human in hazardous situations [13]. Often considered mobile robots, the first of such were developed as a test bed for a DARPA-funded artificial intelligence work at Stanford Research Institute [14]. At a recent DARPA Urban Challenge that was held on November 3, 2007, at the former George AFB in Victorville, CA. Building on the success of the 2004 and 2005 Grand Challenges, this event required teams to build an autonomous vehicle capable of driving in traffic; performing complex maneuvers such as merging, passing, and parking; and negotiating intersections. This event was truly groundbreaking as the first time autonomous vehicles have interacted with both manned and unmanned vehicle traffic in an urban environment [15].

Car Intelligent System

The purpose of intelligent care systems is to be a communication portal for the driver, other cars, and the "grid" to control such functions as speed and direction and to have provisions for accidence avoidance [16]. This is accomplished through the use of advanced sensor technology operating through a ubiquitous environment integrated through an onboard computer. Flexible display systems will be the means by which the information will be communicated [17]. A recent example of the rise of popularization and demand of intelligent car systems is the MS Detroit Project [18] versus SIRI-Inside Car by Apple.

7.3.1.2 Market Drivers: Eco-friendly

The environmental factors that are considered in the context of display systems include the efficiency, power consumption, and harm to the environment. The damage to the environment usually comes in the form of the materials that are used to create the displays. OLED technology consumes generally 40 % less energy when compared to LCD displays [8]. This power advantage is due to the fact that OLED displays do not need power to display black pixels [17]. Additionally, according to [19], new technologies such as OLED that incorporate energy-adaptive display subsystems align the display's energy output/consumption to the functionality currently being asked of it. Systems such as this allow OLED's to consume less power than traditional LEDs, Plasma, and LCD display technology.

Additionally, because OLED technology does not require backlighting, the presence of mercury is removed, making it a more environmental conscious product when compared to other display technologies.

7.3.1.3 Market Drivers: Driver Experience and Safety

As previously mentioned, the increased web connectivity, smartphone capability, entertainment (the total In-Car Entertainment market is expected to reach billion by 2016 at a CAGR of 12.1 % from 2011 to 2016 [20]), and HVAC management functions have led to the need for large intelligent informatics displayed in a well-designed platform that is all encompassing and enhances the drivers' experience while not intrusive to the driving function [11]. The designers of the flexible display revolution are concentrated on human-centered design and functional HMI integration for intelligent vehicle and cooperative systems [18], thus making the operating environment safe. The emergency of flexible OLED display systems fills this void, enhancing the drivers' experience. Additionally, due to the composition of these display systems and the materials utilized, these display systems are designed to be impact resistant.

7.3.1.4 Market Drivers: Economic

The exponential growth of in-vehicle information is triggering a revolution in the design of display systems in the automotive infotainment market. New analysis from Frost & Sullivan (http://www.automotive.frost.com), Strategic Analysis of European and North American Markets for Display and Instrument Clusters, finds that in Europe, the market size for central displays, touch screens, and head-up displays is estimated to reach 9.5 million, 2 million, and 0.5 million, respectively, by 2017. Additionally, as previously mentioned in North America, the market size for central displays, touch screens, and head-up displays is anticipated to reach 6 million, 3 million, and 0.4 million, respectively, by 2017 (Fig. 7.2) [21].

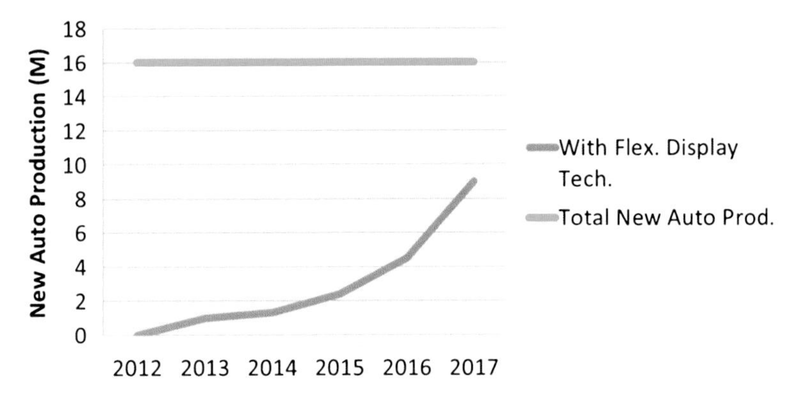

Fig. 7.2 Economic growth – flexible display

7.3.2 *Product Analysis*

Product value in the application of flexible display in automotive industry reflects buyers' desire to retain or obtain a product [22]. The best product value propositions focus on the key benefits – not features or attributes – that matter most to buyers in the target market. Moreover, the best value propositions specifically document the worth/superiority of the seller's offering, relative both to competitors and to customer needs [23]. According to the researched market drivers in automotive industry, we have pointed out some of the key automotive product features (see Fig. 7.3) for short- and long-term viability within the market place. Based on these features, we grouped the similar features and defined our future products (see Fig. 7.4).

The quality function deployment (QFD) analysis method linked customers' needs to product characteristics, which helped us transform user demands into design quality, to deploy the functions forming quality, and to deploy methods for achieving the design quality into subsystems and component parts, and ultimately to specific elements of the manufacturing process [24]. We developed a QFD table to connect our "product features" and "market driven" and get their relationships and priorities for our TRM (see Fig. 7.5).

7.3.3 *Technology Analysis*

Determining the proper mix of existing and to-be-developed technology to realize future products is a critical problem. Our development process was to use the existing technologies to support each product component where permissible. Then to try to find the opportunities for the future development of existing or related technologies and threats from the development of new technologies which it may cause the

Group	Product Features	Code
Information	Onboard Navigation	PF1
Information	Multi-information display	PF2
Efficiency	Vehicle Interior / Exterior lighting	PF3
Safety	Back window alerts and messaging	PF4
Information	Computer Telephony Integration	PF5
Information	Entertainment System	PF6
Efficiency	Solar Roof Panel Integration	PF7
Information	Dashboard Display	PF8
Information	Wider viewing angles and improved brightness	PF9
Efficiency	Display response time - immediate	PF10
Information	Photo-sensitive	PF11
Safety	Durable, Ultra Thin and Lightweight	PF12
Efficiency	Rollable Display	PF13

Fig. 7.3 Product features – flexible display

Products		Code	Present	Gap
Informative Displays	Windshield Display	P1	Laser Base	Curved Display
	Dashboard Display	P2	LCD (FPD)	Curved Display
	Passenger Seat Display	P3	LCD (FPD)	Rollable Display
Safety or Lighting Devices	Flexible Light-emitting Devices	P4	Prototype	Curved Display

Fig. 7.4 Products and gaps – flexible display

potential substitution on existing technologies. Therefore, our first step is to understand the market drivers' and customers' needs. Second, we define the product features based on the market drivers. Lastly, we need to map the existing or developed technologies to our defined product features (see Fig. 7.6). To do this, we defined the priority of each of the technologies and found the gaps between product features and technology features. This is helpful for us to know the cost of using and

Product Features VS. Market Drivers	
Strong Relationship	
Medium Relationship	
Weak Relationship	

Priority	
High	
Midium	
Low	

		Smart		Eco-friendly				Driver Experience				Safe		Economic		
		Unmanned Vehicle Technology	Car Intelligent System – provide interface	High Energy Efficiency	No Toxic Material	Environmental Regulations	Greater likelihood to purchase green products	Car Entertainment System	More Flexible, Dynamic and Adaptable interior/Exterior	Wireless Communication Connectivity	Color Tunability and immobility	More durable, safer & impact resistant	Free from distraction and overload.	Increase market share	Reduce total product cost	
Produt Features		D1	D2	D3	D4	D5	D6	D7	D8	D9	D10	D11	D12	D13	D14	Priority
Onboard Navigation	PF1															
Multi-information display	PF2															
Vehicle Interior / Exterior lighting	PF3															
Back window alerts and messaging	PF4															
Computer Telephony Integration	PF5															
Entertainment System	PF6															
Solar Roof Panel Integration	PF7															
Dashboard Display - "heads-up"	PF8															
Wider viewing angles and improved brightness	PF9															
Display response time - immediate	PF10															
Photo-sensitive	PF11															
Durable, Ultra Thin and Lightweight	PF12															
Rollable	PF13															

Fig. 7.5 QFD- product features versus market drivers

Technology Features	Technologies	Code	Present Status	Gaps
Safety & Energy	Intelligent Safety Features	T1	Developing	Light car-Open source Technology
	Onboard Navigation	T2	Existing	Present
	Safety Alerts	T3	Developing	Light car-Open source Technology
	Better energy consumption	T4	Existing	Present
	Impact Resistant	T5	Existing	Present
Driver Experience	Pristine Surface - Coating Technique	T6	Existing	Present
	Exceptional Optical Clarity - Flex Features	T7	Developing	Advanced Coating Technology
	Interactive-multifunction	T8	Developing	Interactive OLED Micro wall Technology
	Frameless Design	T9	Developing	MFG

Fig. 7.6 Technology features – flexible display

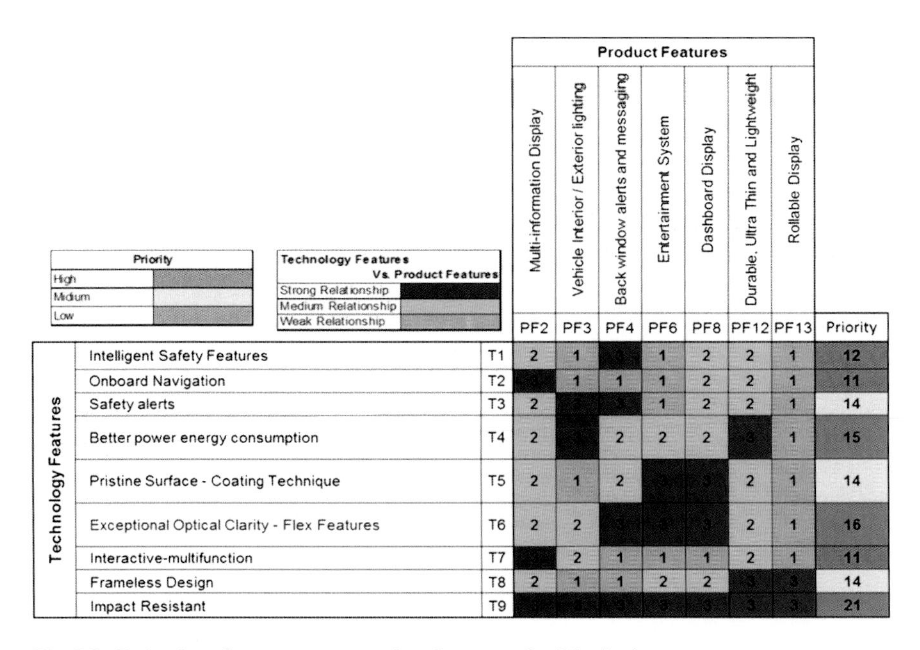

Technology Features		PF2 Multi-information Display	PF3 Vehicle Interior / Exterior lighting	PF4 Back window alerts and messaging	PF6 Entertainment System	PF8 Dashboard Display	PF12 Durable, Ultra Thin and Lightweight	PF13 Rollable Display	Priority
Intelligent Safety Features	T1	2	1	3	1	2	2	1	12
Onboard Navigation	T2	3	1	1	1	2	2	1	11
Safety alerts	T3	2	3	3	1	2	2	1	14
Better power energy consumption	T4	2	3	2	2	2	3	1	15
Pristine Surface - Coating Technique	T5	2	1	2	3	3	2	1	14
Exceptional Optical Clarity - Flex Features	T6	2	2	3	3	3	2	1	16
Interactive-multifunction	T7	[illegible]	2	1	1	1	2	1	11
Frameless Design	T8	2	1	1	2	2	3	3	14
Impact Resistant	T9	3	3	3	3	3	3	3	21

Fig. 7.7 Technology features versus product features – flexible display

developing technologies and what we need to do to develop or find more new technologies or partners. Figure 7.7 concludes all the related technologies we already have, we need to develop, or to cooperate with a third party, or to buy the technology outright.

7.3.3.1 Multi-information Display

The multi-information display provides a fast overview of all relevant vehicle information. Recently, many automotive companies launched MID into the flexible display technology. With this technology, it presents ergonomically superior visibility through vibrant self-luminescent characters.

Vehicle Interior/Exterior Lighting

The flexible display technology is able to integrate into the car sunroof, windows, and body appearance. With this technology, the car interior illumination and the exterior appearance can be changed, as we mentioned in the beginning of the Introduction, the Toyota Fun Vii.

Back Window Alerts and Messaging

This technology is able to alert drivers to cars or objects in drivers' blind spot and provides a wide-open shot of what is happening behind the vehicle. Also, the message is showing on the rear window to warn the driver behind if there is an accident ahead.

Entertainment System

There are many options available for car entertainment systems. In September 2011 Kia unveiled a new concept car called the GT, which uses an intelligent system for the dashboard display: three layers of transparent OLED panels that create a unique 3D display – showing instrument data, entertainment info, and the navigation system [25].

Rollable Display

The rollable display is a thin OLED display flexible enough to roll around 4 mm object. Engineers could use the technology to develop electronic displays that mimic the features of paper. Although rollable displays are still at least 5 years off, ITRI is working on versions of its current bendable technology for organic LED displays and touch screens [26].

With the product feature set prioritized (Fig. 7.5), we were then able to compare those products against what we identified as key technology features. Based on these findings, we then grouped the top technology features as follows (Fig. 7.6):

TIER 1

Impact Resistant – via transparent sheets of plastic or metal foils, the OLED can withstand greater collision/impact than that of other visual displays currently being offered.

Exceptional Optical Clarity – clean and crisp, the flexile OLED will deliver picture quality far greater than LCD technologies.

Energy Efficiency – does not rely on backlighting to deliver any visual, provides greater lumens or images per watt compared to that of LCD technology [27].

TIER 2

Safety Alerts – though important, and a key feature offered with other technologies, the use of safety alerts dovetail nicely into our existing platform.

Pristine Surface – a polyimide-coated substrate and direct-emission RGB subpixels, makes OLED clear, stronger, and thinner [28].

Frameless Design – cutting-edge technology, frameless design allows for wide range of applications, whereby the OLED can be placed or over-imposed in and on almost any shape and surface.

TIER 3

Onboard Navigation – allows for a hands off and somewhat artificial intelligence experience for both driver and passengers.

Interactive Multifunction – as a stand-alone technology feature, allows the user to interact with things on the screen [28].

Intelligent Safety Features – as stand-alone technologies may not be considered disruptive in their delivery, yet when bundled, offer an impressive increase from today's safety offerings.

7.3.4 Resource Analysis

The resource analysis must not only give attention to economic costs but also has to determine if it is feasible to obtain the needed physical material and manpower in the required time period. Therefore, we need to understand the current and required level of technological capabilities and its gaps. We developed a table (see Fig. 7.8) to analyze our technological capabilities, i.e., the resources, which are composed of a variety of sources of knowledge. The integration of new technology systems requires the mastering of previous technologies, allowing economic agents to build competencies in a cumulative manner. The various sources of technological capability are more likely to be complementary rather than interchangeable. So, the creation and improvement of technological capabilities involve a crucial element of technological "effort" [29].

7.3.4.1 Government Organizations and Academia

From the viewpoint of public role in technology innovation, the investment or funds in the flexible display technology have been drawn by governmental organizations and the academic world in the United States. For instance, in 2004, the US Army

Resources			Contents	Code
Governmental Org. & Academia	ASU+US Army	Flexible Display Center (FDC)	· Government-Industry-Academia Partnership · Display Technology · Manufacturing Technology	R1
	DARPA+Various Universities	The DARPA Grand Challenge	· Unmanned Vehicle Technology	R2
Industry	Hewlett-Packard		· Manufacturing (Roll-to-Roll Process)	R3
	XEROX	PARC	· Plastic Electronics	R4
	Display Companies	Samsung Display LG Display Universal Display etc.	· Manufacturing · Display Techology	R5
	Material Companies	Corning Dupont 3M etc.	· Substrate Material Technology · Coating Technology · Manufacturing	R6
	Automotive Component MFG	Continental Automotive Delphi Automotive Bosch EDAG etc.	· Application · Design	R7
	Automakers	Mercedes Benz BMW Toyota Ford etc.	· Application · Design	R8
Alliance	FlexTech Alliance	87 Organizations in North America participated	· Facilitating Partnerships · Ensuring R&D Support · Developing Product Demonstrators · Identifying and Addressing Manufacturing Issues · Equalizing Funding v. Overseas Competition	R9
Standard		SAE	· Electrical, Electronics and Avionics · Human Factors and Ergonomics · Parts and Components	R10
		ISO	· ISO 9000 (Quality Management) · ISO 26262 (Functional Safety)	

Fig. 7.8 Resources analysis – flexible display

and Arizona State University established the Flexible Display Center (FDC) because the US Army figured out the benefits which flexible displays will bring to commercial markets as well as military markets. The center is not only conducting fundamental research for display and manufacturing technologies but also trying to strengthen partnership among government, academia, and industry [30].

Moreover, some governmental organizations such as the Defense Advanced Research Projects Agency (DARPA) and the Sandia National Laboratory have promoted related technologies by giving funds and working on grant programs. For instance, in 2004, 2005, and 2007, DARPA held the Grand Challenge in which various teams competed for conducting given missions with autonomous vehicle technology. The derivative technologies from this competition have led to variety of innovations in automotive technology. In special, diverse control and sensor systems enabling fully autonomous driving can be used for more advanced vehicle intelligent systems [15].

7.3.4.2 Industry

In common with governmental organizations and academia, numerous companies from substrate material companies like Corning and DuPont to automobile companies have also developed and invested in the flexible display technology. Some display manufacturing companies such as Samsung Display, LG Display, AUO, and Universal Display are focusing on accelerating commercialization by various researches of display technology including substrate materials and devices as well as manufacturing technology. Also, other companies which have concentrated on precedent technologies, such as Hewlett-Packard (HP) and Xerox, have researched those technologies. In particular, HP has researched roll-to-roll process which enables extreme cost reduction for a long time [31]. Furthermore, automobile companies have announced new concepts adopting the flexible display technology such as BMW and Toyota's Fun Vii [1, 32]. By showing their future concepts or applications, they cannot only advertise their ability but also lead markets and suppliers.

7.3.4.3 Alliance and Standard

As an emerging technology, it is impossible for some organizations to solve all problems or bottlenecks without collaborations or alliance. Fortunately, in the beginning stage of this technology, various kinds of collaborations have been formed and developed. One of representative collaborations is FlexTech Alliance. This commercial alliance consists of over 80 organizations that include display manufactures, material companies, governmental organizations, and academic organizations [33]. Furthermore, typical automotive component markets require more strict standards in quality management. Here, ISO 9000 series and ISO 26262 series are representative examples. According to Vojak and Chambers, active participation in these alliances and standards can be required for component suppliers and developers because it can be opportunities not only for reading market trends but also leading technology [34] (Fig. 7.9).

7.4 Conclusion

The automotive industry was slow in adopting LCD flat panel display technology because of concerns over safety and performance in extreme environmental conditions [28]. Since then, the automotive industry is looking for an alternative to replace the glass substrate. The emergence of OLED technology opened up new opportunities in the industry. OLED technology is viewed as the future solution because of it being able to be constructed on a plastic substrate and operate in extreme conditions, as well as because of its ultrathin size and flexibility, all of which caught the attention of automakers. Companies like Audi, Toyota, and Mercedes are spending huge amounts on research and development of flexible displays [35]. Some of these companies succeeded in implementing small OLED applications and also were able to produce prototypes for unique applications like rear-view mirror displays and rollable displays. With this early success, OLED flexible displays show a promising future in the coming years. It is evident from the current development in OLED technology that we will see more flexible displays in vehicles in the next 2–7

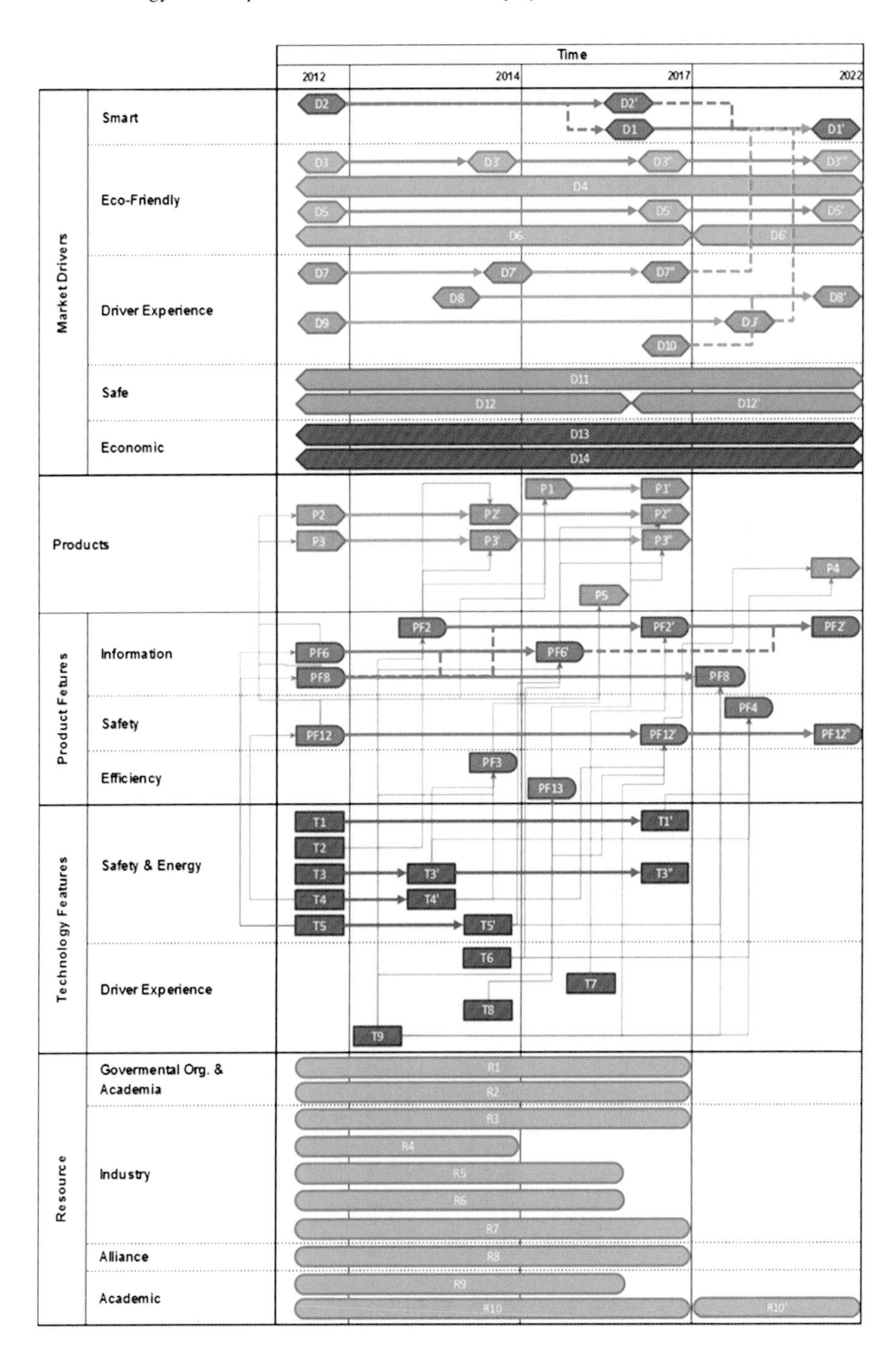

Fig. 7.9 Technology roadmap – automotive flexible display

years. One of the main issues with OLED flexible display today is it's expensive to produce. However, with improvement in manufacturing technology, the cost of OLED is expected to come down, thus encouraging the automakers to explore more areas of its application.

7.5 Future Research

As stated in the beginning, the objective of this report is to develop a roadmap for the flexible display in automotive industry. The research report meets the goal by collecting, analyzing, and presenting the research data in the form of a technology roadmap. The report presents the current state of flexible OLED displays in the automotive industry and where the industry should and will be heading in the next 5 years. Factors like manufacturing technology and display technology and the related research by industry and government-industry-academia partnership are well accounted. This report can be expanded to other industries of flexible display beyond automotive industry. This roadmap needs to be maintained for the changes that happen in a particular interval.

References

1. Patton P (2011) Toyota Fun-Vii: the car as mobile mood ring. The New York Times [Online]. http://wheels.blogs.nytimes.com/2011/11/30/toyota-fun-vii-the-car-as-mobile-mood-ring/
2. Allen K (2005) Markets and applications of flexible displays. In: Crawford GP (ed) Flexible flat panel displays. Wiley, Chichester, pp 495–523
3. Phaal R, Farrukh CJP, Probert DR (2004) Technology roadmapping—a planning framework for evolution and revolution. Technol Forecast Soc Change 71(1–2):5–26
4. Stein HU (1989) Light emitting diode display. US Patent 4,853,593, 1 Aug 1989
5. Ferrell JF (1989) Dense LED matrix for high resolution full color video. US Patent 4,857,801, 15 Aug 1989
6. Colak SB (1990) Wide band gap semiconductor light emitting devices. US Patent 4,894,832, 16 Jan 1990
7. Tang CW, Van Slyke S (1987) Organic electro-luminescent diodes. Appl Phys Lett 51:913
8. Tsujimura T (2012) OLED display fundamentals and applications. Wiley, Hoboken, pp 5–36
9. Howard WE (2004) Better displays with organic films. Sci Am 290:76–81
10. Sawyer C (2008) The reconfigurable display revolution, Automotive Design and Production, http://www.autofieldguide.com/articles/the-reconfigurable-display-revolution
11. Feick K (2012) Frost and Sullivan: Deluge of in-vehicle information to trigger a revolution [Online]. http://www.frost.com
12. Isele R (2011) Flexible displays as key for high-value and unique automotive design. Advances in display technologies; and e-papers and flexible displays, vol 7956, SPIE, Bellingham
13. Ványa L (2003) Excerpts from the history of unmanned ground vehicles development in the USA. Acad Appl Res Mil Sci 2(2):185–197
14. Nelson NJ (1969) A mobile automation: an application of artificial intelligence techniques. In: Proceedings of the first international joint conference on artificial intelligence. Washington DC, May 1969, pp 509–520

15. Seetharaman G, Lakhotia A, Blasch EP (2006) Unmanned vehicles come of age: the DARPA grand challenge. Computer 39:26–29
16. Jain K, Klosner M, Zemel M, Raghunandan S (2005) Flexible Electronics and Displays: High-Resolution, Roll-to-Roll, Projection Lithography and Photoablation Processing Technologies for High-Throughput Production, Proceedings of the IEEE 93(8):1500–1510
17. Wiley R (2011) OLED TV vs. LCD TV [Online]. http://oled.lcdtvbuyingguide.com/oled-tv-articles/oled-tv-vs-lcd-tv.html
18. Bosch R (2008) Automotive HMI: current status and future challenges. In: AIDE final workshop and exhibition, Gothenburg, 15–16 Apr 2008 [Online]. http://www.aide-eu.org/pdf/final_workshop/day1/round_table/aide_day1_round_table_all.pdf
19. Harter T et. al (2004) Energy-aware user interfaces: an evaluation of user acceptance. CHI 2004, Vienna, 24–29 Apr 2004
20. In-Car Entertainment (Infotainment) [ICE] System Market – Global Forecast & Analysis by OEM & Aftermarket (2011–2016), marketsandmarkets.com, March 2012, SE 1738 [Online]. http://www.marketsandmarkets.com/Market-Reports/in-car-vehicle-infotainment-ici-systems-market-538.html
21. Frost & Sullivan: Deluge of in-vehicle information to trigger a revolution in the design of automotive display and instrument clusters. Frost & Sullivan, London, 27 June 2012 [Online]. http://www.frost.com/prod/servlet/press-release.pag?docid=262400812
22. Neap HS, Celik T (1999) Value of a product: a definition. Int J Value-Based Manage 12(2):181–191
23. Mohr J (2012) Crafting the value proposition for innovative products and services, Wisepreneur, Innovation Marketing. http://wisepreneur.com/innovation-marketing-2/crafting-the-value-proposition-for-innovative-products-and-services
24. Akao Y (1994) Development history of quality function deployment. In: The customer driven approach to quality planning and deployment. Asian Productivity Organization, Minato, Tokyo, p 339. ISBN 92-833-1121-3
25. OLED panels in cars. OLED-Info.com [Online]. http://www.oled-info.com/oled-cars
26. Merritt R (2010) Researcher: rollable displays unfold in 2015. EE Times, News & Analysis, 11 Apr 2010 [Online]. http://www.eetimes.com/electronics-news/4210430/Researcher-Rollable-displays-unfold-in-2015
27. Kanellos M (2012) Seven reasons why OLED TVs could really be real this time. Forbes [Online]. http://www.forbes.com/sites/michaelkanellos/2012/01/12/seven-reasons-why-oled-tvs-could-really-be-real/
28. Archibugi D, Coco A (2004) A new indicator of technological capabilities for developed and developing countries (ArCo). World Dev 32(4):629–654
29. Xu E (2011) Toyota Fun-VII vehicle concept: flexible OLED for changeable body display. The cool gadgets, 2 Dec 2011 [Online]. http://thecoolgadgets.com/toyota-fun-vii-vehicle-concept-flexible-oled-for-changeable-body-display/
30. Morton D, Forsythe E, Forsythe E (2007) Flexible display development for army applications. Inf Display 23:18–23
31. Greene K (2010) Roll-to-Roll plastic displays. Technology review [Online]. http://www.technologyreview.com/news/417307/roll-to-roll-plastic-displays/. Accessed 12 Aug 2012
32. Isele R (2011) Flexible displays as key for high-value and unique automotive design. In: Proceedings of SPIE, 2011, vol 7956, pp 79560A–79560A-6
33. FlexTech Alliance's White Paper (2009) The Flextech Alliance. http://www.flextech.org/ii-white-papers-archive.aspx
34. Vojak BA, Chambers FA (2004) Roadmapping disruptive technical threats and opportunities in complex, technology-based subsystems: the SAILS methodology. Technol Forecast Soc Change 71(1–2):121–139
35. Knight S (2012) LG preparing flexible OLED display plant for production. Techspot, Industry News, 14 May 2012 [Online]. http://www.techspot.com/news/48578-lg-preparing-flexible-oled-display-plant-for-production.html

Chapter 8
Technology Roadmap for Next Generation PC: Hybrid PC

Zack Khalifa, Mohamed Burgan, Tila Bregaj, and Manar Almallak

Abstract Technology roadmap (TRM) is a powerful management tool for technology planning process. The uniqueness of this tool enables firms to identify and develop technology alternatives that are required to meet a set of product or service needs. In this framework, we utilized this powerful tool to measure the pace of the next hybrid PC generations. The main catalyst behind this study is attempting to answer the question of why PC sales have shrunk recently. We started conducting our research by applying the macroeconomics forces at the macroscale to have a clear vision of the exerted forces on PC industry—namely, the impact of tablets, ultrabooks, laptops, and smartphones on PCs. Accordingly, we conducted an intensive literature review followed by a survey to understand the trends of PC industry as well as the end users' needs. Based on the knowledge extracted from the literature and the survey, we constructed the technology roadmap of the next hybrid PC generations. The developed roadmap—consisted of drivers, products, technology, and resources—empowered us to evaluate the current state of PC industry and revealed technological gaps implicitly. We believe the technological gaps discovered by this framework will help any hypothetical manufacturer pioneer in the PC industry to cope up with the dynamic of PC market for the next 5 years. Market research is conducted using Porter's five force model, and the data for other layers of technology roadmap are from literature research and surveys.

Z. Khalifa (✉)
Schlumberger, Denver, CO, USA
e-mail: zack.kh@gmail.com

M. Burgan • M. Almallak
Portland State University, Portland, OR, USA

T. Bregaj
Intel Corporation, Hillsboro, OR, USA

T.U. Daim et al. (eds.), *Planning and Roadmapping Technological Innovations: Cases and Tools*, Innovation, Technology, and Knowledge Management,
DOI 10.1007/978-3-319-02973-3_8,

8.1 Introduction

8.1.1 History of the PC

The PC, or personal computer, has revolutionized today's society in several different ways. When computers first came on the scene and started being used to help the government and businesses work more efficiently, this was seen as a major step forward in technology. At first, however, nobody dreamed that the computer would find its way into our homes, where it would help to change the way people communicated, sought information, purchased goods, and took care of everyday tasks. These days, PCs are almost as commonplace in the home as televisions and are used almost as frequently. The computer history timeline that is the foundation for the history of the PC begins way back in the 1930s. The first automated computer was invented by a man named Konrad Zuse, a German aircraft engineer who needed something that could help him calculate, and save in some sort of memory, complex math equations [1]. This first primitive computer paved the way for more research into computer technology. By the late 1930s and early 1940s, computer technology had advanced to the point where computers could perform math calculations at amazing speeds and store several of these calculations in a digital memory system. With the creation of the UNIVAC in the late 1940s, the computer began to be used by government and businesses, mostly for math-related functions. The age of advanced technology was clearly underway. In the late 1960s and early 1970s, a man named Ed Roberts, after running an electronic device assembly kit business, began to work on a computer assembly kit that could be sold to consumers for use in their homes. He named this computer kit, and subsequently the assembled computer, the Altair. Upon hearing of and purchasing a couple of the Altairs, two computer processors named Bill Gates and Paul Allen decided to develop software programs for it. Gates and Allen were successful with these software programs, which allowed the Altair to perform many more tasks than it originally could. Bill Gates used his success to go on to create the company Microsoft, which Paul Allen later joined.

Tracing the history of the computer is a fascinating task; one that is filled with surprising achievements and giant technological leaps forward. Following this history shows one how computers have changed society in a relatively short amount of time. What computer history shows us is that the invention of the computer made it possible to make many more technological advances—ones that may not have been possible without the help of computers. Later on the computer history timeline continues with the invention of the personal computer, the handheld computer, the Internet, up to now with laptops, netbooks, tablets, ultrabooks, and smart handheld devices. The history of computing has often been told as a succession of paradigms (mainframes, time-sharing, personal computing, and networking), driven mainly by the technical processes of miniaturization and Moore's Law. Each of these models for the organization of computer systems, however, was simultaneously a model for the politics and social relations of a coming information society. The replacement of one model with another owed not only to technological changes but also to changes in the political and cultural landscape, which shaped ideas about how computer technology could and should be brought to a mass audience [1].

8.1.1.1 Moore's Law

Intel cofounder Gordon E. Moore postulated in his famous 1965 paper that the number of components in integrated circuits had doubled every year from their invention in 1958 until 1965 and then predicted that the trend would continue for at least 10 years. Later, David House, an Intel colleague, after factoring in the increase in performance of transistors, concluded that integrated circuits would double in performance every 18 months [1]. Soon after the realization of Moore's law, the suspicion on this law reaching an end persisted. Now, the concern is as serious as it can get. Not only has the feature size to be scaled down, the manufacturing cost also has to be contained. At the core of it are the lithography tools and processes to sustain Moore's law of scaling and Moore's law of economy. It includes the three viable candidates to push lithography beyond the 20 nm logic node. In 1975, Moore refined his component count estimation to a doubling every 2 years and thus a reduced exponential growth compared to his initial estimation. Indeed, looking at the history of integrated circuits from 1975 to 2008, a doubling of transistor counts every 2 years was a good estimation [1]. This prediction known as Moore's Law has become a business dictum for the whole semiconductor industry [1].

This source is from 1999, and back then it predicted that in 2010 we would be at one billion transistors per chip. Today in 2012 with Intel's new 3rd Generation Intel Core, the 22 nm 3D technology named "IVY Bridge" has surpassed that prediction with 1.4 billion transistors in each processor [2]. For almost 50 years, the transistors used to fabricate chips have been flat or planar. With the new 3D tri-gate structure, the transistors are formed on very tall and very skinny silicon "fins," with current flowing along the top and along the sides of these fins. The result is that these new transistors provide significantly improved energy efficiency, especially at low operating voltages, and increase the chips' performance. Intel is the first company to offer these new transistors and it took almost 10 years of research (Fig. 8.1).

8.1.1.2 PC Manufacturers Market Share

Market research firm Gartner paints a grim picture of the PC market in the second quarter this year as shipments dropped more than 5 % in the United States and stayed flat globally. HP remained the world's top PC vendor worldwide as shipments of HP desktops and laptops slid 12.1 % to 13.04 million, and Dell dropped 11.5 % to ship 9.35 million units. Asian vendors Lenovo, Acer, and ASUS each showed growth during second quarter, but not enough to offset tepid ultrabook demand [2]. In the United States, every top vendor lost ground except for Apple, according to Gartner's numbers. Apple, the country's No.3 vendor, showed growth last quarter, with shipments climbing 4.3 % to 1.91 million units. HP shipments slid 12.7 % to 3.98 million units; Dell dipped 9.5 % to 3.46 million. Worldwide Lenovo, Acer Group, and ASUS are holding strong [2] (Fig. 8.2).

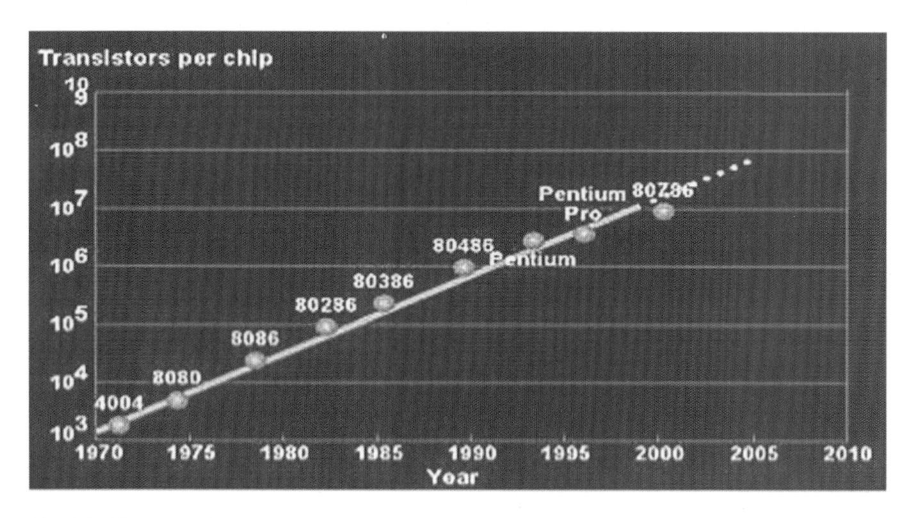

Fig. 8.1 Illustrates the amount of transistors per chip through years publically available [3]

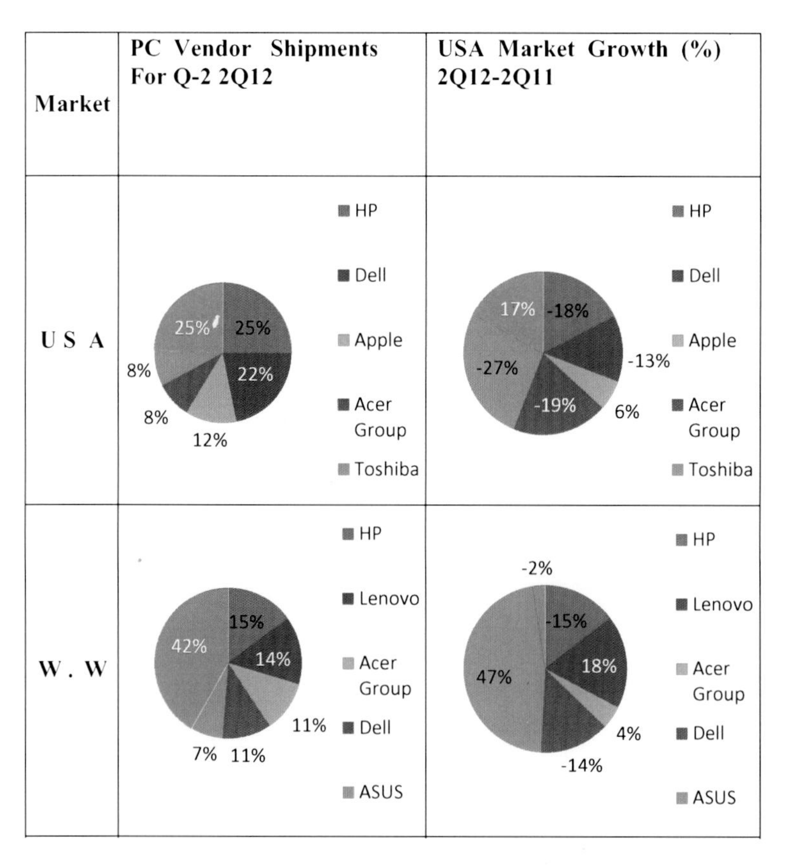

Fig. 8.2 PC Market analysis worldwide and in the United States according to Gartner [4]

According to Gartner's analysts, some of the key influencers of slow PC shipment growth were uncertainties in the economy in various regions as well as consumer's low interest in PC purchases. Consumers are less interested in spending on PCs as there are other technology product and services, such as the latest smartphones and media tablets that they are purchasing. This is more of a trend in the mature market as PCs are highly saturated in these markets. Despite the high expectations for the thin and light notebook segment, ultrabooks shipment volume was small and has a little impact on overall shipment growth. From a regional perspective, EMEA, Asia/Pacific, and Japan registered low single-digit growth while all Americas markets posted year-over-year shipment declines.

8.1.1.3 Technology Roadmapping

In this framework, the team utilized the technology roadmapping to map out the next PC generation. The strength of this tool helps any type of organization to link business strategies to technology—product or services—and market needs. The tool organizes the planning process with respect to time to reveal all parameters that are relevant to the technology and organization. Moreover, technology roadmapping can be defined as an incursive approach than can help accommodate technology and science into product and business for strategy planning [5]. Creating a roadmap can provide three main benefits: first, it creates a forecasting mechanism for the developed technology; second, it produces a unified collection of requirements, needs, and values along with the developed technology; and third, it helps construct a framework to plan and assist the development of the technology or the product [6–8] Furthermore, technology roadmap can provide other values to organizations like enhancing the plan ownership and communication, setting plan priorities, and linking values, products, technologies, and resources plans together [5].

8.1.2 Problem Statement

As the maturity of high-tech markets increases, replacement acquisitions become the dominant proportion of sales [9]. Therefore, the change in demand and new innovation will keep changing the position of the PC industry in the coming years significantly [10]. Demand on low cost of ultraportable PC has generated high competition among the pioneers of PC industry by forcing them to change their business model—in order to move swiftly with the dynamic of today's market of new innovations [10]. The core of this project is focusing on measuring the pace of the next PC generations using technology roadmap. The main question that arises while doing this research is why the sales of PCs has shrank recently? We attempted to answer this question by conducting a thorough literature review to understand the impact of tablets, smartphones, laptops, and ultrabooks on the market growth of PC.

The global PC market in the last few years has seen noticeable changes with a new wave of tablets, iPads, notebooks, ultrabooks, and smartphones that have entered the market. As a result of this, technology analysts have said that the PC market is "flat" or even "dead." In this paper, we will analyze and evaluate where the PC market stands worldwide, looking at both emerging markets, particularly Asia and Brazil, and mature markets like the United States and Europe. After we lay down this landscape, by the use of surveys and research, we will illustrate a technology roadmap for what we call "the next generation of hybrid PCs." Roadmaps are now established instruments for designing future policies and strategies. They provide an operational approach to help organizations see where they are going and how they are going to get there. Roadmaps integrate science and engineering to develop future products. Roadmaps look at market drivers, product and technology gaps, and resources. Technology roadmapping is driven by a need, not a solution [11, 12]. Technology planning is important for many reasons. Globally, companies are facing many competitive problems. Technology roadmapping, a form of technology planning, can help deal with this increasingly competitive environment. Our methodology is explored by looking at trends and drivers and answering the following questions: Where are we now? Who are our competitors? What are the current trends? What are the main drivers? Who are the present leaders in the field? What are the gaps in technology? Where do we want to be? What is stopping us from getting there? What needs to overcome the barriers? In this project, the team thoroughly looked at smartphones, tablets, ultrabooks, their features, and use and came up with a hybrid convertible laptop-tablet that consumers can work and play at the same time. They can create and they can consume. What attracts consumers are the sleek user interfaces, quality components, extended battery lives, portability, competitive price points, excellent functionality, and access to content and apps. The idea is that in emerging markets, a consumer could spend their worth earned money on a product that they can use both as a laptop for work or school and then detach it into a tablet for other convenient, creative uses. Our survey of 70 participants included young working professionals mostly in the Portland area.

8.2 Methodology

Across the PC industry, pioneers face combined and complicated factors stemmed from the heat of the competition in the market place and many other problems that are associated with accelerating the R&D of both radical and incremental innovation. Such problems are generated due to the challenges of the short life cycle of the gadgets which forces PC manufactures to come up with breakthrough technologies in this industry, thereby cope up with the dynamic of the market in this era. Consequently, it is imperative for the PC industry leaders to develop mechanisms/ approaches that enable them to incorporate the industry requirements as well as the market need—i.e., linking business strategies to technology. Technology roadmap is a powerful tool that serves these purposes effectively and efficiently. The strength of this tool enables firms to map out all their business plans and link them

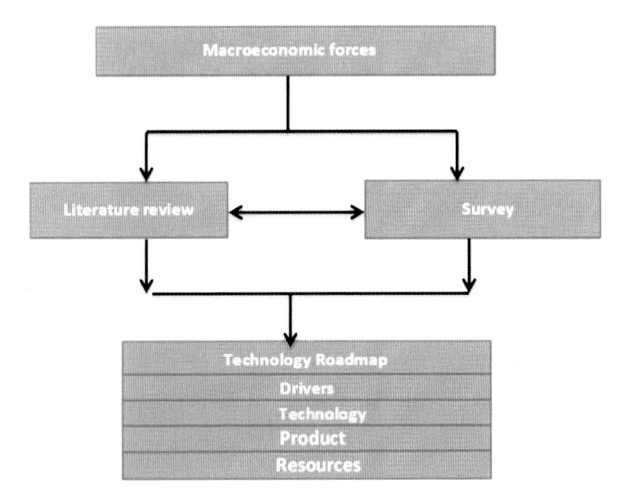

Fig. 8.3 Flowchart for technology roadmap development

accordingly to the technologies with respect to the time. Moreover, it helps roadmappers to understand the drivers that are driving technology—either if it is a product or service—thus highlighting/lowlighting all possible factors that seem to be significant from the market and industry point of view with respect to the time. Upon developing the drivers, roadmappers can recognize patterns that cannot be discerned using conventional planning tools—technology gaps. Furthermore, technology gaps can give an insight into what the customers' needs are in terms of desired features on a product or service. Accordingly, roadmappers can start initiating the pipeline of R&D starting from the discovery phase—by innovating ideas to fulfill the end users' needs—all the way through commercializing/launching the products into the market space.

Thus, to tailor the layers of the TRM, we relied on three approaches in order to have a broad view of the PC industry. These approaches are described as follows:

Macroeconomic Forces: In order to have an oriented path of research of this framework, we developed a macrocosmic forces analysis at the macro level of the PC industry in a brief manner. The five forces enlightened us with factors that we need to look at while conducting the research and developing the survey.

Literature Review: An intensive research was conducted in an in-depth induction in order to understand the impact of laptops, tablets, smartphones, and ultrabooks on the growth of PC. This was done by looking at blog reviews by customers, new articles from technology journals, and reports by IDC and some other reporters.

Survey: In order to have a tangible sense of what end users expect from PC, we developed a survey. The survey has many questions categorized into personal information as well as information about portable devices being owned by the customers and potential devices that end users are looking forward to have. The template of the survey is attached in Appendix A.1 (Fig. 8.3).

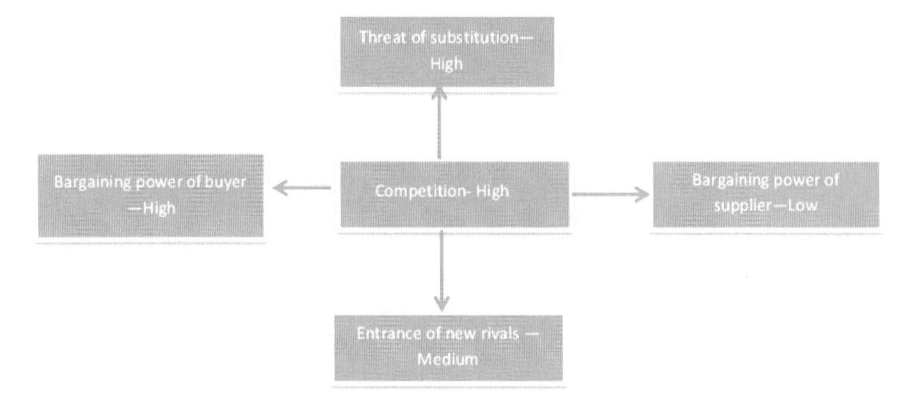

Fig. 8.4 Macroeconomic forces in PC industry

8.2.1 Macroeconomic Forces

In order to have a good vision of this framework at the macroscale level, the team decided to apply the Porter's five forces, as shown in the Fig. 8.4, to have a generic orientation to develop the elements of the "master roadmap." The uniqueness of this analysis enabled us to have a deep understanding of the PC industry in terms of what is "out there." In other words, understand the external forces being exerted on the PC industry at the macroscale [13]. The description of each of the five forces is described as follows:

Entrance of New Rivals

This force evaluates the degree of the severances that new comers to the market might encounter, thus highlighting possible threats that might confront new comers [13].

Threat of Substitution

This force asses the degree of replacing an exciting product by new disruptive and cool products that seem to have a magnificent value to the end users [13].

Bargaining Power of Supplier

This force examines the strength of the supplier in terms of how strong a supplier is with respect to launching disruptive services/products that add value to the final version of product/supplier [13].

Bargaining Power of Buyers

This force appraises the power of the supplier in terms of how purchasing power embodies threat to the market. Somehow, this force is associated with product/services image [13].

Competition

This force tests whether an existing competitor is creating an intense competing environment in the market space [13].

Now after identifying the five forces, below we apply them in a brief manner on the PC industry—where any hypothetical manufacture can perform at the macroscale.

Entrance of New Rivals

The entrance of new comer to the market space is classified as medium. Such an assumption is made because PCs are not something that are as disruptive as they have been in the market for a long time. Yet, new coalitions of manufacturing pioneers from the PC industry may render this force to be high—this is not surprising if it happens.

Threat of Substitution

We believe this force is classified to be very high for the PC industry, as end users can displace PC by smartphones, laptops, tablets, and ultrabooks. Thus, PC manufactures need to take into account such an impact that might be generated from these products which almost can serve the same functions that PC does.

Bargaining Power of Supplier

This power is characterized to be low, since the main supplier of PC industry is Intel, and it has a strong position in the PC industry, surpassing the pace of Moore's law as described in the introduction of this framework.

Bargaining Power of Buyers

We believe this power is very high as end users have so many alternatives to choose from as far as computing device is the main concern. Customers can perform almost the same functions that can be done on a PC on a laptop, smartphone, tablet, or ultrabook, which has a small-size screen, is lightweight, easy to carry, sleek looking and is a cool product.

Competition

As far as the competition force is a concern in the PC industry, we believe this force to be very high. This is evidenced by the product being released by Apple and the rest of the manufacturing pioneers in the PC industry. It is tangible in the market that we see PC manufactures coming up with innovative ideas to be incorporated into the PC. For instance, Sony coming up with the "Blu-ray" technology formed high competition forcing other manufactures in this industry to develop some other ideas to attract customers. Such examples are very sensible to the end users which eventually encourage customers to favor "A" product from "A" manufacture that brings out the best innovative idea. Thus, in this industry, "if you snooze you lose."

The Porter's five forces for any hypothetical company that wants to invest and develop in the PC industry are shown in Fig. 8.4.

8.2.2 Literature Review

A comprehensive research has been conducted for each of the products that has an impact on the growth of the PC industry. This section describes the impact of each, viz., tablets, ultrabooks, laptops, and smartphones, as follows:

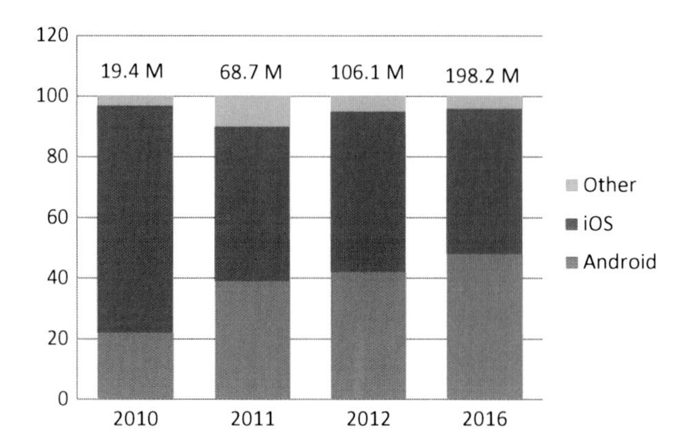

Fig. 8.5 Tablets shipment with respect to OS historical forecast from 2010 until 2016 in million units [14]

8.2.3 Tablets

The idea of tablet computer was first presented to the public in the 1950s. The concept of the tablet was based on handwriting recognition as an interface instead of a keyboard. In the 1980s, several companies had started commercializing the tablet concept based on pen computing technology. Pen computing technology refers to a pen that is used as a user interface rather than other input devices such as a keyboard or mouse. Since the 1980s the tablet was used for note taking. Also, it was used in the health-care sector for data capture [14].

In April 2010, Apple launched its first iPad; the iPad was an introduction to the tablet market revolution [14]. In fact, iPad reinvigorated the tablet market with touch interface, which differentiates the tablet from the traditional PC and identifies the tablet computer as a new portable device platform. According to IDC report, global tablets shipment reached 19.4 million units in 2010 [14]. In 2011, the shipments have increased to 68.7 million units and it is expected to reach 200 million units in 2016 [14]. The large growth in tablets sale in 2011 was due to consumer's response to Apple's, Samsung's, and Amazon's tablets that had been launched in that year [14]. Also, tablets market has been drastically growing due to the features that tablets provided to their customer such as long battery lives, durability, apps, better display screen, and portability. Figure 8.5 shows tablets shipment with respect to OS historical forecast from 2010 until 2016 in million units.

8.2.4 Market Share Trend of Tablets

The chart below (Fig. 8.6) depicts the historical market share trend for the recent years based on quarter sales. The chart shows clearly that Android is gradually

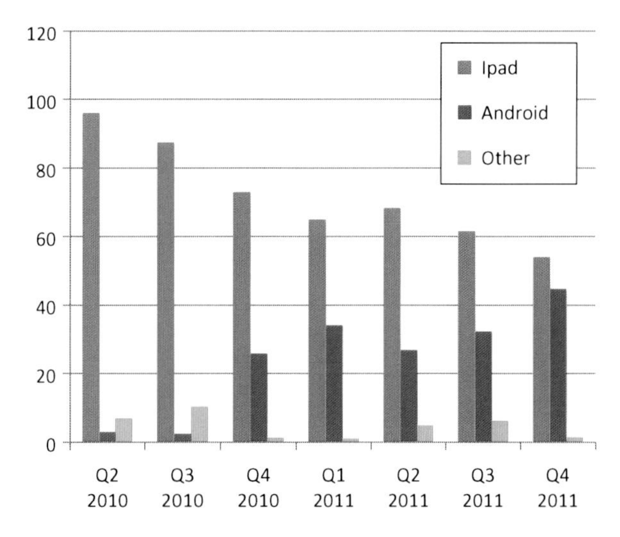

Fig. 8.6 Market share trends of tablets from Q-2 of 2010 to Q-4 of 2011 [14]

Table 8.1 Vendors, worldwide media tablet shipments, second quarter 2012

Vendor	2012 shipments	Market share	2011 shipments	Market share	2012/2011 growth
Apple	17,042	68.2 %	9,248	61.5 %	84.3 %
Samsung	2,391	9.6 %	1,099	7.3 %	117.6 %
Amazon.com	1,252	5.0 %	0	NA	NA
ASUS	855	3.4 %	397	2.6 %	115.5 %
Acer	385	1.5 %	629	4.2 %	−38.7 %
Others	3,067	12.3 %	3,668	24.4 %	−16.4 %
All vendors	24,994	100 %	15,042	100 %	66.2 %

gaining market share from Apple. Also, the chart shows that Apple has lost part of its market share in each consecutive quarter where there was no new iPad launched. In the second quarter of 2011 with launch of the iPad2, Apple was able to gain more market share; on the next quarter, Apple partially lost some of its market share. Despite the rival competition between Apple and Android, Apple still has over 60 % of the tablet market share. The biggest threat that Apple will face this year is the two major product launches—the new Kindle Fire and the Nexus.

Table 8.1 shows top 5 vendors' worldwide media tablet shipments, in the of second quarter 2012 (preliminary) (unit shipments are in thousands [14]).

According to NPD Display Search, by 2016 tablets are expected to surpass the note book shipment, and by 2019 the ratio is expected to be 2 to 1, with tablets in the lead. Consumers who focus on mobile computing devices shift from notebook to tablet PCs [15]. Also, it is hard to imagine tablets taking over notebooks, but it seems that the two segments are moving toward each other to the hybrid PC which is considered a tablet and notebook merged together. In fact, consumers are looking for a mobile platform PC to be integrated between a consumer product and a commercial product, with the following features: lighter, faster, better battery life, and cheaper [15].

8.2.5 Ultrabook

Ultrabook is the name trademarked by Intel to describe a new category of thin and light mobile computers that have a new level of responsiveness, long battery life, are built on Intel's newest platform security technologies, and are around 18 mm thick. The goal with these new machines is to combine the performance of a laptop with tablet-like features such as sleek design, instant on, always connected, touch, and easy software delivery. Momentum for what would become the ultrabook began to build in 2010 as many consumers were looking into sleek, sexy devices of smartphones and tablets. Ultrabooks continue to build momentum. Early indicators are that ASUS, Acer, Samsung, Lenovo, and of course Microsoft will have sleek, highly refined tables available in time for Windows 8's launch [16]." In the pipeline, Intel has 140 ultrabook designs, including 40 touch-enabled models [17]. What Intel was aiming at when it came up with the ultrabook concept was to start with the user experience first and incorporate that into their product planning. The added bonus is when the touch-enabled "Metro" interface of Windows 8 becomes available. Thus, consumers will be able to buy a touch screen ultrabook with a detachable screen, giving them a tablet and notebook functionality [18]. According to technology analysts, the fourth quarter may prove to be a "perfect storm" of refreshed ultrabooks with 3rd-generation Core processors, a new window operation system, and the holiday buying season.

8.2.6 Laptops

A laptop is a small portable computer that can sit on your lap. Sometimes it is referred to as a notebook computer by manufacturers. However, technically notebooks are smaller in size (weight and thickness) compared to laptops [19, 20]. A laptop is a battery or AC-powered computer that usually weighs between 4 and 5 pounds and 3 cm or less in thickness. They usually cost more than desktop PCs because of the difficulties in manufacture, design, and fragility. A laptop can be turned into a regular desktop PC by connecting it to a "docking station [20]." Traditionally, the screen's diameter is used to measure the size of the laptop, e.g., 13- or 15-in. models [21].

A docking station is a hardware device that can be plugged into a laptop to get extra functionality, like full-sized monitors, keyboards, mice, printers, external hard drives (HDDs), and scanners [22]. This accessibility to all these peripherals and more via the docking station through one single plug is very helpful when the laptop has few USB, VGA, or FireWire ports [20, 22]. Laptops use thin-screen technology displays like the active matrix screen or the thin film transistor, which can provide a better angle view and brighter interface than the dual-scan screen or STN. Newer laptop monitors have the Super-TFT screen technology, which has a glossy coating that provides the normal screen with an enhanced contrast and colors that are richer [20, 21]. Nevertheless, laptops use different ways to integrate the capabilities of the regular mouse into the keyboard, e.g., trackball, touch pad, and pointing stick [20]. The touch-sensitive pad is the most common method used as an alternative to the mouse; it can be described as an oblong strip located in the front side of the keyboard. Some of the newer laptops or notebooks have a touch screen functionality enabled on their monitors. Pointing stick on the other hand is a rubber dial that has been integrated into the keyboard [21].

Consequently, there are several styles of keyboards like the "isolation" style, where the keys are cut through a hole individually in the laptop's chassis. This type is the most popular one because it provides more space for fingers to type freely [21]. Other types of keyboards are also available like the ones that have the "hot keys and single-use keys" for extra functionalities. Other keyboards have a backlight (for working or gaming) in dark places [21].

Laptop products can vary, depending on the brands and manufacturers. The vast majority of laptops on the current market are produced by small handful of original design manufacturers (ODM [23]). Some of the best laptops that are available and/or launched in 2012 according to computers.toptenreviews.com are [24]: HP ENVY 17, Sony S Series, Dell XPS 15z, Apple MacBook Air, Acer Aspire Ethos, HP Pavilion dv7t series, MacBook Pro, Toshiba Portege R835-P56X, Lenovo ThinkPad X220, and HP ENVY 14 series.

8.2.7 Laptops Market Share

A prediction from IDC analyst says that PC sales will be lower this year than it has been initially predicted. One of the main reasons that led to this is the declaration of Apple that it is willing to downgrade Mac and PC to be just a device. On the contrary, starting from next year there should be a PC market recover led in specific by laptop sales [25–27]. Despite the fact that PC sales this year is hitting a slow pace, the long-term predictions show more positive figures (see Fig. 8.7):

Twenty percent of laptops compound growth from 2012 to 2015 including 7 % of mature markets and emerging technologies' market [25]. Newer, thinner, and lighter PC designs will provide a boost to the market; the newer laptop PCs will have longer battery life, touch, thinner design, and other improvements, e.g., Intel's sub-$1,000 ultrabooks and Lenovo's ThinkPad X1 [25, 27]. Having these new innovations in mind, optimism grows for this year's PC sales by some companies such as Intel. While PC growth prediction for 2011 is from 7 % to 4 % according to IDC,

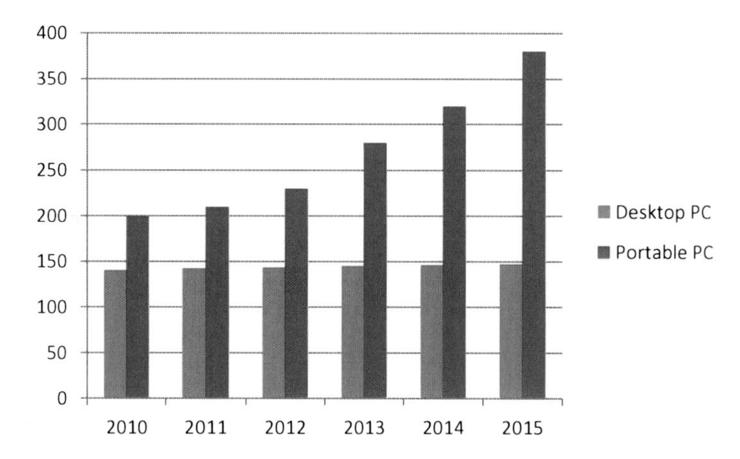

Fig. 8.7 Desktop and PC sales 2010–2015 [25, 26]

Intel is not willing to change its predictions of an 11 %. Intel's prediction is depending on the possibility of tablets "cannibalizing" 32 % of laptop sales [25, 26].

8.2.8 Smartphones

Smartphone users have fallen in love with smartphones as a result of having many great applications that come along with them. The abundance of features on smartphones has rendered the adoption of smartphones increasing rapidly, making this product as the mainstream in different end user segments. The iTunes app store and the Android market have grown considerably over the past few years, which make smartphones account for half of all phones sold [28]. As a result, simple cell phones are dying in the global space as apps are booming leading more users to shift towards smartphones [29].

The worldwide smartphone market grew by 42.5 % in Q1 of 2012 as opposed to 2011—this growth was 1 % higher than IDC's forecast of 41.5 % for the Q1 of 2012 [30]. At the same time, 398.4 million mobile phones were shipped in Q1 of 2012, which represents a decrease of 1.5 % compared to 2011 [30]. The high share of smartphones is an indicator that the majority of end users believe in this product and are adopting it for different uses—phone calls, web browsing, gaming, listening to music, etc. (Fig. 8.8).

The substantial growth of smartphones has led to a dramatic change in the world of personal technology. In the past 30 years, PCs represented the main computing device in many several forms of usage [31]. In fact, PCs were the first machines to be used for computing purposes and giving people access to the cyberspace—via the Internet—to different types of services from their homes and offices. Nowadays, the growth of smartphones and tablets threatens and is diluting the dominance of PCs [31]. In 2011, smartphone sales surpassed PC sales for the first time [32].

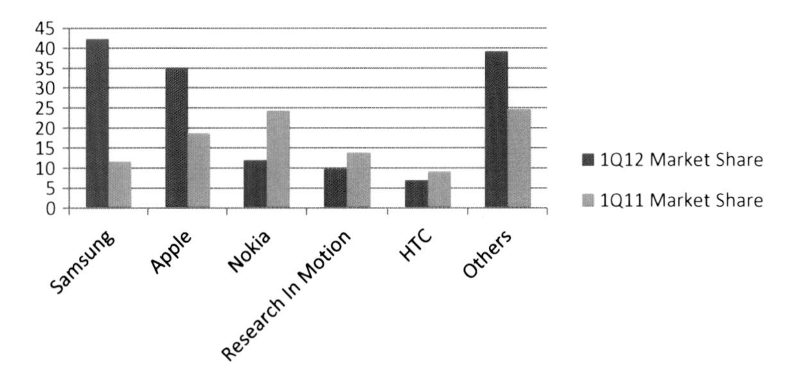

Fig. 8.8 Worldwide market share of smartphones by vendors

According to Alex Cocotas, tablets and smartphones will not displace PCs, yet they will quickly disturb them in the units' sales [32].

The new technology landscape is embodying form that provides consumers access to computing from anywhere on several different types of device. Smartphones are representing the "forefront" of such significant change in the era of technology.

It is surprising how the technology has matured and what can people do on a "tiny" screen. It was reported in the *Economist* that in one of the flights of America's space shuttle, two iPhones were carried using an app that measures parameters such as altitude and orbital location [33]. This is an evidence of how the new world of personal technology reached a degree where the "sky is no longer the limit "of innovation in this industry.

Lots of consumers in each of the five key global markets now have an Internet-capable mobile device than having conventional computers—desktop or laptops [34]. Morgan Stanley said "Within the next 5 years, more users will connect to the Internet over mobile devices than desktop PCs [34]." In one of her other reports she said "Rapid Ramp of Mobile Internet Usage Will be a Boon to Consumers and Some Companies Will Likely Win Big (Potentially Very Big) While Many Will Wonder What Just Happened [35]." Figure 8.9 shows the usage of global mobile vs. desktop Internet.

The aforementioned research indicates that personal computers are turning out to be less of a necessity and more of an old device as a result of the increase in the innovation of the mobile world.

8.2.9 Survey

Based on the macroeconomic forces and the literature review, a survey was developed targeting young professionals to identify customer needs (people who favor gadgets). Seventy responses were received from the participants. Basically the

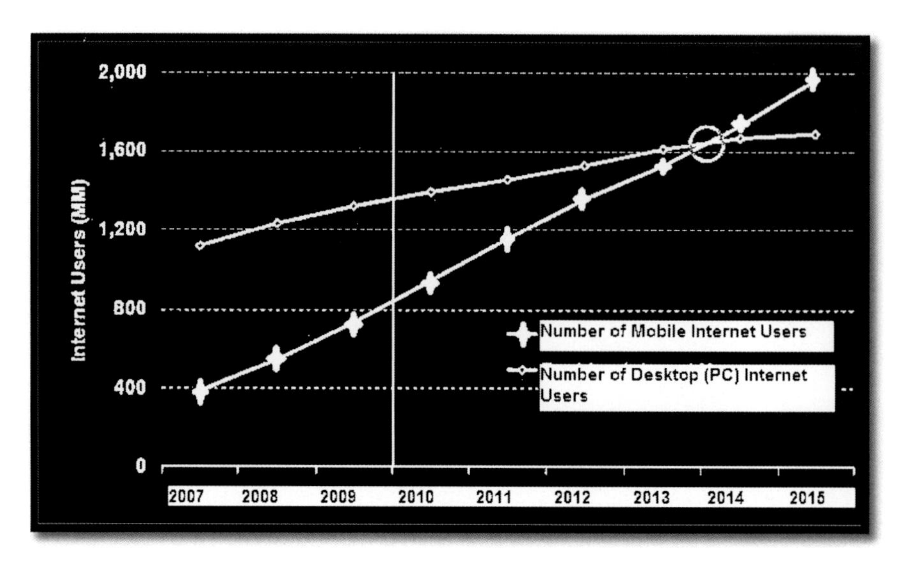

Fig. 8.9 Usage of global mobile vs. desktop Internet projection 2007–2015—publically available [35]

survey consist of two sections, the first section had four questions to identify age, gender, work status, and frequent features used in Portable PC by the participants. The second section was focused on portable device information and it contains five questions. The survey questionnaire and its result are in presented in the Appendix.

8.3 Technology Roadmap Development

In this section of this framework, we construct the technology roadmap by mapping out the drivers, products, technology, and recourses that are needed for the "next generation PCs." We describe each of the elements/layers of the roadmap based on the literature review we carried out. Therefore, we outline the layers of the roadmap as follows.

8.3.1 Drivers

Throughout our literature review, blogs and end users review, macroeconomic forces, and survey, we developed a strong sense of what are the key drivers that seem to be significant towards driving the next PC generations. Our deep assessment and thoughtful analysis enabled us to a have a better insight of the main drivers that seem to be significant for driving the next generation PC. Therefore, we outline and condense our drivers as follows:

8.3.1.1 Social

We believe social drivers play a center role driving the PC of next generations. The validity of such hypothesis is intensified by the elements that social drivers consist of, which are: education, preferences, income levels, and other cultural factors. These elements have a strong effect on the demand in different regions; thereby, they influence business models, dynamic of a firm, and how companies run their operations in a region [10]. For instance, the education level and the income seem to be very critical in terms of how they affect the brand image of computer manufactures. As illustrated in Fig. 8.10, intuitively, households with higher income seem to adopt Apple computers. This reflects the fact that households with higher income can afford and desire Apple computers. Such desire carries with it emotional attachment towards Apple's computers—which encourages end users with high demand to have Apple's product. The high price of Apple's computer along with diffusing its emotional value into the customers enabled Apple to sustain its strategy of premium pricing as opposed to Windows PCs [36], thus, increase its market share of the total laptop and PC market [10].

Additionally, education is also appearing to be a considerable element as a social factor. According to the report conducted by MetaFacts, the majority of household, who hold or own Apple computers, are end users with a higher educational level—people who have completed a 4-year degree course or higher as shown in Fig. 8.11 [37]. Aside from this view, new computers have been developed for deprived users in developed countries like Africa such as what is called ultraportable OLPC (one laptop per child [10].) Such facts embody the evidence of how education levels can influence product demand and preference.

Furthermore, cultural traits are also another social factor that seem to influence the seasonal sales of PCs. For example, towards the holiday seasons in United States, people tend to buy lots of gadgets for family members and their beloved ones as a gift for some occasions/events in the holiday seasons. Therefore, the culture factor seems to stimulate the sales of PCs in some seasons as consequences of end users wanting to buy something precious for their friends, family members, etc. This also explains the reason why customers get lost in the product and want to buy something that they think to be "super cool" for their beloved ones.

8.3.2 Value

The advancement of the global innovation in the PC industry has been driven mainly by economic factors followed by relational drivers that involve interdependencies of activities along with social networks that often influence the choice of suppliers or location [38]. Such statement is supported by the example of the interdependency between the development and manufacturing of notebook PCs and the "guanxi" social networks that link Taiwanese firms and managers [38].

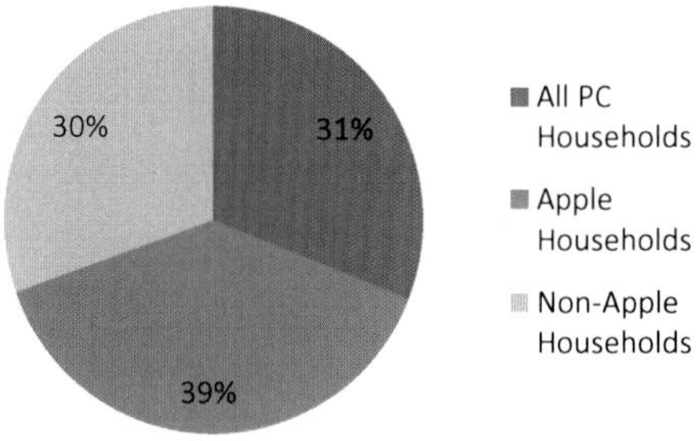

Fig. 8.10 Socioeconomic characteristics of households with income of $60 K or higher

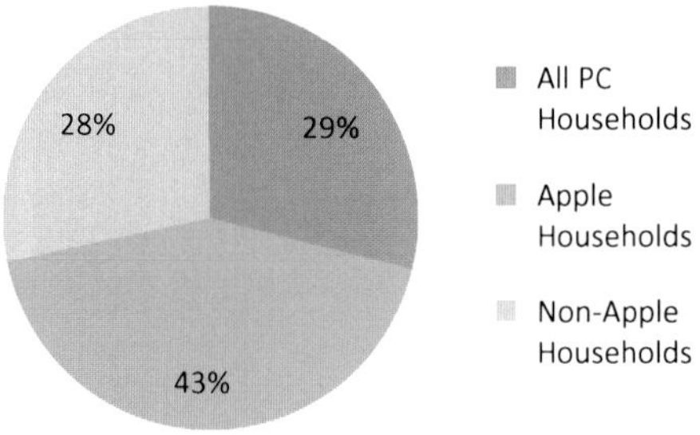

Fig. 8.11 Socioeconomic characteristics of households with 4-years degree or high

Economic factors are classified to be the main drivers of the PC industry due to the fact that manufacturing of PCs has been shifted offshore [38]. This endeavor took place for the sake of decreasing the manufacturing cost as well as reach out for new customers across the global.

In addition, the significant development and innovation in the PC industry by pioneers such as Intel have led to an increase in the power and performance of PC processers with considerable reduction in both power consumption and cost. Such progression has not only led to an increase in the market share of the PC industry globally, but also opened the doors to new ideas of innovations. The miniaturization of technology has boosted the world of PC by going to the nanoscale as described in Moore's law—in the introduction of this report. Going deeper into the nanoscale opened the doors for tons of innovative ideas where the "sky is the limit" of the outcomes. This is evidenced by the high performance of the PCs that are around us in the market place. Moreover, the miniaturization enabled the PCs to be presented in a sleek product with light weight and high energy efficiency. Aside from these values, Intel has recently come up with an innovative idea for security system. The new security system—as will be discussed in the product features section of this report—has added remarkable values to the PCs as security is a big concern for the end users. This system carries with it OS guard to safeguard users' data and personal identities. Furthermore, the latest processors of Intel have improved the efficiency of the PCs in a way that attracts customers who are concerned about the environment. For instance, lots of organizations in the northwest area are working diligently towards developing green buildings. PCs are one of the elements that seem to generate an overall considerable heat load dissipated to the environment which eventually reflects on the atmosphere. However, with Intel's massive

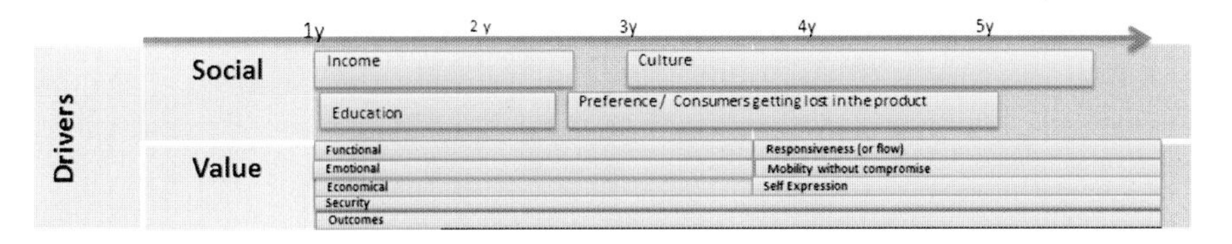

Fig. 8.12 Market drivers—hybrid PC

endeavors, the energy consumption of the new processors has shrunk dramatically, which favors the new PCs to industrial organizations. All these described generic features about the advancement of the technology seem to stimulate PCs in the market as they carry with them combined attractive values to the end users.

According to the description of both drivers—social and value— the drivers are mapped out as depicted in the Fig. 8.12 with respect to time.

8.4 Product

In the TRM timeline we have placed the Products section right below the Drivers. We divided the Products section into four main categories: Tablets, Smartphones, Laptops, and Ultrabooks. Then, based on our research and survey results, we created a list of the best 2012 products/devices for every one of the four categories. For better visual representation and to make the TRM look less crowded, the complete list of all the products has been placed separately from the main TRM timeline; see Fig. 8.13. According to Laptopmag.com [39], the Tablets category contains the following products/devices: Apple iPad 2, Google Nexus 7, ASUS Transformer Pad Infinity TF700, Samsung Galaxy Tab 2 7.1, ASUS Eee Pad Transformer Prime, Lenovo ThinkPad Tablet, Amazon Kindle Fire, Barnes and Noble Nook Tablet, and Samsung Galaxy Tab 2 10.1. These products were available during the time we were conducting this study. The list of the Tablet products has been identified with orange boxes to recognize them from the other product categories.

In the same way, according to *PCWorld* [40], the Smartphones category contains the following products/devices: Samsung Galaxy S III, Sony Xperia Advance, Lava Xolo X900, Nokia Lumia 900, Samsung Galaxy Beam, HTC One Series, Motorola Droid Razr Maxx, HTC EVO 4G LTE, Nokia PureView 808, Samsung Galaxy Exhilarate, Apple iPhone 4S, Apple iPhone 4, and Sony Ericsson Xperia Arc. These products are either about to get launched in the market or were available during the time we were doing this study. The list of the smartphone products has been identified with green boxes to recognize them from the other product categories.

According to Computers.toptenreviews.com [41], the Laptops category contains the following products/devices: HP ENVY 17, Sony S Series, Dell XPS 15z, Apple MacBook Air, Acer Aspire Ethos, HP Pavilion dv7t series, Macbook Pro, Toshiba Portege R835-P56X, Lenovo ThinkPad X220, and HP ENVY 14 series. These

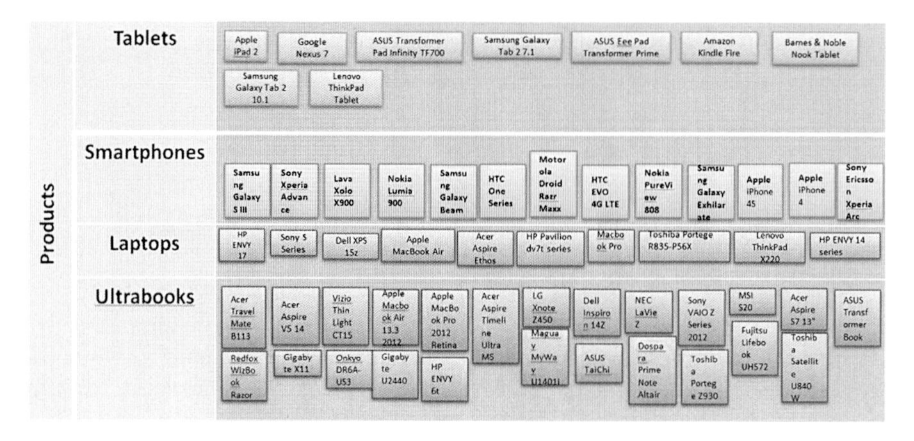

Fig. 8.13 Product—hybrid PC

products were available during the time we were conducting this study. The list of the Laptop products has been identified with purple boxes to recognize them from the other product categories. Following this further, according to Ultrabooknews.com [42], the Ultrabooks category contains the following products/devices: Acer TravelMate B113, Acer Aspire V5 14, Vizio Thin Light CT15, Apple Macbook Air 13.3 2012, Apple MacBook Pro 2012 Retina, Acer Aspire Timeline Ultra M5, LG Xnote Z450, Dell Inspiron 14Z, NEC LaVie Z, Sony VAIO Z Series 2012, Redfox WizBook Razor, Gigabyte X11, Onkyo DR6A-US3, Gigabyte U2440, HP ENVY 6 t, Maguay MyWay U1401i, ASUS TaiChi, Dospara Prime Note Altair, and Toshiba Portege Z930. These devices are either about to get launched in the market or were available during the time we were conducting this study. The list of the Ultrabook products has been identified with light-red boxes to recognize them from the other product categories as depicted in Fig. 8.13.

8.5 Technology

Personal computing has a crucial turn when it comes to portability and size. Business makers are determined to design a device which allows users to compute portably like they do it on their desktops. This led to the laptop; ultrabooks, tablets, and smart phones evolved [43].

To identify the technology needed for the next generation PC, a survey was conducted targeting young professionals to identify the desired product features. The survey template and its results are presented in Appendix A.1 and A.2. The primarily end user devices are integrated units such as laptops, smart phones, tablets, ultrabooks, and hybrid-PCs [44]. Numerous activates can be done using these mobile appliances with easy-use user interface, activities such as communication, socializing, entertainment, learning, and creating, sharing, managing information, etc. In addition, these mobile devices extended the office work by allowing users to work anytime and anywhere they want, and became business tools. Also in the work environment, these appliances provide an intuitive interaction with customers and co-workers which enhances productivity, and enables efficient use of both resources and time. These different platforms made communication and collaboration more mobile with rich media and multitasking [45, 46].

The technologies needed were identified according to the desired features from the survey results. Based on the numerous activities which can be done with mobile PCs, there are combinations of technology which can be integrated in the mobile PC platform. These technologies were categorized on the following categories:

8.5.1 Camera

Cameras are considered standard equipment in mobile PC devices. The numbers of pixels in camera is continuously increasing to enhance the quality of the images. The number of pixels is directly correlated to data traffic from the camera to storage units such as memory and also required processing power, compression, noise reduction, and other picture processing algorithms. The digital zoom and focus function such as smile-shot are important features in mobile devices' cameras. Camcorder is required for video recording which produce extremely large amounts of data to be processed and stored. Hardware acceleration is needed to process the large amount of encoding and decoding for both video and pictures. Face recognitions and motion detectors are considered a technology gap for the next generation PC [47].

8.5.2 Social Networking

Users are becoming content and service providers, and the amount of data is increasing and will be available to all. Users with mobile PCs will be socializing more without the constraint of locations and time. Users will socialize virtually by establishing communities on the social media hubs. The new PC generation should consider the importance and influence of the social media, moreover mobile devices will enhance the interaction of the users with the social media by implementing new technology to increase the level of interactions, technologies such as Geo-tagging and social hub [45].

8.5.3 Connectivity

All connectivity links tend to become faster generation after generation and the speed is accomplished by sophisticated algorithms which require more computation processes. Bluetooth, Wi-Fi, WiMAX, Wireless USB, etc., are connectivity methods that use unlicensed frequency bands. The speed of these radio links will grow, and for the local area connections WLAN will evolve from the current 802.11a/b/g to the n-version which will provide high transfer rate. In addition, antennas with high gain will be implemented to enhance the mobile device connectivity such as the Two Omni Antennas. The Two Omni Antennas was identified as a technology gap for the next PC generation [48, 49].

8.5.4 Display

The displays and graphics will grow in size and in the number of pixels. The quality required rises with users watching different multimedia video streaming and play games from their mobile devices screens. Videos and video games require fast response time from the display and create a lot of data traffic to process. With faster operating systems, display resolution will be improved and a variety of different displays will be installed in the mobile PC appliances, technologies such as LED IPS (Retina), LED-Backlit LCD, TFT Display Tech, and 3D gaming display. Graphic cards technology such as Nvidia Geforce, Intel HD Graphic, Highly flexible touch sensors [50], and Readeon HD will be used to accelerate graphics processing.

Interactive touch screens could be installed in these devices, but capacitive touch screens and multi-touch touchpad with vapor inscrutable screen features are considered as technology gaps. Another way for better and especially bigger displays is to use external display technologies such as built-in interactive projectors and the use of projected laser keyboard which is a technology gap need to be fulfilled.

8.5.4.1 Physical Properties and User Interfaces

Many types of human input are developed. A type aid that is used for predicting writing and voice recognition is already in use. In addition, magnetic keyboard technology is going to be used for faster response in typing. Also, hand writing recognition is another input technology gap that needs to develop for PCs. Other demonstrated ways for user input are gestures and moving/turning the device. Moreover, Magnesium case is being used to provide devices with lighter weight and more durability. Vending on both screen sides and energy star qualifications are technology gaps.

8.5.5 Biometric

Biometric implies the authentication and identification of humans by their characteristics such as face recognition, fingerprint, voice recognition, DNA, and signature. Mobile PC devices are used to carry and access personal and confidential information, therefore biometric authentication technology has become an important part of security due to the increase in unauthorized access and frauds. Using biometric technology will provide an accurate authentication and narrow down the margin of duplicity or error. Iris recognition technology is a gap needed to be accomplished in the next generation PC [51].

8.5.6 Processors

With no doubt, computing has made a great growth in the recent years. But as long as it has enhanced in the last decades, in the coming decades, the migration and emergence of new workload and the heavy mainstream computing will put large demands on future computing platforms. The demands for much higher performance, for lower power, and for enormous expanded functionality are really required for the next generation PC's processors. It is mandatory for the future to satisfy not only computation, but interface and infrastructure requirements as well. The microprocessor has the most significant transformation since its creation in order to achieve the prediction of Moore's law. Increasing the number of transistor is vital with accommodating the basic foundation such as process technology, architecture, and software. To achieve the future desired microprocessor, the following technologies need to be reached: Chip Level Multiprocessing CLM, Special Purpose Hardware, Large Memory Subsystem, Virtualization, Microkernel, Silicon and Process Technology, and Compatibility and Ecosystem Enabling. Also, IV-Bridge technology has started to be implemented in new platforms. Fabrication technology processes of 10, 7, 5 nm are considered a gap that needs to be archived for processors technology [52, 53].

8.5.7 Sounds

Sound process requirement are evolving with different kinds of contents. Music content require small amount of processing, but for video content more amount of computing processing is required. Movie standards like Dolby Digital and DTS have been installed in mobile PC devices, moreover 3D virtual sound technology was implemented too.

After evaluating the exciting technology for the next generation PC, we identified technology gap needed to acquire the desired features. The chart above (Fig. 8.14) shows the technology needed, and the time period for each technology to be achieved according to Survey results and the literature review. The technology was classified in different categories.

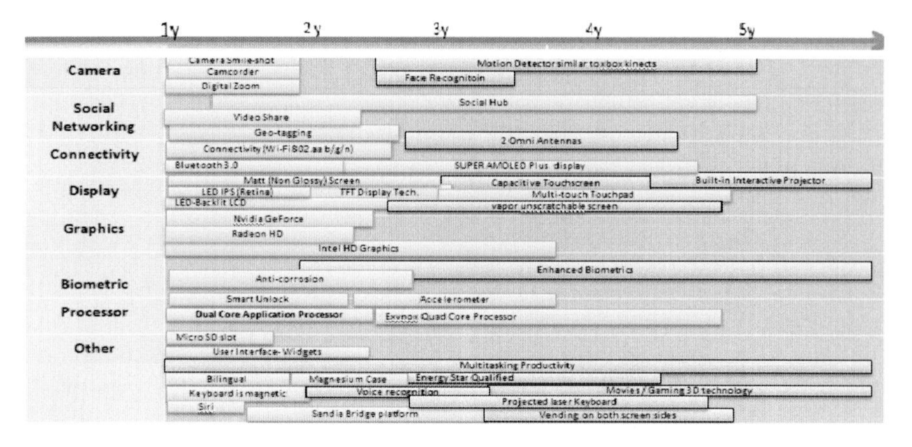

Fig. 8.14 Technology—hybrid PC

8.6 Resources

R&D is a crucial area for any product development and planning. We must do effective technology planning particularly in R&D to identify and develop the technologies required to make a product. Once identified, technology enhancements or new technologies may be developed internally or collaboratively with external partners. Most of the big high-tech companies have R&D centers where collaboration has been done between universities and partnerships. As far as PC is the main concern in this framework, R&D is categorized into three categories: R&D manufacture, R&D materials and R&D engineering/scientist capabilities. Having a well-structured R&D management with these three critical elements of R&D, any hypothetical PC manufacture can boost the outcomes of its respective R&D in both radical innovation and incremental innovation. These approaches can be modeled with respect to firms' business strategies and end users' expectations. For example, IBM since the 1990s formed a "radical collaboration" model and formed R&D alliances with several of its competitors in order to deal with the high cost of R&D and manufacturing [54]. In a similar approach, our "Next generation of PCs-hybrid product" will need similar R&D approach where then the product would be handed to the OEMs for manufacturing. For example, for Intel's Ultrabook, a big portion of R&D spending has been allocated to their development, together with Intel's massive investments to establish the market segment. Intel set up a $300 million fund to help manufacturers ramp up the component supply chain and devise new ways to keep costs down [55].

The advancement of the display technology has fascinated researchers for many years. Many companies are working diligently to incorporate the flexible display technology to Smartphones in this era—like Samsung, Nokia, and LG. Thus, it is certain that the "heat" of the market will force the pioneers of the PC industry to

Fig. 8.15 Shows roll able PC

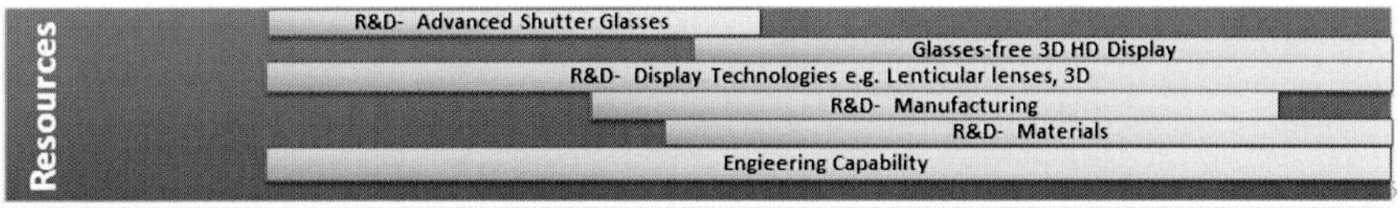

Resources
R&D- Advanced Shutter Glasses
Glasses-free 3D HD Display
R&D- Display Technologies e.g. Lenticular lenses, 3D
R&D- Manufacturing
R&D- Materials
Engieering Capability

Fig. 8.16 R&D layer—hybrid PC

incorporate the flexible technology on PCs. Such features will lead to have a super cool product—namely rollable PCs as depicted in Fig. 8.15.

Figure 8.16 depicts the R&D actions needed to transform next generation PCs.

8.7 Master TRM and Discussing the Linking

8.7.1 Coding of TRM Items

Every item within the master TRM has been identified with a significant code, for instance, in the Drivers section, the first Social item 'Income' now is called: S1 and the second Social driver now is called: S2 and so on.

Here's a list of the used TRM item codes:

- Drivers
  - Social
    - S1: Income
    - S2: Education
    - S3: Culture
    - S4: Preference/Consumers getting lost in the product

- Value
    - V1: Functional
    - V2: Emotional
    - V3: Economical
    - V4: Security
    - V5: Outcomes
    - V6: Responsiveness (or flow)
    - V7: Mobility without compromise
    - V8: Self-Expression
- Products
    - P1: Tablets
    - P2: Smartphones
    - P3: Laptops/PC
    - P4: Ultrabooks
- Technologies
    - Camera
        - Ca1: Camera Smile-shot
        - Ca2: Camcorder
        - Ca3: Digital Zoom
        - Ca4: Motion Detector similar to MS Xbox Kinect
        - Ca5: Face Recognition
    - Social Networking
        - SN1: Social Hub
        - SN2: Video Share
        - SN3: Geo-tagging
    - Connectivity
        - Co1: Connectivity (Wi-Fi 802.11 aa/b/g/n)
        - Co2: 2 Omni Antenna
        - Co3: Bluetooth 3.0
    - Display
        - Ds1: Super AMOLED Plus display
        - Ds2: Matt (Non Glossy) screen
        - Ds3: LED IPS (Retina)
        - Ds4: LED-Backlit LCD
        - Ds5: TFT Display Technology
        - Ds6: Capacitive Touchscreen
        - Ds7: Multi-touch pad
        - Ds8: Vapor unscratchable screen
        - Ds9: Built-in Interactive Projector

- Graphics
  - Gr1: Nvidia GeForce
  - Gr2: Radeon HD
  - Gr3: Intel HD Graphics
- Biometric
  - Bi1: Enhanced Biometrics
  - Bi2: Face Identification
  - Bi3: Smart Unlock
- Processor
  - Pr1: Accelerometer
  - Pr2: Dual Core Application Processor
  - Pr3: Exynox Quad Core Processor
- Other
  - O1: Micro SD slot
  - O2: User Interface—Widgets
  - O3: Multitasking Productivity
  - O4: Bilingual
  - O5: Magnesium Case
  - O6: Energy Star Qualified
  - O7: Keyboard is Magnetic
  - O8: Voice Recognition
  - O9: Movies/Gaming 3D technology
  - O10: Siri
  - O11: Projected Laser Keyboard
  - O12: Sandia Bridge Platform
  - O13: Vending on both screen sides

- Recourses
  - R1: R&D—Advanced Shutter Glasses
  - R2: Glasses-free 3D HD Displays
  - R3: R&D—Display Technologies, e.g., Lenticular Lens, 3D
  - R4: R&D—Manufacturing
  - R5: R&D—Materials
  - R6: Engineering Capability

8.7.2 TRM Linking

Following this further, we established linking the items starting from the Resources section all the way up to the Drivers (Fig. 8.17). The linking was based on the dependency of every item on the other items. Most of the arrows start from an item that is located underneath the dependent one, e.g., the product items receive the

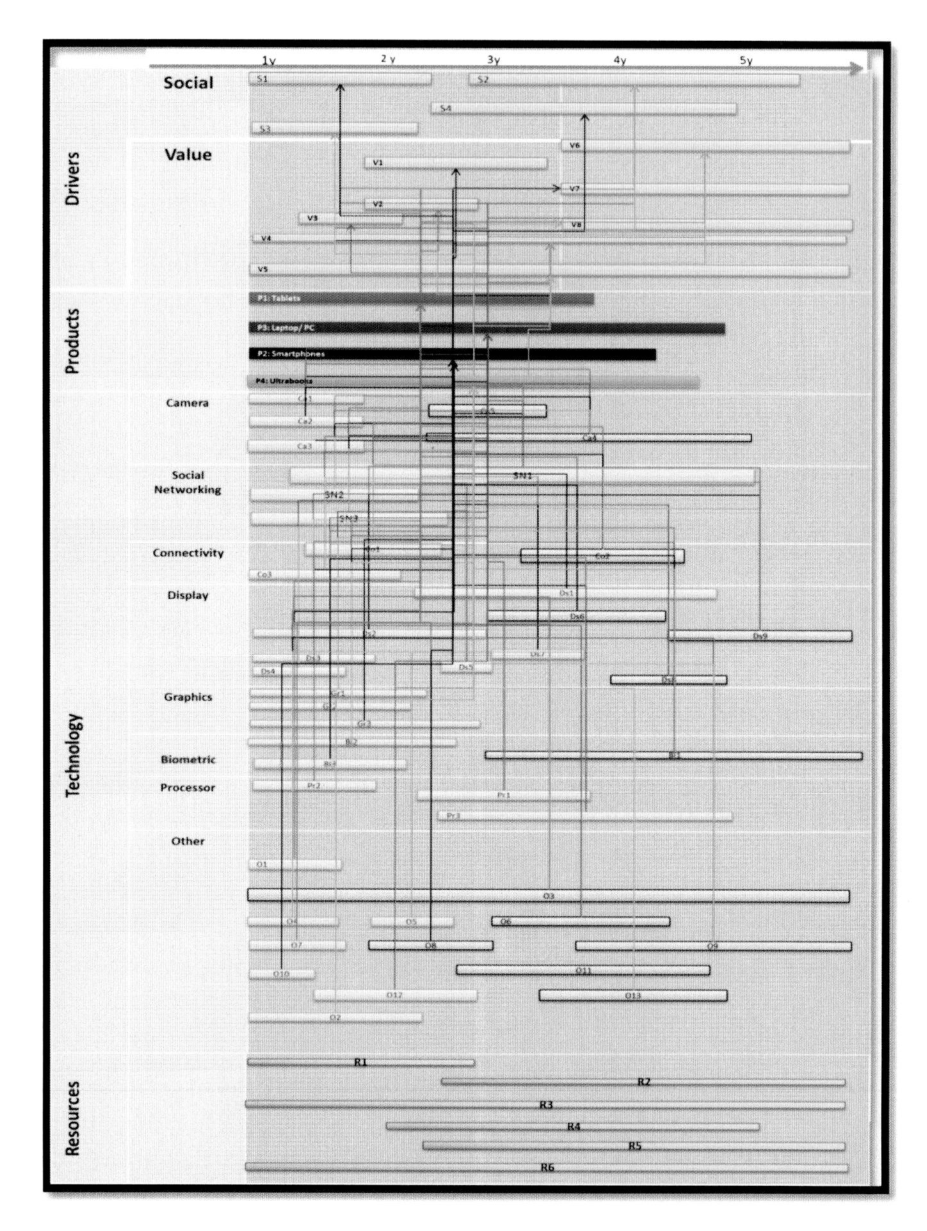

Fig. 8.17 Master roadmap—hybrid PC

arrows from the technologies that are located below and are linked to the Drivers that are located above. To identify the difference between every category and the relevance they have to every product, we made four significant colored arrows for every product: P1: Tablets' arrows are in blue color, P2: Smartphones' arrows are in black color, P3: Laptops/PCs' arrows are in red color, and P4: Ultrabooks arrows are in light-green. The purpose of this version of the TRM is to prepare for the final

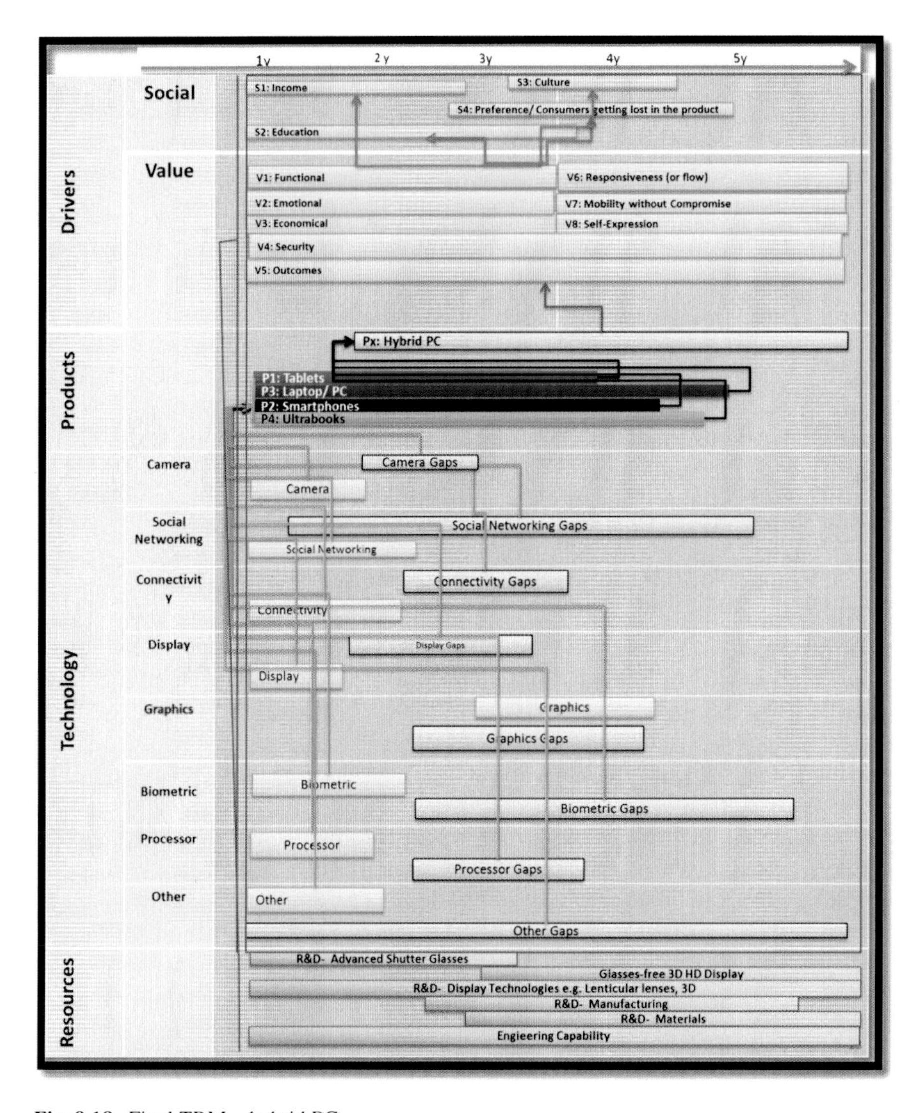

Fig. 8.18 Final TRM—hybrid PC

Master version that contains hybrid-PC as our proposed product. Notice the connection and the dependency between every item in their section to the above and below sections within a 5-year timeline.

Networking, Display, Graphics, Biometric, Processor and others have been combined together. For better visual representation, they have been linked to the section above (Products). In the Products section, all the products Laptops/PCs, Tablets, Smartphones, and Ultrabooks have been combined as one entity. This new Products' entity filters the needed features and overcome the gaps via the new product/device "hybrid-PC" which receives the other product outputs to satisfy the Drivers (see Fig. 8.18).

8.8 Conclusion

Technology roadmap is a form of technology planning; better technology planning can help companies better position themselves and their products to deal with the increasingly competitive environment. The main benefit of technology roadmapping is to provide information that makes better technology investment by identifying the critical technologies and the technology gaps that need to be bridged, and identify ways to leverage R&D to fulfill technology gaps. In this study, TRM is used to identify the next PC generation platform. This study started by applying macroeconomics forces at a macro scale level to provide a clear image of the impacts of tablets, ultrabooks, laptops, and smartphones on PCs. Based on macroeconomics forces, an intensive literature review was done followed by a survey to understand the customers' needs and the trend of the PC market. From the survey results and the literature review a technology roadmap was constructed for the next generation PC, by identifying drivers, identifying the products to meet the drivers, identifying of technologies to support the products, and assigning resources to accomplish the technologies. All the previous layers were identified with their time line. The following are the major finding of this study:

- Although still in its relative infancy, the tablet market and associated ecosystem are developing quickly as OEMs are utilizing knowledge and relationships from previous mobile computing efforts.
- Tablet PCs and the mobile computing phenomena are threatening to cause a shift in industry leadership and dynamics in both the technology and telecom sectors.
- The notebook market is most threatened by the introduction of tablet PCs and smartphones.
- Demand for tablets is high in both the consumer and enterprise markets. Mobility, in combination with real-time access to content and services, are the major factors driving adoption.
- It is hard to imagine tablet PCs replacing ultrabooks or other mobile computing devices, but these platforms segments do seem to be moving toward each other creating the hybrid PC. The hybrid PC will contain the features of tablet, ultrabook, laptop, and smart phone in one single platform.

8.9 Future Research

As stated throughout this framework, the team conducted the study at the macro level. However, using technology roadmapping for R&D planning proposed by Sungjoo Lee and et al. as an extension of this work, any PC manufacture proponent can carry out this technology effectively [56]. The uniqueness of this tool will enable PC manufactures to have a systematic approach by mapping out explicit plans for the revealed technology gaps generated from this framework. Moreover, the tool's strength can cover both sector-level planning process as well a PC manufacture-level process. Hence, providing clear, feasible, and reliable plans for the required R&D activities to bridge the gaps—highlighted by this framework. Furthermore, the tool allows a PC manufacturer to build both macro TRM and micro TRM. Micro TRM can be used to decompose the gaps—proposed by this framework—to their main components. Such approach is very robust and provides a reliable pipeline carrying all the desired activities from the discovery phase of the gap all the way through making tangible products or features to the end users. Astonishingly, the TRM for R&D proposed by Sungjoo has many management tools embedded into as follows [56]:

- TRM initiation
- Subject selection
  - Requirements analysis module
  - Environment analysis module
  - Technology valuation module
- Technology needs assessment
  - Decomposition analysis module
  - Portfolio analysis module
  - Priority analysis module
- Technology development plan
  - Performance measure module
  - Technology evaluation module
  - Risk assessment module
- TRM implementation
- Follow-up activities

Each of the management tool embedded in the pipelines allows technology roadmappers to model each stage efficiently with all the possible criteria and releases its outputs to the subsequent stage. This systematic approach will carry through all of the R&D actions needed for PC manufacture by assessing the technology and operate productively within the constrained resources the PC manufacture proponent has.

Appendix

Technology Roadmapping Survey

The aim of this framework is to establish an insight for a marketing plan for next generation PC. The study is being conducted as a part of technology roadmap in the field of engineering and technology management.

Section 1: Personal Information

i. Which age group do you belong to?

☐ 19 and under ☐ 20-29 ☐ 30-39 ☐ 40-49
☐ 50-59 ☐ 60+

ii. What is your Gender?

☐ Male ☐ Female

iii. Are you currently working?

☐ Yes ☐ No

iv. How often are these features used on computer?

	Never	Rarely	Sometimes	Often	Always
Email	•	•	•	•	•
Web browsing	•	•	•	•	•
Social networks	•	•	•	•	•
Video games	•	•	•	•	•
Listening to music	•	•	•	•	•
Watch movies	•	•	•	•	•
School/work related Software	•	•	•	•	•

Section 2: Portable (laptop/tablet/ultrabook) device information

v. Do you currently own a portable computer (Tablet/Laptop)?

☐ Yes ☐ No

vi. What is the make of your current portable computer(s)? (Mark all that apply)

☐ Apple ☐ Toshiba ☐ Dell
☐ COMPAQ ☐ SONY ☐ LG
☐ MOTORALA ☐ SAMSUNG

vii. What is the most common reason(s) for changing your portable computer? (Mark all that apply)

☐ Software/hardware issues ☐ damaged screen
☐ Damage laptop/tablet ☐ Lost/stolen
☐ Lack of features ☐ never change laptop/tablet
☐ Other

viii. What is the ranking of the following features of your current laptop/tablet?

	Worst	Bad	Average	Good	Best
Durability	•	•	•	•	•
Software	•	•	•	•	•
Battery life	•	•	•	•	•
Laptop/tablet size	•	•	•	•	•
Weight	•	•	•	•	•
Touch screen	•	•	•	•	•
Energy efficiency	•	•	•	•	•
Polished look	•	•	•	•	•

ix. When you buy a laptop/tablet, how important are the following feature(s)?

	Least important	Less important	Average	More important	Most important	N/A
Brand	•	•	•	•	•	•
Price	•	•	•	•	•	•
Quality	•	•	•	•	•	•
Uniqueness	•	•	•	•	•	•
Weight	•	•	•	•	•	•
Sleekness	•	•	•	•	•	•
Size	•	•	•	•	•	•
Sound quality	•	•	•	•	•	•
Screen size	•	•	•	•	•	•
Processor speed	•	•	•	•	•	•
Hard drive capacity	•	•	•	•	•	•
Anti-theft protection	•	•	•	•	•	•
Durability	•	•	•	•	•	•
Graphics	•	•	•	•	•	•
Battery efficiency	•	•	•	•	•	•

Survey Results

Feature usage	
Email	61 %
Web browsing	54 %
Social networks	45 %
Video games	9 %
Listening to music	32 %
Watch movies	8 %
School/work related software	27 %

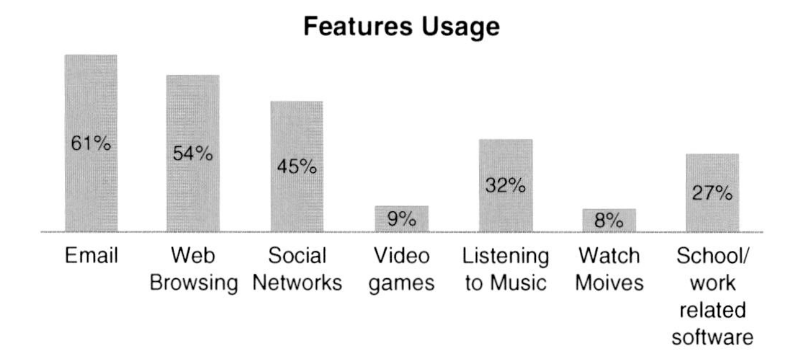

Customer needs (customer value)	
Durability	30
Software	30
Laptop/tablet size	20
Weight	24
Touch screen	14
Energy efficiency	16
Polished look	37

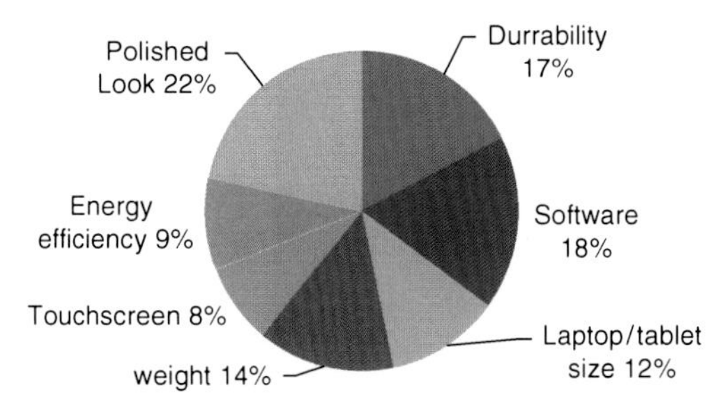

Importance of product features	
Brand	25 %
Price	27 %
Quality	51 %
Uniqueness	16 %
Weight	16 %
Sleekness	12 %
Size	19 %
Sound quality	14 %
Screen size	19 %
Processor speed	38 %

(continued)

(continued)

Importance of product features	
Hard drive capacity	24 %
Anti-theft protection	22 %
Durability	30 %
Graphics	32 %
Battery efficiency	40 %

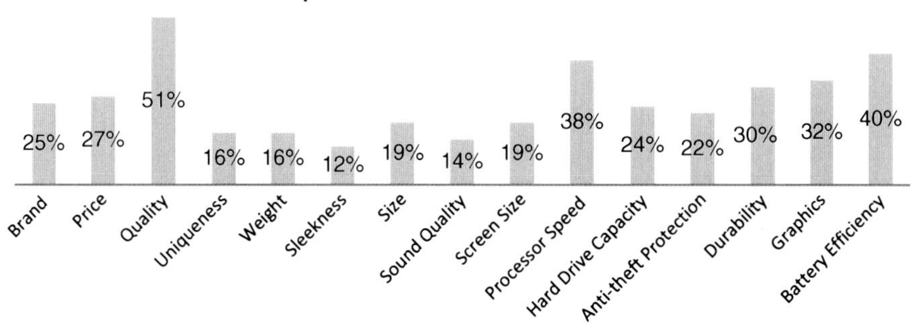

References

1. The History of the PC (2012) http://www.historyofthepc.com. Accessed 30 July 2012
2. McDonald CF (2011) Building the information society: a history of computing as a mass medium, Princeton University, Princeton, 345 pages; 3480114
3. Joel Birnbaum (1999) Innovation observatories: technology roadmapping. In: HP lecture at APS Centennial, Atlanta
4. Gartner Newsroom (Apr 11, 2012) Gartner says worldwide PC shipments grew 1.9 percent in first quarter of 2012. http://www.gartner.com/it/page.jsp?id=1981717. Accessed 20 July 2012
5. Phaal R, Farrukh CJP, Probert DR (2004) Technology roadmapping—a planning framework for evolution and revolution. Technol Forecast Soc Change 71(1):5–26
6. Garcia ML, Bray OH (1997) Fundamentals of technology roadmapping. Sandia National Laboratories, Albuquerque
7. Alexander P, Tech Crunch (Jan 1, 2010) Creating a technology road map. http://www.entrepreneur.com/article/83000. Accessed 11 Aug 2012
8. Petrick IJ, Echols AE (2004) Technology roadmapping in review: a tool for making sustainable new product development decisions. Technol Forecast Soc Chang 71(1–2):81–100
9. Gordon BR (2009) A dynamic model of consumer replacement cycles in the PC processor industry. J Market Sci 28(5):846–867
10. Aditya Shah, Abhinav Dalal (Apr 13, 2009) The global laptop industry. http://srl.gatech.edu/Members/ashah/laptop_industry_analysis_aditya_abhinav.pdf. Accessed 20 July 2012
11. Tolfree D, Smith A (2009) Roadmapping emergent technologies. Troubador, Leicester
12. Garcia ML, Bray OH (1997) Fundamentals of technology roadmapping SAND97-0665. Sandia National Laboratories, Albuquerque
13. Porter M (1980) Competitive strategy: techniques for analyzing industries and competitors. The Free Press, New York

14. IDC (July 20, 2012) Strong apple shipments drive robust tablet market growth in second quarter, according to IDC. http://www.idc.com/getdoc.jsp?containerId=prUS23632512. Accessed 24 July 2012
15. Samanth Murphy (Jul 3, 2012) Tablets surpass labtop in 2016. Internet.http://mashable.com/2012/07/03/tablets-to-surpass-tablet-growth/. Accessed 10 Aug 2012
16. Phillip Davis, Intel Corporation (2012) Windows 8 release date revealed. employeecontent.intel.com. Accessed 20 July 2012
17. Intel (2012) The story behind the Ultrabook. employeecontent.intel.com. Accessed 5 July 2012
18. Philip Davis (2012) Gushing review for Ultrabook. employeecontent.intel.com. Accessed 6 July 2012
19. Webopedia. What is a laptop computer? http://www.webopedia.com/TERM/L/laptop_computer.html. Accessed 01 Aug 2012
20. Rouse M, Search Mobile Computing (2012) Laptop computer. http://searchmobilecomputing.techtarget.com/definition/laptop-computer,Jul. Accessed 01 Aug 2012
21. Parsons J, What Laptop (Feb 11, 2011) Laptops explained: everything you need to know. http://whatlaptop.techradar.com/2011/11/what-is-a-laptop-2/. Accessed 01 Aug 2012
22. Wise Geek. What is a docking station? http://www.wisegeek.com/what-is-a-docking-station.htm. Accessed 1 Aug 2012
23. Canon Pro1, Whirlpool (Feb 8, 2007) Notebook OEM/ODM. http://forums.whirlpool.net.au/archive/679605. Accessed 1 Aug 2012
24. Top Ten Reviews (Aug 01, 2012) 2012 best laptop computer reviews and comparisons. http://computers.toptenreviews.com/laptops/. Accessed 01 Aug 2012
25. Pinola M, PCWorld (Jun 07, 2011) PC sales expected to rebound in 2012. http://www.pcworld.com/article/229607/pc_sales_expected_to_rebound_in_2012.html. Accessed 04 Aug 2012
26. Davies L, Software.Intel (Feb 28, 2012) Transforming the laptop gaming experience@GDC 2012. http://software.intel.com/en-us/blogs/2012/02/28/transforming-the-laptop-gaming-experiencegdc-2012/. Accessed 04 Aug 2012
27. Schonfeld E, Tech Crunch (Jun 17, 2012) Forrester projects tablets will outsell netbooks By 2012, desktops By 2013. http://techcrunch.com/2010/06/17/forrester-tablets-outsell-netbooks/.Accessed 04 Aug 2012
28. MacTrast (2012) The explosive growth of smartphones and the app economy (Infographic). http://www.mactrast.com/2012/03/the-explosive-growth-of-smartphones-and-the-app-economy-infographic/. Accessed 14 July 2012
29. Martin Michalik (Feb 19, 2012) Booming growth of smartphones and apps. http://www.viralblog.com/mobile-and-apps/booming-growth-of-smartphones-and-apps/. Accessed 14 July 2012
30. IDC (May 01, 2012) Worldwide smartphone market continues to soar, carrying Samsung into the top position in total mobile phone and smartphone shipments. http://www.idc.com/getdoc.jsp?containerId=prUS23455612. Accessed 14 July 2012
31. The economist (Oct 8, 2011) Beyond the PC: mobile digital gadgets are overshadowing the personal computer, says Martin Giles. Their impact will be far-reaching. http://www.economist.com/node/21531109. Accessed 14 July 2012
32. Alex Cocotas (Feb 14, 2012) Sales will reach nearly 500 million units a year by 2015. http://articles.businessinsider.com/2012-02-14/research/31057816_1_tablets-smartphones-pc-sales. Accessed 14 July 2012
33. The economist (Oct 8, 2011) Smart thinking is needed about smart gadgets' influence. http://www.economist.com/node/21531113. Accessed 15 July 2012
34. Sharp Innovation, inc. (Mar2012) Smart phones vs. the personal computer. http://www.sharpinnovations.com/blog/2012/03/. Accessed 20 July 2012
35. GIGAOM (Apr 12, 2010) Mary meeker: mobile internet will soon overtake fixed internet. http://gigaom.com/2010/04/12/mary-meeker-mobile-internet-will-soon-overtake-fixed-internet/. Accessed 21 July 2012
36. Mel Martin (Apr 02, 2009) Apple market share continues to climb, Windows drops. http://www.tuaw.com/2009/02/02/apple-market-share-continues-to-climb-windows-drops/. Accessed 24 July 2012

37. METAFACTS (Apr 5, 2009) Just how "different" and elite are Apple customers – socioeconomically, behaviorally, and attitudinally? http://technologyuser.com/2009/04/05/just-how-different-and-elite-are-apple-customers-socioeconomically-behaviorally-and-attitudinally/. Accessed 24 July 2012
38. Jason Dedrick, Kenneth L. Karemer (May 1, 2008) Globalization of innovation: the personal computing industry. http://web.mit.edu/is08/pdf/Globalization%20of%20Innovation%20PC.PDF. Accessed 28 July 2012
39. Laptopmag (Aug 11, 2012) Top 10 tablets available right now. http://blog.laptopmag.com/top-10-tablets-now?slide=10. Accessed 11 Aug 2012
40. Cassavoy L, PCWorld (Jun 5, 2012) Smartphones 2012: the best are yet to come. http://www.pcworld.com/article/256908/smartphones_2012_the_best_are_yet_to_come.html. Accessed 1 July 2012
41. Top Ten Reviews (July 01, 2012) 2012 best laptop computer reviews and comparisons. http://computers.toptenreviews.com/laptops/. Accessed 01 July 2012
42. Ultrabook News (2011) Ultrabook comparison. http://ultrabooknews.com/product-databank/. Accessed 01 July 2012
43. Lee Chyen Yee, Clare Jim (June 8, 2012) Hybrid "ultrabooks" blur line between tablets, laptops. http://www.reuters.com/article. Accessed 2 Aug 2012
44. Mihovska A, Fanny P, Karetsos G, Kyriazakos S, Van Muijen R, Guarneri R, Pereira JM (2007) Towards the wireless 2010 vision: a technology roadmap. Wireless Personal Commun 42:303–336. doi:10.1007/s11277-006-
45. Alahuhta P, Jarvansu M, Pentikanem H (Nov 2004) Roadmap for network technology and services. http://nordicictfore.vtt.fi/materiaali/roadmap_network_technologies.pdf. Accessed 10 Aug 2012
46. Iannucci (2005) Connected lifestyle: the next big wave, Presentation at Infotech day, Oulu, 11 Nov 2005
47. Greg Scoblete (July 27, 2012) 2012 camcorder tech trends. http://camcorders.about.com. Accessed 3 Aug 2012
48. Roivainen Etelapera, Soinien Hyysalo (2007) Smart phone technology roadmap, 10 Jan 2007
49. Danny Stiebe (Jul 16, 2012) Wireless alphabet soup explained. http://www.makeuseof.com/tag/wireless-alphabet-soup-explained-4g-3g-lte makeuseof-explains/. Accessed 6 Aug 2012
50. Ed Oswald (Apr 6, 2012) Atmel's flexible touch sensors will revolutionize mobile device design. http://www.extremetech.com/electronics/125325-atmels-flexible-touch-sensors-a-revolution-in-device-design. Accessed 8 Aug 2012
51. marketsandmarkets.com (June 2012) Next generation biometric technologies market – global forecast & analysis (2012–2017). http://www.marketsandmarkets.com/Market-Reports/next-generation-biometric-technologies-market-697.html. Accessed 8 Aug 2012
52. Gareth Halfacree (May 14, 2012) Intel details 10nm, 7nm, 5nm process roadmap. http://www.bittech.net/news/hardware/2012/05/14/intel-process-roadmap/1. Accessed 8 Aug 2012
53. Ramanathan RM, Thomas V, Intel Corporation (2006) Platform 2015: Intel® processor and platform evolution for the next decade. White paper by Intel
54. The Story Behind the Ultrabook (2012) employeecontent.intel.com. Accessed 5 July 2012
55. King A, Pisano G, Shih W (2008) Radical collaboration: IBM microelectronics joint development alliances. Harvard Business School, Boston
56. Lee S, Kang S, Park YS, Park Y (2007) Technology roadmapping for R&D planning: the case of the Korean parts and materials industry. Technovation 27(8):433–445

Chapter 9
Technology Road Map for Tesla Motors Sedan EV

Abrahim Abdulsater, Aparna Balasubramanian, Bing Wang, Farshad Madani, Mohammad Mansour, and Rajasree Talla

Abstract In order for the USA, as well as other nations, to decrease their dependency and reliance on imported fossil fuel, to control and reduce the largest source of their carbon emission, and to secure their national transportation system, a faster transition from the internal combustion engine to the electric vehicle has to be promoted. The public and private sectors will have to work hand in hand to ensure reaching such a national goal.

This chapter lays out a technology road map for a private company "Tesla Motors," proposing a balanced mixed basket of technology push and market pull strategy in order to get closer and closer to the desired goal. Fossil fuel does not have to run out in order for the transition to take place. After all, the reason why humanity came out of the Stone Age was not due to the lack of stones; there's still plenty out there. Tools like STEEP analysis, gap analysis, and QFD are used to come up with the technology road map.

9.1 Introduction

The ongoing increase in the fossil fuels' consumption, the uncontrollable rise in the price of crude oil, the natural and logical increase for energy demand due to global population growth which is expected to reach ten billion by 2050 [1], and the

A. Abdulsater (✉) • M. Mansour
Intel Corporation, Hillsboro, OR, USA
e-mail: abrahimsater@hotmail.com

A. Balasubramanian
FEI Company, Hillsboro, OR, USA

B. Wang • F. Madani
Portland State University, Portland, OR, USA

R. Talla
GE Healthcare, Portland, OR, USA

T.U. Daim et al. (eds.), *Planning and Roadmapping Technological Innovations: Cases and Tools*, Innovation, Technology, and Knowledge Management,
DOI 10.1007/978-3-319-02973-3_9, © Springer International Publishing Switzerland 2014

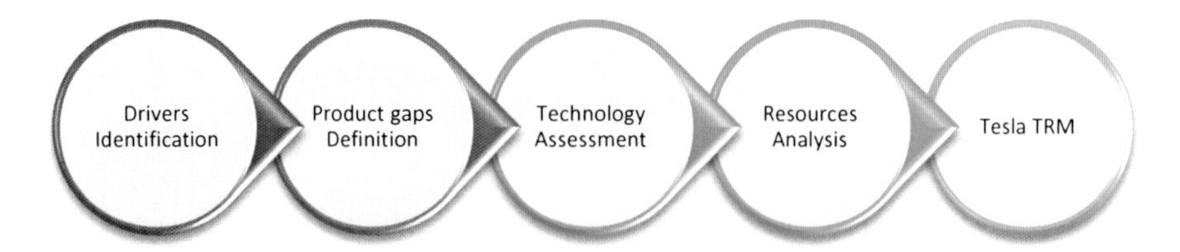

Fig. 9.1 Flow of technology road mapping (TRM) analysis [2]

general environmental awareness, added to the growing importance of sustainability and preserving natural resources and ecosystems in recent years, have been major factors in product innovation. Efficiency has also been pursued by all energy-related industries and been promoted for its immediate and long-term positive financial benefits. For the auto industry leading manufacturers, those were key business drivers to develop and produce vehicles that rely less on fossil fuel. Electric vehicles, whether being pure electric or hybrid (EV/HEVs), that once were a dream are now becoming a reality and commercially available and have been gaining acceptance among the mainstream consumers. Toyota, Honda, Ford, Nissan, BMW, and Audi are among the leading automobile manufacturers that introduced hybrid and electric vehicle models. Tesla Motors decided to differentiate itself by solely manufacturing electric vehicles that will stand out in the market and survive the competition with the major well-established brands in the market.

This chapter will focus on Tesla Motors, an American electric vehicle (EV) company. As it will be defined in a later section, EV technology has a wide range of products; in this chapter, a technology road map for an affordable Tesla Sedan is the goal to be achieved. We will analyze the market to identify its drivers, define the market needs to fulfill the gaps with new products, suggest the technological capabilities needed to achieve the realization of the product gaps, and finally identify the necessary resources and link them to the suggested needed technologies. Figure 9.1 shows the flow to the final outcome, a Tesla technology road map that will allow the newly established electric auto manufacturer to stand ground and gain more market share.

9.1.1 *The Electric Vehicle*

9.1.1.1 Definition and History

An electric vehicle (EV), as defined by the encyclopedia Britannica, is a motor vehicle powered by battery that originated in the late 1880s and that has been used for private as well as public transportation [3]. An electric vehicle can be a bicycle, a motorcycle, or any type of four-wheeled automobile, being private or commercial. The electric automobiles competed very well with the petroleum-fuelled ones from the early days of the auto industry up until the 1920s. They were preferred for their quietness and low maintenance costs. But with the highway system coming into use, automobile owners wanted to travel longer and faster. The electric car fell short on fulfilling that desire, while the fuel-powered vehicle, with internal combustion engine (ICE) that continued on improving, did [4]. Nowadays, after almost a whole century of ICE vehicle dominance of the private transportation sector, it seems like the EVs are back in the picture with tremendous opportunities to revolutionize and reshape the transportation sector during this current decade [5].

9.1.2 Forecasted Growth

Multiple service companies, PricewaterhouseCoopers, the international research consulting firm McKinsey & Company, and Deloitte Consulting LLP to name a few, have reported promising forecasted growth figures for the electric vehicle market globally and in the USA. PricewaterhouseCoopers forecasts that the global market will continue to grow in a way that by the year 2020 the EV market could be as large as almost 2.5 million or as low as 750,000 but more realistically around 1.5 million vehicles [6]. Deloitte Consulting LLP also provided three scenarios for the US electric vehicle market penetration and trend. The aggressive, most probable, and conservative vehicle forecasted figures for the year 2015 are 75,000, 60,000, and 45,000, respectively, and for the year 2020 the figures are 840,000, 465,000, and 285,000 units [7].

The task is not an easy one; the success and survival of the EV require lots of effort and collaboration among multiple players: the auto industry, the policy makers, the financial institutions, the energy sector, the media industry, and importantly the general public, to name a few. Figure 9.2 graphically displays the relation or the nature of collaboration needed for EV's success. A later section of the chapter will also identify the drivers for electric vehicle's positive trend which are rooted in various life aspects. Social, technological, economic, environmental, and political factors are directly or indirectly linked to the success or failure of the electric vehicle survival.

9.1.3 Tesla Motors

Tesla Motors is a fairly new and ambitious American company that started operation in the year 2003. Ever since, Tesla Motors differentiated itself by making it clear that the company will solely focus on the development, manufacturing, and delivery of nothing short than a high-end performance electric vehicle, a pure electric vehicle (EV). The first vehicle, Tesla Roadster, was delivered to its new owners in 2008. The introduction of this first model was very important to the company. It was a showcase to the advanced technologies used and proof of Tesla Motors' ability and

Fig. 9.2 Collaboration cycle needed for success

willingness to lead the pure EV market. The advanced battery pack, along with other sophisticated parts of the vehicle, allowed the newly delivered EV a longer range on a single charge, a decent 236 miles.

In 2010, the company secured a long-term loan from the Department of Energy to finance further development of EVs, powertrains, and purchasing and retooling of manufacturing facilities. Tesla even negotiated with its suppliers an integrated manufacturing approach to manufacture parts on Tesla's sites to alleviate the dependency on the suppliers' performance. The positive indications to Tesla's success were noticeable and translated into actions by some of the automaker leaders. Daimler uses Tesla's battery pack in its a-class EV. Daimler also invests in the outstanding capital stock of Tesla by owning a good 8 %. Furthermore, Toyota has a 3 % equity investment in Tesla Motors in addition to the agreement of relying on the company (Tesla) as a source for major parts to the all-electric versions of RAV4. Such actions are strong assurances to the investors about the young Tesla's products and in the house designed and developed technologies. The following is part of a long innovations list backed by multiple patent applications.

- An advanced and efficient battery system
- A sophisticated battery cooling, power, safety, and management system
- An exclusive alternating current 3-phase induction motor and its power electronics
- An all-encompassing software system to manage safety, efficiency, as well as the overall vehicle control.

As mentioned in the previous section, the path of the EV or EV manufacturers is not free of obstacles. In the case of Tesla, the company has to focus on bringing the EV high tag price down a bit, a focusing point of this chapter. Also, the company has to maintain its standards high in order to keep on gaining consumers appreciation and trust in an environment where the general public is lacking the awareness of EVs. As for the infrastructure, the slow but steady rollout and development plans may hinder Tesla's and the EV industry's ambitious expansion efforts.

9.2 Technology Road Map Development

9.2.1 Electric Vehicles Market Drivers

In recent decade, car buyers have inclined using EVs due to several drivers in the US environment. These drivers have been emerged from social (S), technological (T), economic (E), environment (E), and political (P) environments. To explain how these drivers affect the electric car market, STEEP analysis is used. Recognized factors are shown in the Table 9.1.

Table 9.1 STEEP factors affecting EV market

Factor	Social/market	Technological	Environmental	Economic	Political
Increasing demand for green transportation	✓		✓		
Tax benefits and US government's incentives			✓	✓	✓
Increasing demand for lower cost transportation	✓			✓	
Smart grid implementation with relation to V2G technology		✓			
Emerging new technologies in EV's main parts (battery, electric motor, etc.)		✓			

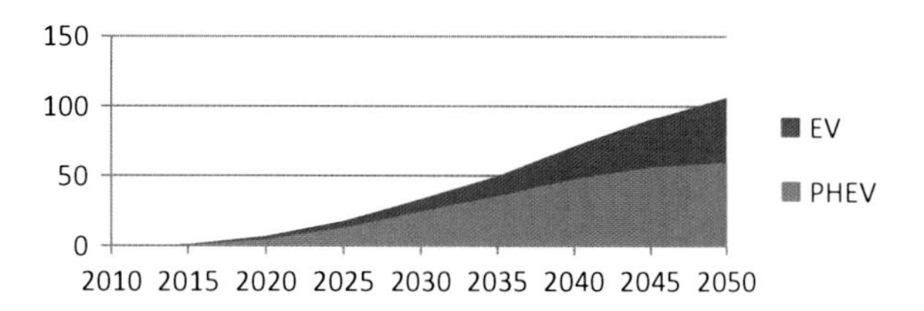

Fig. 9.3 Annual global EV and PHEV sales in BLUE map scenario

9.2.2 Increasing Demand for Green Transportation

According to increasing anxieties about environmental issues such as CO2 emissions and increasing GHGs, green transportation including public transportation like bus, walking, and bicycling has been noticed more and more. Electric vehicle as one of the modes of green transportation has been noticed widely by societies and governments, as a result annual sales of different types of electric cars will have a remarkable growth by 2050 and the number of sold conventional gasoline and diesel cars will be decreased dramatically by that time [8]. The International Energy Agency's study shows that the number of EV and PHEV cars sold globally by 2050 would be around 106.4 million cars – Fig. 9.3 above.

9.2.3 Tax Benefits and US Government's Incentives

Increasing gas prices in recent years made energy security as a one of the federal and state governments' main concerns. Moreover, environmental issues and related international commitments led the governments to enact some incentives. The most important incentive is the Recovery Act Funds. As part of DOE's $12 billion investment in advanced vehicle technologies, the Department is investing more than $5 billion to make the US transportation system electrified. These investments are supporting the development, manufacturing, and deployment of the batteries, components, vehicles, and necessary charging infrastructure and facilities [9].

9.2.4 Increasing Demand for Lower Cost Transportation

Dramatic changes in gasoline, have been a big challenge for car drivers over recent years. Increasing gasoline price more than 200 % between 2009 and 2012 indicates that fuel consumption cost is going to be a big problem in transportation cost. Also Kenny Ham, vice president of Apocalyps EV, reported [10] that 70 % of America's daily oil consumption relates to automotive transportation. Despite of the high price of EVs, cost analysis on advanced EVs shows they could be competitive with gasoline-powered vehicles over time due to less maintenance cost and energy cost reduction [11].

9.2.5 Smart Grid Implementation with Relation to V2G (Vehicle to Grid) Technology

Smart grid implementation is a basic prerequisite to promote using EVs nationwide. Upgrading distribution level transformers to make a reliable service to homes and charging locations, investing in smart meters and smart charging software, and investing in IT infrastructures to support applications including EVs are the main parts of smart grid development that utilities have to follow. $3.4 billion was assigned in 2010 by the federal government as stimulus fund to develop smart grid and modernize the current one.

According to the US Department of Energy's Alternative Fuels Data Center, there are currently around 4,150 EV charging stations in the USA. It is reported that the number of EV charging stations will be 4.1 million by 2017 [12].

9.2.6 Emerging New Technologies in EV's Main Parts (Battery, Electric Motor)

The technology of batteries has had great progress after emerging lithium-ion batteries in 1999. With the emergence of lithium batteries, the dream of riding electrical vehicles for long distances got more possible. Today's automotive Li-ion cells are capable of supporting higher mileage around 70 miles for a 200 kg pack. It is predicted that Li-ion batteries will reach 400 Wh/kg by using high-capacity cathode materials and alloy anode materials. Li-air batteries, which will emerge in the near future, potentially will surpass the battery technology used today. Li-air batteries may reach 400 Wh/kg. Theoretically, achieving 1,000 Wh/kg is attainable if some technological obstacles would be overcome. This generation of batteries makes it possible to drive more than 380 miles on a single charge [13].

9.3 Product Road Map and Gaps

Tesla Motors is well known for its premium cars. They maintained the top score features in all their products [14]. To understand what should be done for Tesla's product road map, we performed gap analysis between the current features and features that are required for Tesla to make a difference in the market. We focused on identifying potential gaps and also tracking known gaps [15]. We are also focusing on electric vehicles.

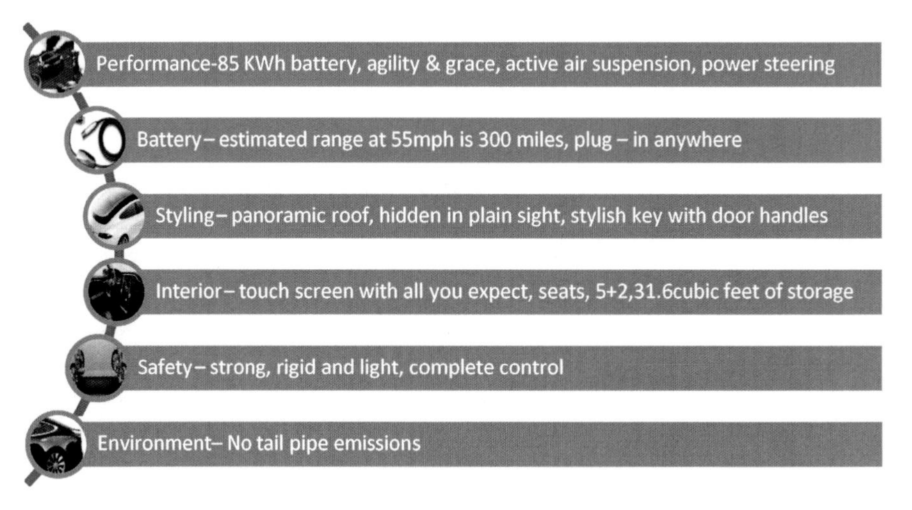

Fig. 9.4 Present features of Tesla motors' latest model S [15]

9.3.1 Current Position

Performance: It has one of the best performances in electric vehicle industry. It rises from 0 to 60 mph in just 5.6 s. 125 mph is the top speed with zero tail pipe emissions. Few of the important features include its 85 Kwh battery and its active air suspension [16] (Fig. 9.4).

Battery: Battery is the major part of the electric car. There is a lot of research going on to optimize the performance of the battery [17]. Understanding the issues with the battery and improving its performance are important for electric vehicle's success. Currently, Tesla is leading in this with 85 kWh batteries which enable the car to reach up to 130 mph [16].

Styling: Focusing on the premium, this car delivers all the features that most luxury cars deliver. Comparing with the competitors it has all the panoramic view with maximum efficiency. It has all the features that are expected in a premium car [16].

Interior: It has 5+2 seats with maximum capacity for the size of the car and also the touch screen with top most features in the present internal electronics. Few of them include integrated media, navigation, communications, and cabin controls [16].

Safety: This is one of the most important features. Tesla exceeds in the safety domain also with the rigid battery. The traction and stability also give a complete control over the car. With high strength steel it provides maximum capacity for occupant safety [16].

Environment: Being an electric vehicle it is already favoring the environment. With zero tail pipe emission, it is more efficient than any of the gasoline or petroleum-burned vehicles. The sources of electricity are also efficient technologies. Thus, it is less harmful to the environment [16].

What Will It Cost: With all of this we also looked into the price range for different performance levels as shown above.

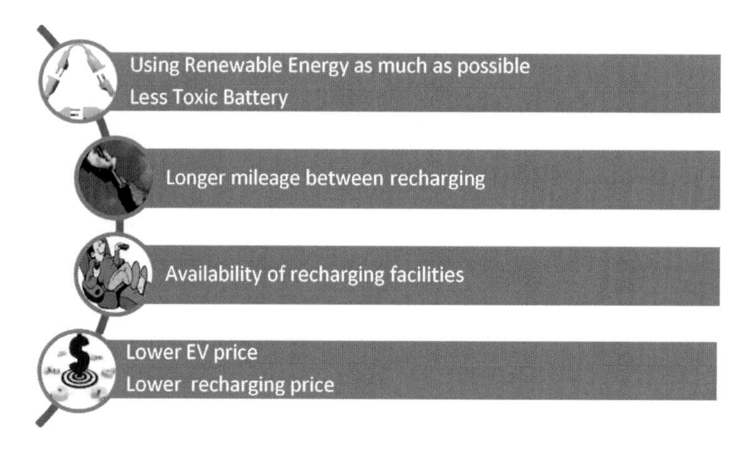

Fig. 9.5 Features – Tesla market leader [18–23]

9.3.2 Future of Tesla

Understanding the current features and also looking into the future of EV, we identified the potential gaps and known gaps [15]. Surveys on the Internet and literature review provided the information on what customers want to see in an electric vehicle. Figure 9.5 depicts our understanding on where Tesla should be in the future to become a market leader.

9.3.3 Known Gaps

1. *Lower Electric Vehicle Price*
   Electric vehicles are now not being purchased by regular-salaried persons. They are mostly targeting the premium vehicle range. The most expensive part of the electric vehicle is the battery. We need to consider reducing the cost by reducing the cost of the battery [18, 19]. Understanding Tesla's design we came up with negative gaps like reducing the interior features and styling to make the car affordable.
2. *Less Toxic Battery*
   To improve battery as environment friendly, the toxic battery needs to be changed. There is research going on this subject and lithium-ion battery is an alternative that is being considered [18]. Considering this will make the vehicle greener to the environment.

9.3.4 Potential Gaps

1. *Using Renewable Energy as Much as Possible*
   Even though electric cars are considered environmental friendly, there are still ways to make it absolutely environmental friendly. One of which is using photovoltaic power to improve the efficiency and performance of electric vehicles. Power can be generated from the PV-powered vehicle and PV-powered charging stations [20].
2. *Longer Mileage Between Recharging*
   The major part of the EV is the battery. Increasing the performance of battery will increase the mileage, and also other technologies that are covered in technology will increase the mileage between recharging [18, 19, 21]. This is one of the major gaps in the market. The target for mileage keeps on increasing with technological changes.
3. *Availability of Recharging Facilities*
   This is considered to be a gap for the entire EV market. Because the availability of charging stations is currently less, rolling out new facilities and improving these stations in collaboration with technology and electricity companies is essential. Measures have to be taken to standardize the availability by government and companies [19, 22]. Plug-in station is also a priority from customer surveys [21, 23].
4. *Lower Recharging Price*
   Lowering the recharging price is another gap that needs to be addressed. This is mostly related to technological changes that are coming up in the EV industry like smart grid and PV-powered stations [20, 22]. This is a potential gap that is dependent on continuous improvements of the technologies.

The next step after identifying the product gaps is to map them to the market drivers. In the technology road mapping process, understanding the market will give the insight to understand the product needs. This gives the opportunity to set the targets for the market. To map this product gaps with the market drivers, we used a QFD (quality function deployment) tool. The house of quality process will provide the relation between each of these gaps and help to analyze the priorities. We can understand the immediate needs of the market and proceed with focusing on them [24, 25]. Table 9.2 shows the implementation of QFD matrix between the drivers and product gaps.

All of them have equal importance. But considering the availability of technology and the top market drivers, the prioritization for product features was selected. Understanding the prioritization and mapping them to the market needs help to understand the implementation of the product and its life cycle. We focused on the Sedan model for attracting the market as it drives towards satisfying the market needs. The table below represents the product features delivered with each product and also gives an idea on the time line (Table 9.3).

The products are designed for implementation for the road map only focused on Sedans. This is planned for a time interval of 5 years. The first target is to make

Table 9.2 QFD matrix – drivers versus product gaps

Drivers	Green transportation	Emerging technological changes	Tax benefits and US government's incentives	Lower cost of transportation	Performance
Using renewable energy as much as possible	✓✓	✓✓	✓		
Efficient power electronics	✓✓	✓✓		✓	✓
Longer mileage between recharging	✓	✓✓		✓✓	✓✓
Charging interface		✓✓		✓	✓
Lower EV price		✓✓	✓✓	✓✓	

Table 9.3 Product gaps versus products

	1	5	10
Time (years)	Sedan B	Sedan XY	EV – powered by PV
Efficient power electronic	✓	✓	
Longer mileage		✓	✓
Lower price	✓	✓	
Charging interface	✓	✓	✓
Using renewable energy			✓

the Sedan affordable and add the technology changes that improve efficiency of the battery and charging interfaces. But lowering the price is the main focus for the short-term goal. The next step is to understand the technology gaps and mapping them to the product gaps.

9.4 Technology Road Map and Gaps

Technology road mapping is a process that can be applied to identify any existing technology gaps, critical system requirements, and milestones that are critical to the development of a product. It is a method by which one can assess the different pathways, if any, for meeting a requirement and is especially useful when there are high-risk elements in the product development process. In which case, one could pursue more than one path for fulfilling a specific requirement and help in reducing the risk of execution. This sort of strategy management is ideally done before making any technological investments or starting the execution phase of the project or product. For a given set of needs and a time frame, TRM provides a method to organize and analyze information about critical requirements, targets, performance metrics, etc.

Table 9.4 EV product targets

	Current	~1 years	~5 years	~10 years
Model	Sedan	Sedan B	Sedan XY	PV powered Sedan
Car cost	≈ $50 K	$40 K	$50 K	$60 K
Battery RE-charging time	45 min	45 min	30 min	30 min
Battery range	≈ 160 miles	200 miles	500 miles	500 miles
Motor efficiency (KW)	≈ 245	≈ 275	≈ 500	≈ 500

and the time frames by which they have to be accomplished so as to meet the needs of the product rollout planned. It also helps in identifying alternative pathways and making trade-offs among them to better mitigate the risks identified [26]. In this first stage, typically the time lines are more or less defined, but not the means to achieve it. Within the scope of this project, the targets and time lines have been decided as shown above (Table 9.4)

These technology gaps and challenges have been identified based on market drivers and product gaps, and further technological assessment and adoption rates can help in multistage product development.

The following are some of the limitations with proposed solutions in the current state of the art EVs:

(a) *Battery Technology and Performance: Need for Improved Reliability and Capacity* Energy density in existing batteries is by far the biggest limitation in EV industry in terms of the amount of power that can be delivered per unit weight of the battery. It also plays a huge part in determining the overall price of the EV. So far, the only way to overcome this has been to use heavier batteries to improve the working range of a car for a single charge. However, this leads to a reduction in responsiveness of the car due to the extra weight and slower acceleration in uphill climbs. One of the emerging technologies for improving energy density is to go for lithium-air-based batteries as demonstrated by the engineers at IBM [27].

In terms of reliability, while current estimates for nickel-metal hydride (NiMH)-based batteries suggest that their life could be as high as 15 years based on regular usage of the EV, these estimates are based on projections based on extrapolated data, and higher reliabilities would be a welcome addition to the existing list of market drivers [18]. One way of ensuring higher reliability is to slow the rate of charge–discharge cycles, and in this context, the usage of ultra-capacitors [18] for short-term booster power or for storage of energy in regenerative braking would likely answer some of the abovementioned challenges. Another competing technology as demonstrated by scientists in Stanford University has been the usage of nickel-iron batteries for intermediate-term storage supplementing the storage of the main batteries [28]. These batteries have a much larger life based on the charge–discharge cycles and hence can definitely pave the way to improved reliabilities.

(b) *Safety: Thermal Management of Batteries*
Storage of energy in a confined space whether it be liquids, gases (such as petrol, compressed natural gas), or batteries (fuel cells, lead acid) could lead to safety hazards and give rise to regulations by government or its agencies. One such example is the fire hazard in vehicles such as the Nano developed by Tata Motors [29]. The solution of this problem is an important step in addressing market and human concerns and is an important gap to be addressed. Interestingly, the temperature control of the battery is not only an important step in mitigating fire hazard, it is also a means to improve battery efficiency and usable life. A team at Fraunhofer Institute in Germany devised a phase change material as a coolant to keep the battery temperature at an optimum level between 20 °C and 35 °C to improve the efficiency of the battery as well as reduce fire hazards [35].

(c) *Environmental Issues: Battery Recycling and Repurposing*
Primary costs of the batteries come from the cost of lithium and other scarce metals. Proper recycling and repurposing of such metals is essential to ensure lower costs and also to ensure zero total emissions of EVs. Thus, development of a mechanism that allows end users to trade in their used batteries is essential to recover some cost and protect the environment and as such adds to the appeal of owning a zero-emission vehicle. Possible usage models include repurposing these batteries into indoor converters or in utility vehicles for which the range may not have the same requirements as passenger vehicles. Existing companies such as Toxco already provide a range of services which could be tapped for closing the gap in this area [36]. Tesla currently ships the end of life batteries to Toxco for dismantling and reuse, recycling.

(d) *Use of Renewable Energy: Photovoltaic (PV)*
Even though EVs have zero emissions, they are still reliant on electricity which is available from the grid, and more often than not, the electricity is produced by coal-fired plants, and hence, EVs are not truly zero emissions. One of the readily available technologies is the use of solar PV panels which provide a truly zero-emission renewable energy-based transport solution. Cost of electricity by PV is expected to be equal to or drop below that of coal-based electricity by 2025 [37], and this is within the time frame for using PV-based sources for EVs. These could either be in the form of in-vehicle charging capabilities or using rooftop PV panels (say in the garage) for providing charging and vehicle-to-grid technology.

9.4.1 Implementation Steps

The resources for these gaps could either be in-house R&D or existing commercial or emerging solutions. There could also be outsourcing and negotiations with partners or alliances with national labs and standards institutes such as NIST. Manufacturing concerns are not as important due to the already existing leadership role taken by Tesla in the EV/automobile manufacturing sector. Tesla already provides services to other auto giants and could even rely on the goodwill to develop partnerships in other areas as well.

In order to accomplish the time line set for the product rollout, Tesla would need to address the above gaps using the methods recommended so that the technology is available in a timely manner.

9.5 Resources

9.5.1 The R&D Resources

Resource management is to manage the investment of the company's R&D resources, which includes human resource, information resource, monetary resource, and material resource. There are concerns about the availability of skilled workforce, information, and material resources when needed. The cost of securing these resources is usually determined by their usefulness and scarcity. The ability to get all the needed resource in a cost-efficient way is significant to the success of R&D programs and hence to the success of the future of the company. Firms need to utilize strategic decision making during the acquisition of the R&D resources to maximize the utility and eliminate the risks in R&D process. The point of concern is to maximize R&D overall productivity of resources, which is beyond R&D job itself, and the purpose is to find the best balance between internal and external R&D productivity. There are four ways to acquire the R&D resources, i.e., in-house R&D, alliances/partnerships, outsourcing, and acquisition. The definitions, pros, and cons of all four ways of getting R&D resources are listed in Table 9.5 below.

1. *Strategic Decisions in Resources Acquisition*
   There has been research about the strategic decision of adopting in-house R&D, alliances, or outsourcing [38]. Rajneesh Narula suggested when and under what circumstances it is advantageous for firms to engage in R&D activity internally or externally, distinguishing between the use of in-house R&D activity, R&D outsourcing, and R&D alliances. Granstand et al. viewed the competences of technology-based firm as four types as demonstrated in the figure below. Rajneesh Narula maps the four quadrants to in-house R&D, outsourcing, and alliance as the oval circles show (Fig. 9.6).

   Rajneesh Narula then looked into the dynamic view of the evolution of technological paradigms and came up with a decision tree for selecting mode of R&D for pre-paradigmatic technology shown in Appendix 1. Instead of using a decision tree to express the decision model as in Rajneesh Narula's research, a decision table was used to express the decision modes as shown in Appendix 2.
2. *Tesla's R&D Resources Decision*
   Several technological gaps were identified based on the earlier research performed above. Based on the R&D resource selection framework defined in

Table 9.5 The comparison of four ways to acquire the R&D resources

	Definition	Pros	Cons
In-house R&D	Do it by yourself, with your employees, your R&D facilities	1. Ownership of technology 2. Exclusiveness 3. Core competencies in the value chain 4. Strategic advantages	1. High fixed costs 2. Mobility of researchers 3. Risks of substituted by disruptive technological progress
Alliances/ partnership	Do it together with partners with knowledge share within alliances	1. Help to get more resources at low prices 2. Complimentary in the vertical alliance	1. Safety of exclusive technology 2. Competition from partners usually in horizontal alliances 3. Knowledge and brain drain among alliance partners
Outsourcing	Pay the R&D suppliers to do it; get the outcome of R&D as the result	1. Quick progress in R&D 2. Less cost of R&D team 3. Flexibility when disruptive technologies bring substitution	1. Dependency on the R&D suppliers 2. Lack of control to the technology progress 3. Knowledge shared by the R&D suppliers
Tech acquisition	Buying the technology in the form of patents, business secrets, etc.	Get the required technology fast, when a specific technology is need	Conducting a technology acquisition project every year would be very costly (therefore, you should do your best to select a vendor and a technology that can grow with your business for the next 2–3 years) [38]

the previous section, we will identify the appropriate R&D resource for each of these technological gaps. The technological gaps to be analyzed are:

- Economic Sedan design
- Charging interface standard
- Coolant system
- Battery recycling
- Li-air battery
- Photovoltaic R&D
- Sensors and electronic
- R&D for integration.

The appropriate R&D resource for each technological gap is derived by evaluating each of the gaps above against the selection model utilizing Tesla's strategy and current market status. Table 9.6 shows the recommended R&D resource outcome of each technology based on the selection model.

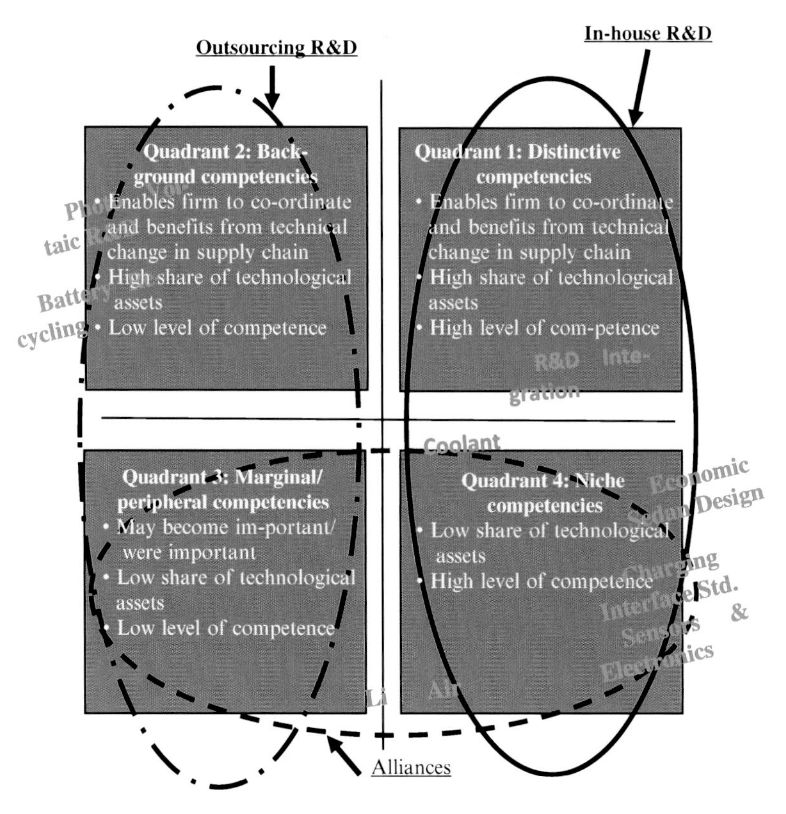

Fig. 9.6 Static view: relationship between distributed competencies and internal/non-internal R&D

Tesla's R&D alliances: Based on the above analysis, we try to identify the potential external resources required for Tesla, as shown in Table 9.7 below.

After Tesla has got the decisions of selection between in-house R&D, outsourcing, and alliances, it still needs to set up the outsourcing provider and the alliance partnership. There are five steps to do this:

- Step 1: to find out the available providers/partners.
- Step 2: to do technology assessment, make sure that the technology is what Tesla needs.
- Step 3: to select some of the providers to negotiate with according to the result of Step 2.
- Step 4: to negotiate with the candidates.
- Step 5: to make decisions about the selection of providers/partner.

Table 9.6 Tesla's decision among in-house R&D, outsourcing, or alliances

	Economic Sedan design	Charging interface standard	Coolant system	Battery recycling	Li-air battery	Photovoltaic R&D	Sensors and electronic	R&D integration
Slow/rapid technical change?	Rapid	Rapid	Slow	Slow	Slow	Rapid	Slow	Rapid
Systematic effect/marginal effect on existing technology?	Systematic	Systematic	Systematic	Marginal	Systematic	Marginal	Marginal	Systematic
Is internal resource available?	Yes	Yes	Yes	No	No	No	Yes	Yes
Multiple substitutable sources available?	Yes	Yes	Yes	Yes	Yes	Yes	Yes	No
Is the entrance to the technology late?	No	No	No	No	No	No	No	No
Decision	In-house R&D supported by alliance	In-house R&D supported by alliance	In-house R&D supported by alliance	Outsource	Alliance	Outsource	In-house R&D supported by alliance	In-house R&D

Table 9.7 External resources pool for Tesla

	Decision	Available partners/vendors	Negotiation result
Economic Sedan design	In-house R&D supported by alliance	Daimler and Toyota Fresno Design Alliance	TBA
Charging interface standard	In-house R&D supported by alliance	SAE International China Enterprise Confederation and China Electric Power Research Institute International Electrotechnical Commission	TBA
Coolant system	In-house R&D supported by alliance	Fraunhofer Inst. DENSO Corporation Alliances with SAE (Society of Automotive Engineers)	TBA
Battery recycling	Outsource	Interstate Batteries, Inc. Toxco Battery Solutions, Inc.	TBA
Li-air battery	In-house R&D supported by alliance	IBM Chengdu Jianzhong Lithium Battery	TBA
Photovoltaic R&D	Outsource	Kyoecera Mitsubishi SunPower Corporation, CleanTech Institute Toyota	TBA
Sensors and electronic	In-house R&D supported by alliance	Large number of providers (634)	TBA
R&D integration	In-house R&D supported by alliance		TBA

9.6 Proposed Sedan EV Road Map

Road map is an integrated plan linking all factors in market, product, technology, and resources parts, so three main tasks must be accomplished to make an integrated road map: timing, prioritization, and naming product generations. To make a reasonable foresight and adjust our timing to the realities of the business, we divided our timing to:

- Short range: 1 year, to make more economic current product
- Medium range: 5 years, to make more improvements in the main parts of the product and its performance
- Long range: 10 years, to apply new technologies, particularly photovoltaic, to make new generation of EVs

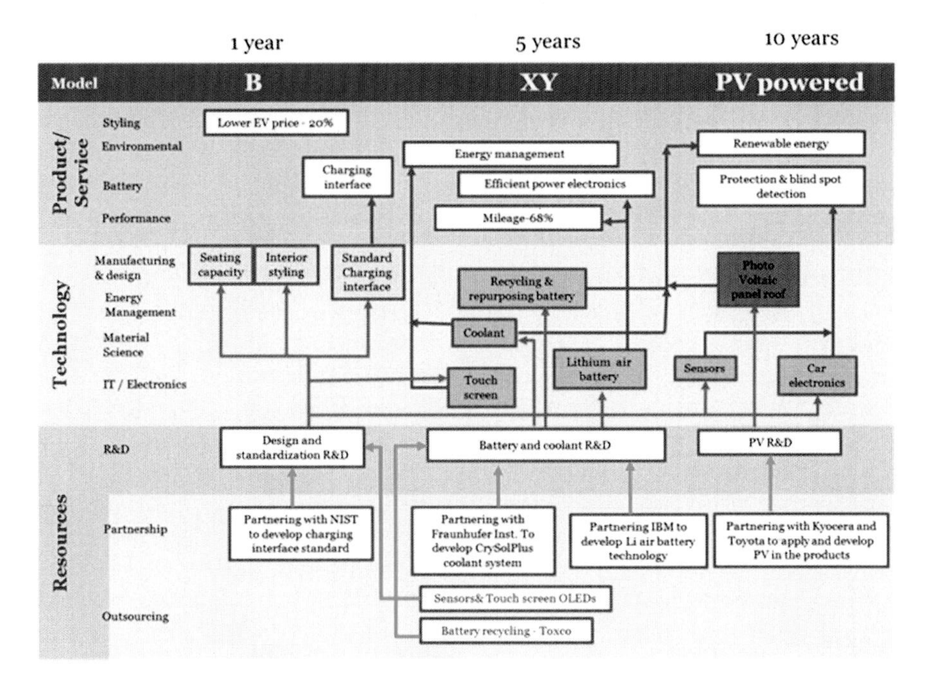

Fig. 9.7 Technology road map – electric vehicle

To make priority among all factors and anticipated activities, each was discussed and its relationship with others was determined. Timing was another point considered in making prioritization. The road map focuses on three main product generations offerings to support the described market drivers discussed earlier. The product offering will be derived by R&D programs that are precisely linked to the technology and product requirements. The three product generations in the road map are:

- Basic (B): introducing the product with some minor design changes to the current product in order to make it more affordable
- XY: introducing the product with significant environmental, performance, and operational enhancements at an affordable price
- PV powered: explaining next generation of Tesla's products which will be powered by photovoltaic technology

The integrated road map of Tesla's Sedan EV is shown in Fig. 9.7 above and Appendix 3.

9.7 Conclusion

In order to maintain sustainability in today's diverse and competitive automobile market, it is imperative for Tesla Motors to design, develop, and integrate TRM as a strategic planning tool to align their technology strategies with business strategies. A preliminarily technology road map was created to address the short and long-term business strategy and market penetration for Tesla Sedan EVs. A typical TRM development model was adopted throughout this study which focuses on analyzing the market to identify its drivers, defining the market needs to fulfill the gaps with new products, suggesting the technological capabilities needed to achieve the realization of the product gaps, and finally identifying the necessary resources and linking them to the suggested needed technologies. Throughout the study, some specific tools and/or frameworks were utilized during each stage of the road mapping development process. As an example, STEEP analysis was used during the market driver's definition stage. To map product gaps with the market drivers, QFD technique was used during the technology analysis stage. At the resource analysis stage, a combination of decision tree and decision tables was used to determine the best and most effective method of securing the required resources for each technology defined.

9.8 Future Research

The study focused on creating a high-level road map for one product segment which is the Sedan EV. Additional research can focus on expanding this road map to include other segments such as compact and SUV vehicles. This might entail using addition or new tools, models, and/or frameworks during the road map development stage. This study was done based on the current market and technology status and taking into the consideration Tesla's current positioning in the market. Additional research can be performed in the areas of providing a continuous maintenance to the road map and adapting to future market and technology changes. Finally, Tesla should plan for the after-technology road map development stage, which is the continuous integration and implementation of TRM into an ongoing strategic planning process.TRM integration and implementation will require adopting change in some business process, organizational structure, or even working culture. Additional research can be conducted on how Tesla can effectively integrate this road map into its business process, and organizational changes are required.

Appendix 1: R&D Decision Tree

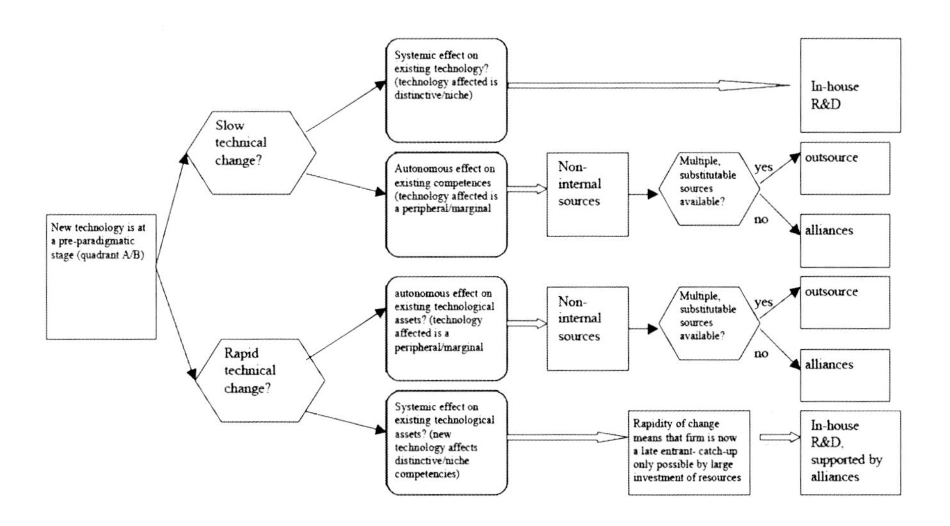

Appendix 2

	1	2	3	4	5	6	7	8	9	10	11	12	13	14	15	16
Slow/rapid technical change?	Rapid	Rapid	Rapid	Rapid	Rapid	Rapid	Rapid	Rapid	Slow	Slow	Slow	Slow	Slow	Slow	Slow	Slow
Systematic effect/marginal effect on existing technology?	Systematic	Systematic	Systematic	Systematic	Marginal	Marginal	Marginal	Marginal	Systematic	Systematic	Systematic	Systematic	Marginal	Marginal	Marginal	Marginal
Are Internal resources available?	Yes	Yes	No	No	Yes	Yes	No	No	Yes	Yes	No	No	Yes	Yes	No	No
Multiple substitutable sources available?	Yes	No	Yes	No	Yes	No	Yes	No	Yes	No	Yes	No	Yes	No	Yes	No
Is the entrance to the technology late?	No	No	No	No	No	No	No	No	No	No	No	No	No	No	No	No
Decision	In-house R&D Supported by alliances	In-house R&D Supported by alliances	In-house R&D Supported by alliances	In-house R&D Supported by alliances	In-house R&D with support from alliances	In-house R&D	Outsource	Alliance	In-house R&D	In-house R&D	In-house R&D	In-house R&D	In-house R&D with support from alliances	In-house R&D	Outsource	Alliance

Slow/rapid technical change?	Rapid	Rapid	Rapid	Rapid	Rapid	Rapid	Rapid	Rapid	Slow	Slow	Slow	Slow	Slow	Slow	Slow	Slow
Systematic ef-fect/marginal effect on existing technology?	Sys-tematic	Sys-tematic	Sys-tematic	Sys-tematic	Mar-ginal	Mar-ginal	Mar-ginal	Mar-ginal	Sys-tematic	Sys-tematic	Sys-tematic	Sys-tematic	Mar-ginal	Mar-ginal	Mar-ginal	Marginal
Are Internal resources available?	Yes	Yes	No	No	Yes	Yes	No	No	Yes	Yes	No	No	Yes	Yes	No	No
Multiple substitutable sources available?	Yes	No	Yes	No	Yes	No	Yes	No	Yes	No	Yes	No	Yes	No	Yes	No
Is the en-trance to the technology late?	Yes	Yes	Yes	Yes	Yes	--------	Yes	Yes	Yes	Yes	Yes	Yes	Yes	Yes	Yes	Yes
Decision	In-house R&D	In-house R&D	In-house R&D	In-house R&D	In-house R&D	In-house R&D	Out-source sup-	Alli-ance	In-house R&D	In-house R&D	In-house R&D	In-house R&D	In-house R&D	In-house R&D	Out-source sup-	Alliance

Appendix 3: Technology Road Map for Tesla EV Vehicle: Sedan

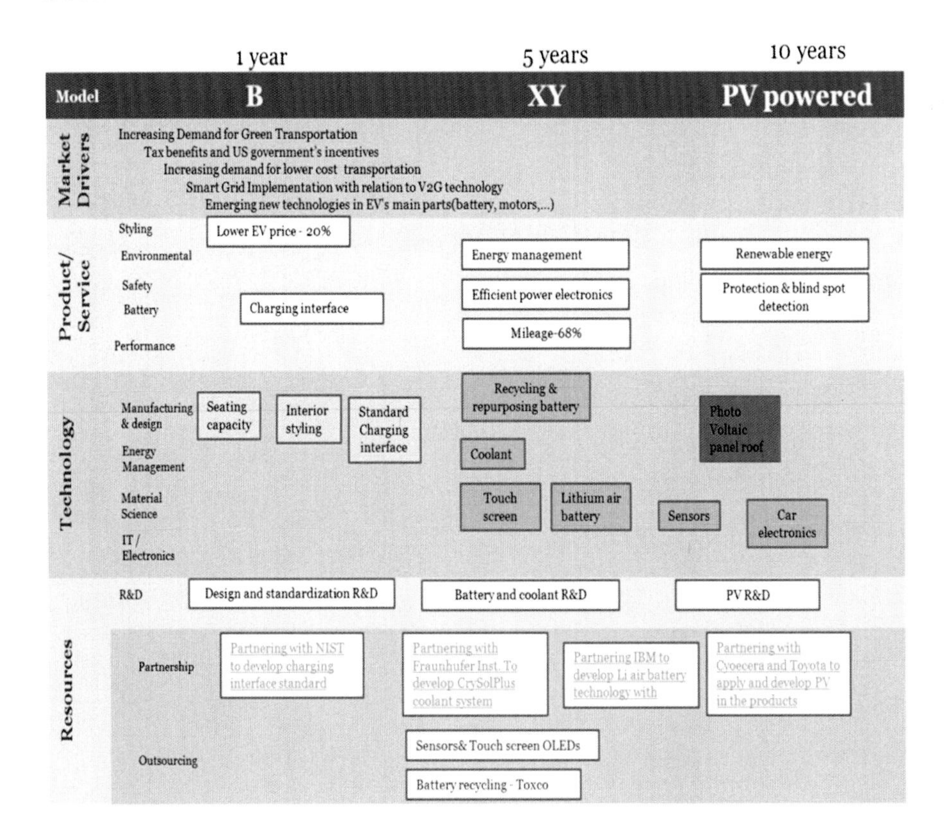

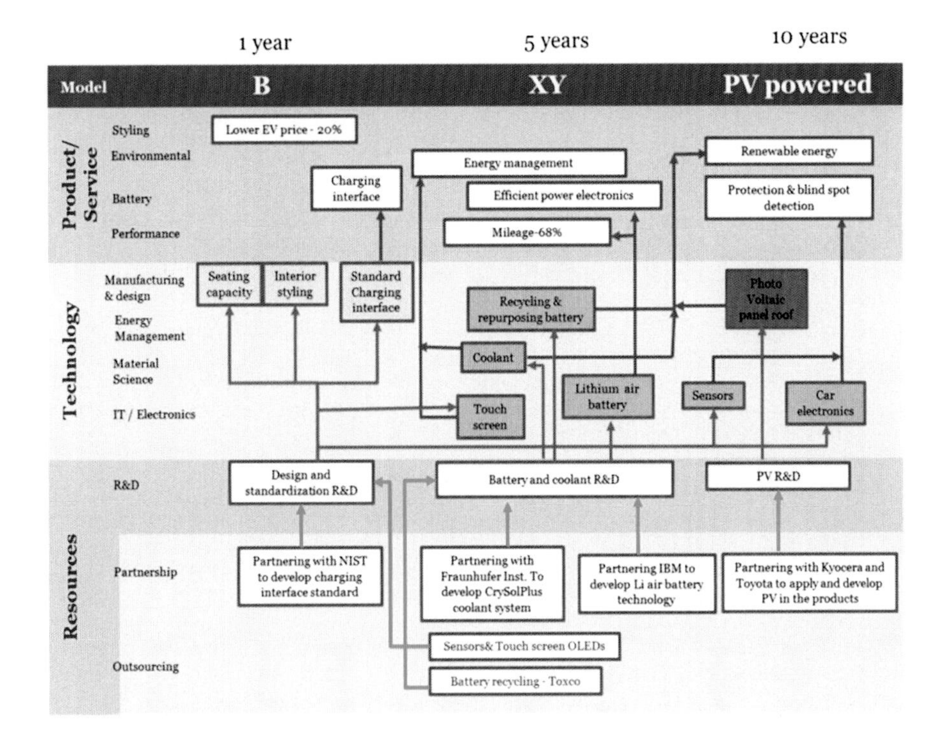

References

1. Chan CC, Wong YS (2004) Electric vehicles charge forward. IEEE Pow Energ Mag 2(6):24–33
2. Phaal R, Farrukh CJP, Probert DR (2004) Technology roadmapping–a planning framework for evolution and revolution. Technol Forecast Soc Change 71(1):5–26
3. Encyclopedia Britannica. http://www.britannica.com/. 31 July 2012
4. Chan C (1993) Present status and future trends of electric vehicles. In: Advances in power system control, operation and management. APSCOM-93., 2nd international conference, Hong Kong
5. Brown S, Pyke D, Steenhof P (2010) Electric vehicles: the role and importance of standards in an emerging market. Energ Policy 38(7):3797–3806
6. Macrae C, Mckenzie M (2009) Price water house coopers automotive institute analyst report. Price Water House Coopers, 9 Jan 2009
7. Giffi C et al. (2010) Gaining traction – a customer view of electric vehicle mass adoption in the U.S. automotive market. Deloitte Consulting LLC
8. International Energy Agency (2011) Technology roadmap: electric and plug in hybrid electric vehicles. International Energy Agency, Paris France, http://www.iea.org/publications/freepublications/publication/EV_PHEV_Roadmap.pdf
9. Department of Energy (2010) The recovery act: transforming America's transportation sector s.l. Department of Energy, Washington, DC
10. Ham K (2011) Why the USA needs small electric vehicles. Vice President, Apocalyps EV
11. Office of Technology Assessment, Congress of the United States (1994) Saving energy in U.S. transportation. Office of Technology Assessment, Congress of the United States, Washington, DC

12. Frost & Sullivan (2012) Strategic technology and market analysis of electric vehicle charging infrastructure in North America, Frost & Sullivan
13. Christensen J et al (2012) A critical review of Li/Air batteries. J Electrochem Soc 159:R1–R30
14. Tesla Motors Company Overview Summer 2011.http://files.shareholder.com/downloads/ABEA-4CW8X0/1404747030x0x494001/dd297293-ec2d-4dc5-8db4-63d491fb6bd0/Company_Overview_Q3_2011.pdf
15. White Paper: 5 steps for gap analysis. http://jthawes.com/pdf/5StepsforGapAnalysis.pdf
16. Tesla Motors website. http://www.teslamotors.com/models/features. Viewed 8 Nov 2012
17. Battery manufacturing for hybrid and electric vehicles: policy issues, Bill Canis specialist in industrial organization and business 22 Mar 2011. Congressional Research Service. http://www.fas.org/sgp/crs/misc/R41709.pdf
18. Elwood M Electric vehicle technology roadmap for Canada 2010. http://canmetenergy.nrcan.gc.ca/transportation/hybrid-electric/329. Viewed 8 Nov 2012
19. Electric Vehicles (EVs). http://www.fueleconomy.gov/feg/evtech.shtml/. Viewed 8 Nov 2012
20. Performance of a PV powered charging station for electric cars. http://www.cede.psu.edu/users/alau/ASESPVChrgingStation95.pdf. Viewed 8 Nov 2012
21. Electric vehicle survey reveals consumer preferences. http://www.gizmag.com/electric-vehicle-survey-reveals-consumer-preferences/17418/. Viewed 8 Nov 2012
22. Electric vehicle charging infrastructure. http://www.mpoweruk.com/infrastructure.htm. Viewed 8 Nov 2012
23. Survey: Consumers express concerns about electric, plug-in hybrid cars. http://news.consumerreports.org/cars/2012/01/survey-consumers-express-concerns-about-electric-plug-in-hybrid-cars.html. Viewed 8 Nov 2012
24. House of quality- Steps in understanding house of quality. http://www.public.iastate.edu/~vardeman/IE361/f01mini/johnson.pdf
25. Hauser JR, Clausing D The house of quality. Harvard Business review reprint 88307. http://www.csuchico.edu/~jtrailer/HOQ.pdf
26. Garcia ML, Bray OH (1997) Fundamentals of technology roadmapping. Strategic Business Development Department Sandia National Laboratories. www.sandia.gov/PHMCOE/pdf/Sandia%27sFundamentalsofTech.pdf
27. Wilcke W The battery 500 project. http://www.ibm.com/smarterplanet/us/en/smart_grid/article/battery500.html. 8 Aug 2012
28. Wang H et al. (2012) An ultrafast nickel–iron battery from strongly coupled inorganic nanoparticle/nanocarbon hybrid materials. Nature Commun 3. http://www.nature.com/ncomms/journal/v3/n6/pdf/ncomms1921.pdf
29. Mishra AK Tata's nano: fire! http://www.forbes.com/2010/05/20/forbes-india-wheels-of-fire-tata-moters.html. 21 May 2010
30. Tesla Motors website. http://www.teslamotors.com/models/options. Viewed 8 Nov 2012
31. Tesla Motors, Inc. Annual report, filed Mar 03 2011 for the period ending 31 Dec 2010
32. Loanzon E, Mansour M, Torres T (2011) No gas required: a marketing plan for Tesla motors' model S electric car. Portland State University, Spring term of 2011
33. Ciarcia D (2011) Charging ahead GE EV solutions. General Electric
34. Economic Briefing: Economics & Statistics Administration. Economics & Statistics Administration Web Site. [Online] United States Department of Commerce, 22 Feb 2012 http://www.esa.doc.gov. 22 Feb 2012
35. Czyzewski A (2012) EV battery coolant offers better temperature buffering. http://www.theengineer.co.uk/sectors/automotive/news/ev-battery-coolant-offers-better-temperature-buffering/1013127.article. 13 July 2012
36. Sherman D (2010) When electric-car batteries die, where will they end up? http://www.nytimes.com/2010/06/13/automobiles/13RECYCLE.html?_r=1&pagewanted=all. June 11, 2010
37. Cowan KR, Daim T (2009) Comparative technological road-mapping for renewable energy. Technology Soc, 31:333–341
38. Narula R (2012) Choosing between internal and non-internal R&D activities: some technological and economic factors. Viewed on line at http://arno.unimaas.nl/show.cgi?fid=306 7 Aug 2012

Chapter 10
A Proposed Road Map for Cybersecurity in Cloud Computing at Portland State University

Emy Loanzon

Abstract In 2011, Portland State University (PSU) transitioned its email and office applications suite to Google Apps. Google Apps for Education is a suite of Internet-cloud-based services provided by Google, which include email, calendar, document sharing, and access to these applications from Windows and Macintosh computers, as well as mobile devices (Google FAQ [Available Online] http://oit.pdx.edu/google-faq#4. Accessed 10 July 2012). PSU, like most higher education institutions, is now using cloud computing services for applications and data. As colleges and universities increase their business and academic use of cloud services, cybersecurity technologies and governance practices need to evolve. The current research proposes a technology road map for creating a more secure and stable computing environment for a higher education institution such as PSU.

10.1 Introduction

> Security is a negative deliverable.
> You don't know when you have it.
> You only know when you've lost it.
> Jeffrey I. Schiller, Security Architect, Massachusetts Institute of Technology (MIT) [1]

We need not look very far to find evidence that Jeffrey Schiller's description of security is a disturbing reality every day. Barely a week goes by when we do not find news about the latest security breaches into major companies, from Sony PlayStation in 2011, Global Payment Networks (GPN), a major payments processing firm in 2012 to government agencies such as the Pentagon in 2011 and the Federal Aviation Agency in 2009. Higher education institutions, with their more open and collaborative computing environments, are particularly vulnerable to these security breaches.

E. Loanzon (✉)
SAIF Corporation, Salem, OR, USA
e-mail: emlpdx@gmail.com

T.U. Daim et al. (eds.), *Planning and Roadmapping Technological Innovations: Cases and Tools*, Innovation, Technology, and Knowledge Management,
DOI 10.1007/978-3-319-02973-3_10, © Springer International Publishing Switzerland 2014

In 2011, 48 higher education institutions reported significant security breaches in their network, with Virginia Commonwealth University recording the most number of confidential records compromised at 176,567 [2]. Indeed, the growing number of cybersecurity breaches has become a major concern for governments, organizations, and individuals. Statistics show that over 430 million people have been victims of cyber crime in 2011 [3]. The Obama administration has declared cybersecurity threats as "one of the most serious economic and national security threats our nation faces" [4]. The growing menace of security breaches makes preventing and containing the impacts of these threats more challenging and critical.

Organizations have shown renewed interest in cybersecurity in the context of disruptive technologies. One such technology is cloud computing. Cloud computing is becoming a more prevalent technology for organizations aiming to reduce costs, expand services beyond geographic locations, and provide 24×7 services to customers. The National Institute of Science and Technology defines cloud computing as "a model for enabling convenient, on-demand network access to a shared pool of configurable computing resources (e.g., networks, servers, storage, applications, and services) that can be rapidly provisioned and released with minimal management effort or cloud provider interaction" [5]. Cloud computing offers organizations several benefits such as provisioning services and adapting to changing requirements faster, meeting enterprise requirements based on business priorities, and enables standard and on-demand services to customers.

However, these same cloud computing benefits create challenges in ensuring security and protecting privacy. As more higher education institutions such as Portland State University adopt cloud-based solutions such as Google Apps for Education, what drivers form the bases for ensuring that academic computing is secure? What current cybersecurity products and services are being deployed to address these drivers? How could higher education institutions bridge the gap in current security products and services to implement ones that address the requirements of cloud computing?

These questions will be addressed in the current study by proposing a technology road map for cybersecurity in cloud computing that a higher education institution, such as Portland State University, could reference. Technology road mapping is one of the processes that organizations have employed to ensure that they are addressing the global challenges of economic growth, technological innovation, industry collaboration, and other critical milestones. It is a technology planning process that helps identify, select, and develop technology alternatives that is based on organizational needs [6]. Technology road mapping enables organizations to identify critical requirements in technologies that need to be met in certain time frames and helps identify technologies that need to be developed to meet these requirements [6]. Indeed, technology road mapping acts like a compass for organizations to help them identify their business and strategic goals, which technologies to invest resources in, and develop plans to accomplish those goals.

The current study on technology road mapping aims to investigate these questions with the following goals:

(a) Determine the key drivers for cybersecurity at PSU's cloud computing environment.
(b) Describe current cybersecurity products and services in PSU's computing environment.

(c) Identify gaps in current cybersecurity products and those that are required in cloud computing.
(d) Present emerging technologies and IT governance practices that address cybersecurity requirements in cloud computing.
(e) Provide resources that PSU can utilize to address cybersecurity goals in cloud computing.
(f) Identify implications for managing a mixed environment of on-premise and cloud computing environments.

A study proposing a technology road map for cybersecurity in cloud computing in higher education institutions is significant for several reasons. First, research of this nature demonstrates the application of technology road mapping for strategic planning involving disruptive technologies. As cloud computing becomes a ubiquitous computing environment, its features and benefits also pose new challenges for cybersecurity and privacy. A technology road map will help determine the drivers and goals for cybersecurity in this scenario, identify appropriate processes and technologies to meet these goals, and present a planning horizon to meet these requirements. Second, the current study will describe traditional network security products and services and present anticipated cybersecurity technologies and IT governance for cloud computing. The discussion will highlight the gaps in providing an improved cybersecurity in cloud computing in higher education. Finally, the current study contributes to existing research on technology road mapping, as well as research on cybersecurity in cloud computing.

The review of literature presents research developments in technology road mapping in recent years. Studies that support best practices, as well as those that identify limitations will be presented. A brief background on cloud computing will be provided and another section of the review of literature will highlight research on traditional technologies for cybersecurity and best practices for cybersecurity in cloud computing. These studies will be instrumental in creating a proposed technology road map for cybersecurity in cloud computing at PSU. Background information on PSU and its academic computing environment will be provided.

A survey of literature and interviews with subject matter experts in cybersecurity are the main sources of data for creating a proposed technology road mapping for this study. Finally, the management implications of the proposed technology road map will be presented in the conclusion of the study.

10.2 Research Methodology

10.2.1 Literature Review

10.2.1.1 Technology Road Mapping

Several studies and industry applications have shown that technology road mapping can play a key role in strategic planning, ensuring that an organization has the appropriate resources and technologies aligned to its main goals. Garcia and Bray's publication on the fundamentals of technology road mapping from the Sandia National Laboratories in New Mexico focused more on technology road mapping as a process instead of a product [6]. They divided the technology road mapping process as consisting of three phases, which are preliminary activity, development of the technology road map, and follow-up activity. The preliminary activity involves meeting requirements, securing sponsorship, and defining the scope of the technology road map. The development phase determines the system requirements and targets of the road map, as well as their technology drivers. Finally, the follow-up activity focuses on critiquing and validating the road map, as well as developing its implementation plan.

In their 2003 research, Phaal, Farrukh, and Probert adopted a similar perspective that technology road mapping is a multilayered process. They further proposed that technology road mapping can be viewed from two perspectives—a company perspective and a multi-organizational perspective. Technology road mapping from a company perspective enables the organization to integrate technology developments to be part of business planning, thereby allowing the organization to evaluate new technologies and market developments [7]. On the other hand, technology road mapping from a multi-organizational perspective considers "the broader environmental landscape, threats and opportunities for a particular group of stakeholders in a technology area" [7]. Phaal and his coauthors acknowledged the need for a technology road mapping framework that is more robust and multilayered. With this perspective in mind, they developed the fast start technology road mapping framework. The T-plan road mapping approach has two parts, namely, the standard and customized approaches. The standard approach involves workshops that focused on the market, product and technology, and constructing the timelines for the road map. The customized approach goes beyond these workshops and incorporates elements that are particular to the organization and the industry that it operates under [7].

Technology road mapping continues to evolve and demonstrate flexibility in addressing the needs of industries and organizations. The growing significance of renewable sources of energy in terms of the environment, energy security, technological breakthroughs, and jobs is one of the central themes behind the creation of the 2011 International Technology Roadmap for Photovoltaics (ITRPV), released by the Crystalline Silicon Technology and Manufacturing (CTM) Group. This technology road map aims to inform suppliers and customers of solar energy systems about expected technology trends in the field of crystalline silicon photovoltaic and required improvements and standards [8]. On a national level, several technology road maps address regulatory mandates, such as the 2007 Energy Independence and Security Act, which assigned to the National Institute of Standards and Technology (NIST) the "primary responsibility to coordinate development of a framework that includes protocols and model standards for information management to achieve interoperability of Smart Grid devices and systems…" [9]. Based on this mandate, Fitzpatrick and Wollman developed a three-phase plan to accelerate the identification of standards, coordinate a framework based on them and their longer-term evolution, and establishment of a testing and certification framework for Smart Grid devices and systems [9]. The growing shift to renewable sources of energy and concerns about energy costs were major environmental and business drivers for a technology road map for wind energy in the Pacific Northwest as proposed by Daim, Amer, and Brendan [10].

Customizing technology road maps to an organization's business goals is important to enable an organization to meet its goals and remain relevant in its industry. However, this process is more complex than it appears to be. Lee and Park contend that technology road maps need to be flexible to accommodate changes and unusual situations. While Lee and Park recognized that technology road mapping software tools have been developed, particularly those with graphical features that help communicate the relationships between products, markets, and technologies, these software tools do not support the level of customization that organizations require [11]. In their study, they recommended a framework to meet customization and standardization requirements. The researchers also suggested web-based and modularized technology road maps to accommodate changes in the environment. Martin Rinne's study envisioned technology road mapping as a driver of innovation, suggesting a scenario where innovation will be virtualized with computer models and simulations [12]. Rinne proposes the possibility of applying the concept of object technology in virtualizing technology mapping. Object technology could help address the need for various technologies and products to find their relevant linkages in technology road maps.

10.2.1.2 Cloud Computing: A Game Changer for Cybersecurity

Cloud computing presents a paradigm shift in how organizations architect, manage, and allow access to remote computing resources. Tim Berners-Lee, founder of the World Wide Web, noted that "The big benefit of cloud computing is ubiquity. The downside of traditional computing is you need your computer to access your data. With cloud computing, you can have your environment...available from any interconnected terminal [13]". The NIST described cloud computing deployment and service models, which could impact the security and privacy controls that organizations implement. Cloud computing deployment models can be grouped as into four: public, private, hybrid, and community. Public clouds have their infrastructure and computational resources available to the general public over the Internet [5]. Amazon's Elastic Compute Cloud (EC2), Google App Engine, and Windows Azure services are examples of this deployment model. Private clouds are managed and maintained exclusively for an organization [5]. VMware with virtual servers hosting given applications and desktops delivered to a user via a client is an example.

A community cloud has characteristics from both public and private clouds. The infrastructure and computational resources are exclusive to two or more organizations that have common privacy, security, and regulatory considerations, instead of just a single organization [5]. As an example, all government agencies within California may share computing infrastructure on the cloud to manage data related to residents of California [14]. Finally, the NIST describes a hybrid cloud as the most complex, since this involves a combination of two or more public, private, and community clouds. Salesforce cloud computing model is an example of hybrid computing.

The cloud computing service model involves the organization's scope and control over its remote computing resources and the level of abstraction of this environment [5]. The three cloud computing service models are:

(a) IaaS (Infrastructure as a Service) – offers hardware related services which include storage services or virtual servers. Rackspace Cloud servers and Amazon EC2 are examples.
(b) PaaS (Platform as a Service) – offers a development platform on the cloud. Google App Engine and Microsoft Azure are providers of this service model.
(c) SaaS (Software as a Service) – offers complete software suites on the cloud. Users can access software programs hosted by the cloud vendor on a pay-per-use basis. Examples of SaaS providers are Salesforce, Google, and Microsoft [14].

Of the three cloud service models, most higher education institutions implement SaaS. Free email services such as Gmail, Yahoo! Mail, and Microsoft Hotmail became popular communication and messaging tools in colleges and universities. "The 2010 Campus Computing Survey reported that over 80 % of U.S. colleges and universities use hosted email solutions; of these institutions, 60 % use Gmail, and the remaining 40 % use Zimbra and Hotmail" [15]. Higher education institutions such as the University of Arizona, University of Central Florida, and Ohio State University have adopted Gmail and Hotmail for their email services [15]. This trend is only expected to grow as higher education transitions more computing resources and services to the cloud.

As early as 2008, a survey of 263 IT executives from Fortune 500 companies conducted by IDC identified the major benefits that organizations expect from cloud computing:

However, the same survey also yielded concerns that IT executives have about adopting cloud computing. As the results indicate, security is a major source of concern—not surprisingly, it is one of the obstacles that keep organizations from adopting cloud computing.

The US Department of Defense (DOD) defines cybersecurity as "all organizational actions required to ensure freedom from danger and risk to the security of information in all its forms (electronic, physical), and the security of the systems and networks where information is stored, accessed, processed, and transmitted, including precautions taken to guard against crime, attack, sabotage, espionage, accidents, and failures" [16]. As the Internet, e-commerce, social networks, and mobile communication devices become more ubiquitous, cybersecurity threats become serious concerns. "Cyber-security risks may include those that damage stakeholder trust and confidence, affect customer retention and growth, violate customer and partner identity and privacy protections, disrupt the ability or conduct or fulfill business transactions, adversely affect health and cause loss of life, and adversely affect the operations of national critical infrastructures" [16]. The Identity Theft Resource Center reported 213 security breaches in the USA alone, with 8,524,426 confidential records exposed—by July 2012 alone [17]. These alarming statistics prompted the

Obama administration to declare cybersecurity threats as "one of the most serious economic and national security threats our nation faces" [4].

The Cloud Security Alliance (CSA), the non-profit organization that promoted best practices for cloud computing security, identified seven major security threats to cloud computing. These include "Abuse and Nefarious Use of Cloud Computing, insecure Application Programming Interfaces, Malicious Insiders, Shared Technology Vulnerabilities, Data Loss/Leakage, Account, Service & Traffic Hijacking, and Unknown Risk Profile" [18]. Bisong and Rahman's research underscored the importance of IT governance, active management involvement and effective communication between the organization's management team and its cloud service providers as critical to implementing a secure cloud computing environment [19].

Shue and Lagesse encouraged organizations to be aware of the impact of cloud computing on cybersecurity. A key benefit of cloud computing is less company time and resources spent on maintaining and managing on-site systems while providing data and services on-demand to customers. The authors foresee a shift in focus for cybersecurity—rather than spending resources on securing desktop computers and removable media, organizations should focus on securing communications with remote systems. Shue and Lagesse listed six areas of limitations in cloud computing, which are lack of control and interoperability, lack of privacy, safety of cloud servers, client authentication, resource allocation, and connectivity and mobility [20]. These limitations present opportunities in researching and implementing technologies that secure pervasive systems, such as cloud computing.

Khorshed, Ali, and Wasimi's study on cybersecurity surveyed the gaps in cybersecurity that slow down adoption of cloud computing. The authors contend that current threat remediation mechanisms are only implemented after a security breach. Khorshed et al propose a proactive approach by detecting the cyber attacks in cloud computing using machine learning techniques, such as Naive Bayes, Multilayer Perception, Support Vector Machine, Decision Tree, and PART [21]. Of these techniques, the authors concluded that the Support Vector machine technique showed the best results in detecting cyber threats for cloud computing services [21]. Liu and Chen proposed a model for retrospective detection of malware attacks in cloud computing [22]. A retrospective detection is a part of malware postmortem analysis, which includes memory and hard drive examination. Testing this detection model demonstrated that it was able to find identical files of malware with various file attributes [22].

IT auditing has become critical and challenging in cloud computing. Chen and Yoon noted that data life cycle in the cloud has unique features as it constantly moves from different storage locations and security domains [23]. In this context, the researchers proposed customized IT audit checklists for public, community, and private cloud environments. Chakraborty et al. explored the differences in information assurance practices in cloud computing compared to conventional computing environments [24]. End-to-end security, privacy, and data integrity are more complex in a cloud environment. Their research revealed that information assurance depends on the cloud service model. For example, PaaS vendors place less emphasis on privacy assurance than IaaS and SaaS vendors. On the other hand, privacy and business integrity are perceived as a universal requirement, defying the potential segmentation of the cloud market based on the level of service [21]. Research on cybersecurity in the cloud continues to grow and expand into key areas ranging from identifying new security threats, mobile device management, to legal compliance and governance.

Of the three cloud service models, most higher education institutions implement SaaS. Free email services such as Gmail, Yahoo! Mail, and Microsoft Hotmail became popular communication and messaging tools in colleges and universities. The 2010 Campus Computing Survey reported that over 80 % of US colleges and universities use hosted email solutions; of these institutions, 60 % use Gmail, and the remaining 40 % use Zimbra and Hotmail [2].

10.2.2 Organization Profile: Portland State University

Portland State University (PSU) was first established as the Vanport Extension Center in 1946 to meet the education needs of American soldiers returning from World War II [25]. In 1955, it was granted a 4-year college status by the Oregon Legislature and has grown since then to full university status by 1969 [25]. Today, PSU prides itself as "an urban research university encompassing 50 city blocks, eight schools, 226° programs, 29,000 students, including 1,700 international students from 91 countries, and 126,000 alumni" [25].

The Office of Information Technology (OIT) works with the university community and with external partners to serve more than 40,000 technology users each year [26]. OIT is organized into seven areas:

(i) Academic and Research Computing – web development, research and academic computing, and programming
(ii) Business Intelligence – provides business reporting, data analytics, and information management
(iii) CIO Administrative Office – direction, communication, and strategic planning
(iv) Computing Infrastructure Services – data center, server hardware, storage, operating systems, and applications
(v) Enterprise Information Technology Systems – administrative applications programming and support
(vi) Instructional Technology Services – support for faculty and students using technology, labs, and classroom technology
(vii) Network and Telecommunications Services – data networks, telephones, switchboard, and campus wiring
(viii) User Support Services – helpdesk, publications, training, and software sales [26]

OIT maintains several academic and instructional computer labs and computer kiosks at PSU. Several departments at PSU such as the School of Business,

Department of Engineering, and School of Education, to name a few, maintain and manage their own computer labs.

Higher education institutions, such as Portland State University (PSU), have been on the forefront in implementing cloud computing in their computing environments. Portland State University became one of several universities to adopt Google Apps for Education in 2011, based on a contract between Google and the Oregon University System (OUS) [27]. Google Apps for Education is a suite of Internet-cloud-based services provided by Google, which include email, calendar, document sharing, and access to these applications from Windows and Macintosh computers, as well as mobile devices [27].

PSU migrated to Google Apps for Education to provide much needed and often requested services. Google meets these needs and also provides our faculty, staff, and students with many additional benefits including:

(ix) Free, high-quality, easily accessible, and modern email and calendar system (with 25+ GB of storage).
(x) An improved web interface with new functionality.
(xi) Access to innovative services as Google implements them.
(xii) A unified all-campus solution for both email and calendaring.
(xiii) Collaboration services, such as Google Docs for file sharing, Google Talk for instant messaging, and Google Sites for web-based group collaboration.
(xiv) Better data resiliency: Google provides more extensive disaster recovery services than we can offer at PSU [27].

As state funding for colleges and universities suffer more reductions, higher education administrators are focusing on operational efficiencies that new technologies such as cloud computing bring. This changing technological landscape sheds a new light on the significance of cybersecurity.

The current study applied literature review and interviews to address the goals of the research. The literature review presented studies that showed developments in technology road mapping in recent years, a background on cloud computing, and the growing significance of cybersecurity, particularly in cloud computing. Attempts to schedule interviews with the Chief Information Security Officer at PSU and other IT managers were not successful due to time constraints in the summer term. The researcher interviewed other subject matter experts in cybersecurity best practices from various state agencies in Oregon instead. Current information on PSU's cloud computing environment and information security policies were also obtained from information published in PSU's website. The researcher also used research studies published by leading professional associations for higher education such as EDUCAUSE and its Network Security Task Force.

The main goal of the research is to propose a technology road map for cybersecurity in cloud computing for PSU. The information gathered from the review of literature and interviews of subject matter experts in cybersecurity best practices will be presented and discussed later in the chapter.

10.3 Drivers Behind a Secure Cloud

Migrating computing resources to a cloud environment presents a challenging set of drivers for cybersecurity in higher education in the USA. While security and privacy are among the important drivers for cybersecurity in a traditional, on-site computing environment, the significance of these two drivers is elevated into prominence in cloud computing. Higher education officials, together with federal and state agencies, and private organizations continue to increase their collaboration and alliance to provide network infrastructures that are more secure and protect privacy of information. The significance of security and privacy of data can be demonstrated in a collaboration on cybersecurity on a national level through the EDUCAUSE/Internet2 Computer and Network Security Task Force, which was organized in 2000 [22]. The task force created a framework for action, which are divided in five parts:

(xv) Make IT security a higher and more visible priority in higher education.
(xvi) Do a better job with existing security tools, including revision of institutional policies.
(xvii) Design, develop, and deploy improved security for future research and education networks.
(xviii) Raise the level of security collaboration among higher education, industry and government.
(xix) Integrate higher education work on security into a broader national effort to strengthen critical infrastructure [28].

Legal and regulatory compliance underscore these national collaboration efforts for cybersecurity in higher education. The information and communication resources of the Internet are now considered a vital part of national infrastructure. The growing number of federal and state regulations around security and privacy are making a tremendous impact on higher education. At the federal level, the key regulations that higher education institutions such as PSU have to comply with are as follows:

(xx) Electronic Communications Privacy Act (ECPA) – broadly prohibits the unauthorized use or interception by any person of the contents of any wire, oral, or electronic communication.
(xxi) Computer Fraud and Abuse Act (CFAA) – criminalizes access to a "protected computer" with the intent to obtain information, defraud, obtain anything of value, or cause damage to a computer.
(xxii) Family Educational Rights and Privacy Act (FERPA) – requires confidentiality around student records, prohibiting institutions from disclosing "personally identifiable education information" such as grades or financial aid information, without the student's written permission.
(xxiii) Health Insurance Portability and Accountability Act of 1996 (HIPAA) – Colleges and universities are required to provide written notice of their health-care providers' electronic information practices.

(xxiv) USA Patriot Act – enacted as a result of the 9/11 terrorist attacks, grants law enforcement increased access to electronic communications and, among other things, amends FERPA, ECPA, and the Foreign Intelligence Surveillance Act of 1978 (FISA), enabling law enforcement personnel to gain access to otherwise confidential information [29].

In addition to compliance with federal laws on security and privacy, higher education institutions need to abide by state laws. Higher education institutions such as PSU in Oregon have to comply with the state's administrative rules and revised statutes for student records, as well as the state's identity theft protection act, created in 2007.

Financial cost is another significant driver behind cybersecurity in the cloud. PSU is facing a $23 million budget shortfall by 2015 [30]. The operational efficiencies that cloud computing promises are becoming attractive options for administrators to consider. In addition, higher education institutions need to keep up with technological developments which will eventually be part of their academic, research, and business environments. Containing costs related to equipment and software was also cited in interviews of cybersecurity professionals for this study [31]. Cloud computing is fast becoming an integral part of the computing environment in higher education. The emerging trend of BYOD (bring your own device), which allows students, faculty, and staff to bring their personal mobile computing devices to access computing resources from higher education institutions, instead of accessing these resources from on-site work computers or computer labs, serves to further hasten the adaptation of cloud computing in colleges and universities. Implementing cloud computing technologies in the academic and research environments require higher education institutions to invest in the appropriate security models and technologies that will ensure security and privacy of information. IT spending in higher education in the USA is expected to top $56 billion in 2012, with most of the expenditures in telecommunications, collaborative technologies, and outsourced IT services [32].

Recovery costs from a security breach are typically very high. A recent study from Symantec, the antivirus software manufacturer, estimates the cost of global cybercrime at $114 billion annually, significantly more than the annual global market for marijuana, cocaine, and heroin combined [33]. Colleges and universities are particularly vulnerable to security breaches on data such as financial, research, and student records, to name a few. Social media, mobile devices, and file-sharing programs in the Internet have become avenues for malware, worms, and spyware that gain access to protected information such as student records, network passwords, and financial information, among others. In 2010, faculty and student names, social security numbers, and other personal information were compromised by hackers at Ohio State University, costing the university an estimated $4 million to investigate, notify, and remediate the security breach [15].

PSU will not only incur financial costs when security breaches occur. The negative publicity of these cyber attacks could have a more far reaching impact on the institution's reputation and the public's trust. In May 2012, a computer server in the

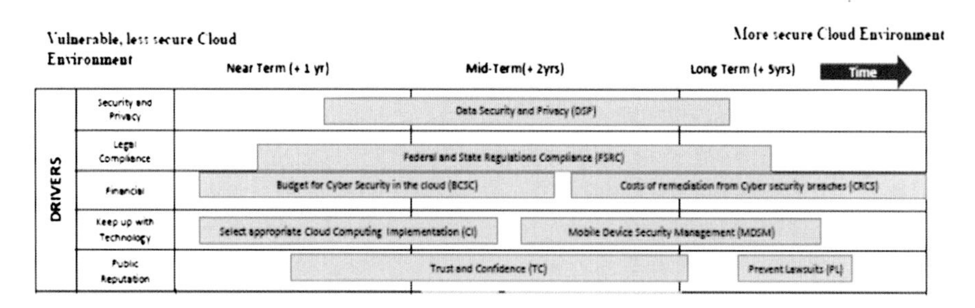

Fig. 10.1 Cybersecurity drivers for cloud computing in higher education

University of Maine was hacked, potentially exposing personal information such as credit card numbers and social security numbers of customers from campus-based stores [15]. The security breach not only costs the university $900,000.00 to mitigate the issue but also created negative publicity and complaints from individuals from other universities that purchased from its online store. Most colleges and universities have created Information Security and Risk Management offices focused on implementing programs on best practices in information security and privacy. One of the major objectives of these programs is to prevent lawsuits arising from security breaches.

These drivers for cybersecurity at PSU can be summarized in a graphical representation. These drivers have a lot in common with other colleges and universities. These drivers set the context for developing a secure cloud environment in higher education in the near, middle, and long terms. Most of them will be critical in these three time spans. In summary, the drivers for cloud cybersecurity in higher education can be illustrated in Fig. 10.1 above:

10.4 Products and Services

The following section identifies the current cybersecurity products and services that PSU uses to address the drivers for cybersecurity.

The different cybersecurity products in this section are grouped into two—network security and enterprise applications, and data access points. Network security refers to technologies that secure and protect the internal network infrastructure from unauthorized and malicious intrusions from the Internet. Enterprise applications are programs that are widely used by students, faculty, and staff such as office productivity suites, email, finance, and registration applications, among many others. These enterprise applications involve client–server systems and web-based programs. Data access point security refers to technologies used that secure access to data from personal computers and, increasingly, mobile devices. Most of these products are expected to be around for the next several years, with their next generation versions improving on features and capabilities.

The services include campus-wide cybersecurity awareness training, training for IT professionals, information assurance, and periodic review of cybersecurity policies and risk management plans.

10.4.1 Network Security and Enterprise Applications

A firewall allows or blocks traffic into and out of a private network or the user's computer [26]. Firewalls are widely used to give users secure access to the Internet as well as to separate a company's public web server from its internal network [34]. Leading companies that offer firewall technologies such as Cisco, Checkpoint, and SonicWall currently provide firewalls that detect and block sophisticated attacks as well as enforce granular security policy at the application (versus port and protocol) level [35]. However, current firewall technologies suffer from processing capability as broadband speeds increase. With additional security policies to verify, the firewall's performance degrades even more. The next generation firewall products combine improved software and hardware design, with a proprietary security chip as its core [36].

Intrusion detection systems (IDS) are another key component in network security. IDS collect information from a variety of systems and network resources and then analyze the information for possible security problems. IDS provides monitoring and analysis of user and system activity, auditing of system configurations and vulnerabilities, and a statistical analysis of activity patterns based on the matching to known attacks [37]. IDS currently fall into two groups—passive and active. The passive IDS watch data traffic that flows through them and then capture and log any suspicious data based on policies and rule sets [38]. On the other hand, the active IDS detect and attempt to prevent potential threats and attacks from intruders [38]. Current IDS technologies fail to monitor traffic between internal hosts; thus, internal attacks may not be detected. External connections from wireless and dial-up devices are also not monitored by current IDS technologies. Next generation IDS are expected to address these technical and security issues.

For a user to gain access to network resources, his or her account needs to first be authenticated. User authentication identifies a user and verifies that he or she is allowed to access the network and its resources. For nonmobile users, the current user authentication technologies include password, personal identification number (PIN), PKI, 2FA software token, and 2HA hardware token. Two-factor authentication (2FA) uses a combination of two different factors to gain access or authenticate to say online banking: something you know, such as a password or PIN, and something you have, such as a loaded mobile phone [39]. The 2HA includes a hardware token device that resembles a thumb drive and users will install their digital certificate on the hardware token [40].

User accounts have access to computer resources in various systems. An increasing number of organizations are deploying identity management systems to help manage user access to various systems. Identity management is the combination of business process and technology used to manage data on IT systems and applications about users. Managed data includes user objects, identity attributes, security entitlements, and authentication factors [41]. Current IDM implementations include context-based solutions that help users access data stored across complex and heterogeneous enterprise environments, with risk scoring. Key limitations include disparate IDM systems and the lack of a widely accepted process for defining and managing digital identities that supports requirements for different levels of identity assurance.

Encryption is a procedure used in cryptography "to scramble information so that only someone knowing the appropriate secret can obtain the original information (through decryption)" [42]. Encryption is a method of converting an original message of regular text into encoded text. The text is encrypted by means of an algorithm (type of formula). If information is encrypted, there would be a low probability that anyone other than the receiving party who has the key to the code or access to another confidential process would be able to decrypt (translate) the text and convert it into plain, comprehensible text [42]. Current storage encryption technologies include full disk encryption, virtual disk encryption, and volume encryption and file/folder encryption [43]. Current encryption standards include the 64-bit and 128-bit data encryption standard (DES) and Secure Sockets Layer (SSL) authentication. Application encryption programs vary in their implementation of security policies and may have limited compatibility with other programs.

Enterprise applications are business-oriented software used by colleges and universities for finance, registration, online learning course tools, word processing, and email, among other business functions. These applications can be client–server-based or web-based programs. The current technologies for enterprise applications security include static application security testing (SAST), dynamic application security testing (DAST), web application firewalls (WAF), database auditing and protection (DAP), and static data masking (SDM) [44].

10.4.2 Data Access Points

PSU faces the challenge of providing an open, but secure, network for academic and research collaboration. Several higher education institutions also provide residential facilities such as student dormitories and guest hotels for visitors and guests. As a result, computer hosts in the campus and these residential areas are more susceptible to security hacks. Majority of colleges and universities install antivirus software and system updates and patches in host computers. However, these computers could be managed by different academic departments and not the central IT department. As a result, antivirus software updates and system security patches may not be regularly updated.

Access to academic and research data are increasingly being done from mobile phones and tablets. A January 2012 survey of 768 IT professionals in North America, Europe, and Japan by Dimensional Research revealed that 89 % use smartphones or tablets to connect to corporate networks [45]. The same survey participants also identified these mobile devices as main contributors to recent security risks. While mobile devices allow users to access data anytime and anywhere, these devices are also targets of cyber hackers. Current mobile security management technologies either use a messaging server's management capabilities (usually from the same vendor that made a particular phone) or use a third-party product, which is designed to manage one or more brands of phones [46]. Use of untrusted mobile devices and untrusted networks susceptible to man-in-the-middle attacks could still be done and information can be intercepted and modified.

PSU, like several higher education institutions, is in the forefront of supporting "bring your own device" (BYOD) for students and faculty. This is not surprising since these groups purchase their own computing and handheld devices for years. The current baseline security policies for managing these devices are commonly provided by Microsoft Exchange ActiveSync (EAS) policies. Current MDM solutions offer features such as the ability to do software and hardware inventory, manage configurations, and distribute software updates. However, as BYOD becomes more prevalent and the amount and type of data accessed by mobile devices grow, MDM solutions with more advanced security management features are recommended.

According to the Pew Research Center, 83 % of US adults have a cell phone of some kind and that 42 % of them own a smartphone [47]. Recent technologies include authenticating users via cell phones, such as one-time password (OTP) sent as an SMS text message to a mobile phone, Mobile soft token, Mobile PKI, and other technologies such as Voice and Mobile TAN [48]. Although there are some vendors that currently provide these technologies, user authentication by cell phone remains problematic due to variations in network latency by phone service providers.

Biometric authentication is currently the most secure way of authenticating users, since it is based on physical characteristics of individuals. Attempts have been made to incorporate biometric authentication such as voiceprint with user authentication. However, biometric authentication still faces a lot of challenges in implementation. Not all systems are equipped to use it, and it is still considered intrusive and expensive to implement. Market studies indicate that it could take a few more years for this technology to mature and be accepted as a standard form of user authentication.

10.4.3 Services

Security awareness, education, and communication are critical in promoting best practices for data security and privacy on campus. At PSU, the Office of Information Security and OIT work closely together to oversee efforts to provide these services, protect the information assets of the institution, and comply with regulations. Many colleges and universities require students, faculty, and staff to attend security training programs and disseminate information about security best practices in their websites and providing them with security CDs that will auto-configure computers to receive the latest security updates and ensure that virus protection is installed and updates in their computers. The popularity of mobile devices and social media websites continues to pose challenges in security awareness in colleges and universities.

Some colleges and universities have started integrating cybersecurity as part of the academic curriculum in degree programs such as computer science and other information technology courses. Current challenges in integrating cybersecurity in the academic curriculum include faculty members that lack the knowledge in this field and lack a comprehensive approach that address business and management aspects of computer security.

As cybersecurity becomes increasingly important in a cloud environment, there is an acute shortage of the number of qualified IT professionals with the necessary training and experience in cybersecurity best practices and technologies. Jim Gossler, Founding Director of the CIA's Clandestine Information Technology Office, stated that there are about 1,000 security people in the USA who have the specialized security skills to operate effectively in cyberspace—we need 10,000–30,000 [49].

Like many organizations dealing with the shortage of qualified IT security professionals, providing security training for PSU's IT staff has been impacted negatively by budget cuts. Like other colleges and universities, PSU is investing in online learning to provide much needed security training for their IT staff. Several higher education institutions are offering online cybersecurity graduate programs, such as the one offered by the Polytechnic Institute of New York University. Currently, PSU's computer science program offers a graduate computer security certificate [50]. Various computer security professional certifications are offered by government agencies, vendors, and professional associations. These certifications could help address gaps in security-related training for IT professionals in a relatively shorter period of time than obtaining an academic degree.

The Committee on National Security Systems defines information assurance as "measures that protect and defend information and information systems by ensuring their availability, integrity, authentication, confidentiality, and non-repudiation. These measures include providing for restoration of information systems by incorporating protection, detection, and reaction capabilities" [51]. Information assurance is more complex in a cloud environment compared to the conventional on-premise computing environment. Chakraborty et al. concluded in their research that information assurance varies depending on the cloud service model an organization chooses to implement [24]. Since higher education institutions often implement the SaaS cloud service model, the study concluded that such organizations require more privacy, control over data, and business integrity in the service assurance offerings they negotiate with cloud service providers. Best practices for information assurance in cloud computing are evolving, and there is a need for standardized practices to meet the computing needs of the academic community and address regulatory compliance goals.

Higher education institutions such as PSU should conduct periodic reviews of their information security policies to keep up with the changing security

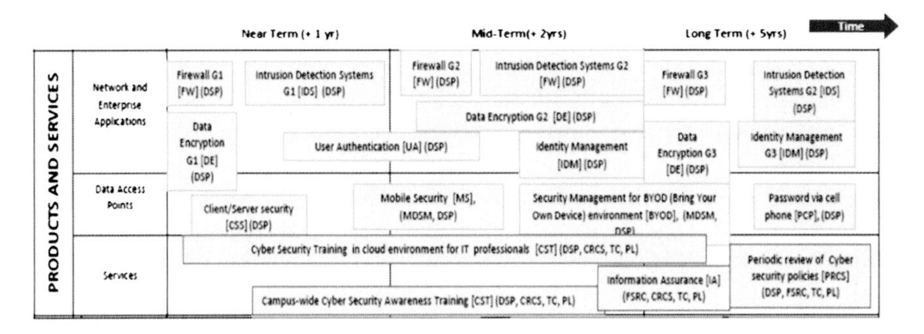

Fig. 10.2 Cybersecurity products and services

requirements of new and emerging technologies and remain up to date with regulatory compliance. Security audits and findings from these audits should be implemented within a reasonable and responsible time frame [29].

Cloud computing and the emerging BYOD computing environment bring serious security concerns in developing cybersecurity policies and risk management plans in higher education. The system complexity and loss of control of data in a cloud environment, in addition to the risks introduced by untrusted mobile devices and networks, are just beginning to be evaluated and considered in cybersecurity policies of colleges and universities.

Cybersecurity products and services continue to evolve in their next generation versions in the coming years. Most of the features in next generation product versions address security and improved capacity features. The current cybersecurity products will continue to be used for applications and data that are on premise. Transition to cloud services will create a hybrid computing environment of on-premise and cloud computing environments. As described in this section, current cybersecurity technologies are more appropriate for on-premise computing resources and have limitations when applied in a cloud environment. Services such as security awareness training, relevant security training for IT professionals, and review of cybersecurity policies will continue to evolve as well to address the security risks and vulnerabilities that cloud and mobile computing bring. The progression of these products and services is illustrated in Fig. 10.2 above:

10.5 Technology and Governance for Cloud Computing Security

The next section discusses the emerging technologies for cybersecurity in cloud environments and the changes in governance and management it brings for a higher education institution such as PSU.

10.5.1 Technology

In some aspects, cybersecurity for the cloud shares similarities with traditional on-premise computing environment security. While SaaS is the most common cloud service model deployed in higher education, the computing environment in most colleges and universities is projected to be a mixed environment where some applications are offered in the cloud, while some, due to business requirements and security policies, will continue to be provided within the campus. Colleges and universities will continue to deploy current and next generation versions of technologies for firewalls, IDS, IDM, VPN, data encryption, and user authentication. In both computing environments, managing security for data access points from mobile devices and managed hosts will continue to be critical.

However, while several cybersecurity technologies used for protecting data provided by on-site data centers can be extended to the cloud environment, several aspects of the cloud infrastructure are significantly different from conventional computer network infrastructure. Even though third-party vendors provide services for an organization in a cloud environment, organizations will always retain the responsibility—and liability—for exposure and loss of customer information in the event of security breaches. The cloud architecture is a significant departure from the traditional computing environment in the following aspects:

(xxv) System complexity – Since many components make up the public cloud, there are several possible security attack scenarios. The computing components, such as deployed applications and virtual machines; the management components, such as data replication and recovery; and resource metering can be implemented with different layers of cloud providers.

(xxvi) Shared multi-tenant environment – Client organizations share resources with other customers that are unknown to them. Cloud computing has a greater dependence on logical separation at multiple layers than using physical separation.

(xxvii) Internet facing services – Applications and data that used to be accessed only within organizations are now accessible in a public cloud, thus exposing these to more security threats.

(xxviii) Loss of control – In a cloud environment, organizations rely on cloud service providers to manage and control applications and data. The organization's ability to maintain situational awareness, set priorities, and implement changes is diminished. Compliance with security and privacy regulations become a joint coordination with the cloud services provider [5].

These disparities are more likely to require different cybersecurity technologies for cloud computing. In the SaaS cloud service model, the cloud service provider is responsible for physical and environmental security, but also for the infrastructure, the applications, and the data. Colleges and universities that implemented the SaaS model have alleviated these direct responsibilities to their cloud service providers. It is very critical for PSU which has implemented the SaaS cloud services model by using Google Apps, to make security an explicit clause in its service contracts with cloud providers.

How then can cloud service providers work with their higher education customers in testing application security? Gartner proposed three models of application testing in the cloud [52]. The first model involves the prospective cloud customer and the cloud services provider to agree to a third-party security testing, with the results reported back to the prospective cloud customer for review. In the second model, the cloud provider applies independent security testing and provides evidence of such testing to the prospective cloud customer. Finally, the third model adopts application testing technologies, trains its own staff on these technologies, and conducts its own security testing. Gartner states that the first two models benefit from independent testing, while the third model, while providing cost benefits to the provider, suffers from lack of transparency [52]. Technologies that play major roles in application testing for the cloud include dynamic application security testing (DAST) and static application security testing (SAST). These two technologies for testing applications in the cloud are described below:

(xxix) DAST testing of cloud services: DAST technology analyzes web applications for security vulnerabilities, such as SQL injection, XSS, XSRF, and buffer overflow. The process for DAST cloud services calls for an agreement by the prospective client (which can be the cloud provider) and the DAST vendor. The cloud provider then gives the DAST vendor the web address of the application to be tested, and the DAST vendor conducts remote testing and sends back a report containing vulnerability discoveries and remediation advice [52].

(xxx) SAST testing of cloud services: SAST technology is designed to analyze application source code, byte code, or binaries for coding and design conditions that indicate security vulnerabilities. SAST tools are used to analyze applications in a nonruntime state, in contrast to DAST tools, which analyze applications in a runtime state. The SAST cloud services process is similar to the DAST process, with one important difference: The code that is to be tested is sent to the SAST vendor, or the SAST vendor's specialists are permitted to use its technology to perform testing on the cloud provider's premises [52].

As an increasing number of applications are being transitioned into the SaaS cloud service model, user authentication plays an even more critical part in security. The user authentication process for a conventional computing environment requires users to authenticate separately to each application that he or she has access to. This user authentication process requires multiple credentials to remember and manual logins to several systems. As more applications are transitioned to SaaS, this conventional user authentication method contributes to cybersecurity threats and becomes cumbersome and frustrating for end users. Federated Single Sign-On (SSO) eliminates the need for multiple user credentials and multiple logins. Federated SSO for SaaS cloud services authenticates users against an organization's preferred user information repository, then sending only the authorized attributes to both on-site and cloud applications to automatically authenticate the user and control privileges without requiring a manual login [53]. Users can have a simpler authentication experience, since they only need one set of credentials to login and access on-site and applications provided by SaaS. System administrators can perform regular audits and reports on user authentication and access to internal and SaaS applications, as well as easily provision new user accounts, modifications to user access, and revocation of user privileges.

As web browsers become common user interface for applications, particularly those delivered via SaaS cloud services, web browser optimization becomes important. Fan et al. created "Godson-T," a model for an optimized web browser based on a state-of-the-art 64-core architecture [54]. The "Godson-T" model takes advantage of multi-core processors to speed up processing of URL requests. The model reduces latency for HTML data from web servers and provides improved security for web applications because the URL requests are separated from the source data [44]. Singh et al proposes the use of another protocol, HTTPi that offers end-to-end web integrity. HTTPi supports progressive page loading on the client browser, handling mixed content and defining access control policies among HTTP, HTTPi, and HTTPS from the same domain [55]. Developers of modern web browsers have optimized their JavaScript engines and have begun implementing isolation to prevent actions in one web browser window from affecting other windows. This isolation allows the browser to continue functioning, even if one window malfunctions [20].

Mobile devices such as smartphones and tablets are outpacing the use of personal computers. In 2011, vendors shipped 158.5 million smartphones, up to 57 % on the 101.2 million units shipped in 2010 [46]. The global client PC market grew only 15 % in 2011 to 414.6 million units, with 274 % growth in iPad shipments [56]. This trend underscores the demand for data and services provided in the cloud—in particular, the security and protection of data. Mobile device management (MDM) tools play a major role in data security and privacy. MDM software is used for policy and configuration management tool for mobile handheld devices such as smartphones and tablets based on smartphone operating systems [57]. MDM enforces security management through standard device security, authentication, and encryption. The security management component of an MDM include remote wipe, remote lock, secure configuration, policy enforcement password enabled, encryption, authentication, firewall, antivirus, and mobile VPN.

Several current MDM tools provide management features for mobile devices in their own enterprise, but none of these are making the most of cloud environment capabilities. Liu et al. from the IBM research center presented a web portal design that provides management access to virtualized device management servers hosted in a service cloud [58]. The design hides the details of the device management behind a standard-based, uniform control interface that can be viewed from a cross-platform agent that can run on multiple mobile platforms [58]. Future versions of MDM software will include document management systems with secure storage and transfer of enterprise content [57].

Biometric technology will provide key solutions to user identification issues in the long term. Current biometric security technologies for mobile users include (a) fingerprint recognition, (b) voice identification, (c) face recognition, and (d) iris recognition [59]. The next generation biometric identification technologies will focus on the following developments:

(xxxi) Fusion of biometric with different technologies: One of the future developments of biometric security solutions are to combine different technologies.

(xxxii) Combining biometric security with RFID technology is one of the enhancements the fusion between the two technologies brings an extra security mean for mobile commerce applications, like mobile banking and payment systems [59].

(xxxiii) Live face identification: Due to the limitation of existing biometric face identification technologies, it is possible for an illegitimate user to show the still picture of a legal mobile user during a face image capture process. A "liveness detection" solution, by 2D Fourier spectra analysis based on the face images, has been provided to deal with this issue. This solution is capable to differentiate between a fake face and a live face using vein map of faces taken from an ultraviolet camera, although this mechanism is expensive [59].

Current user authentication technologies such as smart cards and browser certificates fail to go past the specific systems that they are authenticating a user against. Providing user authentication for cloud services requires a more robust and comprehensive approach. Homomorphic encryption, developed by Craig Gentry from IBM, allows a company to encrypt its entire database of emails and upload it to a cloud. Then it could use the cloud-stored data as desired—for example, to search the database to understand how its workers collaborate [60]. The results would be downloaded and decrypted without ever exposing the details of a single email [60]. Homomorphic encryption is ideally suited for cloud computing, where the computing environment is untrusted, but given the task of performing computational tasks on a client's confidential data, the client can protect its confidential data from the untrusted cloud if it can encrypt its data using a homomorphic encryption function and use the cloud to do the computing on the encrypted data [60]. Gentry's breakthrough research has inspired others to apply the homomorphic encryption scheme for cloud computing security. Gomathisankaran et al. proposed applying the homomorphic encryption scheme using the residue number system (RNS) to develop security technologies for cloud computing [61].

A common application framework for cloud computing, which includes developer tools, documentation, and automated processes to build and test applications that will operate in the cloud, needs to be created. One such framework was introduced in 2010 by Joseph Hellerstein, at the University of California, Berkeley. His application framework modifies database programming languages so that they can be used to quickly build any sort of application in the cloud—social networks, communication tools, games, and more [62]. For years, these programming languages have been refined to hide the complexities of shuffling information in and out of large databases. In a cloud-friendly version, programmers could just think about the results they want, rather than micromanaging data. Hellerstein's application development framework, called Bloom, builds into the language the notion that data can be dynamic, changing as it is being processed. Hellerstein's group has used the Bloom language and its predecessors to quickly rebuild and add major features to popular cloud tools such as Hadoop, a platform used to manipulate very large amounts of data [62]. By making applications development in the cloud less complex, these languages should increase the number of developers willing to work with cloud programming, resulting in ideas for new types of powerful and secure applications.

10.5.2 Governance and Management

The NIST describes governance as "implies control and oversight by the organization over policies, procedures, and standards for application development and information technology service acquisition, as well as the design, implementation, testing, use, and monitoring of deployed or engaged services" [5]. While cloud computing enables agility in project implementations, it does not release the client organization from taking responsibility of protecting and securing their data. Higher education institutions are still accountable for documenting how they protect data and applications, the level of encryption used, and what business transactions are allowed to access their data.

The paradigm shift from a conventional, on-premise computing environment to one that mixes private and public clouds demands a new set of governance skills in the academic community. Organizations such as PSU need to negotiate with cloud services providers on meeting the security requirements of applications and data, disaster recovery, and network infrastructure resources in the cloud that will be assigned to them. As Dave Roberts, the VP of strategy at ServiceMesh, a cloud services provider, sums it: "You need governance that works in a way that respects the creative process and fosters it, yet at the same time, ensures that things get verified and checked." [63]. Indeed, higher education institutions need to review contract management, SLA management, and the management of policy and regulatory compliance in third parties when it comes to working with cloud service providers. Colleges and universities can find guidance in these areas in organizations like EDUCAUSE (information technologists), NACUBO (business officers), NACUA (attorneys), ACUA (auditors), and others to meet these critical goals in governance [64].

The emerging requirements for cybersecurity in cloud environments uncover the shortage of qualified IT professionals. US colleges and universities are not producing enough US graduate students in computer science, math, and science and most especially graduate students in cybersecurity. The current immigration laws and government regulations contribute to this shortage by limiting foreign students who want to specialize in these areas. These foreign students who want to specialize in cybersecurity research are often denied by the NIST due to technology restrictions against them [65].

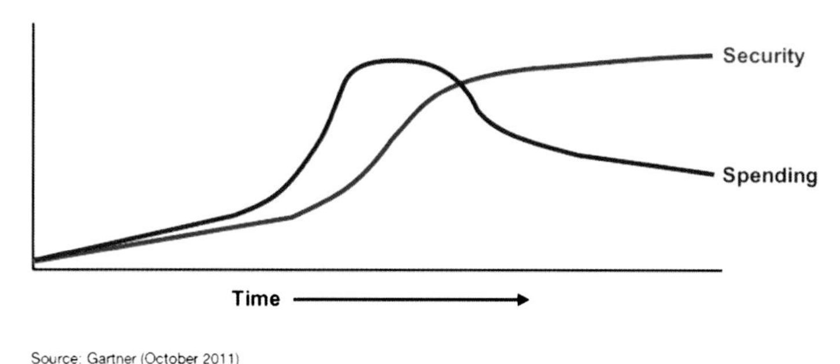

Fig. 10.3 Relationship between security and security spending

Allocating the necessary budget for cybersecurity spending for cloud services is a major consideration for migrating computing services to the cloud. Gartner research's general rule of thumb is that enterprises should be spending between 3 % and 6 % of their IT budget on IT security; lower in the range if they have mature systems, higher if they are wide open and at risk [66]. The relationship between IT budgets and spending on security is shown in Fig. 10.3 above:

Following Gartner's recommendation, expenditures for IT security in cloud computing is expected to be high in the early periods of its adoption, since cloud computing is still a new and evolving technology. Compliance and security breaches reported in the general media will continue to be key incentives driving these security expenditures. However, organizations rarely follow a consistent spending allocation for IT spending due to pressures to reduce costs, emerging security threats, technological developments, and industry changes. Cybersecurity research is vital in keeping organizations such as colleges and universities current in protecting data and privacy. Unfortunately, the lack of adequate research funding for cybersecurity in cloud computing is one of the main barriers for cloud's adoption in organizations. Available funding is random and inconsistent and lacks structured programs that allow universities to establish centers of excellence which are clearly paramount from an academic perspective [65].

The shared tenancy and complexity of cloud environments are compelling incentives for colleges and universities to review and update their secure policy and compliance policies. Information system security policies define the goals and strategies of an organization's information system and how it addresses security threats and vulnerabilities. By integrating cloud computing in their information systems, higher education institutions need to work with cloud service providers in planning these policies. Colleges and universities should need to periodically review and update these policies and discard those that are no longer applicable. Secure mobile strategies and policies play significant roles in providing a secure and stable computing environment. A mobile device security policy should define which types of mobile devices are permitted to access the organization's resources, the degree of access that various classes of mobile devices may have—for example, organization-issued

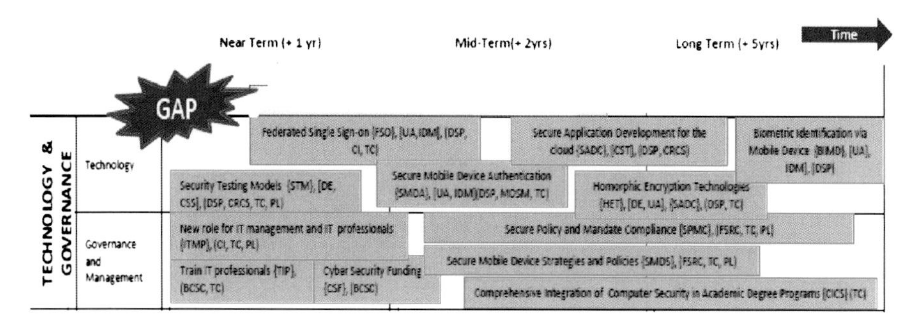

Fig. 10.4 Cybersecurity technology and governance

devices versus personally owned (bring your own device) devices—and how provisioning should be handled [46]. The SANS institute provides mobile security templates that colleges and universities could reference and integrate in creating their mobile device security policy [67].

Integrating security training in current computer science and other IT-related academic programs could help address the shortage of IT professionals with cybersecurity training. Yang proposed a combination of workshops integrating cybersecurity into existing technologies, revision of existing computer science courses to incorporate cybersecurity best practices, and adding a new track for cybersecurity specializations in existing computer science programs [68].

Figure above presents a graphical summary of the emerging technologies and services in cybersecurity that will be used within a year (near term), in the next 2 years (midterm), and 5 years from now (long term) (Fig. 10.4).

10.6 Resources

Cloud computing introduces a paradigm shift in cybersecurity technologies and governance. Addressing the technical, management, and compliance requirements that cloud computing introduces would require PSU to work with other higher education institutions, federal and state agencies, cloud services providers, and other professional associations. Establishing and maintaining these collaborative efforts become even more important when transitioning or integrating existing technologies to a cloud environment.

Research and development of cybersecurity technologies is a critical area of collaboration among higher education institutions, federal and state agencies, and the private sector. Research in emerging technologies for the next generation encryption, user authentication, and prevention of security breaches in a cloud environment are being undertaken in joint projects at a multi-sector level. Georgia Tech Information Security Center (GTISC) at the Georgia Institute of Technology has initiated research projects in cryptography, virtualization, network security, and usability of security solutions [69]. These research projects are supported by grants from the National Science Foundation, DARPA, Army Research Office, and the private sector. GTISC's academic degree programs and professional certificates in information security have earned the institution the Center of Excellence in Information Assurance Education designation by the National Security Agency [69]. The University of Maryland (UMD) and Massachusetts Institute of Technology (MIT) Lincoln Laboratory entered a 3-year partnership agreement with UMD's Maryland Cybersecurity Center to focus on collaborative research, student engagement, and the development of innovative security technologies [70]. Northrop Grumman Corporation created the Cybersecurity Research Consortium, with leading cybersecurity research institutions such as the Massachusetts Institute of Technology, Carnegie Mellon and Purdue University, to advance research in cybersecurity and develop solutions to counter the complex cyber threats facing our economy, freedom of information, and national security [71]. A number of higher education organizations are engaged in discussions, plans, and actions that might position them as cloud service providers. These include large universities and university systems like Carnegie Mellon University, Indiana University, the University of California, North Carolina State University, and others as well as national organizations like EDUCAUSE, Internet2, the Kuali Foundation, the Quilt, the CampusEAI Consortium, and regional organizations like the regional optical networks (RONs) [64].

Significant developments have also been made in providing funding for cybersecurity research and technologies. In 2011, the Department of Homeland Security has announced a program offering $40 million in funds for cybersecurity research and development [72]. The decision to fund such efforts underscores the need for increased cooperation among public and private sectors in addressing the challenges of cybersecurity efforts. For fiscal year 2013, cybersecurity is identified as a priority for basic research, with millions of dollars from the $140.8 billion requested to go towards cybersecurity R&D at the departments of Defense and Homeland Security, the National Science Foundation and the National Institute of Standards and Technology, in addition to funding for operational cybersecurity programs [73]. The US senate is considering a bill that would create scholarships and fellowships for students who agree to conduct research on cybersecurity [74]. In 2011, Indiana University received $800,000 federal funding to create tools to collect and share cybersecurity threat data and intelligence [75].

Multi-sector conferences on cybersecurity demonstrate the multi-sector perspective of cybersecurity in the age of cloud computing and mobile computing. One such conference was sponsored by Georgetown University in April 2012, brought together senior officials at the Federal Communications Commission, the US Department of Defense, faculty from the Georgetown Institute of Law, and cloud services providers to prevent potential threats and enhance cybersecurity overall [76]. The Cloud Security Alliance (CSA) is a broad coalition of industry practitioners, corporations, associations, and other key stakeholders in promoting cybersecurity. Its mission is to promote the use of best practices for providing security assurance within cloud computing and to provide education on the uses of cloud computing to help secure all other forms of computing [CSA-about]. It sponsors conferences, such as "SecureCloud 2012," as a venue for educational and networking event on cloud computing security and privacy [77].

Information sharing centers at the state and national levels help breakdown "industry silos" in cybersecurity by promoting collaboration and alliances among organizations in public and private sectors. Federal agencies such as the US Department of Homeland Security's National Cyber Security Center (NCSC) and the US Computer Emergency Readiness Team (US-CERT) are at the forefront of these initiatives. State and local governments share threat intelligence and best practice information through the Multi-State ISAC (Information Sharing and Analysis Centers). EDUCAUSE, a nonprofit association for IT leaders and professionals in higher education, and the Higher Education Information Security Council (HEISC) work with colleges and universities in information sharing of best practices in cybersecurity.

In recent years, cybersecurity competitions have been tapped by public and private sectors for fresh and innovative strategies to prevent security breaches and malware attacks. These competitions are increasingly being viewed as another means to resolve the shortage of cybersecurity professionals by promoting interests in research and education in the field. The US Cyber Challenge's (USCC) mission is "to significantly reduce the shortage in the cyber workforce by serving as the premier program to identify, attract, recruit and place the next generation of cyber security professionals" [78]. It partners with high schools, community colleges, universities, state and federal agencies, corporate sponsors, and national labs and research facilities to promote and motivate students and professionals to pursue education, development, and career opportunities in cybersecurity. Some colleges and universities sponsor cybersecurity competitions as well. The Polytechnic Institute of New York University sponsors annual cybersecurity competitions to promote invention, innovation, and entrepreneurship in the field of cybersecurity [79].

Finally, legislation that promote public and private partnerships to improve security and privacy in cyber space are key to promoting best practices, the creation of standards, and innovation in cybersecurity for cloud computing. Recent examples of these are the following:

(xxxiv) The Homeland Security Act of 2002 (HSA) gave the Department of Homeland Security (DHS) some cybersecurity responsibilities in addition to those implied by its general responsibilities for homeland security and critical infrastructure.

(xxxv) The Cyber Security Research and Development Act, also enacted in 2002, established research responsibilities in cybersecurity for the National Science Foundation (NSF) and NIST.

(xxxvi) The Federal Information Security Management Act of 2002 (FISMA) clarified and strengthened NIST and agency cybersecurity responsibilities, established a central federal incident center, and made OMB, rather than the Secretary of Commerce, responsible for promulgating federal cybersecurity standards [80].

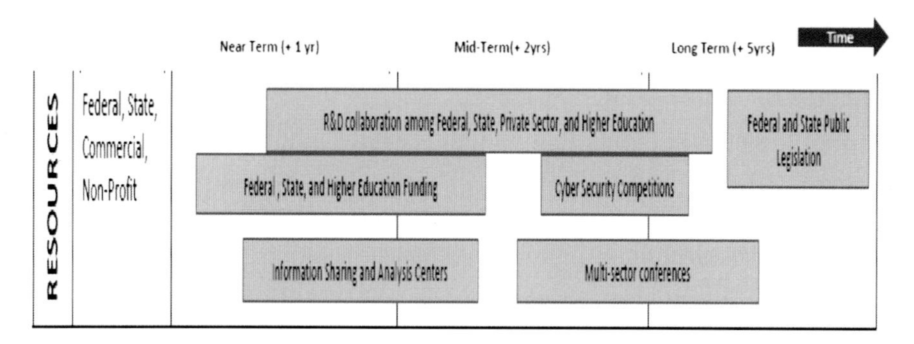

Fig. 10.5 Resources for cybersecurity in cloud computing

The resources that PSU and higher education institutions can reference and access in implementing a more robust cybersecurity model in a cloud environment emphasize the importance of public and private partnerships, collaboration across industry, and the need for all agents in the ecosystem to do their part. These resources are presented in Fig. 10.5 above:

10.7 Technology Road Map for Cybersecurity in Cloud Computing for PSU

The technology road map for cybersecurity in cloud computing for a higher education institution such as Portland State University is based on the technology road map for strategic business planning identified as one of by Phaal et al.'s research on types of technology road maps. This road map focuses on the development of a vision of the future business in terms of markets, business, technologies, skills, among others [Phaal]. Gaps are identified and strategic options explored to bridge the gaps. A graphical representation of this technology road map is shown in Fig. 10.6 below.

The graphical representation helps visualize the drivers, products and services, technology, governance and management skills, and resources needed to move from a vulnerable, less secure cloud environment to realize the goal of a more secure and stable cloud computing environment for a higher education institution against a timeline. The timeline is provided based on estimates given in research studies about the viability and availability of the technology or service. The road map has four layers, each with its own subcategories. Each subcategory identifies key components of each layer.

The components of each layer share the same color code. To show the linkages among market drivers, products and services, and technology and governance, the abbreviation of a component is indicated in the component from another layer that it is linked with. This method was used as an alternative to indicate the linkages of the components, in lieu of arrows, due to space constraints. For example, data

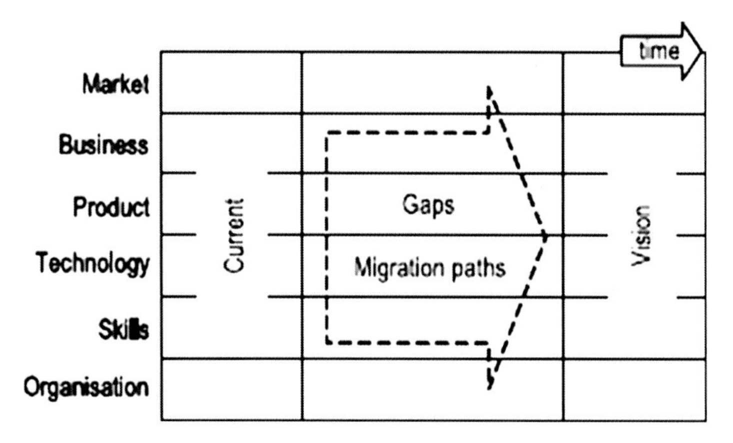

Fig. 10.6 Road map graphical representation

security and privacy is one of the market drivers. This market driver is abbreviated as (DSP) and designated within parenthesis. In the Products and Services layer, Data Encryption G2 (second generation) is abbreviated as [DE] in square brackets. Within the Data Encryption G2 component, we can see the (DSP) component. This means that this product addresses the data security and privacy driver. In the Technology and Governance layer, the security testing models is abbreviated as {STM} with curly braces. Inside this component, we can find [DE, CSS], (DSP, CRCS, TC, PL). This indicates that this emerging technology will improve data encryption [DE] and client server security [CSS] and addresses drivers such as data security and privacy (DSP), cost of remediation from cybersecurity breaches (CRCS), trust and confidence (TC), and prevent lawsuits (PL). A list of the abbreviations is presented following the technology road map graphic. The components in the resources layer address the components in the drivers, products and services, and technology and governance. The relationships among the components are based on functionality, research, and future assumptions from research conducted in these areas.

The technology road map is designed to meet future requirements of cybersecurity in cloud computing at Portland State University and can be modified as needed. Each layer is color-coded and contains the abbreviations of the current component, as well as other components from other layers of the road map it is linked with. The drivers' layer has four subcategories which are addressed in the Products and Services layer and the Technology and Governance layer. The subcategories of "Network and Enterprise Applications" and "Data Access Points" identify products that are currently used today at PSU and other higher education institutions. These products will continue to evolve in their next generation versions with improved security features and capabilities. These products will continue to be used even as PSU migrate some applications in the cloud, while some applications remain supported by its on-premise data center. The services subcategory identifies initiatives and activities that relate to promoting cybersecurity at PSU and its cloud services vendor, Google.

The "Technology and Governance" layer identify technologies that are still being developed that have potential prospects of addressing cybersecurity issues in a cloud environment. In the technology subcategory, examples of these are security testing models, secure application development for the cloud, and homomorphic encryption technologies. Migrating applications to the cloud does not only require technologies that will ensure security and privacy of data, but a new set of governance and management skills as well. Examples of these skills are "new role for IT management and professionals" and "Secure Mobile Device Strategies and Policies."

Finally, the "Resources" layer present the means by which PSU and other higher education institutions can use in order to bridge the gap between the current products and services for cybersecurity to those that cloud environments will require. Research show that a number of collaborations and alliances among government agencies, higher education institutions, private sector, and nonprofit organizations in the areas of research and development, funding, and multi-sector conferences to fund and develop new technologies, as well as providing guidance in governance and management of resources in a cloud environment (Fig. 10.7).

Legend (abbreviations' key)

Drivers	
Security and privacy	Data Security and Privacy (DSP)
Legal compliance	Federal and State Regulations Compliance (FSRC)
Financial	Budget for Cyber Security in the cloud (BCSC)
	Costs of remediation from Cyber security breaches (CRCS)
Keep up with technology	Select appropriate Cloud Computing Implementation (CI)
	Mobile Device Security Management (MDSM)
Public reputation	Trust and Confidence (TC)
	Prevent Lawsuits (PL)

Products and Services	
Network and enterprise applications	Firewall G1 (FW)
	Intrusion Detection Systems G1 (IDS)
	User Authentication (UA)
	Data Encryption G2 (DE)
	Identity Management G3 (IDM)
Data access points	Client/Server security (CSS)
	Mobile Security (MS)
	Security Management for BYOD (Bring Your Own Device) environment (BYOD)
	Password via cell phone (PCP)
Services	Cyber Security Training in cloud environment for IT professionals (CST)
	Information Assurance (IA)
	Periodic review of Cyber security policies (PRCS)
	Campus-wide Cyber Security Awareness Training (CAT)

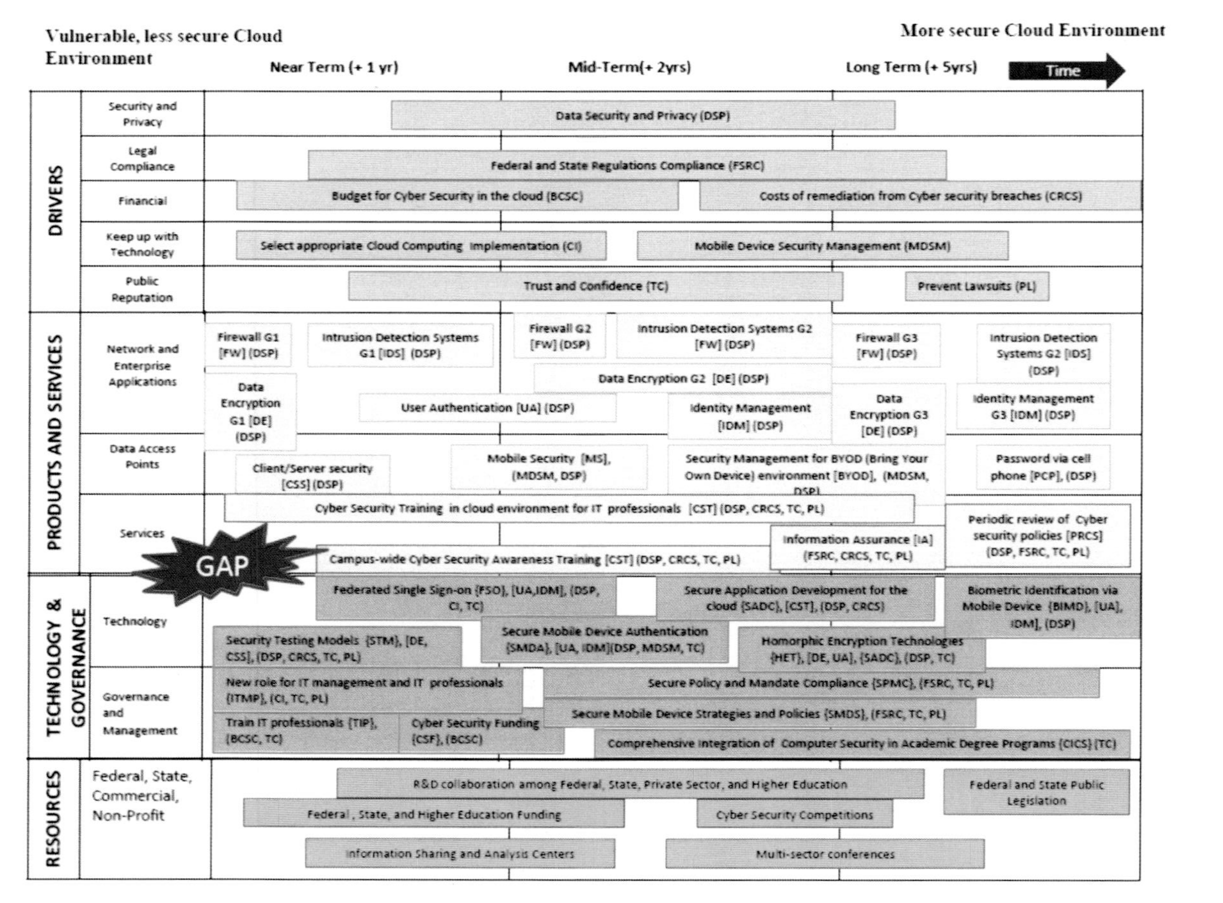

Fig. 10.7 Technology roadmap or cyber security in cloud computing for PSU

Technology and Governance	
Technology	Federated Single Sign-on (FSO) Secure Application Development for the cloud (SADC) Biometric Identification via Mobile Device (BIMD) Security Testing Models (STM) Secure Mobile Device Authentication (SMDA) Security Testing Models (STM) Secure Mobile Device Authentication (SMDA) Homomorphic Encryption Technologies (HET)
Governance and management	New role for IT management and IT professionals (ITMP) Secure Policy and Mandate Compliance (SPMC) Train IT professionals (TIP) Cyber Security Funding (CSF) Secure Mobile Device Strategies and Policies (SMDS) Comprehensive Integration of Computer Security in Academic Degree Programs (CICS)

Resources	
Federal, state, commercial, non-profit	R&D collaboration among federal, state, private sector, and higher education Federal, state, and higher education funding Cyber security competitions Information sharing and analysis centers Multi-sector conferences Federal and state public legislation

10.8 Conclusion

Using the business strategic model for technology road mapping from Phaal et. al.'s research, the proposed technology road map for PSU is an effort to encapsulate the drivers, the products and services, the technology and governance, and the resources in order to advance the current unstable, less secure cybersecurity cloud environment to one that has improved cybersecurity systems and processes. The proposed technology road map for cybersecurity at PSU's cloud environment identified security and privacy concerns stemming from the limitations of current products and services that are more appropriate for on-premise computing environments. Cloud computing environments, due to their multi-tenancy, vast geographic location of data centers which are not known by clients, and distinct contract agreements with cloud service providers and clients, pose different security requirements. Its shared environment amplifies security concerns about user identification and authentication, data encryption, and identity management, to name a few technical security issues.

Cloud computing introduces changes in IT governance and managing the access and use of applications and data in the cloud is an area that cloud computing brings major changes to. Even though organizations could work with third-party vendors to provide services in a cloud environment, organizations will always retain the responsibility—and liability—for exposure and loss of customer information in the event of security breaches. Negotiation, process management, IT auditing, and financial literacy, in addition to technical skills, are just a few of the desired skills for technology managers and IT professionals to successfully manage services and people in a cloud and on-premise computing environments. Technology managers need to have a good understanding of procurement and supply processes [81].

Another key management implication is multi-sector collaboration. This collaboration is vital for the successful delivery of computing resources and services in a cloud environment. There are so many new aspects in cloud computing that are just beginning to surface and need to be learned. The newer the technology, the higher the risks involved when using it. For this reason, higher education institutions such as PSU will benefit with knowledge sharing, discussions, and other collaboration efforts with other colleges and universities, state and federal agencies, the private sector, and nonprofit associations to learn and promote best practices and technologies for a more secure cloud computing environment.

With all the security risks that the cloud computing environment poses, it is not without benefits and opportunities for creating a more stable and secure computing environment. Applications and data accessed from a cloud have better high availability, since cloud service providers can scale data center facilities to accommodate availability. Backup and recovery of data and applications are more robust and allow for no or very minimal downtime at all. Data accessed from the cloud could be less risky for an organization such as PSU, instead of storing data in host computers, thumb drives, or mobile devices. With data and application management now migrated to the cloud, IT professionals do not have to spend a lot of time on daily operational tasks involving systems management and troubleshooting. This provides opportunities to learn other skills, whether it be additional technical, financial, or management skills.

10.9 Future Research

While not all applications and data will be transitioned in the cloud in the short term, there is no denying that cloud computing is fast becoming a part of the mainstream landscape of academic computing. Managing a mixed environment of on-premise and cloud computing environments will be a common scenario for higher education. Such complex computing environments bring about cybersecurity risks but also opportunities to leverage cloud computing for a more secure and stable computing environment.

The proposed technology road map for cybersecurity in the cloud for PSU needs to be reviewed and updated as environmental factors such as business drivers, technology, and security compliance requirements change. This technology road map involves an ongoing process, and it will evolve, as cloud computing developments amplify the need for a more robust cybersecurity environment.

References

1. Effective Cyber security Practices for Higher Education [online]. net.educause.edu/ir/library/powerpoint/SER0539A.pps. Accessed 21 July 2012
2. Wlasuk A. A higher education student database is an identity thief's dream come true… [online]. http://www.securityweek.com/higher-education-perfect-security-storm. Accessed 21 July 2012
3. Nigam H. 2011s cybercrime explosion and your 3 cyber security resolutions for 2012 [Online]. http://blogs.discovery.com/criminal_report/2012/01/2011s-cybercrime-explosion-and-your-3-cybersecurity-resolutions-for-2012.html#4. Accessed 15 July 2012
4. Department of Homeland Security. Cyber security [Online]. http://www.dhs.gov/files/cyberse curity.shtm. Accessed 16 July 2012
5. NIST Definition of Cloud Computing [Online]. http://csrc.nist.gov/groups/SNS/cloud-computing/index.html. Accessed 17 July 2012
6. Garcia M, Bray O (1997) Fundamentals of technology road mapping. Strategic Business Development Department, Sandia National Laboratories, April 1997, pp 1–31
7. Phaal R, Farrukh CJP, Probert DR (2004) Technology roadmapping—a planning framework for evolution and revolution. Technol Forecast Soc Change 71(1):5–26
8. Crystalline Silicon Technology and Manufacturing (CTM) Group (2012) International Technology Roadmap for Photovoltaics (ITRPV) Results 2011. 3rd edn.
9. Fitzpatrick G, Wollman A (2010) NIST interoperability framework and action plans. Power and energy society general meeting, (IEEE 2010), MN, USA. 25–29 July 2010, pp 1–4
10. Daim T, Amer M, Brenden R (2012) Technology road mapping for wind energy: case of the Pacific Northwest. J Clean Prod 20:27–37
11. Lee S, Park Y (2005) Customization of technology roadmaps according to road mapping purposes: overall process and detailed modules. Technol Forecast Soc Chang 72:567–583
12. Rinne M (2004) Technology roadmaps: infrastructure for innovation. Technol Forecast Soc Change 71:67–80
13. Rayport JF, Hayward A (2009) Envisioning the cloud: the next computing paradigm. In: Marketspace point of view. http://www.egov.vic.gov.au/trends-and-issues/information-and-communications-technology/cloud-computing/envisioning-the-cloud-the-next-computing-paradigm.html. Accessed 20 March 2009, pp 1–57
14. Types of Cloud Computing [Online]. http://thecloudtutorial.com/cloudtypes.html. Accessed 20 July 2012
15. Britto M (2012) Cloud computing in higher education [Online]. http://www.librarystudent journal.org/index.php/lsj/article/view/289/321#microsoft2010. Accessed 23 July 2012
16. DOD Cyberspace Glossary [Online]. http://www.pcmag.com/encyclopedia_term/0,1237,t=D OD+cyberspace+glossary&i=62535,00.asp. Accessed 14 July 2012
17. Identity Theft Resource Center. 2012 data breach stats – known vs. unknown totals [Online]. http://www.idtheftcenter.org/artman2/uploads/1/ITRC_Breach_Stats_-_Known_vs_Unknown_Summary_1H_20120630.pdf. Accessed 16 July 2012
18. Cloud Security Alliance (2010) Top threats to cloud security computing. https://cloudsecurity-alliance.org/topthreats/csathreats.v1.0.pdf .v1.0, pp 1–14
19. Bisong A, Rahman S (2011) An overview of the security concerns in enterprise cloud computing. Int J Netw Secur Appl (IJNSA) 3(1):30–45
20. Shue C, Lagesse B (2011) Embracing the cloud for better cyber security. In: 8th IEEE international workshop on middleware and system support for pervasive computing, Seattle, WA, pp. 245–250
21. Khorshed M, Shawkat A, Saleh W (2011) Trust issues that create threats for cyber attacks in cloud computing. In: 2011 IEEE 17th international conference on parallel and distributed systems, Tainan Taiwan, pp 900–905
22. Liu S, Chen Y (2010) Retrospective detection of malware attacks by cloud computing. In: 2010 international conference on cyber-enabled distributed computing and knowledge discovery, CyberC, Huangshan, China, pp 511–517

23. Chen Z, Yoon J (2010) IT auditing to assure a secure cloud computing. In: 2010 IEEE 6th world congress on services, Miami, pp 253–259
24. Chakraborty R, Ramireddy S, Raghu TS, Rao H (2010) The information assurance practices of cloud computing vendors IT Professional, July/August 2010 12(4):29–37
25. Portland State University History [Online]. http://pdx.edu/portland-state-university-history. Accessed 14 July 2012
26. About OIT [Online]. http://www.pdx.edu/oit/about. Accessed 14 July 2012
27. Google FAQ [Online]. http://oit.pdx.edu/google-faq#4. Accessed 10 July 2012
28. Luker M, Petersen R (2003) "Preface", computer and network security in higher education. In: Luker M, Petersen R (ed) EDUCAUSE, pp xv–xxii
29. Salomon K, Cassat P, Thibeau B (2003) IT security for higher education: a legal perspective. EDUCAUSE/Internet2 Computer and Network Security Task Force, pp 1–19
30. Pardington S PSU prepares for stark budget outlook [Online]. http://pdx.edu/news/psu-prepares-stark-budget-outlook. Accessed 26 July 2012
31. Voll, Scott, e-mail interview, 17 July 2012
32. Nagel D. Education IT spending, fueled by telecom, to top $56 billion by 2012 [Online]. http://campustechnology.com/articles/2008/09/education-it-spending-fueled-by-telecom-to-top-56-billion-by-2012.aspx. Accessed 26 July 2012
33. Serrano A. Cyber crime pays: a $114 billion Industry [Online]. http://www.thefiscaltimes.com/Articles/2011/09/14/Cyber-Crime-Pays-A-114-Billion-Industry.aspx#page1. Accessed 22 July 2012
34. Definition of Firewall [Online]. http://www.pcmag.com/encyclopedia_term/0,2542,t%3Dfirewall&i%3D43218,00.asp. Accessed 22 July 2012
35. Young G, Pescatore J (2011) Magic quadrant for enterprise network firewalls. Gartner research, pp 1–29
36. SifoWorks. Firewall for the next generation [Online]. http://www.o2security.com/library/SifoWorks%20White%20Paper%20(OD0700WPE01)%20EN%201.0.pdf. Accessed 22 July 2012
37. SANS Institute. Understanding intrusion detection systems [Online]. http://www.sans.org/reading_room/whitepapers/detection/understanding-intrusion-detection-systems_337. Accessed 19 July 2012
38. Tett M. Detection and prevention: 6 intrusion detection systems tested [Online]. http://www.zdnet.com/detection-and-prevention-6-intrusion-detection-systems-tested-1139156750/. Accessed 19 July 2012
39. Security Token [Online]. http://www.aradiom.com/SolidPass/2fa-OTP-security-token.htm. Accessed 19 July 2012
40. The Hardware Token [Online]. http://www2.exostar.com/l/4632/2010-12-09/5GRF. Accessed 19 July 2012
41. Defining Enterprise Identity Management [Online]. http://hitachi-id.com/password-manager/docs/defining-enterprise-identity-management.html. Accessed 19 July 2012
42. What is Encryption? [Online]. http://www.hhs.gov/ocr/privacy/hipaa/faq/securityrule/2021.html. Accessed 19 July 2012
43. Scarfone K, Souppaya M, Sexton M (2007) Guide to storage encryption technologies for end user devices. National Institute of Standards and Technology, NIST Special Publication 800-111, Gaithersburg
44. Feiman J, MacDonald N (2012) Application security road map beyond 2012: breaking silos, increasing intelligence, enabling mass adoption. Gartner research, pp 1–9
45. Dimensional Research (2012) The impact of mobile devices on information security: a survey of IT professionals. http://www.checkpoint.com/downloads/products/check-point-mobile-security-survey-report.pdf. pp 1–7
46. Souppaya M, Scarfone K (2012) Guidelines for managing and securing mobile devices in the enterprise (Draft). National Institute of Standards and Technology, NIST Special Publication 800-124, Gaithersburg

47. Pew Internet and American Life Project 35% of American adults own a smartphone [Online]. http://pewresearch.org/pubs/2054/smartphone-ownership-demographics-iphone-blackberry-android. Accessed 22 July 2012
48. Goode Intelligence (2009) The mobile phone as an authentication device 2010–2014, pp 1–3
49. Langevin J, McCaul M, Charney S, Raduege H (2010) A human capital crisis in cyber security. Center for Strategic and International Studies, pp 1–53
50. Computer Science Programs [Online]. http://pdx.edu/computer-science/programs. Accessed 26 July 2012
51. Committee on National Security Systems (2010) National Information Assurance (IA) Glossary. CNSS instruction no. US Government, Washington DC. 4009, pp 1–103
52. Feiman J (2011) Application security testing of cloud services providers is a must. Gartner research, pp 1–8
53. Fischer International. Federated single sign-on for higher education [Online]. http://www.fischerinternational.com/press/collateral/IDMOverviewHigherEd.pdf. Accessed 23 July 2012
54. Fan L, Shi W, Tang S, Yan C, Fan D (2011) Optimizing web browser on many-core architectures. In: 12th international conference on parallel and distributed computing, applications and technologies, Gwangju, pp 173–178
55. Singh, End to End web integrity. Singh K, Wang H, Moshchuk A, Jackon C, Lee W (2012) Practical end-to-end web content integrity. In: World wide web conference 2012, Lyon, pp 659–668
56. Canalys (2012) Smart phones overtake client PCs in 2011 [Online]. http://www.canalys.com/newsroom/smart-phones-overtake-client-pcs-2011. Accessed 23 July 2012
57. Redman P, Girard J, Basso M (2012) Magic quadrant for mobile device management software. Gartner research, pp 1–34
58. Liu L, Moulic R, Shea D (2010) Cloud service portal for mobile device management. In: IEEE international conference on E-business engineering (ICEBE 2010), Shanghai, pp 474–478
59. Jobanputra N, Vijayendra K, Dinkar R, Gao J (2009) Emerging security technologies for mobile user accesses. San Jose State University, San Jose, pp 1–12
60. Naone E (2011) Homomorphic encryption [Online]. http://www.technologyreview.com/article/423683/homomorphic-encryption/. Accessed 23 July 2012
61. Gomathisankaran M, Tyagi A, Nauduri K (2011) HORNS: a homomorphic encryption scheme for cloud computing using residue number system. In: Information sciences and systems conference, Baltimore, MD, USA, pp 1–5
62. Naone E (2010) TR: cloud programming [Online]. http://www.technologyreview.com/article/418545/tr10-cloud-programming/. Accessed 24 July 2012
63. Stackpole B (2012) Governance meets cloud: top misconceptions [Online]. http://www.informationweek.com/cloud-computing/infrastructure/governance-meets-cloud-top-misconception/232901483. Accessed 24 July 2012
64. Katz R, Goldstein P, Yanosky R (2010) Cloud computing in higher education. http://net.educause.edu/section_params/conf/CCW10/highered.pdf
65. Internet Security Alliance (2008) The cyber security social contract policy recommendations for the Obama administration and 111th congress, pp 1–48
66. Wheatman V (2011) Identifying the real information security budget. Gartner research, pp 1–9
67. SANS Institute Mobile security policy templates [Online]. http://www.sans.org/security-resources/policies/mobile.php. Accessed 24 July 2012
68. Yang A (2001) Computer security and impact on computer science education. Indiana University of Pennsylvania, pp 1–14
69. Georgia Tech Information Security Center [Online]. http://www.gtisc.gatech.edu/history.html. Accessed 28 July 2012
70. UM and MIT Lincoln Lab Partner on Cyber security (2011) [Online]. http://www.eng.umd.edu/html/news/news_story.php?id=5957. Accessed 28 July 2012
71. MIT joins Northrop Grumman's new cyber security research consortium (2009) [Online]. http://web.mit.edu/newsoffice/2009/csail-grumman.html. Accessed 28 July 2012

72. DHS Funds $40 Million Program for Cyber Security Research [Online]. http://infosecisland.com/blogview/11466-DHS-Funds-40-Million-Program-for-Cyber-Security-Research.html. Accessed 28 July 2012
73. Jackson W Cyber security research feels the love in 2013 budget request [Online]. http://defensesystems.com/articles/2012/02/14/cybersecurity-2013-federal-budget-request.aspx. Accessed 28 July 2012
74. Laster J Senate considers paying for cyber security scholarships [Online]. http://chronicle.com/blogs/wiredcampus/senate-considers-paying-for-cybersecurity-scholarships/21417. Accessed 28 July 2012
75. Indiana University (2011) [Online]. IU center awarded funding for cyber security. http://www.insideindianabusiness.com/newsitem.asp?id=49656. Accessed 28 July 2012
76. Georgetown University [Online]. Cyber security conference brings FCC chair, others to Georgetown. http://www.georgetown.edu/news/cybersecurity-conference-fcc-chair.html. Accessed 1 Aug 2012
77. Cloud Security Alliance. About cloud security alliance [Online]. https://cloudsecurityalliance.org/about/. Accessed 1 Aug 2012
78. National Board of Information Security Examiners. Welcome to U.S. cyber challenge [Online]. https://www.nbise.org/uscc/. Accessed 1 Aug 2012
79. Polytechnic Institute of New York University [Online]. About CSAW cyber security competition 2012. http://www.poly.edu/csaw2012/about. Accessed 1 Aug 2012
80. Fischer E (2012) Federal laws relating to cyber security: discussion of proposed revisions. Congressional Research Service, Washington, DC, pp 1–65
81. Woodford, Melissa, e-mail interview, 17 July 2012

Printed by Publishers' Graphics LLC
CAMZ140126.20.06.144